MW01039209

The Enduring Lost Cause

The Enduring Lost Cause

AFTERLIVES OF A REDEEMER NATION

EDITED BY Edward R. Crowther

Knoxville / The University of Tennessee Press

Copyright © 2020 by The University of Tennessee Press / Knoxville.
All Rights Reserved. Manufactured in the United States of America.
First Edition.

Library of Congress Cataloging-in-Publication Data

Names: Crowther, Edward R., editor.
Title: The enduring Lost Cause : afterlives of a redeemer nation /
    edited by Edward R. Crowther.
Description: First edition. | Knoxville : The University of Tennessee Press,
    [2020] | Includes bibliographical references and index. | Summary:
    "The year 2020 will mark the fortieth anniversary of the publication of
    Charles Reagan Wilson's classic study Baptized in Blood: The Religion
    of the Lost Cause, 1865–1920. Conceived in part to honor this mile-
    stone, this multiauthor volume seeks to show how various aspects of Lost
    Cause ideology persist into the present. Among the contributors to this
    work are Carolyn Dupont, Sandy Dwayne Martin, Colin Chapell, Keith
    Harper, and Charles Reagan Wilson himself. Among the many aspects
    of the Lost Cause to be considered are the impact of Lost Cause ideol-
    ogy on southern Christianity; the difficulty of evading neo-Confederate
    narratives in education; and the influence of Confederate catechisms in
    keeping Lost Cause ideology alive and well."— Provided by publisher.
Identifiers: LCCN 2019053593 (print) | LCCN 2019053594 (ebook) |
    ISBN 9781621903895 (hardcover) | ISBN 9781621905752 (pdf)
Subjects: LCSH: Christianity—Southern States. | United States—
    History—Civil War, 1861–1865—Religious aspects. | Southern
    States—Civilization.
Classification: LCC BR535 .E53 2020 (print) | LCC BR535 (ebook) |
    DDC 277.5/081—dc23
LC record available at https://lccn.loc.gov/2019053593
LC ebook record available at https://lccn.loc.gov/2019053594

For Lori

Contents

Acknowledgments

While no book is solely the product of a single writer, this collection of essays results from the efforts of its various writers, their respective mentors and muses, and all of the archivists, librarians, and others who make their work possible. It is genuinely a team project. In addition, it has benefited from the expert assistance of Scot Danforth and the splendid staff of The University of Tennessee Press and advice and encouragement from external reviewers Edward J. Blum and Joe Cocker. Although it is not intended to be a Festschrift, this collection was inspired by the work of one of its contributors, Charles Wilson Reagan, whose *Baptized in Blood* compelled the rest of us to think about the cultural power and persistence of the Lost Cause. Finally, I would like to thank Charles, my other fellow contributors, and especially my wife, Lori Tanner. Consistently witty and patient, she has lived with the digital and physical clutter this endeavor entailed.

Introduction

EDWARD R. CROWTHER

His commanding likeness stood as a sentinel over New Orleans's Tivoli Circle for 133 years. Over time, the massive figure even lent its name to the circle itself, obliterating the original name of the traffic loop. At sixteen and a half feet tall, the bronze statue of Robert E. Lee, with arms folded and stern countenance, recollects the larger-than-life image of the Confederacy's greatest general in cultural memory. But in May 2017, a construction crew removed the statue from its sixty-foot-high pedestal. Supporters of the move considered it a long-overdue effort in interracial healing, in which public spaces would no longer glorify those who fought a war to create a slaveholding republic. Others countered that a politically correct and present-minded agenda sought to deprive white southerners of their history and heritage. Both sides acknowledged that many of these memorials had been erected as a result of efforts of former Confederates to make sense of their defeat and to inculcate in their children and grandchildren a perspective on the South and the Civil War known as the Lost Cause.[1]

Building on themes that had emerged during the Civil War emphasizing the righteousness of the Confederate cause and especially the valor of its generals and fighting men, the Lost Cause reflected the efforts of the Confederacy to claim a privileged place in cultural memory after its defeat. After the Civil War, the substance of the emerging Lost Cause competed with other traditions—the Emancipationist, the Unionist, and the Reconciliationist—in the tempestuous decades following Lee's surrender at Appomattox, as the various participants in the Civil War sought to valorize their perspectives about its meaning. As many historians have shown, white supremacy in the forms of political redemption in the states comprising the former Confederacy and scientific racism among whites in general quickly marginalized the Emancipationist view. Although partisan expressions of the Unionist and Lost Cause views persisted into the twentieth century, the Reconciliationist view—which emphasized common sacrifice and heroism, buoyed by a powerful and national sense of white supremacy—facilitated sectional reunification around a shared sense of nationalism. And yet, the Lost Cause managed to carve out a privileged niche in the national discourse and largely a dominant one in the former Confederate States, one that continues to inform in varying degrees how the Civil War era is remembered throughout the United States.[2]

Taking its name from an eponymous tome written by Edwin Alfred Pollard in 1866, the Lost Cause refers to ideas, symbols, and rituals that sought to vindicate the antebellum South and the Confederate War that was fought to preserve it. Although other figures such as Jubal Anderson Early and John William Jones helped frame the corpus of Lost Cause beliefs, at least four themes come directly from the forty-four chapters that chronicle what Pollard termed "the most gigantic struggle of the world's history." The first of these diminished slavery's importance in bringing on secession and civil war. In his explanation, slavery versus free labor was only one symptom of many sectional divergences resulting in the development of "two distinct nations" under the label of the United States of America. "Sectional Animosity" was the root cause of sectionalism, secession, and civil war. Slavery "was merely an incident," although it incorrectly "came to be regarded as the main subject of controversy." He even objected to the term slavery because "the system of servitude in the South . . . was really the mildest in the world."[3]

Secondly, states' rights, Pollard asserted, was the immediate cause of secession and war. His narrative chronicles the consistent violation of Southern state rights by the "North," which supported the federal union for monetary gain and "sectional aggrandizement." The South, in contrast, "worshipped that picture of the Union drawn by John C. Calhoun: a peculiar association" characterized by "sovereign states." To promote their own interests, the North pursued policies like the protective tariff to enrich itself as the South's expense. Union under such unfavorable terms no longer commanded the "affection" of eleven of the Southern states, so they seceded.[4]

Pollard's third theme calls into question the beliefs and actions of President Abraham Lincoln. The sixteenth president carried the Northern "doctrine of consolidation" to its logical conclusion by waging war on those states that seceded. Lincoln's view, said Pollard, "was that all former statesmen of America had lived, and written, and labored under a great delusion; that the States, instead of having created the Union, were its *creatures*; that they obtained their sovereignty and independence from it, and never possessed either until 1787."[5]

According to Pollard, perhaps Lincoln's greatest misdeed was his manipulation of the issue of compensated emancipation to permit his issuing the Emancipation Proclamation in September 1862. It was "an act of malice toward the master rather than one of mercy to the slave." In the short run, the measure strengthened Confederate resolve and led to conservative electoral victories in the 1862 elections in the Union. Lincoln had done "that which was repugnant to civilization and to morals," at once seizing property while "adding severity and bitterness to a wicked and reckless war." But in the end, emancipation led to an enlarged federal state, including the creation of the Freedmen's Bureau, and the Thirteenth Amendment, further constitutional consolidation under the guise of radical anti-slavery.[6]

Pollard's final Lost Cause theme is its deep taproot into the virtue of Confederate military leaders and the dauntless courage of common Southern fighting men. In Pollard's telling, Southern leaders and soldiers, thus threatened by Northern interests and then invasion, and to secure their rights as states and their property in persons, waged war to the bitter end, under noble leadership by heroic men such as Robert E. Lee and Thomas J. "Stonewall" Jackson, whom Pollard described as "a machine of conscientious motives . . . intense religious character . . . epicene . . . [and of] almost superhuman endurance." Waxing eloquent, Pollard concluded that Jackson's death harmed the Confederate cause, but also constituted "a calamity to the world: a subtraction from the living generation of genius: the extinction of a great light in the temples of Christianity."[7]

Under such exemplary leadership, Confederate soldiers fought to the point of utter exhaustion, honorably capitulating only when they were worn down by superior numbers. Pollard narrates the denouement of the Army of Northern Virginia following Lee's surrender: "It was a most affecting scene. Rough and rugged men, familiar with hardship, danger, and death in a thousand shapes, had tears in their eyes, and choked with emotion as they thronged around their old chieftain, uttering words to lighten his burden and mitigate his pain." He resurrects glory from the surrender of soldiers and their leaders: "The Confederates have gone out of this war, with the proud, secret, deathless, *dangerous* consciousness that they are THE BETTER MEN, and that there was nothing wanting but a change in a set of circumstances and a firmer resolve to make them the victors."[8]

In sum, the Lost Cause holds that southern secessionists understood the true nature of the Union under the Constitution as a league of states. The more populous north used its legislative powers to reward its manufacturing base at the expense of the agrarian south. Having grown weary of northern cupidity and facing its continuance under the Lincoln administration, eleven southern states seceded. Lincoln made war on the Confederacy, despite the right of southern states to secede, and immorally seized their property. Confederate troops under superior leadership fought heroically until the bitter end. For Pollard, perpetuating these ideas mattered in transcendent ways: "The war has left the South its own memories, its own heroes, its own dead. Under these traditions, sons will grow into manhood, and lessons sink deep that are leaned from the lips of widowed mothers."[9]

Considered a "caricature of the truth" by most historians, the Lost Cause remains woven into the fabric of United States culture. In April 2017, President Donald Trump demonstrated as much by articulating his own understanding of the Civil War that included a major Lost Cause theme: the Civil War was tragically unnecessary. Trump may have learned such a concept from the textbooks he encountered at the Kew-Forest School or at the New York Military Academy, as schoolbooks north and south often delivered the Lost Cause message. But other cultural forces continue to convey its ideas. Gary Gallagher has shown how the Lost Cause shaped cinema and art, powerful media that invite emotional connection more than they inspire reflection on the historical accuracy of their themes. Military posts bear names of Confederate generals, such as Ambrose Powell Hill. Hence, the Lost Cause persists and endures, despite scholarship documenting its inaccuracies, especially about the nature of slavery and the reason for the secession of eleven states.[10]

Over the years, numerous scholars have undertaken a systematic study of the origins, manifestations, and meaning of the Lost Cause; indeed, a contemporary analysis of Lost Cause historiography merits its own volume, and contributors to this one take pains to locate their works in the rich loam of Lost Cause scholarship. But critical to the idea of persistence is how the Lost Cause manifests itself across generations, sometimes triggered by contemporary events that seemingly—at least superficially—have little to do with maintaining the memories of 1865. Its perpetual vitality attests to the power of marble and myth.

Certainly, physical structures, imposing stone and bronze likenesses, explain part of the doggedness of the Lost Cause. Celebrating in tangible and visible ways the visages and actions, especially of heroic Confederates who dot battlefields and town squares, these memorials not only assuaged the "fear of abstraction" in Southern minds but also nurture the mental image of soldiers' bravely fighting, rather than prompting investigation of the motive for their fighting. Gendered rituals, from decoration days to active participation in organizations like the United Daughters of the Confederacy, link the Lost Cause to social events and gatherings. Its assumptions become those of polite white society, and its influences begin early in a white person's life. As recent research has shown regarding race, young people—especially white southerners—come of age surrounded by parental messages and concrete reminders of the Confederate cause. Acceptance, rather than analysis of contradictions and ambiguities, is a likely result.[11]

In the end, as it was in its beginning, the Lost Cause persists because it is fundamentally an expression of faith and devotion. The Confederate cause was "just" and its historical claims inerrant because Lost Cause believers think it was so. In 1980, Charles Reagan Wilson powerfully demonstrated the marriage between Southern religion as a mental and ritual force and Southern culture in *Baptized in Blood: The Religion of the Lost Cause*. One reviewer presciently predicted the monograph was "destined to be the definitive essay on the relation of religion and southern regional patriotism." And so it was. Another noted that Wilson's analysis not only explained the South from Appomattox to 1920 but also explained Southern history from *Brown v. Board of Education* to the present. Although the review appeared in 1982, his conclusion still seems valid in the twenty-first century.[12]

What Wilson did so successfully was to delineate and analyze a Southern Civil Religion which at once sacralized key features of Southern society while explaining how a righteous God could have permitted white Southerners to have experienced military defeat. The Lost Cause belief system permitted an acceptance of national reunification while preserving the ideal of a righteous Confederacy whose white population embodies special virtues and values, an upright and honorable people who sought to maintain their identity through secession and, once defeated, maintained their identity through their pure regional ideas and culture. For its acolytes, the Lost Cause was a world view, which gave order, purpose, and meaning in a mythic and psychological sense. It not only undergirded Southern white sectional pride, it gave providential meaning to the regional culture and offered a vantage to view subsequent United States history through a Southern lens. And as he and scores of others have noted, Southern Civil Religion, like postbellum reconciliation efforts between white Northerners and white Southerners, was silent on race and accepting of white supremacy and segregation. The experience of African Americans was marginal.[13]

The Lost Cause emerged as an effort to transform Confederate defeat into cultural victory. Because it is designed to provide emotional and cultural balm and not to promote deep, empirically informed reflection, its contradictions and plain falsehoods remain unexamined to those who drink at its spring. Since it engrafts itself deeply in important rituals, displays itself in public and private spaces, appears consistent with cultural values like white supremacy, and is easily passed on from one generation to the next —sometimes with an emphasis on certain themes to fit the needs of the times—it endures in numerous and important ways. The essays that follow illustrate some of these manifestations persisting from Reconstruction to the twenty-first century.

Christopher C. Moore offers a fresh reading of John William Jones, whom Charles Reagan Wilson deemed the movement's "Evangelist." To Moore, Jones was the principle instigator of the various patterns and practices of Lost Cause apologetics. His published early biographies of Lee and Davis; his *Christ in the Camp* transmogrified the Army of Northern Virginia into a disciplined band of righteous saints; his work as editor of the *Southern Historical Society Papers* developed the lines of argument and the rhetoric to vindicate the Confederate cause. And, of course, Jones was pivotal in the effort to make the Confederate battle flag the symbol of the solider rather than an emblem of treason.

Colin Chappel demonstrates how gendered rituals begun after the Civil War to commemorate the Confederate dead morphed into vehicles for defining gender roles that delimited the proper activities for men and women, and by extension, set them apart from less-virtuous Northern men and women. The United Daughters of the Confederacy and the Sons of Confederate Veterans exemplify this effort, and their ongoing saga demonstrates one avenue by which the Lost Cause perpetuates itself into the twenty-first century. In a rapidly changing world, Lost Cause ideology contains a bedrock of gendered certainty to succor its adherents.

While women have often done the heavy lifting of disseminating the Lost Cause, Keith Harper shows how a president's son, Lyon Gardiner Tyler, labored indefatigably in the production of Confederate catechisms. Not only do these catechisms contain the elemental assertions of Lost Cause claims, as they evolved in form after 1920, they increasingly assailed both Lincoln and the growing power of the federal state, a prologue to efforts to delegitimize the image of Lincoln and to undermine the New Deal and, later, the Great Society state in the name of states' rights. Simultaneously, he engaged in textbook wars to ensure that the South in general and the Confederacy in particular received the most favorable treatment possible.

Although its white devotees construct a Lost Cause in which African Americans play only a marginal role, Sandy Dewayne Martin re-centers the Lost Cause on black actors, especially focusing on the ideas of W. Bishop Johnson, whose sermons and writings sought to explain why a benevolent God would permit so many horrors to be visited on black people. This exercise in theodicy and civil religion served to discipline the black community to fulfill a higher purpose, including the Christianizing of Africa.

Charles Reagan Wilson delineates and analyzes the tensions between the Lost Cause symbols, rituals, and ideologies and their interactions with the modernizing forces of the twentieth century. Often the Lost Cause symbols were trivialized, commercialized, and decontextualized, but they also served as a white Southern totem against imposed changes in traditional social, commercial, and racial norms. And the Lost Cause proved remarkably adaptive, as radio, film, and even the names of United States highways injected key emblems of the Lost Cause into the body of national symbols.

Clearly race-based and gender-based perspectives add hue and contrast to the rich tapestry of the Lost Cause. It withstands but is sometimes rent by the ravages of time. Lee McWhite explores the themes of continuity and change by examining the Lost Cause-rich environment of the University of Mississippi. Perhaps no public space more closely identified with physical Confederate symbols and rituals, reaching a fever pitch in 1962. But demography compelled the campus to begin to debate and to change, in meaningful ways, its close identity to the Lost Cause. Simultaneously the university struggles to market an image of openness and inclusivity while maintaining support from an older alumni base that is deeply invested in preserving its traditions, including those associated with the Lost Cause.

Certainly the need for the University of Mississippi to attract black athletes who perform before largely white fans demonstrates how context shapes the Lost Cause over time, often in ironic ways. As Alan Scot Willis shows, the needs in a particular context—mobilizing men and women as Christian soldiers in the crusade against Communism—challenge dominant tropes, nurtured by the Lost Cause, about gender roles. In its crusade against Godless Communism in the 1950s, the Southern Baptist Convention offered alternative notions of household politics, making men and women appear as partners. When many Baptist women embraced this egalitarianism and sought to push for more equality in church matters, the Southern Baptist Convention found itself pushing back toward tradition against a movement it had unwittingly nurtured.

Carolyn DuPont's nuanced study of Mississippi's Methodists during the era of civil rights shows not only the limits of the Lost Cause in affirming identity and regional dissent, but also how Lost Cause themes, especially the notion of a special destiny, permit the Lost Cause to persist. The concept of a pure religious heritage, exemplified by Mississippi Methodism, seen as besieged by Northern liberalism and global Communism provided an ecclesiastical glue to hold the white denomination together against internal discord. Rather than defect to more extreme religiously based massive resistance, most Mississippi Methodists remained in their church.

Since a major purpose of ritual is to recreate a sense of an earlier event, Civil War re-enacting is a major demonstration of continuity and change of the Lost Cause. Bradley Keefer, himself a re-enactor, demonstrates how the historical script of a battle often yields to Lost Cause tropes to ensure that Confederate re-enactors display excessive courage. At the same time, he also delineates how re-enactment becomes a bond that reaches across sectional and political lines, as re-enactors value their comrades over occasional efforts to bring contemporary agendas into a backward-looking activity.

Ed Stetzer offers an interesting examination of how Lost Cause ideas spread outside of the former Confederacy and how these ideas persist. His study of Southern Baptist missiology shows how intentionally and inadvertently Lost Cause ideas frame missionary activities whose main goal is conversion, not cultural indoctrination. The result is the promulgation of Lost Cause assumptions as the product of successful Baptist missionary endeavors.

Contemporary events demonstrate the continued power of the Lost Cause which, as Bill Leonard compellingly shows, has a strange, seemingly symbiotic relationship with a belief in American exceptionalism. Both themes revel in the notion of a special relationship between cause and God. Sadly, the outcome is often a justification for abusing minorities—seizing their land and their labor. He offers a four-part tactic for an increasingly diverse population to come to terms with these powerful themes and avoid the negative behaviors they often justify.

Edward R. Crowther demonstrates through a case study of the Social Studies Standards in Texas how Lost Cause ideas have become part of a larger conservative agenda in the culture wars. Under the rubric of tradition and patriotism, Lost Cause themes with peculiar specificity appear in curricular materials that badly distort how Civil War history is represented in textbooks and assessed. Proponents of these measures have no direct connection with heritage organizations, but have simply imbibed Lost Cause ideas as part of their encounter with conservative politics and beliefs about United States history.

The protean persistence of the Lost Cause remains a major feature of both Southern and United States history. Its ubiquity often masks its presence, especially among those who either celebrate its tenets or find little that is offensive about commemorating those who supported and fought for the Confederate States, especially if Lost Cause rhetoric supplants what Confederate leaders and commoners said and did when they began their quest to create a slaveholding republic. The prominent and lasting expressions of the Lost Cause highlighted in this volume are episodic in part because the strands of the Lost Cause appear in so much of the tapestry of United States culture. Much scholarly work remains to demonstrate how the Lost Cause has shaped physical environments, challenged and informed how the United States has projected its image abroad, how the Lost Cause shapes the ways in which foreign interests have interpreted the Civil War and its legacy, and even how Lost Cause tropes shape efforts at humor, such as the bizarre persistence of blackface. While scholars have shown how African Americans have kept the flame of the emancipation legacy of the Civil War brightly lit, a study of the welter of voices who have challenged the Lost Cause remains to be written. Given the ongoing power of the Lost

Cause to shape the contours of United States history and animate debates about its meaning, scholars have hardly begun to exhaust the mythopoetic force of the Lost Cause.

Popular revulsion against Lost Cause symbols has led to change and pushback. Following the vengeful murders of nine African Americans at Emanuel African Methodist Episcopal Church in Charleston in 2015, state lawmakers yielded to demands to cease flying the Confederate battle flag over South Carolina's statehouse. A year later, using a makeshift flagpole, Confederate re-enactors apparently affiliated with the South Carolina Secessionist Party raised their own Confederate battle flag on the statehouse grounds, where it flew for some five hours. And the debate over the flag at first obscured the continued presence of the Confederate soldier monument on those same grounds, bedecked by inscriptions worthy of Edward A. Pollard. [14]

Hence, the Lost Cause endures in at least three ways: one, it informs contemporary Confederate partisans and white supremacists, who are vocal, but perhaps no longer representative of mainstream white society; two, because of its long-standing place in Southern and United States culture, Lost Cause displays and ideas enjoy the status and inertia of tradition; and three, the Lost Cause has engrafted itself into the larger conservative ideology and rhetoric that resists globalization and multi-culturalism, and endorses United States exceptionalism, ironically by deploying tropes from the losing side of a rebellion against the same United States. A durable relic of military and political defeat in 1865, the Lost Cause has proven to be malleable and remarkably long lived.

NOTES

1. "The Lee Monument. An Account of the Labors, etc.," *The Daily Picayune,* February 22, 1884; Mitch Landrieu, "New Orleans Mayor: America Is Stuck 'In a Mentality Where They Could Lynch You,'" *Time,* March 19, 2018, http://time.com/5203614/mitch-landrieu-in-the-shadow-of-statues/.

2. See generally David Blight, *Race and Reunion: The Civil War and American Memory* (Cambridge: Harvard Univ. Press, 2001); Edward J. Blum, *Reforging the White Republic: Race, Religion, and American Nationalism, 1865–1898* (Baton Rouge: Louisiana State Univ. Press, 2005); and the numerous studies cited in the essays below. On the continuity of Lost Cause themes with efforts to interpret the course of the Civil War as it was occurring, see Edward R. Crowther, "John the Evangelist Revisited: John William Jones and the Lost Cause," *Journal*

of Southern Religion 17 (2015): http://jsreligion.org/dev/issues/vol17/crowther.html. Of course, among African Americans, the Emancipationist view persisted and found powerful counterpoints in works such as W. E. B. Du Bois, *Black Reconstruction in America: An Essay Toward a History of the Part Which Black Folk Played in the Attempt to Reconstruct Democracy in America, 1860–1880* (New York: Harcourt, Brace, 1935) and John R. Lynch, *The Facts of Reconstruction* (New York: Neale Publishing Co., 1913).

   3. Edward A. Pollard, *The Lost Cause: A New Southern History of the War of the Confederates.* (New York: E. B. Treat & Co., 1866), 46–47. It is both important and true that Pollard revised his views even further, making violations of the rights of southern states as the cause of the war in his *The Lost Cause Regained,* published two years later. But my point is simply to show how the diminution of slavery as the cause of war, a central trope of Lost Cause history, began before Pollard's mysterious ideological pilgrimage. On this point, see Jack P. Maddex, *The Reconstruction of Edward A. Pollard: A Rebel's Conversion to Postbellum Unionism* (Chapel Hill: Univ. of North Carolina Press, 1974).

   4. Pollard, *Lost Cause,* 52.

   5. Pollard, 175.

   6. Pollard, 359–61.

   7. Pollard, 379–83.

   8. Pollard, 711, 729.

   9. Pollard, 751. Pollard proved eerily prescient on this last point. Carolyn E. Janney, *Burying the Dead but Not the Past: Ladies Memorial Associations and the Lost Cause* (Chapel Hill: Univ. of North Carolina Press, 2008) and Karen L. Cox, *Dixie's Daughters: The United Daughters of the Confederacy and The Preservation of Confederate Culture* (Gainesville: Univ. Press of Florida, 2003) splendidly explore and explain how southern mothers and daughters shaped and maintained the culture of the Lost Cause.

   10. Alan Nolan, "The Anatomy of the Myth," in *The Myth of the Lost Cause and Civil War History,* ed. Alan T. Nolan and Gary W. Gallagher (Bloomington: Univ. of Indiana Press, 2000), 29 (quote); Matt Ford, "What Trump's Generation Learned About the Civil War," *The Atlantic,* August 28, 2017, https://www.theatlantic.com/education/archive/2017/08/what-donald-trump-learned-about-the-civil-war/537705/; Gary W. Gallagher, *Causes Won, Lost, & Forgotten: How Hollywood and Popular Art Shape What We Know About the Civil War* (Chapel Hill: Univ. of North Carolina Press, 2008), 42–43, 56–58, 89, 136–84; Michael Hill, "A Question of Treason?: Confederate Generals and U.S. Army Post Names" (master's thesis, Adams State Univ., 2013).

   11. Thomas Connelly and Barbara Bellows, *God and General Longstreet* (Baton Rouge: Louisiana State Univ. Press, 1982), 1–5; Kristina DuRocher, *Raising Racists: The Socialization of White Children in the Jim Crow South* (Lexington: The Univ. Press of Kentucky), 153–58.

   12. Carey J. Gifford, review of *Baptized in Blood: The Religion of the Lost Cause, 1865–1920,* in *Journal of Southern History* 48 (May 1982): 294; Dallas A. Blanchard, review of *Baptized in Blood: The Religion of the Lost Cause, 1865–1920,* in *Review of Religious Research* 24 (September 1982): 82.

   13. Charles Reagan Wilson, *Baptized in Blood: The Religion of the Lost Cause, 1865–1920* (Athens: Univ. of Georgia Press, 1980), 15–17; Blight, *Race and Reunion,* 3–4. Civil Religion

refers to the beliefs and supporting rituals that link the structural secular values of a nation or culture with transcendent religious meaning. See Robert N. Bellah, "Civil Religion in the United States," *Daedalus* 96 (Winter 1967): 1–21.

14. *Charleston Post and Courier,* July 10, 2017, https://www.postandcourier.com/news /confederate-flag-temporarily-flies-again-at-the-south-carolina-statehouse/article _35b03f6e-6573–11e7-b38e-63407c94f72f.html.

The monument inscriptions read: "This monument perpetuates the memory of those who, true to the instincts of their birth, faithful to the teachings of their fathers, constant in their love for the state, died in the performance of their duty . . . who have glorified a fallen cause by the simple manhood of their lives, the patient endurance of suffering, and the heroism of death . . . and who in the dark hours of imprisonment, in the hopelessness of the hospital, in the short sharp agony of the field, found support and consolation in the belief that at home they would not be forgotten." And "Let the stranger, who in future times reads this inscription, recognize that these were men whom power could not corrupt, whom death could not terrify, whom defeat could not dishonor, and let their virtues plead for just judgement of the cause in which they perished. . . . Let the South Carolinian of another generation remember that the state taught them how to live and how to die, and that from her broken fortunes she has preserved for her children the priceless treasures of her memories, teaching all who may claim the same birthright that truth, courage and patriotism endure forever."

Confederate Symbology and the Prophecy of J. William Jones

CHRISTOPHER C. MOORE

With the perennial maelstrom surrounding monuments and symbols of the Confederacy, understanding the roots of white Southern memory is of paramount importance. Even more than a century and a half after the Civil War, the ubiquity of Confederate images is striking. The Southern Poverty Law Center (SPLC) has published telling numbers, including the estimate that there are more than fifteen hundred "publicly sponsored symbols" of the Confederacy in the United States. The spirits of Confederates roam nearly every corner of the South, from public schools to military bases. In particular, there are more than seven hundred Confederate monuments on public property.[1] While these figures are revealing, it is important to note that long before they had carved icons like Robert E. Lee and Thomas J. "Stonewall" Jackson into stone, ex-Confederates had emblazoned a carefully crafted narrative into the minds of white Southerners.

The remarkable staying power of the Lost Cause[2] mythology—a sacralization of white Southern history that often entailed an apology for the Confederate cause and a veneration of Confederate heroes—is owed to a number of factors, but perhaps none as wide-reaching as the life and career of former Confederate chaplain and Baptist minister, J. William Jones. A prolific writer and editor, Jones codified a host of Lost Cause tenets through seminal publications on Lee, Jefferson Davis, and wartime Confederate revivals, as well as through editorship of the *Southern Historical Society Papers* (*SHSP*) from 1876 to 1887. Jones's opuses on Lee and Davis set the standard for future biographers, and through his work with the *SHSP*, he mainstreamed the Lost Cause. So influential was Jones as editor that historian Gardiner Shattuck maintains he "literally controlled the shape of the Lost Cause."[3]

While Jones was a key player in Southern mythmaking, he has often received only passing treatment from historians.[4] This lacuna is unfortunate for a number of reasons, not the least of which is the fact that modern-day controversies over Confederate memory bear Jones's indelible imprint. From monuments and flags to slavery's role in the onset of the Civil War, self-appointed defenders of Southern heritage allege to have recovered a strand of history that is now being actively suppressed. Yet in reality, these advocates continue to imbibe from the deep well of Lost Cause mythology, drawing heavily from the rhetorical strategies of Jones and his fellow ex-Confederates. The contention here is not merely that Jones set the stage for current-day controversies, but that he presaged them. His work functioned prophetically for white Southerners, as Jones anticipated—and deployed defensive measures against—many of the most serious and enduring challenges to Lost Cause orthodoxy. Today's Confederate partisans are thus indebted to Jones, who was largely responsible for establishing the rubric by which future white Southerners could interpret the past and defend against the ideological onslaught of the Yankees.

JONES'S LIFE AND CAREER

Jones was born on September 25, 1836 in Louisa County, Virginia.[5] He was converted in the summer of 1855 while attending a Baptist protracted meeting, and thereafter religion would play a central role in his life. Later the same year, Jones enrolled at the University of Virginia (UVA). Graduating in 1859, he went on to attend the Southern Baptist Theological Seminary (SBTS) in Greenville, South Carolina. Ordained in the summer of 1860, he envisioned serving as a missionary in east Asia, but sectional tensions in the United States stymied his funding and thus his departure. In December 1860, he married Judith Page Helm (1836–1924). The couple had five children, four of whom became Baptist ministers. In the same month that Jones married, South Carolina seceded from the union, and the trajectory of Jones's life shifted radically.

After Virginia's secession in the spring of 1861, Jones joined a volunteer company, the "Louisa Blues," which would eventually become Company D of the Thirteenth Virginia. Two of Jones's younger brothers also joined the Thirteenth (both were wounded in action and died from their injuries soon after). The Thirteenth was involved in numerous engagements, including

Gaines' Mill, Second Bull Run, Antietam, Fredericksburg, and Chancellorsville. Jones became a regimental chaplain in October 1861, a post he had longed for ever since joining the army. As chaplain, and later as army evangelist, he participated in the flurry of revivals that swept through the Army of Northern Virginia beginning in late 1862. He preached up to three sermons a day and calculated that during the course of the war, he had baptized 410 of the approximately fifteen thousand converts in Lee's army.

After the war, Jones continued his ministry in Southern Baptist churches. In addition to his multiple (and sometimes simultaneous) pastorates over the course of his lifetime, he served in various denominational roles for Southern Baptists: agent for both the Foreign Mission Board and Southern Baptist Theological Seminary, general superintendent of the Sunday School and Bible Board of Virginia, staff writer for Virginia Baptists' *Religious Herald*, and assistant corresponding secretary of the Home Mission Board. One of his early pastorates after the war was in Lexington, Virginia, which put him in close proximity with Lee, who served as president of Washington College until his death in 1870. Jones led services at the college, and it was during this time that he developed a close friendship with Lee, a relationship that Jones believed added credence to his later writings on the general.

Jones gave frequent speeches about his time with the Confederate Army, and in 1874 he published *Personal Reminiscences, Anecdotes, and Letters of Gen. Robert E. Lee*, a book he hoped would provide an intimate look at Lee's personal character. Jones also became permanent secretary of the Southern Historical Society (SHS) in 1875, and as such, he edited fourteen volumes of the *SHSP* from 1876 to 1887. While his responsibilities at the *SHSP* largely involved editing the articles of others, Jones was an assiduous writer himself. His publications included the *Army of Northern Virginia Memorial Volume* (1880), *Christ in the Camp* (1887), *School History of the United States* (1896), *Davis Memorial Volume* (1889), and *Life and Letters of Robert Edward Lee: Soldier and Man* (1906). Later in life, he ministered as chaplain at the University of Virginia and the University of North Carolina, served as secretary and superintendent of the Confederate Memorial Association, and served as chaplain-general of the United Confederate Veterans. He died on March 17, 1909 in Columbus, Georgia.

By the time Jones died, he had bequeathed to white Southerners a quiver full of arguments with which to defend Confederate memory. Of the many Lost Cause doctrines Jones fashioned or honed, three deserve special mention for their applicability and resiliency today. The first involves George Washington, whom Jones bound so tightly to Lee that distinguishing the two Virginians became practically impossible. The second concerns Jones's treatment of former Confederate general James Longstreet, on whom Jones casted ultimate culpability for the South's defeat. The third focuses on Jones's role in expunging slavery from prevailing treatments of secession and the Civil War.

WASHINGTON REDIVIVUS

Almost immediately after Lee's death in 1870, the college where he had served as president changed its name: Washington College would henceforth be Washington and Lee University. For the faculty and trustees, the move made perfect sense. George Washington's financial support had saved the struggling institution in the late eighteenth century, and Lee's five-year presidency had sustained and grown the college in the wake of the Civil War. "How fit it is," the trustees reflected, "that two of the most renowned names of their respective centuries as Washington and Lee be forever hereafter associated indisputably, as Founder and Restorer of our beloved College!"[6] That Washington's and Lee's names would be forever linked was no mere chance. White Southerners had long felt a unique connection with Washington; the icon even featured prominently on the Confederate seal. Thus the Lost Cause alchemy that transformed Lee into Washington was as unsurprising as it was deliberate. One individual chiefly responsible for this merger was Jones, whose 1874 biography of Lee inextricably bound together two of the Old Dominion's most revered sons. The book garnered Jones high praise, as well as an honorary doctorate of divinity, appropriately enough, from Washington and Lee University.[7]

Jones's first significant meeting with Lee was in the winter of 1864. As a part of Jones's role with the Chaplains' Association of the Second and Third Corps, Army of Northern Virginia—an interdenominational group organized in March 1863 for the purposes of improving camp morality and recruiting chaplains—Jones had visited the general in order to request a reduction of military work on the Sabbath (Lee gladly agreed). Even though Jones had interacted with Lee during the war, it was only after the war that Jones came to know Lee on a deeply personal level. Lee began serving as president of Washington College in 1866. That same year—likely influenced by a desire to be near Lee—Jones accepted a pastorate in Lexington, Virginia. He reconnected with the general and began leading services for the students of Washington College.[8]

Within a month of Lee's death, Jones began work on a memorial volume to his champion. Lee's colleagues at what was now Washington and Lee University began a similar project. When the faculty's initiative fell through, however, Jones offered to pick up the mantle. With access to Lee's papers, as well as to a copy of the faculty's incomplete manuscript, Jones published *Personal Reminiscences, Anecdotes, and Letters of Gen. Robert E. Lee* in 1874.[9] The book not only blazed a trail for subsequent Lee biographers but also exemplified Jones's intimate and absolute devotion to the South's great hero. Jones's plaudits knew no bounds. He praised Lee's "transcendent abilities," deeming him the greatest solider, and even the greatest college president, that the nation had ever produced. The general was Spartan in his needs, temperate in his consumption, and measured in his speech. He also represented the epitome of Christian piety, and Jones declared that he had never met an individual whose religious sincerity rivaled that of Lee.[10]

In addition to his prodigious praise of the general, Jones seldom missed an opportunity to compare Lee to Washington. Jones set about on this mission not only in his 1874 work on Lee, but also in a 1906 book, *Life and Letters of Robert Edward Lee: Soldier and Man.*[11] Some connections were obvious. Both Lee and Washington were Virginians, Episcopalians, and generals. There were also connections between the men through both friendship and family. Lee's father, General Henry "Light-Horse Harry" Lee, had served with Washington during the American Revolution, and Jones quoted an address that described the admiration of Lee's father for Washington as "almost idolatrous." Lee's father also coined what is perhaps the most well-known adulation of Washington: "First in war, first in peace, and first in the hearts of his countrymen." Jones wrote that while Lee was reticent to leave the union, "there could be little doubt on which side the sword of Robert Lee would be drawn. He was the son of 'Light Horse Harry,' and a Virginian of the Virginians." Jones even quoted Lee's father as proclaiming, "Virginia is my country; her will I obey, however lamentable the fate to which it may subject me." By connecting Lee's father (and by extension, his son) to Washington, white Southerners fused Southern secession and the Civil War to the Declaration of Independence and the American Revolution, respectively.[12]

Jones also identified the familial connections between Lee and Washington. George Washington Parke Custis, Lee's father-in-law, was Martha Washington's grandson from a previous marriage. After Custis's father died, George Washington reared the young boy as a son. Jones cited an address by James P. Holcombe, a law professor at the University of Virginia, who observed that Lee, having married into the Washington family, "was brought still more closely within that gracious and hallowed influence which already like a tutelary genius overshadowed his life." To Holcombe, Lee evidenced this "hallowed influence" from an early age. Holcombe detailed Lee's childhood: "In the simple yet manly tastes and habits, in the dignity of carriage which forbade too familiar approach, in the unequaled modesty, in the command of temper, in the noble self-restraint, in the impartial justice, in the inflexible adherence to truth, in the uniform and scrupulous discharge of duty, in the chastened ambition of young Lee, they saw reflected, as in the mirror of youth, the severe and majestic image of Washington."[13] For Holcombe and Jones, the young Lee's temperament not only resembled that of Washington, but heralded that Lee was to *be* the next Washington. In their efforts to establish the incredible similarities between the two men, white Southerners mythologized Lee's entire life, infusing in his genealogy and childhood an air of destiny. "Much has been written of what the world owes to 'Martha [*sic*], the mother of Washington,'" Jones recounted, "but it owes scarcely less to 'Anne, the mother of Lee.'"[14]

For Jones, Lee's entire life and career mirrored Washington's. Once again tethering the American Revolution with the South's struggle for independence, Jones deemed Washington the "great 'rebel' of 1776." Jones quoted an address from former Confederate senator Benjamin Harvey Hill, who described Lee as a "Caesar without his ambition; a Frederick without his tyranny; a Napoleon without his selfishness; and a Washington without his reward." Hill recalled a conversation with Lee regarding Washington in which Lee maintained that there had been none like the father of the country, who excelled in both military and political leadership, and yet had not become a tyrant. "Surely Washington is no longer the only exception," Hill demurred, "for one like him, if not greater, is here."[15]

Lee's similarities to Washington even extended into Lee's postwar career as a college president. Referencing an occasion when Lee declined a financial gift to Washington College, Jones observed (with an accompanying jab), "The refusal of General Lee to receive presents or gratuities was but one of the many points in which he resembled George Washington, 'the Father of his Country.' How far he differed from many of our leading public men of the present day, we will not here discuss." Jones also cited resolutions from the faculty of Washington College, issued upon Lee's death. Leaders justified changing the name of the institution, referencing "the immortal names of Washington and Lee, whose lives were so similar in their perfect renown."[16]

Present-day advocates for Confederate monuments have been quick to draw upon similarities between Lee and Washington. Both men were of the highest moral integrity, the argument goes, and both fought valiantly against tyranny (or at least government overreach). Incidentally, however, both men also owned slaves. Here, Lee devotees contend, the parallels continue. Although a slaveholder himself, Washington grew opposed to the institution, even writing in a private letter, "I never mean (unless some particular circumstances should compel me to it) to possess another slave by purchase; it being among my first wishes to see some plan adopted by . . . which slavery in this Country may be abolished by slow, sure, & imperceptible degrees." Washington's will stipulated that his slaves be freed upon Martha's death.[17]

Lee's views on the South's peculiar institution were similarly complicated. In 1856, he wrote his wife, admitting that "there are few I believe, but what will acknowledge, that slavery as an institution is a moral & political evil in any country." Lee continued by opining that slavery was more detrimental for whites than for slaves, and that the "painful discipline" slaves endured was "necessary for their instruction as a race."[18] As had Washington (albeit in his will), Lee manumitted his slaves. Lee had inherited the slaves from his father-in-law, and as stipulated in Custis's will, the slaves were to be freed within five years of his death. Concerned about the financial solvency of the Arlington plantation, Lee did so only after keeping the slaves for the entire time allotted.[19]

Washington's and Lee's perspectives on slavery are key for defenders of Confederate monuments and boil down to inevitable (if not slippery) questions: If Lee's statues are removed, then what is to become of Washington's? Should the Washington Monument be renamed? Furthermore, do the same standards apply for the slaveholding Thomas Jefferson? While an analysis of Washington's and Jefferson's legacies is beyond the scope of this study, essential to recognize here is that ex-Confederates like Jones imbedded certain safeguards within Lost Cause mythology that have endured for well over a hundred years. In the event that the apotheosis of Lee failed to preserve the general's pristine image, perhaps melding his legacy with that of the incorruptible Washington would prove more successful.

In an 1896 article for the *Confederate Veteran*, Jones epitomized the efforts of white Southerners to reincorporate Lee into the American narrative. Lionizing the contributions of Southerners to the United States, Jones asserted that "no section has a better right to be proud of our country's history, or to labor for its future prosperity, greatness, honor and glory, than our Southland—the home of Washington, Jefferson, Jackson, Davis, and Lee."[20] This was a classic case of absolution by association, as Jones blurred any distinction between revolutionaries and rebels. To shun Lee, Jackson, or Davis was to disown Washington and Jefferson. Stated differently, advocates for Confederate monuments could find no better friend than Jones. Lee's foremost disciple understood well that while stone and bronze could preserve Lee's visage, they were insufficient to protect Lee's name. Inasmuch as Jones's redaction sanitized the South's past, his prescience secured the South's future.

THE SACRIFICE OF JAMES LONGSTREET

If Jones recognized the glory of George Washington in Robert E. Lee, equally did Jones sense the specter of Benedict Arnold in James Longstreet (1821–1904). The story of Longstreet's fall from grace, as well as his eventual expulsion from the Confederate pantheon, reveals the lengths to which postwar white Southerners would go in order to muzzle anyone who dared challenge established Lost Cause precepts. As many ex-Confederates well knew, nothing was quite as effective, or quite as dangerous, as a compelling counternarrative.

Based purely on his service in the Confederate Army, Longstreet seems an odd candidate for postwar scapegoat. He was born in South Carolina, reared in Georgia, and ostensibly a dyed-in-the-wool Southerner. A graduate of West Point, his military record in the Civil War—while not perfect—was impressive. His battle résumé was nearly unparalleled: First Bull Run, Seven Days, Second Bull Run, Antietam, Fredericksburg, Gettysburg, Chickamauga, and the Wilderness. He rose to the rank of lieutenant general, and he became an indispensable subordinate to Lee, especially after the loss of Stonewall Jackson in the spring of 1863. With a mixture of gratitude and affection, Lee called Longstreet the "staff in my right hand" and "my old war horse." Longstreet served with Lee until the surrender of the Army of Northern Virginia at Appomattox. When Longstreet left the army in April 1865, he carried with him a wound from May 1864 that had severely damaged his right arm. As had been the case with Stonewall Jackson, Longstreet had been fired upon by his own men.[21] Ironically, he would spend the rest of his life trying to evade attacks from fellow Southerners.

For Longstreet, the trouble began in 1867. In March, he responded to an invitation from the *New Orleans Times* to reflect on the country's political situation. Longstreet acknowledged that Southerners were a "conquered people" and then counseled: "Recognizing this fact fairly and squarely, there is but one course left for wise men to pursue. Accept the terms that are offered us by the conquerors!" He continued, "We have made an honest, and I hope that I might say, a creditable fight, but we have lost."[22] While some Southern newspapers defended the general, many white Southerners were outraged. With each subsequent letter Longstreet published, the animosity toward him deepened.

In April 1867, Longstreet expounded on his views, admitting that defeated Confederates had surrendered both the "*claim* to the right of secession," as well as the "former political relations of the negro." He advised his fellow Southerners to "relieve ourselves from our present embarrassments by *returning to our allegiance, in good faith, to the General Government under the process laid down by Congress, or seek protection under some foreign Government.*"[23] By the summer, Longstreet was openly questioning Democratic platforms, and defending what he believed was the experimental suffrage of African Americans.[24]

The backlash to Longstreet's correspondence was ferocious. One letter printed in Louisiana's *Bossier Banner* declared that "General Longstreet has gone delyerous. In strainin his mind too hard in tryin to maik the n—— all white, and in straitenin thare hare [*sic*]. The work has been so monstrous hard that it has turned him black all over." In the same issue, another contributor concluded that "to all who feel a pride in the military career of General James Longstreet, it has become a subject of regret the wound he received at the Wilderness was not mortal." At least then, the writer continued, Southerners would have been spared witnessing Longstreet ally himself with the "enemies of his country and race."[25]

Longstreet's correspondence was not the only matter that provoked the ire of white Southerners. Besides joining the Republican Party, Longstreet supported and received political appointments from Ulysses S. Grant (with whom Longstreet had been friends since their days together at West Point). Longstreet also cooperated with Reconstruction governments, even leading a racially integrated police force in New Orleans.[26] He persistently and unsuccessfully attempted to vindicate himself, but ex-Confederates dismissed him as a scalawag. With his reputation already gravely damaged, the general then committed the most egregious of his sins—the act that would thereafter sear his infamy into the minds of white Southerners for decades. That offense was Longstreet's public criticism of Lee, specifically with regard to the Battle of Gettysburg. This besmirching of Lee's legacy stirred up a hornets' nest of Confederate veterans, particularly one J. William Jones.

In the ten years following his first letter to the *New Orleans Times*, Longstreet was unable to rehabilitate his image. After 1877, the endeavor would prove virtually impossible. As Reconstruction breathed its last, the campaign against Longstreet revivified. The renewed assault on the general began when Louis Philippe Albert d'Orleans (Comte de Paris)—who had served on the staff of General George McClellan—requested assistance from Jones and the Southern Historical Society (SHS). The Comte was completing a multi-volume work on the war, and in a letter to the SHS, he requested additional perspectives on the Battle of Gettysburg. Specifically, the Comte wanted to know why Confederate initiatives on July 2 had lacked the coordination of previous attacks. Jones and former Confederate general, Jubal Early, now at the helms of the *SHSP* and SHS, respectively, realized the stakes of the Comte's inquiry. As the custodians of Lee's good name, Jones and Early had long resolved to defend the great chieftain at any cost. In order to deflect blame for the Gettysburg defeat from Lee— who himself had claimed full responsibility—Jones and Early set their sights on Longstreet.[27]

In response to the Comte's request, Jones solicited the opinions of leading ex-Confederates. Of the responses Jones printed in the *SHSP*, most pinned the Gettysburg defeat on Longstreet. Early weighed in as well. He accused Longstreet of mishandling Lee's orders to attack early on July 2, a mistake that Early believed cost the Confederacy the entire battle.[28] Other contributors to the series aligned with Early, most of them holding

Longstreet singularly responsible for the Gettysburg failure. In a letter to Jones, Early praised what he felt was his own airtight argument against Longstreet.[29]

The onslaught against the South's great pariah continued in early 1878, when Jones printed an interview that Longstreet had given to the Philadelphia *Times*. Not only did the general defend his actions at Gettysburg, but he recalled expressly disagreeing with Lee's decision to launch the ultimately disastrous third-day attack. The article played right into the hands of the SHS, and in a March 1878 letter, Jones wrote Early, "Of course *I* am anxious for you to slice up what is left of Longstreet."[30] The offensive against Longstreet lasted for more than a year and then continued to surface long after. By 1884, Jones was blaming Longstreet not only for the Confederacy's defeat at Gettysburg, but for the Confederacy's defeat in the war itself. If Lee's invasion of the North had been successful, Jones reasoned, England would have cast their lot with the Confederacy. "The Confederates would have won Gettysburg, and Independence," Jones declared, "but for the failure of *one man*."[31]

Jones and Early's salvo against Longstreet left the general's already tainted character in shambles. Interestingly, Longstreet was not the only high-profile Confederate to defect to the Republicans after the war, or the only one to suffer reprisals as a result. The dashing Confederate colonel, John Singleton Mosby (1833–1916), followed a similar path as Longstreet and nearly suffered a similar fate. During the war, Mosby rose quickly through the ranks, served under General J. E. B. Stuart, and eventually commanded a cavalry battalion. Mosby and his "rangers" launched a number of daring raids against the federals, and his remarkable ability to elude capture earned him the moniker "Gray Ghost."[32]

After the war, as did Longstreet, Mosby aligned with the Republican Party. Also like Longstreet, Mosby supported and befriended Grant. Mosby's relationship with President Rutherford B. Hayes led to Mosby's appointment as both US consul to Hong Kong and as assistant attorney general. With regard to the Lost Cause, Mosby refused to toe the party line, and even went as far as to defend the indefensible Longstreet. In fact, Mosby's heresy seemed to know no bounds. In a letter from 1894, he maintained that slavery was the principal cause of the Civil War, and that Confederate monuments were a "waste of both money & time." After the war, Mosby lived in Warrenton, Virginia. Because of his Republican ties, however, embittered Southerners castigated him as a traitor. Mosby received death threats, had his childhood home set ablaze, and in 1877, survived an assassination attempt.[33]

Worth asking is whether or not Mosby's reputation was as unsalvageable as Longstreet's, especially considering the similarities of the two men's postwar careers. Here again it is important to appreciate the enduring effects of the Jones-Early crusade against Longstreet. Though published after Jones's time as editor, an 1899 issue of the *SHSP* illustrated the point well. The volume contained one article about Mosby's rangers and one about Longstreet. The first piece concerned the dedication of a monument to a group of Mosby's men who had been executed in 1864. Although the story centered on Mosby's rangers rather than Mosby himself, the once-outcast still received high marks. At the unveiling, a former Confederate general "beautifully eulogized Colonel Mosby, to the delight of the veterans." The article even described Mosby as the "idol" of his men.[34]

In contrast to the Mosby article, the *SHSP*'s commentary on Longstreet examined—as might have been expected—the general's role in the Battle of Gettysburg. Written by Henry Alexander White, a professor of history at Washington and Lee University, the treatment was more measured than those of Jones or Early (White even critiqued Early's biases); still, in the end, White made no effort to absolve Longstreet of guilt. In fact, in some ways White's conclusion cast Longstreet in as much of an unflattering light as had *SHSP* articles many years prior. White maintained that Lee did not "vacillate" at Gettysburg, nor did he "yield his judgment to Longstreet." White determined that Longstreet's "fault was not argumentative opposition, but practical disobedience of orders."[35] Readers of White's article were thus left to infer that Longstreet was not merely guilty of incompetence, but of outright insubordination. While White's piece lacked the malignity characteristic of Jones and Early's initiative against the general, the article continued the stock Lost Cause tradition of protecting the Lee legacy. In the end, the *SHSP*'s decades-long preoccupation with the Battle of Gettysburg had less to do with parsing the details of the Confederacy's high-water mark and more to do with distancing Lee as much as possible from the Confederacy's costliest defeat. Because of Gettysburg, as well as Longstreet's postwar comments, he and Lee were inextricably bound in a zero-sum game. For Lost Causers, to anathematize Longstreet was necessarily to canonize Lee. As was the case with Gettysburg, this was a battle that Longstreet was destined to lose.

Certainly, not every Southerner wanted Longstreet to remain in exile. Some Confederate veterans still invited him to reunions, and in 1895, Longstreet gave an address at the dedication of the Chickamauga and Chattanooga National Military Park. He also received an invitation to Richmond in 1890 to participate in the unveiling of Lee's statue[36] (notice, however, that the monument was to Lee, not Longstreet). Even with his partial rehabilitation, when Longstreet died in 1904, many white Southerners could not resist delivering a final barb. In Georgia, a chapter of the United Daughters of the Confederacy (UDC) refused to send flowers to the general's funeral. In North Carolina, one group of ex-Confederates neglected even to convey their sympathies to the Longstreet family.[37]

Longstreet's checkered legacy owes much to Jones and Early's efforts, a campaign that historian Thomas Connelly has described as the "most cynical manipulation that ever occurred in the writing of Civil War history."[38] The character assassination of Longstreet also sheds a needed perspective on perpetual clashes over Confederate monuments. Longstreet was no small-time character in the Southern ranks, and he participated in many of the largest, deadliest, and most pivotal battles of the Civil War. The question, however, hangs heavy: where are Longstreet's monuments? One would be hard pressed to find any subordinate or advisor outside of Stonewall Jackson who was as vital to Lee as Longstreet. Yet one would be equally hard pressed to find many statues, monuments, or other means of tangible memory that relate to the general.

There is a marker in Edgefield, South Carolina, where Longstreet was born, and a statue in Gainesville, Georgia, where he died. In 1998, about a century after the dedication of scores of monuments to the likes of Lee and Jackson, Longstreet advocates finally erected a statue in Gettysburg.[39] Compared to the monuments of other Confederates, the non-pedestaled sculpture is diminutive. While this perceived slight is perhaps unintentional, students of Longstreet's tortuous postwar career can hardly fail to notice.

Arguments from silence (or, in this case, absence) are dicey, but sometimes can speak volumes. In the 150 years since the Civil War, white Southerners shaped much of their history through the erection of monuments. Southerners forged just as much history, however, through the monuments that never were. Thus the dearth of Longstreet memorials is unsurprising. This was the price the general paid for his criticism of Lee, his union with the Republican Party, his cooperation with Reconstruction, and his openness to racially integrated politics. If the monument controversy says anything about the erasing of history, then look no further than General James Longstreet. That is, of course, if you can find him.

SLAVERY AND THE SALTIRE

Disputes surrounding Confederate symbols—be they monuments, flags, or street signs—principally hinge on the question of slavery's role in the onset of the Civil War. Even so, Lost Causers went to great lengths to decentralize slavery as a cause of the conflict. With as much verve as he had forged a link between Lee and Washington, Jones severed any connection between the Confederacy and the South's peculiar institution. Present-day firestorms over Confederate flags are prime examples of how the strategies of ex-Confederates continue to wield substantial influence. In fact, modern discourse over white Southern memory has yet to break free from the parameters that Jones and his ilk established.

The articles Jones printed for the *SHSP* confronted slavery and public memory in ways that were both unusual and expected. While most articles distanced the Confederacy from slavery, some authors acknowledged the connection as a given. There were notable examples in which writers to the *SHSP* let down their guard and suggested that slavery was indeed a central factor in secession. In an 1876 issue of the *SHSP*, one writer acknowledged that, in theory, a defense of slavery was worth fighting a war. In another article, former Confederate general James R. Chalmers contended that Southern paragons like Lee, Davis, and Albert Sydney Johnston had not fought in order to destroy the Union, but "mainly to preserve alive the institution of slavery, guaranteed by the constitution of the United States."[40] Up for debate is whether or not these contributors to the *SHSP* understood that they were chipping away at the foundation of the Lost Cause edifice. The standard approach of most ex-Confederate authors in the *SHSP* was to sidestep the slavery issue altogether and construct a white Southern narrative in which slavery was merely incidental to larger issues at work.

One means of deemphasizing slavery's role in secession was to reinterpret Confederate symbols such as Confederate flags. Perhaps the most illuminating example of this strategy came from former Confederate private, author, and eventual Richmond mayor, Carlton McCarthy. In 1880, Jones printed an article in which McCarthy carefully, if awkwardly, distinguished between Confederate national flags such as the "Stars and Bars" and the Confederate battle flag of the Army of Northern Virginia. McCarthy asserted that the battle flag was "not the flag of the Confederacy, but simply the banner—the battle flag—of the Confederate soldier," and that "as such it should not share in the condemnation which our *cause* received, or suffer from its downfall."[41]

McCarthy also expressed his desire to "place the *battle* flag in a place of security, as it were, separated from all the political significance which attaches to the *Confederate* flag, and depending for its future place solely upon the deeds of the armies which bore it, amid hardships untold, to many victories."[42] McCarthy's approach to Confederate memory essentially bifurcated the motivations of white Southerners. Realizing that he could not successfully detach Confederate symbols from secession and slavery, he opted to sacrifice the "Stars and Bars" (and presumably other iterations of the national flag) in order to preserve the St. Andrew's Cross. The battle flag, he reasoned, simply represented the valor of the common solider.

McCarthy's move to tie the Confederate battle flag into transcendent "American" virtues was not only effective; it was representative of broader impulses among white Southerners. Historian Gary Gallagher identifies four primary strands of postwar memory: Union, Emancipation, Lost Cause, and Reconciliationist. Of particular note is the last of these, which at times overlapped with Lost Cause mythology. For Gallagher, the Reconciliationist strand of memory stressed the "*American* virtues both sides manifested during the war." Such a reconciliation came at a cost, however, as white Southerners (and Northerners) excluded African Americans from the narrative of national reunion.[43] Implicit in this détente was the notion that one could tell the story of secession and war with only tangential reference (or no reference at all) to slavery or to African Americans.

The McCarthy article was just one instance of Jones using the *SHSP* to further reconciliation. He printed a speech in 1881 from former Confederate chaplain J. B. Hawthorne in which the reverend recognized that Union soldiers had fought for "what they believed to be truth and justice."[44] Another piece, this one again from Chalmers, also struck a conciliatory chord: "When Northern men believed it necessary to fight for the Union, we honor those who fought and those who died for their faith. When Southern men fought for their constitutional property and rights, he deserves to be a tyrant's slave who does not honor those who fought and fell for a cause they believed to be right. But while we would cherish all its glorious memories and point our children to the brilliant examples of valor of both sides in the war, we have no desire to revive the bitter hates of the strife."[45]

Perhaps the most fascinating aspect of Chalmers's address was that the general—in a marked break from Lost Cause convention—admitted that slavery had galvanized Southern leaders to secede from the Union. Even more striking, Chalmers asserted that—in addition to the mutual courage of Confederate and Union troops—Southerners (and Northerners!) could be proud of secession. "The very fact that there was a war growing out of a question of constitutional rights should be a source of pride," Chalmers insisted, "as evidence that no large body of our people will ignobly submit to what they believed to be a violation of their rights."[46]

Even though Jones resigned as editor of the *SHSP* in 1887, his impact on white Southern memory persisted long thereafter. Jones's writings and redactions provided for white Southerners the vocabulary by which they would articulate and defend Confederate memory, and today's apologists readily draw from the canons Jones and Lost Causers ingrained in pro-Confederate publications. For example, if *SHSP* contributors' interpretations of Confederate symbols was imaginative, then the vexillology of current-day white Southerners is no less so. As historian John Coski observes:

> The erroneous use of the battle flag (or, more accurately, the naval jack) illustrates the continuing widespread popular belief that the battle flag *is* the Confederate flag. It also reveals the desire to use a flag familiar to most people as a Confederate symbol. That the Stars and Bars is a Confederate flag is immaterial; just as Confederates rejected it in 1863 because it was not distinct enough from the Stars and Stripes, Confederate partisans today reject it because it is not a sufficiently Confederate symbol. Defenders of the public display of Confederate flags complain about the effort to erase or revise history. The insistence on using battle flags instead of historically correct national flags reveals a double standard on the issue of revising history.[47]

Coski rightly notes the ahistoricism of flag advocates who gravitate toward the St. Andrew's Cross. Other polemicists, however, use as leverage the differences among Confederate banners. The ability to make these distinctions serves two functions. First, defenders can use their knowledge of Confederate flags in order to dismiss critics (e.g., a detractor who unknowingly refers to the battle flag or navy jack as the "Stars and Bars" would fall into this trap). Second, flag supporters—taking their cues from Jones, McCarthy, et al.—artfully differentiate between the Confederate national flags and the Confederate battle flag. Whereas the former represent secession and politics, the latter symbolizes courage and honor. More colloquially, inasmuch as national flags characterize a "rich man's war," battle flags signify a "poor man's fight."

For some authors of the *SHSP*, the war at its core was a struggle not just for slavery as an institution, but for white racial integrity as an ideal. The majority of authors, however, extricated slavery from any examination of the conflict. What fueled many white Southerners to do so was a desire to reconcile (on their own terms) with white Northerners. As a result, and as a means of coping with defeat and reincorporating themselves into the narrative of the United States, white Southerners cultivated mutual respect among soldiers from the blue and the gray. They achieved this reconciliation by recasting themselves not as racial purists hell-bent on preserving white dominance in the South, but as intrepid soldiers who had fought valiantly for what they believed to be right. Surely, Southerners reasoned, Northerners could respect that. And, by and large, Southerners were correct. In *Reforging the White Republic*, historian Edward Blum narrates in chilling detail the culpability of Northern Christians in facilitating and endorsing postwar reunion on the basis of shared whiteness. Essentially, mutual respect among soldiers was devastatingly efficient in sanitizing the memories of whites both North and South.

Interestingly, the motivations of twenty-first-century Confederate enthusiasts echo the motivations of nineteenth-century Lost Causers. On one hand, the former appear as the epitome of divisiveness, ready at the drop of a kepi to secede once more and thus embrace the eschatological promise that the South will "rise again." On the other hand, these white Southerners also represent a subconscious desire to be accepted by non-Southerners as having a distinctive identity—one that goes beyond deep-frying, sweet tea, and a funny way of talking.[48] Tragically, this hope for reconciliation is still predicated on the denial of race as fundamental cause for conflict in the United States—whether during the Civil War or today.

Those who support the public display of Confederate symbols are acutely concerned about the erasure of history. As Coski observes, however, "The flag is history, but for many people it is also a symbol with a potent ideological meaning to be preserved and perpetuated; its display does not merely acknowledge a *fact* of history but implies a favorable judgment on that history."[49] Beyond a "favorable judgment," displays of Confederate flags on public property imply that those emblems represent a shared story. As demonstrated in Lost Cause publications, the flags instead testify to a narrative shaped by and for whites. In light of Jones's extensive career as Confederate apologist, the fact that contemporary Southerners condemn the removal of public Confederate symbols as whitewashing history is as inaccurate as it is ironic.

Today, the fiery arguments surrounding Confederate monuments and flags, or the roles of slavery and race in the Civil War, are in many ways testaments to Jones's success in forging a white Southern mythology. His work not only laid the foundation for today's battles over Confederate memory—controversies which acrobatically sever war from slavery, monuments from memorials, and heritage from hate—but also provided the means by which white Southerners could navigate the troubled waters of historical memory. In another touch of irony, Jones's work—for all its prolepsis—still exhibited inspiration from early American history. Jones believed that it was only by honoring a white Southern history that the reunited nation could move forward. In this regard, Jones—who felt that Southerners had as much if not more claim on the "founding fathers" than anyone—did indeed echo voices from the early republic. Disturbingly, these were the voices of compromise, who, from the nation's inception, determined that African Americans would need to be sacrificed in order for whites to get along.

NOTES

1. "Whose Heritage? Public Symbols of the Confederacy," Southern Poverty Law Center (SPLC), accessed April 20, 2018, https://www.splcenter.org/20160421/whose-heritage-public-symbols-confederacy. According to the SPLC, these numbers do not include "markers, battlefields, museums, cemeteries and other places or symbols that are largely historical in nature."

2. There are numerous helpful definitions of the "Lost Cause." Here I am indebted to historian Lloyd Hunter's descriptor, "sacralization." See Hunter, "The Sacred South: Postwar Confederates and the Sacralization of Southern Culture" (PhD diss., Saint Louis Univ., 1978). See also Hunter, "The Immortal Confederacy: Another Look at Lost Cause Religion," in *The Myth of the Lost Cause and Civil War History*, Gary W. Gallagher and Alan T. Nolan (Bloomington: Indiana Univ. Press, 2000). For a sampling of other well-known and variegated perspectives on the Lost Cause, see Charles Reagan Wilson, *Baptized in Blood:*

Religion of the Lost Cause, 1865–1920 (Athens: Univ. of Georgia Press, 1980), 7, 12–13; Wilson, "The Religion of the Lost Cause: Ritual and Organization of the Southern Civil Religion, 1865–1920," *Journal of Southern History* 46 (May 1980): 219–38; Gaines Foster, *Ghosts of the Confederacy: Defeat, the Lost Cause, and the Emergence of the New South, 1865–1913* (New York: Oxford Univ. Press, 1988), 7–8; W. Scott Poole, *Never Surrender: Confederate Memory and Conservatism in the South Carolina Upcountry* (Athens: Univ. of Georgia Press, 2004), 3, 79; Thomas L. Connelly and Barbara L. Bellows, *God and General Longstreet: The Lost Cause and the Southern Mind* (Baton Rouge: Louisiana State Univ. Press, 1982), 4–6, 123–24, 137, 146–48; Roland Osterweis, *The Myth of the Lost Cause, 1865–1900* (Hamden, CT: Archon Books, 1973), x; William C. Davis, *The Cause Lost: Myths and Realities of the Confederacy* (Lawrence: Univ. Press of Kansas, 1996), 175–78.

3. Gardiner H. Shattuck, Jr., *A Shield and Hiding Place: The Religious Life of the Civil War Armies* (Macon: Mercer Univ. Press, 1987), 121.

4. Certainly there are notable exceptions. See William Earl Brown, "Pastoral Evangelism: A Model for Effective Evangelism as Demonstrated by the Ministries of John Albert Broadus, Alfred Elijah Dickinson, and John William Jones in the Revival of the Army of Northern Virginia in 1863" (PhD diss., Southeastern Baptist Theological Seminary, 1999); Christopher Martin, "The Confederate Crusader: John William Jones and the Lost Cause" (PhD diss., Claremont Graduate Univ., 2018). Wilson dedicates a chapter to Jones's life and influence. See Wilson, *Baptized in Blood*, 119–38. See also Edward R. Crowther, "John the Evangelist Revisited: John William Jones and the Lost Cause," *Journal of Southern Religion* 17 (2015): http://jsreligion.org/issues/vol17/ crowther.html. For a less charitable—though not wholly unjustified—take on Jones's career, see Thomas L. Connelly, *The Marble Man: Robert E. Lee and His Image in American Society* (Baton Rouge: Louisiana State Univ. Press, 1977), 41–42.

5. Biographical resources consulted for this sketch include the following: J. William Jones, "Varied Experiences In Work Among Young Men," *Religious Herald* 82 (April 1, 1909): 4–5; Jones, *Christ in the Camp or Religion in Lee's Army* (Richmond: B. F. Johnson and Company, 1887), 17, 321, 391–92 ; Jones, "Reminiscences of the Army of Northern Virginia, or the Boys in Gray, as I Saw Them from 1861 to Appomattox Court-House in 1865," *Southern Historical Society Papers* (*SHSP*) 9 (February 1881): 90–91; Jones, "Reminiscences of the Army of Northern Virginia," *SHSP* 9 (October–December 1881): 561; Wilson, *Baptized in Blood*, 120–23, 125; George Braxton Taylor, *Virginia Baptist Ministers*, 5th Series, 1902–1914 (Lynchburg, VA: J. P. Bell, 1915), 220–23, 225–28; "Chaplain General J. William Jones," *Confederate Veteran* (*CV*) 17 (May 1909): 239; Lyon Gardiner Tyler, *Men of Mark in Virginia, Ideals of American Life: A Collection of Biographies of the Leading Men in the State*, vol. 1 (Washington, DC: Men of Mark Publishing Company, 1906), 250–53; Brown, "Pastoral Evangelism," 55, 109–10; Malcolm Hart Harris, *History of Louisa County, Virginia* (Richmond: The Dietz Press, 1936), 78–79; David F. Riggs, *13th Virginia Infantry* (Lynchburg: H. E. Howard, Inc., 1988), 29, 74–75, 86, 122; Frank L. Hieronymus, "For Now and Forever: The Chaplains of the Confederate States Army" (PhD diss., Univ. of California, Los Angeles, 1964), 78–80, 87; John S. Moore, "John William Jones," *Virginia Baptist Register* 31 (Richmond: Virginia Baptist Historical Society, 1992), 1605–1607; Connelly, *The Marble Man*, 40; J. L. Rosser, "John William Jones," *Encyclopedia of Southern Baptists*, vol. 1 (Nashville, TN:

Broadman Press, 1958), 710; John R. Sampey, *Southern Baptist Theological Seminary: The First Thirty Years, 1859–1889* (Baltimore: Wharton, Barron and Company, 1890), 126; David S. Williams, "J. William Jones (1836–1909)," *New Georgia Encyclopedia*, accessed May 9, 2018; Gardiner H. Shattuck, Jr., "John William Jones," *American National Biography Online*, accessed December 8, 2014.

6. "Our Namesakes: Washington and Lee University," accessed March 16, 2015, http://www.wlu.edu/ about-wandl/history-and-traditions/our-namesakes.

7. Moore, "John William Jones," 1602.

8. Jones, *Christ in the Camp*, 49–50; Hieronymus, *For Now and Forever*, 62; Taylor, *Virginia Baptist Ministers*, 221–22, 225–27; Wilson, *Baptized in Blood*, 120–21, 127–28; Moore, "John William Jones," 1599–1604; Brown, "Pastoral Evangelism," 114–17.

9. Connelly, *The Marble Man.*, 40–42; Moore, "John William Jones," 1602.

10. Jones, *Personal Reminiscences, Anecdotes, and Letters of Gen. Robert E. Lee* (New York: D. Appleton and Company, 1874), 79, 129, 168–69, 416–17, 419, 421–22, 425–27, 440–41, 445.

11. Jones, *Life and Letters of Robert Edward Lee: Soldier and Man* (New York: Neale Publishing Company, 1906).

12. Jones, *Personal Reminiscences*, 491; Henry Lee, "Funeral Oration on the Death of General Washington," 14, accessed May 3, 2018, https://www.nlm.nih.gov/exhibition /georgewashington/education/materials/ Transcript-Funeral.pdf. Jones, *Life and Letters*, 18–19, 125. For more on the parallels between Lee and Washington, see Jonathan Horn, *The Man Who Would Not Be Washington: Robert E. Lee's Civil War and His Decision That Changed American History* (New York: Scribner, 2016). For an analysis of postrevolutionary civil religion, which kindled the sacralization of Washington and the nation's founding documents, see Catherine L. Albanese, *Sons of the Fathers: The Civil Religion of the American Revolution* (Philadelphia: Temple Univ. Press, 1976).

13. Jones, *Personal Reminiscences*, 491.

14. Jones, *Personal Reminiscences*, 147, 366, 491–92; Jones, *Life and Letters*, 24; "George Washington Parke Custis," US National Park Service, accessed May 4, 2018, https://www.nps .gov/arho/learn/historyculture/ george-custis.htm. The name of Washington's mother was Mary, not Martha.

15. Jones, *Personal Reminiscences*, 222–23. Here Hill's phrasing vaguely echoes scripture, e.g., Matthew 12:41 (KJV): "The queen of the south shall rise up in the judgment with this generation, and shall condemn it: for she came from the uttermost parts of the earth to hear the wisdom of Solomon; and behold, a greater than Solomon is here." Cf. Luke 11:31.

16. Jones, *Personal Reminiscences*, 179, 382, 465–66.

17. George Washington to John F. Mercer, September 9, 1786. Transcript available at "George Washington on the Abolition of Slavery, 1786," Gilder Lehrman Institute of American History, accessed May 5, 2018, https://www.gilderlehrman.org/content /george-washington-abolition-slavery-1786. Washington's will applied to his own slaves, but not to slaves Martha owned from her previous marriage. Perhaps fearing an uprising, Martha manumitted her husband's slaves on January 1, 1801, earlier than required. See

"Status of Slaves in Washington's Will," accessed January 19, 2019, https://www.mount vernon.org/library/digitalhistory/digital-encyclopedia/article/ status-of-slaves-in -washingtons-will/.

18. Lee to Mary Randolph Custis Lee, December 27, 1856. Transcript available at *Encyclopedia Virginia*, accessed May 5, 2018, https://www.encyclopediavirginia.org /Letter_from_Robert_E_Lee_to_Mary_Randolph_Custis_Lee_December_27_1856.

19. Lee to W. H. F. Lee, February 16, 1862, George Bolling Lee Papers, 1841–1868, Virginia Historical Society, Richmond, VA. See also Lee to Mary Randolph Custis Lee, November 11, 1863. Transcript available at *Encyclopedia Virginia*, accessed May 5, 2018, https://www.encyclopediavirginia.org/Letter_from_Robert_E_Lee_to_Mary_Randolph _Custis_Lee_November_11_1863.

20. Jones, "Dr. Jones's Rejoinder," *CV* 4 (October 1896): 332. In order to craft his mythology of Lee, Jones relied heavily on mythology surrounding the nation's founders. Historian David Sehat argues that Jefferson in particular contributed to a national mythology that "rhetorically turned the founding era into one of political purity that he himself had channeled." Post-Jefferson political discourse in the US thus consistently (and often inaccurately) appealed to the founders as unified and unerring authorities. See Sehat, *The Jefferson Rule: How the Founding Fathers Became Infallible and Our Politics Inflexible* (New York: Simon and Schuster, 2015), 37.

21. Steven Nash, "James Longstreet (1821–1904)," *New Georgia Encyclopedia*, accessed April 25, 2018; "James Longstreet," *Civil War Trust*, accessed April 25, 2018, https://www .civilwar.org/learn/biographies/james-longstreet.

22. "Gen. James Longstreet on the Situation," *New Orleans Times* 6, March 19, 1867.

23. "Letter from Gen. Longstreet and Judge Campbell, of Louisiana," *The New York Times* (reprinted from *New Orleans Times*, April 7), April 13, 1867. Italics in the original.

24. "General Longstreet," *South-Western* 15, June 19, 1867.

25. "Correspondence," *Bossier Banner* 6, July 6, 1867. The second letter is a reprint from the *Mobile Daily Tribune*. Regarding the *Bossier Banner* letter, I have left the original spelling, but have edited for content.

26. Jeffry D. Wert, *General James Longstreet: The Confederacy's Most Controversial Soldier* (New York: Simon and Schuster, 2015), 31; Cynthia Nicoletti, *Secession on Trial: The Treason Prosecution of Jefferson Davis* (New York: Cambridge Univ. Press, 2017), 97–98; "James Longstreet," *Civil War Trust*; William Garrett Piston, *Lee's Tarnished Lieutenant: James Longstreet and His Place in Southern History* (Athens: Univ. of Georgia Press, 1990), 107–14.

27. See Jones to the Comte de Paris, September 1876, Southern Historical Society Files/ Correspondence: Miscellaneous, Museum of the Confederacy, Richmond, VA. Hereafter as SHS Files, MOC; "History of the Civil War in America," *SHSP* 1 (January–June 1876): i. See also Connelly, *The Marble Man*, 85–90.

28. Jones, "Causes of Defeat of Gen. Lee's Army at the Battle of Gettysburg— Opinions of Leading Confederate Soldiers," *SHSP* 4 (August 1877): 1; "Our Gettysburg Series," *SHSP* 5 (January/February 1878): 87; Early, "Causes of Defeat of Gen. Lee's

Army at the Battle of Gettysburg—Opinions of Leading Confederate Soldiers," *SHSP* 4 (August 1877): 11–16.

29. "Letter from General C. M. Wilcox," "Letter from General A. L. Long, Military Secretary to General R. E. Lee," "Second Paper by Colonel Walter H. Taylor, of General Lee's Staff," *SHSP* 4 (September 1877): 114, 122, 129–30. "Letter from General John B. Hood," "Letter from Major-General Henry Heth," *SHSP* 4 (October 1877): 4, 155; Early to Jones, October 28, 1877, SHS Files, MOC.

30. Jones to Early, March 26, 1878, Early Papers, Library of Congress. See also Harold Eugen Mahan, "The Final Battle: The Southern Historical Society and Confederate Hopes for History," *Southern Historian* 5 (Spring 1984): 32.

31. "General Longstreet's Second Paper on Gettysburg," "Reply to General Longstreet's Second Paper," *SHSP* 5 (June 1878): 6, 8, 13, 287; "Review of the First Two Days' Operations at Gettysburg and a Reply to General Longstreet by General Fitz Lee," *SHSP* 5 (April 1878): 166–67, 175, 177, 185–93; "'Within a Stone's Throw of Independence' at Gettysburg," *SHSP* 12 (March 1884): 111.

32. Ruth Ann Coski, "John Singleton Mosby (1833–1916)," *Encyclopedia Virginia*, accessed April 6, 2018; "John Singleton Mosby," US National Park Service, accessed April 20, 2018, https://www.nps.gov/people/john-singleton-mosby.htm; "John Singleton Mosby," *Civil War Trust*, accessed January 6, 2010, https://www.civilwar.org/learn/biographies/john-singleton-mosby.

33. "John Singleton Mosby," US National Park Service. See also Mosby to Aristides Monteiro, June 9, 1894, photocopy, *Encyclopedia Virginia*, accessed April 20, 2018, https://www.encyclopediavirginia.org/media_player?mets_filename=evm00003514mets.xml; Bradford Richardson, "Confederate Memorial to Anti-Slavery Virginian John Singleton Mosby Upends Battle over Monuments," *Washington Times*, accessed April 20, 2018, https://www.washingtontimes.com/news/2017/aug/17/confederate-memorial-to-anti-slavery-virginian-joh/; John Singleton Mosby, Charles Wells Russell, eds., *The Memoirs of Colonel John S. Mosby* (Boston: Little, Brown, and Company, 1917), xiii.

34. "Ceremonies of the Unveiling at Front Royal, Va., September 23, 1899, of the Monument to Mosby's Men," *SHSP* 27 (January–December 1899): 250, 252, 262.

35. Henry Alexander White, "The Battle of Gettysburg," *SHSP* 27 (January–December 1899): 59.

36. "James Longstreet," *Civil War Trust.*

37. Connelly and Bellows, *God and General Longstreet*, 37.

38. Connelly, *The Marble Man,* 85–90. For a detailed treatment of Jones and Early's operation against Longstreet, see Martin, "The Confederate Crusader," 92–110.

39. Steven A. Holmes, "Where are the Monuments to Confederate Gen. James Longstreet?" accessed January 29, 2018, http://www.cnn.com/2017/08/23/opinions/where-are-monuments-to-confederate-general-longstreet-opinion-holmes/index.html. As Holmes notes, there is no need to portray Longstreet as a "racial saint." Historian William Piston writes that although Longstreet cooperated with Reconstruction governments, he still "sought to *control* the black vote." See Piston, *Lee's Tarnished Lieutenant,* 107.

40. R. M. T. Hunter, "Origin of the Late War," *SHSP* 1 (January–June 1876): 1; James R. Chalmers, "Forrest and his Campaigns," *SHSP* 7 (October 1879): 451–52.

41. Carlton McCarthy, "Origin of the Confederate Battle Flag," *SHSP* 8 (October–December 1880): 497. See also McCarthy, *Detailed Minutiae of Soldier Life in the Army of Northern Virginia, 1861–1865* (Richmond, VA: Carlton McCarthy and Company, 1882), 219–24.

42. McCarthy, "Origin of the Confederate Battle Flag," 499.

43. Gary W. Gallagher, *Causes Won, Lost, and Forgotten: How Hollywood and Popular Art Shape What We Know about the Civil War* (Chapel Hill: Univ. of North Carolina Press, 2013), 2. See also Edward J. Blum, *Reforging the White Republic: Race, Religion, and American Nationalism, 1865–1898* (Baton Rouge: Louisiana State Univ. Press, 2007), 17; David W. Blight, *Race and Reunion: The Civil War in American Memory* (Cambridge, MA: Belknap Press, 2002), 39.

44. J. B. Hawthorne, "The Courage of the Confederate Soldier," *SHSP* 9 (January 1881): 37.

45. James Chalmers, "Forrest and his Campaigns," *SHSP* 7 (October 1879): 452.

46. Chalmers, "Forrest and his Campaigns," 452.

47. John M. Coski, *The Confederate Battle Flag: America's Most Embattled Emblem* (Cambridge, MA: Belknap Press, 2006), 280.

48. As historian W. Scott Poole contends, "[Confederate] symbols now seem meaningless, signs that have no significance beyond a vague dis-ease over the meaning of southern identity, the fear among southern yuppies that their cultural ethos has dwindled to a drawl and a taste for fried foods." See Poole, *Never Surrender: Confederate Memory and Conservatism in the South Carolina Upcountry* (Athens: Univ. of Georgia Press, 2004), 205.

49. Coski, *The Confederate Battle Flag*, 291. Coski also writes that "what is at stake is not so much history as *heritage*." He continues, "Heritage is more akin to religion than history. It is a presentation of the past based not on critical evaluation of evidence but on faith and the acceptance of dogma."

A Pure and Priceless Heritage: Gender Construction and the Lost Cause

COLIN CHAPELL

> "We should ever regard our history as a priceless heritage, cherish and keep green the traditions of the old South, keep alive its chivalrous spirit, and never tire of telling the story of those lion-hearted men, who made this history for us, and around whose names cluster some of the greatest events of the past."
> —Mrs. S. E. F. Rose from *The Ku Klux Klan or Invisible Empire*, 75–76

In her book on the Ku Klux Klan, Mrs. S. E. F. Rose lauded the work of the Invisible Empire.[1] According to her, the Klan "should be our proudest boast, as it was organized and kept up by our best and noblest men, who had proven their worth and valor on so many battlefields, and who preserved the purity and domination of the Anglo-Saxon race."[2] She wrote that the members of that fraternal (terrorist) organization were the South's "best and noblest men," thus demonstrating her belief in the ideas of what historians now call the Lost Cause. Alternately termed a mythology, ideology, or even a civil religion, many of the ideas of the Lost Cause sprang up almost immediately after the defeat of the Confederate forces at the close of the American Civil War.

Despite the war officially ending in 1865, the Lost Cause endures. Whether in the conflicts over taking down the Confederate battle flag or monuments honoring Confederate heroes, statements from the highest office in the United States about the honor of some of the leaders of the Confederacy, or the continuing public arguments over the causes of the American Civil War, it is clear that an understanding of history heavily influenced by the tenets of the Lost Cause continues to influence American life.[3] For some, this veneration of Southern nationalism moves beyond an interpretation of history and into a force that grounds their understanding of the world in a specific interpretation of the past, while at the same time helping them to engage

24

with the contemporary world. These depictions, reified by both symbols and practices, help adherents confront suffering (whether real or perceived) and offer ultimate redemption for the defeated white South. By relying on the Lost Cause mythology to understand their place in the world, adherents create new and organic constructions of personal identity—including specific visions of what true manhood and womanhood entail.[4]

One of the first historians who took seriously the power of the Lost Cause worldview was Charles Reagan Wilson, whose *Baptized in Blood: The Religion of the Lost Cause, 1865–1920* quickly became an authoritative text for those looking to understand the enduring power of the Lost Cause in the United States. First published in 1980, Wilson's argument that significant portions of the general public, particularly whites in the American South, understood their world through the Lost Cause remains an important starting point for understanding the American South.[5] Yet, while Wilson's book demonstrated the continuing power of the Lost Cause as a way for adherents, it did not concentrate on how acolytes used such tenets to construct elements of gender identity. While other scholars have picked up themes not covered in *Baptized in Blood*, it is clear that the Lost Cause, and its enduring power in American culture, is about much more than simply the origins of the Civil War or the reasons for Confederate defeat. It is a way for many people, particularly white Southerners, to understand the world around them.

The tenets of the Lost Cause provide a mythological history—a time when the world was simpler, when (white) families were strong, and where individuals knew their place in the world.[6] In other words, it provided a grounding for adherents during a time when they felt the world had turned against them.[7] By providing a firm foundation of their "heritage," the Lost Cause, with its attendant organizations, symbols, and rituals, not only speaks to the past; it also provides a source of identity for the present. For believers, the enduring influence of the Lost Cause on gender construction, especially for white manhood and womanhood, is powerful and effective.

TENETS OF THE LOST CAUSE

This gendered focus provides further dimension to the familiar outlines of Lost Cause ideology and many of the elements that define this mythology, revealing particularly ways in which Lost Cause thought changes how masculinity and femininity are perceived and constructed. Those who put their hope in the Lost Cause, subscribed to its tenets, and found meaning in the way it presented the world often did so in a quasi-religious fashion. As Wilson writes, one way of understanding the "poverty, confusion, and disorganization" in the South after the Civil War (and during and after Reconstruction) was to create and propagate a particularly virtuous understanding of the white American South.[8] Ministers, whose job it was to provide succor to their congregants already, were sometimes the greatest proponents of this virtuous understanding.[9]

Episcopal Bishop Elliot Capers, who served as a Confederate general during the war, demonstrated this tendency when he composed a prayer that the United Daughters of the Confederacy (UDC) adopted into their annual conference ritual.[10] In part, the prayer that the gathered women read noted, "Almighty God, Our Heavenly Father . . . we thank Thee for our Confederate history. We thank Thee for its pure record of virtue, valor, and sacrifice; and for the inspiring reflection that, despite its bitter disappointments and sorrows, it proclaims for us, to the world, that we came through its years of trial and struggle with our battered shields pure, our character as a patriotic and courageous people untarnished, and nothing to regret in our defense of the rights and the honor of our Southland."[11] Capers and the gathered women of the UDC believed and proudly proclaimed a virtuous understanding of the Confederacy. Indeed, noting the purity, patriotism, and honor of the people of the Confederacy provided a pathway toward reconciling the "bitter disappointments and sorrows" of the war and its outcome.

Capers's prayer also suggests one of the most pernicious and long-lasting arguments of this ideology: the idea that the American Civil War had nothing to do with slavery, but was instead about a state's right to self-government or home rule in the face of an overbearing federal government. This idea shapes one of the more popular catechisms of the Confederate history that the United Daughters of the Confederacy produced to teach children. Lyon Gardiner Tyler's "A Confederate Catechism" was popular enough that the third edition had already been printed in 1929.[12] In it, the first eight questions dealt entirely with the reasons for war, and when question two specifically asked, "Was slavery the cause of secession or the war?" the answer was emphatically, "No."[13] When asked in question eight, "What did the South fight for?" Tyler's catechumens should answer, "IT FOUGHT TO REPEL INVASION AND FOR SELF-GOVERNMENT . . ."[14] While Tyler's catechism was published in 1929, proponents of the Lost Cause, such as the

Sons of Confederate Veterans (SCV), are still recommending it today as a corrective to "propaganda about the South."[15]

While the suggestion that secession and the formation of the Confederate States of America had little to do with slavery is often a key idea in Lost Cause mythology, equally popular but even more damaging is the idea that slavery itself was a net gain for African Americans. While few argue that individual slaves gained from the experience, there are those who hold that, as a group, African Americans benefited from the time in captivity. Tyler's catechism makes this point explicit saying, "The negroes were the most spoiled domestics in the world. The Southerners took the negro as a barbarian and cannibal, civilized him, supported him, and turned him out a devout Christian. Booker T. Washington admitted that the negro was the beneficiary rather than the victim of slavery."[16] Though the idea that slavery was the means that brought African slaves to salvation serves to assuage the consciousness of white Christians, it is not an accurate one, as Christianity in various forms existed throughout the African continent from before 340 AD.[17] Yet, the dominant white American idea of Africa at the time was a singular, essentialized history of barbarism, as this catechism suggests.[18]

Other such catechisms perpetuated the idea that slave owners used "great kindness and care in nearly all cases, a cruel master being rare."[19] Of course, such notions have been roundly disabused by historians such as Edward Baptist, who demonstrated the multitudinous ways that owners increased productivity from their slaves through torture—both physical and psychological.[20] However, the idea of the kind slave owner was a virtual necessity for the other view of slavery in the Lost Cause—that slaves were faithful and happy with their lot.

This idea of the happy slave appeared not only in UDC catechisms but also in articles in the UDC's magazine throughout the twentieth century. For example, an article from 1947 asserted that most African American "Mammies" were not only content, but "willingly faced any danger that threatened the child for whom they cared, and when emancipation came to their race, history tells us the majority of them pleaded to remain with the white family they loved."[21] Not only did slaves prefer to stay with their former masters once freedom came, according to Lost Cause proponents; virtually all slaves proved their true loyalties by faithfully defending both the plantations and the planters' families when the white men served in the Confederate armed forces.[22]

Such devotion from slaves, though, echoed the idea of a united home front among Confederate citizens (white southerners). According to those who follow the Lost Cause, the Confederate home front was of one mind and one heart in supporting its armies. No sacrifice was too great to provide for these fathers, sons, and brothers.[23] The devotion of the united home front sustained the fighting spirit of Confederate soldiers until the lack of resources and severe privations compelled their surrender. Indeed, many Lost Cause apologists held to the idea that the Confederacy was never defeated, it merely surrendered due to lack of resources.[24]

Blended together, the ideas that the Confederate States of America came into existence because of an honorable desire to keep local control and had nothing to do with slavery (and slaves were happy and content in their position under the tutelage of kind and humane masters) and that a united home front supported armies that ultimately had to surrender because of the overwhelming resources of the enemy are at the heart of Lost Cause beliefs. Over the past 150 years, individuals and organizations have written about these ideas, preserving and perpetuating them as truths to be passed down to future generations. While doing so, groups such as the Sons of Confederate Veterans and the United Daughters of the Confederacy have not only continued a specific vision of myth, they have used this myth, or as Wilson describes it, this "religious-moral identity," in the construction of gender ideals. To do so, individuals and groups highlight the manliness of the cause as well as a specific vision of Confederate femininity.

MANLINESS OF THE CAUSE

Lost Cause lore extolls the manly virtues on common soldiers and great generals, but Robert E. Lee stands on the highest pedestal. While one can multiply examples of white men venerating Lee as a Confederate hero, what is not as widely recognized are the ways in which he demonstrates a unique understanding of manhood and manliness.[25] Exhibited as commander of the Army of Northern Virginia and devout Protestant Christian, Lee's masculinity blends ideas of leadership, honor, and white male Christian character to those who espouse the Lost Cause.

The United Daughters of the Confederacy (UDC) especially honor Lee and hold him up as a model of manhood, especially in their catechisms. Not only did they perpetuate a particular understanding of history, they inculcated ideas of proper manhood. For example, question fifty-two of the Cornelia Stone catechism asked, "Who was made commander in chief of all the Confederate forces?" In response, catechumens were to answer, "Robert E. Lee, the best-loved and honored of all the Confederate Generals." Later, in question sixty-four, when students were supposed to understand what the army of the South (it is a common idea that there was merely one army, rather than multiple armies of the Confederacy) was known for, they were instructed that its commanders were "great as soldiers and great as men of stainless character."[26] Throughout Lost Cause writings, honor and Christian character are two of the main traits that adherents attribute to Lee.

Such attributions are marks of the enduring nature and popularity of the Lost Cause and not confined to the turn-of-the-century UDC catechism. In late October 2017, in response to a church taking down plaques honoring both George Washington and Robert E. Lee, President Donald Trump's chief of staff, General John Kelly, praised Lee, telling Fox News host Laura Ingraham that Lee was an "honorable man" who merely chose loyalty to his state over his nation.[27] In similar fashion, for years Reverend Harry Reeder, pastor of Briarwood Presbyterian Church in Birmingham, Alabama, promoted his sermon series, "Christian Manhood Illustrated."[28] To do so, Reeder led seminary-sponsored tours through Civil War battlefields. In some informational pages about the tour, patrons read that they would "learn something about the character" of Robert E. Lee as it was revealed at Appomattox.[29] These tours were not merely advertised in seminary materials, however; in 2011, the *Alabama Confederate*, the official periodical of the Alabama Division of the Sons of Confederate Veterans, advertised Reeder's tours. It was there that Reeder noted how he would "highlight the Christian leadership and character" of Robert E. Lee.[30]

Reeder's veneration of Lee goes beyond simply addressing his exploits on the field of battle. In his book on leadership entitled *The Leadership Dynamic*, Reeder carries forward some of the Lost Cause's most well-known myths about Lee. Reeder writes, "General Robert E. Lee, a devout believer who felt compelled to defend his state in the Civil War even though he opposed secession and despised slavery, was left with practically nothing but hardship when the war ended."[31] The idea that Lee despised slavery, even that he freed his slaves, is sometimes mentioned in Lost Cause writings as a way of absolving Lee of any possible stain on his character. In fact, it is the picture of Lee having a stainless, pure character that seems to be one of the major attractions of his myth.

In Lee, a picture of honor and character-driven manhood is presented as the highest pinnacle of Confederate masculinity when joined with faith-based Protestant Christian ethics and religiosity. Reeder makes this clear in *The Leadership Dynamic* when he writes that after the Civil War, Lee "committed himself to instilling young people with a character-based education rooted in Christian ethics."[32] The commitment to Protestant Christian religiosity (though certainly not always orthodox and historic doctrines of the Christian faith) presents the Lost Cause with a way to absolve its heroes of any possible stain or discrepancy. Rather than being men who fought for a system with its foundation and cornerstone resting on the idea of white supremacy and chattel slavery, these were "honorable" men.

While Lee currently stands at the place of honor in the Confederate pantheon, Jefferson Davis, the president of the Confederate States of America, has frequently occupied a place close by. One of the religious leaders who most admired Davis at the turn of the nineteenth and twentieth centuries was Methodist Bishop Charles C. Galloway. As one of the most influential church leaders in the Methodist Episcopal Church, South at the time, Galloway often used his influence to spread the ideas of the Lost Cause. He praised the leaders of the Confederacy and had a particularly well-known address praising Davis. In it, Galloway opined that Davis's model of Christian manhood was as close to perfection as possible.[33]

Indeed, not only did Galloway believe that Davis was close to perfection; he also extolled Davis as the "greatest of Mississippians, the leader of our armies, the defender of our liberties, the expounder of our political creeds, the authoritative voice of our hopes and fears, the sufferer for our sins, if sins they were, and the willing martyr to our sacred cause."[34] Clearly, Galloway admired Jefferson Davis, but because Galloway helped develop and propagate the ideas of the Lost Cause throughout the Deep South at the beginning of the twentieth century, his spirited defense of Jefferson Davis was not simply an appraisal of someone Galloway thought young men should emulate.[35] Rather, Galloway's veneration of Jefferson Davis portrayed the former president of the Confederacy as having manly traits that fit perfectly into a Christological model. Thus, Jefferson Davis appeared as a Christ figure who gave his people a system of belief, led them to battle, was wounded for their transgressions, and ultimately gave his (political) life on their behalf.

Portraying Davis as a messianic figure allowed Galloway to tell his listeners about the perfect model of manhood that combined Protestant Christian archetypes with the veneration of a Lost Cause hero.[36]

Other writers also picked up on the idea of Jefferson Davis as a model of quasi-messianic manhood. In 1949, Charles Hershberger wrote a portrayal of Davis for *United Daughters of the Confederacy Magazine.* There he proclaimed, "Davis is more than just another man, he is immortal; he is in every sense a martyr. In character and in personality he was infallible. In his love for the South, no one can say that *any man* could have given more."[37] Both Galloway and Hershberger believed Davis was a man who was willing to sacrifice all that he had for the cause he believed in and the people he led. More than this, Davis did so perfectly. Such a man, according to this view, should be held in the utmost esteem and thus presented a model for other men to follow in their quest for masculine dignity and honor.

For Lost Cause acolytes, the archetypal manhood of Lee, Davis, and other individual commanders seems beyond reach for ordinary men. Hence, the Sons of Confederate Veterans and United Daughters of the Confederacy provided other, perhaps more attainable, models of manliness for ordinary white men through their veneration of an essentialized, honorable, brave, and ultimately self-sacrificing rank-and-file Confederate soldier.

As early as 1928, writers in periodicals such as *Confederate Veteran* valorized the ordinary Confederate soldier. In one piece, Captain James Dinkins remarked that "the soldier of the ranks" etched "the record of the South in the field of war."[38] Those who did their duty, who fought for their consciences, and who did not shrink from the field of battle thus proved their manliness. Indeed, according to Dinkins, "A halo of glory hangs around the old Confederate soldier."[39] For those who promoted such ideas of Confederate masculinity, such a picture of glorious manhood was thus not reserved merely for the heroes of the Lost Cause but was attained by the masses of those who answered the call to arms.

The valorization of the enlisted men often accompanied an extended picture of the privations that the Confederate armies faced. Dinkins's writing certainly remarked on the ways in which the ordinary soldier confronted the enemy. He opined, "Against odds overwhelming, without resources, animated by the noble principle of unselfish patriotism and devotion, the Confederate soldier . . . struggled in a forlorn hope against one of the most matchless sections of the world."[40] Such a statement at once glorified the men enlisted in the Confederate armed forces for their fortitude, determination, and stalwart devotion to duty while at the same time absolving them of any misdeeds, imperfections, or lack of manhood that might have changed the course of the war. Indeed, Dinkins follows the general trend started by none other than Robert E. Lee himself who, in his final order to his surrendered forces told them, "After four years of arduous service, marked by unsurpassed courage and fortitude, the Army of Northern Virginia has been compelled to yield to overwhelming numbers and resources."[41] Lee's message to his forces, while gracious in tone to those he commanded, led to the idea long held in Lost Cause mythology that the Confederacy was never defeated, merely overwhelmed. By perpetuating such an idea, men defeated on the field of battle could rest assured that it was not their fault; that there was no lack of manliness or masculinity within them. Nor was the enemy any braver, more skilled, or more devoted than they were. The difference was one of material goods, nothing more.

The notion that ordinary Confederate soldiers solidified their claim to manhood in the face of overwhelming odds was not the end of this line of thought. Not only did Lost Cause adherents remark on the overwhelming resources of the enemy; such writers frequently mentioned the privations that Confederate soldiers faced and their success in spite of such hardships. The UDC Catechism prepared by Cornelia Stone specifically remarked on this topic in question forty-nine. When asked how long the war lasted, catechumens would answer, "Four years, and there is no record, in all the world's history of an army that endured more privations with greater fortitude, or fought more bravely than the soldiers of the Confederacy."[42] Such a statement reified the idea that ordinary men in the armies of the Confederacy demonstrated a superior manhood than all others.

Such statements about superior manliness in the face of deprivation were not limited to turn-of-the-century writers. In 2014, retired historian and one of the founders of the Neo-Confederate Abbeville Institute Clyde Wilson argued, "Man per man, the average Confederate soldier made more hard marches, suffered more privations, risked his life more frequently, was wounded more times, and died more often than the average Union soldiers. Outnumbered and out supplied, Confederate leaders had to show more skill and audacity and take more risks."[43] Clyde Wilson's argument attempted to show why the "average Confederate soldier" had greater manhood than those in the Union forces. As might be expected, such sentiments are also held by various chapters of the Sons of Confederate Veterans (SCV), who proudly sing the praises of both the average Confederate soldier and the Lost Cause's most storied leaders in many of their newsletters and writings.[44]

While groups adhering to the Lost Cause tradition, such as the UDC and the SCV, as well as individual adherents to its tenets, highlighted Confederate masculinity in the face of severe deprivations, such sentiments transition seamlessly into a focus on the bravery of the enlisted men within the Confederate forces. In May 1928, at Chicago's Oakwood Cemetery, J. Lester Williams gave a speech noting how many of the Confederate dead there were unknown to him and to all those gathered there. Yet still they gathered to honor those dead, and Williams believed that those joined together did so because "all of us revere the men whose courage meets the tests of life and never falters even in defeat." In fact, he believed that the ability of the Confederate veterans (both those standing in front of him and those who had already died) were set apart from other men due to the "mastery of their fears."[45] Of course, such language not only elevated the manliness of the Confederate veterans but also denoted their racial stature in the heyday of white supremacy. Noting the courage and mastery of these veterans, both living and dead, was to affirm their supremacy in racial and gendered terms.

But most of the ways that Lost Cause adherents spoke about Confederate bravery had little to do with race. For example, in Stone's version of the Confederate catechism, the "men in the ranks" received praise because they were "dauntless in courage, 'the bravest of the brave,' ever ready to rush into the 'jaws of death' at the command of their great leaders."[46] A separate catechism simplified the matter, telling initiates that when they were asked whether the Confederate soldiers were brave, they could answer, "Yes, the bravest in the world, history says so."[47] To drive home points such as this, Reverend Cowan Ellis wrote an article about living the Confederate principles in the February 1953 issue of *United Daughters of the Confederacy Magazine*. There he let readers know that the young men fighting for the Confederacy (blended into a single "average" soldier for rhetorical value) knew the possibility and the probability of death, but the courage that was a characteristic mark of the Southern soldier took him back to the front."[48] Such bravery in the face of overwhelming odds, despite severe privations, and potential defeat thus helped to define manhood by pointing to the average Confederate soldier for those who held to Lost Cause beliefs.

As Clyde Wilson's 2014 comments demonstrate, this model of manhood did not end during the 1950s. For twenty-first century men who imbibe an enduring Lost Cause ideology, such presentations of masculinity have deep resonance. Part of what composes contemporary Lost Cause masculinity is its focus on heritage. This focus on Confederate heroes and family connections is not apologetic but celebratory in tone.

For example, in fall 2017, the Sons of Confederate Veterans website proclaimed, "The citizen-soldiers who fought for the Confederacy personified the best qualities of America. The preservation of liberty and freedom was the motivating factor in the South's decision to fight the Second American Revolution. The tenacity with which Confederate soldiers fought underscored their belief in the rights guaranteed by the Constitution."[49] Here, the Sons of Confederate Veterans celebrate the average soldiers of the Confederate forces by actually emphasizing their commonness. They were simply "citizen-soldiers" engaged in battle; certainly not battle-hardened, highly trained troops. Much like the mythical yeoman farmer, these citizen-soldiers demonstrated a tenacity that belied their humble origins. At the same time that this statement linked the Confederate forces with an everyman relatability, the SCV also inferred that these men (and they do assume that all the fighting troops were men) were educated, fervent Republicans who were well-versed in Constitutional law. Finally, within this short statement, the note about the "preservation of liberty and freedom" combined with the renaming of the conflict to "the Second American Revolution" to emphasize a Lost Cause narrative in which a beleaguered South had no other option than to attempt to remove itself from an overbearing, tyrannical, and industrial North.[50]

While Lost Cause apologists sometimes emphasize the economic differences between regions as a reason for secession and war, historians such as Charles Dew in *Apostles of Disunion* have demonstrated that secession commissioners spoke unapologetically with fear-mongering language about the loss of slavery and white supremacy, followed shortly by the social equality of the races, and eventually, interracial sex.[51] It is not surprising that the Sons of Confederate Veterans do not include the overtly racist language of secession commissioners in their celebration of "heritage"; yet by whitewashing history, the SCV present a particular type of manhood. The SCV's image of the citizen-soldier as an educated everyman resonates with the picture of the self-sufficient yeoman farmer. Able to provide for and protect his family through the work of his brow, such a construction of independent white manhood seems to move against the grain of the realities of an economic world wherein global markets can make or break the fortunes of hard-working families.[52] Of course, by creating such mythic manliness, Lost Cause acolytes create an understanding of their own manhood in the process. While focused on "heritage," the blend of masculinity based in Lost Cause ideology both glorifies economically independent manhood and highlights a perceived persecution of those who righteously fight against the overbearing powers of their day. Among the SCV, this presents itself as a fight for what they regard as the true history of the conflict of 1861–65.

Throughout their website, the Sons of Confederate Veterans highlight their goal to tell the "truths about the War for Southern Independence."[53] In 2011, Gary Carlyle, the second lieutenant commander of the Alabama Division of the SCV, wrote that the "responsibility of passing down and teaching the truth to our prodigy is OURS. We must see our children and grandchildren know the truth of our heritage." But this truth-telling mission is not without opposition. Carlyle warns, "The truth is hidden and a political agenda is taught in its place."[54] In warning that those who speak about the "truths about the War for Southern Independence" will face persecution, Carlyle presents SCV men with an opportunity to prove their manhood. Are they devout enough believers? Are they strong enough in their faith and knowledge to face such challenges?

Later in the same January 2011 Alabamian newsletter, editor Jimmy Hill wrote about how to become an informed apologist for the ideas of the Lost Cause. Hill encouraged his readers to arm themselves with knowledge, to create their own fact sheets, and most importantly, to "remain cool, calm and collected."[55] In other words, Hill encourages his SCV readers to attain mastery of both knowledge and emotion.

The SCV also attempts to retain a mastery over the symbols of the Confederacy. Following the events in Charlottesville, Virginia in August 2017, the SCV published a statement on their website arguing that the Confederate battle flag "was not and is not a symbol of racism; it is a soldier's battle flag given to the SCV by the Confederate Veterans. The KKK, nor any other group, has legitimate use of our symbols."[56] Recently, the SCV believed their mastery over Confederate symbolism was so strong that only weeks after the 2015 Charleston massacre, when the shooter posted numerous images of himself proudly holding the Confederate battle flag, the SCV used the same flag to decorate the ballroom for their national reunion debutante ball.[57] Believing that they were the only authentic masters of Confederate symbolism, the SVC were confident in their use of these flags and images despite national mourning over a shooter's attempt to start a race war by massacring African American parishioners.

The enduring Lost Cause mythology presents a particular way of understanding and constructing manhood. There are the manly heroes of the Confederate pantheon, such as Robert E. Lee and Jefferson Davis; but Lost Cause constructions of masculinity also highlight the "average" soldiers of the Confederate armed forces in order to present an attainable manhood for adherents. For those who hold Lost Cause beliefs, manhood entails perfection in character, devotion to duty and honorable action in the midst of hardship, mastery over one's emotions in the midst of persecution, and a stainless heritage.

As much as the beliefs of the Lost Cause present a particular model of manhood, ideals of femininity are equally influenced by a Confederate understanding of the world. Confederate femininity presented proper womanhood as a mix of sheltered and strong, genteel, benevolent, and completely self-sacrificial in the midst of a united home front.

CONFEDERATE FEMININITY

According to the tenets of the Lost Cause, the women who remained in their homes throughout the Civil War supported the efforts of the Confederacy with all they had. Recently, retired historian Clyde Wilson argued that despite some "minor" conflict and stress within society, "the obviously significant larger point is that there was so relatively little internal disaffection from the Confederate cause."[58] Despite excellent studies by reputable scholars such as Alice Fahs about riots and revolts by women throughout the Confederate home front, Clyde Wilson downplays such evidence by saying it is the "penchant of feminist historians to make every Confederate woman's private complaint about hardship into evidence of an underground rebellion."[59] Such sexist sentiments deliberately belittle the work of reputable scholars in order to overlook and minimize riots across the Confederacy during the Civil War.[60]

Clyde Wilson's belief in the unity of the Confederate cause, despite the evidence, echoed sentiments from the pages of Albert Bledsoe's 1877 "Women of the Southern Confederacy." Bledsoe wrote that "when the Confederate Government appealed to the women of Virginia for food for the soldier[s]," the women "cheerfully" gave up all the meat they had in their stores.[61] This understanding of Confederate women highlighted not only a united home front but also a self-sacrificing femininity in which those not actively fighting were willing to give all they had in support of the cause.

The view that ideal Confederate femininity was self-sacrificing and willingly devoted to the good of others was repeated throughout Bledsoe's text. He wrote of women learning to deal with the economic measures of the time in order to make plain meals seem sumptuous, of homes being thrown open to receive wounded and ill soldiers, and of "the generosity of the plain farmer's wife, who could not do enough for the 'dear boys' who were fighting their country's battles."[62] Bledsoe then talked about how the women of the Confederacy sacrificed so willingly that they learned to create clothing out of straw and other common materials with "a neatness and dexterity surprising."[63] Lest his lessons somehow not quite be understood, he closed by saying that even in the short study he presented it was clear that "the women of the late Confederacy were in no whit behind their noble predecessors of Revolutionary fame, in piety, patriotism, heroism and long-suffering." Thus, his contemporary Southern women must prove themselves worthy of their ancestors and "verify the eulogy . . . 'Faithful amongst the faithless are the women of the South.'"[64]

Bledsoe clearly believed that the example of the women of the Confederacy presented an ideal of womanhood that women must live up to in order to truly be Southern ladies. In his construction of Confederate femininity, women should be willing to give everything in order for others to flourish. They gave of themselves not for their own goals or ideals, but so the men in their lives might achieve their goals. Such sentiments even made their way into some of the catechisms where children were taught that true Southern ladies "furnished blankets, quilts, and comforts. They cut up carpets, and lined them with cotton, for blankets, also."[65] The United Daughters of the Confederacy certainly continued this line of thinking in their monthly magazine during the mid-twentieth century.

In May 1955, the managing editor of *United Daughters of the Confederacy Magazine* wrote about how the mothers of the Confederate soldiers presented the ideal of womanhood to the entire world. These women in-stilled high ideals in their sons and thus marched along with the fighting men in spirit. The author also asserted that these "mothers of the Confederacy" were also memorable for their "patient endurance, loving services, and great sacrifices."[66] For the editor of the UDC magazine, the women "who stand out as our ideals" displayed an unwavering willingness to patiently endure suffer-ing in the midst of service for others. True womanhood was thus fulfilled in the achievement of men through the sacrifice of women.

While Lost Cause writers employed the trope of the self-sacrificing woman, many constructed femininity within the context of gentility, thus making the self-sacrifice even greater. The UDC magazine employed this rhetoric in a piece entitled "A Woman of the Sixties" (August 1955), in which Mary Noel Estes Moody chronicles a fictionalized account of her an-cestors. Moody describes one of her ancestors as "a lineal descendant of the Indian chief Powhatan. Her negro maid who always accompanied her to school, to church, everywhere was at her back holding her fan." Another ancestor is described as a skilled seamstress, "for the daughters of the old South were not only women of education, but skilled in every household art." A third character, the heroine of the account, while receiving silk from Paris for dresses, decides to wear simple cloth instead so as not to distract others at church.[67] Simply in the description of these ancestors, possibly real but with fictionalized characters and skills, Moody constructs an ideal genteel womanhood.

Moody chose to believe that her female ancestors had enough wealth to order silks from Paris on the eve of war, receive education (which most likely would have required private tutors), and have constant attention from personal slaves. Such wealth would have put the Esteses in a rarified world of genteel life far removed from most Southerners, enslaved or free. Yet Moody was not the only one who wrote as though all white Southern women lived in such lavish surroundings.

In an article comparing the women of the Civil War generations to those of 1959, Clara Hill Carner talks about the women who grew up just be-fore the war. She wrote, "To the Southern woman, tradition, history, poetry, and fiction accorded her beauty, grace, charm, and a delicacy of feeling."[68] Clearly, such a particular description could have only applied to those who were well-educated and had enough leisure time to be able to take advan-tage of their access to literature and other aesthetic works.

Lost Cause enthusiasts constructed ideal women as both sheltered and strong despite their genteel upbringing and surroundings. For example, Carner, who wrote about the "beauty, grace, charm, and a delicacy of feeling" of women, also remarked that during the war itself and afterward during Reconstruction, Southern ladies proved themselves "strong, capable, intelligent, and self-reliant."[69] Moreover, these same women, averred Carner, "Americanized an almost savage race in a few generations."[70] Beyond the racism, white supremacist ideas, and ignorance of history displayed in this statement, Carner sought to demonstrate the matriarchal qualities in Southern women. She believed that they had the ability to essentially rear an entire people group from savagery and barbarism into "adult" white culture.

Interestingly, along with the ideal of the strong but genteel woman who was capable of rearing entire people groups came the notion that proper Southern ladies were also sheltered from the full cares and stresses of the world. In 1947, Mrs. Harry Bates Smith authored an article in the UDC magazine that focused on the "Mothers of the Confederacy." After the essential statement of the "achievement, endurance, and self-sacrificing devotion to loved ones in the lines of Confederate gray," Smith remarked that such devotion marked a special pathos because "the girls of the southland were sheltered or shielded from the actualities of life, never really knowing the sordid side of life, and emerging from girlhoods of ease, they established their own family units with a continuation of the same type of living."[71] Similar to the trope that all white southern ladies were reared in genteel settings, this stated assumption of the sheltered life of young white women in the antebellum South drew more from *Gone with the Wind* portrayals of Southern belles than it did actual history. Yet Smith's claims were not without precedent.

Albert Taylor Bledsoe's "Women of the Southern Confederacy" also asserted that despite being reared in "luxury and refinement, in delicacy and seclusion," proper Southern ladies (and it should be stated here that ladies were always white in this construction of femininity) "made a noble sacrifice of womanly instincts and shrinking timidity, cheerfully surrendering everything to minister to the suffering and wants of their stricken countrymen."[72] In fact, doubling down on this thought that proper womanhood came from within a sheltered setting, Bledsoe argued that it was "not the highest type of woman who willingly sees herself brought before the public, or becomes a candidate for their favor."[73] This idea that only a lower type of woman would engage in public settings set up boundaries of femininity for those who imbibed Lost Cause ideas.

The idea that proper Southern ladies should stay in the background is still echoed today on the UDC website. Patricia Bryson, the UDC president general from 2016 to 2018, issued a statement following the events in Charlottesville, Virginia in August 2017 that reified the ideal that proper UDC members stayed out of the public eye. She stated that the UDC was saddened that "certain hate groups have taken the Confederate flag and other symbols as their own," but argued that UDC "members are the ones who, like our statues, have stayed quietly in the background, never engaging in public controversy."[74] While readers of this volume will likely take issue with Bryson's understanding of the UDC's history of public engagement, the point she makes is that women, when behaving properly, should work behind the scenes.

A common thread throughout the Lost Cause ideals of Confederate femininity is that proper ladies are upper-class white women. The Sons of Confederate Veterans certainly support this understanding of femininity as they hold a debutante ball each year at their annual reunion. The SCV Debutante Planning Guide, written by Chief of Protocol Lee Millar, avers that "a long and honored tradition of Southern society is the formal presentation of eligible young ladies to society."[75] Such eligible young ladies must never have been married or had children (thus assumed to be virginal), must be between sixteen and twenty-three years old, and must never have been previously presented at a national SCV reunion.[76]

In addition, the planning guide outlines some points of refinement that the young women should learn prior to the ball, including graceful ways to walk into the ball with their escort and properly bowing to the SCV commander-in-chief and to the gathered crowd in the ballroom to be "presented to society."[77] During the processional, the debutante should not speak on her own, as the emcee of the ball reads her narrative to the crowd, and she should appear as refined and passive as possible during the event. The emphasis on refined femininity certainly dictates the appropriate clothing for the event. Indeed, the planning guide notes that the dress is of utmost importance by stating, "The main thing that is essential to the deb's presentation is the dress gown." While either modern or period dresses may be worn, the attire must be an entirely white, floor-length dress.[78] The symbolism and ideas implied in the dress are difficult to miss. Not only does it suggest purity of character along with sexual purity; it also suggests the refinement of the family and purity of heritage.[79]

The focus on heritage should come as no surprise in an event hosted by the Sons of Confederate Veterans. Their statement on eligibility emphasizes the continuous line of kinship that must be proven in order to attain membership.[80] Even the Debutante Planning Guide makes the point that it is the heritage of these young women that makes them special.[81] Yet in that uniqueness, nothing about the individual young women is highlighted. Rather, it is what they received passively from their ancestors ("These men bequeathed a heritage of honor to these young Debutantes.") or what they can do for future generations of the SCV ("These young ladies are the mothers of our future SCV sons. If they are proud of their heritage . . . then they will be willing to encourage the SCV.") that provides the reasons for the SCV to celebrate these young women.[82] In this vision of womanhood celebrated by Lost Cause adherents, despite the emphasis on the need to demonstrate refined manners and various forms of purity, nothing inherent in women is worthy of celebration other than their ability to be mothers to future generations of sons.

The United Daughters of the Confederacy also highlight the heritage handed down through Confederate bloodlines. Over the course of the twentieth century, the applications for membership in the UDC emphasized the need to connect applicants to forebears that fought in the Confederate armed forces.[83] Even into the twenty-first century, both the UDC and their organization for youth, the Children of the Confederacy, so fixated on the pure bloodline of their members that they explicitly excluded adopted children from using their parents' heritage, stating that they must only use the heritage of their "natural or biological" family.[84] The focus on this pure-blood heritage is a way of circumscribing racial boundaries on Southern womanhood without ever using racial language. By only allowing membership applications from those women who could trace their bloodlines to those who served in the armed forces of the Confederacy, the United Daughters of the Confederacy preserve true womanhood as solely the realm of Southern white women without sullying their organization with the taint of overt racism.

Passing down a specific vision of femininity neither was nor is the sole purpose of the United Daughters of the Confederacy, however. They both preserve and perpetuate Lost Cause beliefs—beliefs that can be used to reinforce their understanding of true womanhood. Recently, Amy Heyse documented how the UDC created "mythical collective memories by over-simplifying, triggering, forgetting, 'correcting,' and glorifying" both the Old South and Lost Cause narratives.[85] In order to perpetuate these ideas, the catechisms of the UDC teach children the beliefs of the Lost Cause. By using this quasi-religious method of teaching, UDC leaders could retain a vision of womanhood that emphasizes moral leadership rather than political activities or public controversy.[86] This role is even made explicit in some of the catechisms. For example, in the version prepared by Decca Lamar West, questions 167–171 deal with the purposes for which the UDC was founded. These questions aver that the UDC organized not only to "preserve the true history of the Confederacy," but also for the benevolent work of taking care of Confederate veterans and their widows as well as securing pensions for these men and their dependents. These actions are not done in a public manner, but primarily by teaching "children from generation to generation" through scholarships, essay prizes, book collections, and other educational efforts about the "War between the States."[87] Again, by framing these efforts as educational, they were able to avoid the insinuation that they were political efforts intent on rewriting the narrative of the conflict, its causes, and Reconstruction. Their femininity could then be viewed as a moral rather than political influence.

The enduring Lost Cause presented prescriptive ideas of proper Southern womanhood through the writings of both individuals and organizations. Perhaps more influentially than individual writers, the premier groups that preserve and perpetuate Lost Cause beliefs, the Sons of Confederate Veterans and the United Daughters of the Confederacy, used Lost Cause narratives to construct Confederate femininity. According to this worldview, true ladies were self-sacrificial so that others (and specifically men) might excel, operated through moral education while demonstrating refined manners, and had a genteel upbringing that came from their (white) pure-blooded heritage.

The pure heritage of both men and women is a significant issue for acolytes of the Lost Cause. For true believers, such a lineage is not where the ideology ends. Throughout the twentieth and now into the twenty-first century, the Lost Cause presented pre-scriptive ideas of gender construction. Both men and women constructed their sense of identity from the normative ideas offered by writers and organizations preserving and perpetuating this ideology, and yet the persistence of the mythologies of the Lost Cause—its continuing resonance and influence—neither was nor is static. That power waxed and waned with shifts in American popular culture. Its enduring nature and ability to provide a source of identity for many demonstrate that it was and is more than merely a misguided interpretation of historical events: for many who follow its tenets, the Lost Cause offers a starting point to understanding their place in the world.

NOTES

The author wishes to thank Heather Chapell for her invaluable support and incredible patience as well as Catherine Chapell for helping her dad focus on the present.

1. Mrs. S. E. F. Rose, *The Ku Klux Klan or Invisible Empire* (New Orleans: L. Graham Co., LTD, 1914), 75–76.

2. Rose, *Ku Klux Klan*, 75.

3. For examples of the debates over the battle flag, see Aram Goudsouzian, "Does the Confederate Flag Signify Heritage or Hate?" *Al Jazeera*, June 21, 2015, https://www.aljazeera.com/indepth/opinion/2015/06/confederate-flag-heritage-hate-dylann-roof-charleston-150621065209291.html; and Russell Moore, "The Cross and the Confederate Flag," June 19, 2015, http://www.russellmoore.com/2015/06/19/the-cross-and-the-confederate-flag/. For an example of arguments about Confederate monuments, see Steve Holland and Susan Heavey, "Fellow Republicans Assail Trump after he Defends Confederate Monuments," August 17, 2017, https://www.reuters.com/article/us-usa-trump/fellow-republicans-assail-trump-after-he-defends-confederate-monuments-idUSKCN1AX1HF. For a statement from the White House chief of staff about the honor of Confederate heroes, see http://video.foxnews.com/v/5630523067001/?playlist_id=5622526903001#sp=show-clips.

4. Scholars of religious studies will recognize the influence of Thomas Tweed's *Crossing and Dwelling* on this understanding of religion and a religious interpretation of the world. For more, see Thomas Tweed, *Crossing and Dwelling: A Theory of Religion* (Cambridge: Harvard Univ. Press, 2006). Martin Riesebrodt's *The Promise of Salvation: A Theory of Religion* reprint ed., trans. Steven Randall (Chicago: Univ. of Chicago Press, 2012) is also influential in my own definitional work of religion.

5. Charles Reagan Wilson, *Baptized in Blood: The Religion of the Lost Cause, 1865–1920* (Athens: Univ. of Georgia Press, 1980), 10–12.

6. See https://www.washingtonpost.com/news/politics/wp/2017/12/08/roy-moore-america-was-great-in-era-of-slavery-is-now-focus-of-evil-in-the-world/?utm_term=.e0a32105f2e7 for comments about strong families in the time of antebellum slavery.

7. For two examples of this persecution mindset, see Pat Gasson, "Division President's Report," *Confederate Courier* 43, no. 2 (September 2015): 1–3; and Gary Carlyle, "Lt. Commander Reports," *Alabama Confederate* 30, no. 1 (January 2011): 4.

8. Wilson, *Baptized in Blood,* 38.

9. Wilson, *Baptized in Blood,* 139.

10. For more about Bishop Capers, see Wilson, *Baptized in Blood,* 55–57.

11. Bishop Ellison Capers, "A Prayer," in *Yearbook 1931,* Peter Turney Chapter No. 1927, United Daughters of the Confederacy, Winchester-Decherd-Huntland, Frankland County, TN, in United Daughters of the Confederacy: Mary Latham Chapter Collection, Box 1: Memphis and Shelby County Room, Memphis Public Library and Information Center.

12. More on the United Daughters of the Confederacy's catechisms can be found in Keith Harper's chapter of this volume or in Amy L. Heyse, "Teachers of the Lost Cause: The United Daughters of the Confederacy and the Rhetoric of their Catechisms," (PhD diss., Univ. of Maryland, 2006).

13. Lyon Gardiner Tyler, "A Confederate Catechism: The War of 1861–1865," 3rd ed. (Holdcroft, VA: self-published, 1929), 3.

14. Tyler, "Confederate Catechism," 5. Emphasis in original.

15. https://scv-online-store.myshopify.com/products/books-a-confederate-catechism-269.

16. Tyler, "Confederate Catechism," 11.

17. Philip Jenkins, *The Lost History of Christianity: The Thousand-Year Golden Age of the Church in the Middle East, Africa, and Asia – and How It Died* (New York: HarperOne, 2008), 55.

18. For more on this, see Gail Bederman, *Manliness & Civilization: A Cultural History of Gender and Race in the United States, 1880–1917* (Chicago: Univ. of Chicago Press, 1995), 207–15, 220–32.

19. Cornelia B. Stone, "U.D.C. Catechisms for Children," arranged for Veuve Jefferson Chapter UDC, Galveston, TX by Cornelia Branch Stone, 1904, republished by J. E. B. Stuart Chapter No. 10, UDC, 1912. Printed by Stonebruner and Prufer Printers, in Heyse, "Teachers of the Lost Cause," 263. This same question and answer, virtually word for word, also appears in Decca Lamar West, "Catechism on the History of the Confederate States of America," arranged for Children of the Confederacy Chapters by Decca Lamar West, originally written 1926, in Heyse, "Teachers of the Lost Cause," 312.

20. Edward E. Baptist, *The Half Has Never Been Told: Slavery and the Making of American Capitalism* (New York: Basic Books, 2014), 139–42.

21. Mrs. Henry Bates Smith, "Mothers of the Confederacy," *United Daughters of the Confederacy Magazine* X, no. 11 (November 1947): 7.

22. For examples, see William D. Washington, "Burial of Latané," *Confederate Veteran* XXXVII, no. 5 (May 1929): cover image; Smith, "Mothers of the Confederacy," 7; Mary Noel Estes Moody, "A Woman of the Sixties," *United Daughters of the Confederacy Magazine* XVIII, no. 8 (August 1955): 23; and Clara Hill Carner, "Southern Women of Sixties—and Today," *United Daughters of the Confederacy Magazine* XXII, no. 11 (November 1959): 18–19.

23. Albert Taylor Bledsoe, "Women of the Southern Confederacy," *Southern Review* XXI, no. 42 (April 1877): 360. Reproduced in Abbeville Institute, May 2016, accessed February 2, 2017, https://www.abbevilleinstitute.org/review/women-of-the-southern-confederacy/.

24. For examples see Stone, "U.D.C. Catechisms for Children," in Heyse, "Teachers of the Lost Cause," 268; and West, "Catechism on the History of the Confederate States of America," in Heyse, "Teachers of the Lost Cause," 317.

25. For more on the events that took place in Charlottesville, see Kat Chow, "Making

Sense of Charlottesville: A Reader's Guide," August 14, 2017, https://www.npr.org
/sections/codeswitch/2017/08/14/543403461/making-sense-of-charlottesville-a-readers
-guide; and Hunton & Williams, LLP, "Independent Review of the 2017 Protest Events in
Charlottesville, Virginia," November 24, 2017, http://www.charlottesville.org/home
/showdocument?id=59615.

26. Stone, "U.D.C. Catechisms for Children," in Heyse, "Teachers of the Lost Cause,"
268–69.

27. http://video.foxnews.com/v/5630523067001/?playlist_id=5622526903001#sp
=show-clips.

28. The series can be bought on the Briarwood Presbyterian Church bookstore website at
https://briarwood.org/webstore/product/christian-manhood-illustrated/.

29. http://www.rts.edu/Site/Tours/2008_CCT_Information_Registration.pdf.

30. Paid Advertisement for Christian Character and Leadership, 2011 Historical Tours
with Dr. Harry Reeder, *Alabama Confederate* 30, no. 1 (January 2011): 21.

31. Harry L. Reeder III with Rod Gragg, *The Leadership Dynamic: A Biblical Model for Raising
Effective Leaders* (Wheaton, IL: Crossway Books, 2008), 81.

32. Reeder, *The Leadership Dynamic*, 82.

33. Charles B. Galloway, "Jefferson Davis: A Judicial Estimate," given June 3, 1908, in
Bulletin of the University of Mississippi VI (August 1908): 1–48.

34. Galloway, "Jefferson Davis," 47.

35. Wilson notes that Bishop Galloway was "perhaps the best-known Lost-Cause
paternalist in the post-1900 period." For more, see Wilson, *Baptized in Blood*, 109.

36. This paragraph relies heavily on work from the author's book *Ye That Are Men Now
Serve Him: Radical Holiness Theology and Gender in the South* (Tuscaloosa: Univ. of Alabama
Press, 2016), 73–74.

37. Charles E. Hershberger, "Jefferson Davis," *United Daughters of the Confederacy Magazine*
XII, no. 9 (September 1949): 18–19.

38. Captain James Dinkins, "The Army That Has Passed," *Confederate Veteran* XXXVI, no. 7
(July 1928): 244–45.

39. Dinkins, "The Army That Has Passed," 244.

40. Dinkins, 244.

41. Robert E. Lee, General Order 9, April 10, 1865, as recorded in *Recollections and
Letters of General Robert E. Lee by His Son Captain Robert E. Lee* (New York: Doubleday, Page, &
Company, 1904), 153.

42. Stone, "U.D.C. Catechisms for Children," in Heyse, "Teachers of the Lost Cause,"
265.

43. Clyde Wilson, "Nolan's Myth of the 'Lost Cause,'" November 17, 2014, accessed
February 2, 2017, https://www.abbevilleinstitute.org/clyde-wilson-library/nolans-myth-of
-the-lost-cause/. For more on the Abbeville Institute, readers can visit abbevilleinstitute.org.

44. For an example, see *Alabama Confederate* 30, no. 1 (January 2011): 11.

45. J. Lester Williams, "Our Heritage of Courage," in *Confederate Veteran* XXXVI, no. 7
(July 1928): 246.

46. Stone, "U.D.C. Catechisms for Children," in Heyse, "Teachers of the Lost Cause,"
268–269.

47. Mrs. John P. Allison, "A Confederate Catechism for Southern Children," (Concord, NC: Kestler Brothers Printers, 1946). Originally edited and published in 1908 by Mrs. J. P. Allison, re-published in 1946 by Mrs. Charles A. Cannon and Mrs. Guy M. Beaver in Heyse, "Teachers of the Lost Cause," 277.

48. Cowan Ellis, "Living Confederate Principles" in *United Daughters of the Confederacy Magazine* XVI, no. 2 (February 1953): 36.

49. http://www.scv.org/new/.

50. For another contemporary example of this, turn to Wilson, "Nolan's Myth of the 'Lost Cause,'" at https://www.abbevilleinstitute.org/clyde-wilson-library/nolans-myth-of-the-lost-cause/.

51. See Charles B. Dew, *Apostles of Disunion: Southern Secession Commissioners and the Causes of the Civil War* (Charlottesville: Univ. of Virginia Press, 2001).

52. Both Scott P. Marler's *The Merchant's Capital: New Orleans and the Political Economy of the Nineteenth Century South* (Cambridge, UK: Cambridge Univ. Press, 2015) and Edward Baptist's *The Half Has Never Been Told* demonstrate the interconnected global economy of the nineteenth century that would have made such a particular vision of economic independence virtually impossible even prior to the American Civil War.

53. http://samdavis.scv.org/.

54. Carlyle, "Lt. Commander Reports," 4.

55. Jimmy Hill, "Editor's Notes: Is History Repeating Itself?" *Alabama Confederate* 30, no. 1 (January 2011): 24.

56. Thos. V. Strain, Jr., "Sons of Confederate Veterans support for our nation and the rule of law," August 14, 2017, accessed September 4, 2017, http://www.scv.org/new/wp-content/uploads/2017/08/SCV-Press-Release-SCV-Support-to-the-Nation-and-Rule-of-Law-170814-1-4-1.jpg.

57. For more on the Charleston Massacre and the shooter's use of the Confederate battle flag, see Yoni Appelbaum, "Why is the Flag Still There?," *The Atlantic,* June 21, 2015, accessed October 21, 2017, https://www.theatlantic.com/politics/archive/2015/06/why-is-the-flag-still-there/396431/; Timothy B. Tyson, "He Had to be Carefully Taught," *Facing South,* June 22, 2015, accessed October 21, 2017, https://www.facingsouth.org/2015/06/he-had-to-be-carefully-taught.html; Joshua D. Rothman, "The Charleston Massacre and the Rape Myth of Reconstruction," *We're History,* June 22, 2015, accessed October 21, 2017, http://werehistory.org/charleston-rape-myth/. For an example of the decorations at the 2015 Sons of Confederate Veterans National Reunion, held July 15–19, 2015, see their video, "Dixie, at the 2015 National SCV Reunion in Richmond, VA," July 18, 2015, accessed November 21, 2017, https://youtu.be/QB6LFnL-Vjw; and Karen Powers, "Chapter News," in *Confederate Courier* 43, no. 2 (September 2015): 11.

58. Wilson, "Nolan's Myth of the 'Lost Cause,'" https://www.abbevilleinstitute.org/clyde-wilson-library/nolans-myth-of-the-lost-cause/.

59. Alice Fahs, "The Feminized Civil War: Gender, Northern Popular Literature, and Memory of the War, 1861–1900," *The Journal of American History* 85, no. 4 (March 1999): 1461–94.

60. For more on these, see Teresa Crisp Williams and David Williams, "'The Women Rising': Cotton, Class, and Confederate Georgia's Rioting Women," *The Georgia Historical Quarterly* 86, no. 1 (2002): 49–83; or Michael B. Chesson, "Harlots or Heroines? A New Look at the Richmond Bread Riot," *The Virginia Magazine of History and Biography* 92, no. 2 (1984): 131–75.

61. Albert Taylor Bledsoe, "Women of the Southern Confederacy," *The Southern Review* XXI, no. 42 (April 1877): 360.

62. Bledsoe, "Women of the Southern Confederacy," 350.

63. Bledsoe, 362.

64. Bledsoe, 362.

65. Mrs. James A. Fore, "A Catechism for the Children of the Confederacy of the North Carolina Division United Daughters of the Confederacy," prepared by Mrs. J. A. Fore. (Charlotte, NC: Piedmont Printery, n.d., ca. 1930) in Heyse, "Teachers of the Lost Cause," 298.

66. E. B. H. [Likely Mrs. William A. Haggard, the Managing Editor at the time], "Mothers Day Edition of Magazine," *United Daughters of the Confederacy Magazine* XVIII, no. 5 (May 1955): 4.

67. Mary Noel Estes Moody, "A Woman of the Sixties," in *United Daughters of the Confederacy Magazine* XVIII, no. 8 (August 1955): 23.

68. Clara Hill Carner, "Southern Women of Sixties—And Today," *United Daughters of the Confederacy Magazine* XXII, no. 11 (November 1959): 18.

69. Carner, "Southern Women of Sixties," 18.

70. Carner, 18.

71. Mrs. Harry Bates Smith, "Mothers of the Confederacy," *United Daughters of the Confederacy Magazine* X, no. 11 (November 1947): 7.

72. Bledsoe, "Women of the Southern Confederacy," 349.

73. Bledsoe, 334.

74. Patricia Bryson, "Statement from the President General, 08–21–2017," United Daughters of the Confederacy website, accessed September 4, 2017, https://www.hqudc .org/.

75. Lee Millar, "Debutante Planning Guide, revision 3," Sons of Confederate Veterans website, March 2013, 1, accessed September 7, 2017, http://www.scv.org/pdf /DEBUTANTEPlanningGuide(rev3).pdf.

76. Millar, "Debutante Planning," 1.

77. Millar, 6.

78. Millar, 7.

79. For a brief discussion on the purity envisioned in other Lost Cause rhetoric, see Wilson, *Baptized in Blood*, 47–48.

80. http://www.scv.org/new/eligibility/.

81. Millar, "Debutante Planning," 8.

82. Millar, 8, 7.

83. For examples, see Box 4, United Daughters of the Confederacy: Mary Latham Chapter Collection, Memphis and Shelby County Room, Memphis Public Library and Information Center, Memphis, Tennessee.

84. The quoted phrase comes from the Children of the Confederacy's "Purpose and Eligibility" page, accessed November 15, 2017, https://www.hqudc.org /cofc-purpose-eligibility/. However, the UDC's "Membership" page, accessed 15 November 2017, contains virtually the same language, but stating it only for women. See https://www .hqudc.org/membership/.

85. Heyse, "Teachers of the Lost Cause," 252.

86. It is helpful here to look back on Patricia Bryson's statement about the membership of the UDC having always stayed in the background. See Bryson, "Statement from the President General, 08–21–2017," https://www.hqudc.org/.

87. West, "Catechism on the History of the Confederate States of America," in Heyse, "Teachers of the Lost Cause," 323.

"The Truth is Everything": The Confederate Catechism and Perpetuating the Lost Cause

KEITH HARPER

In late 1951 and early 1952 *Tyler's Quarterly Historical and Genealogical Magazine* ran "A Confederate Catechism" in two parts. Penned by Lyon Gardiner Tyler, the catechism stated that the "court of history" functions much like a court of law in that both rely on evidence. In this case, Tyler assured readers that the historical record and eyewitness testimony from the participants themselves provided evidence that called for a verdict. He framed his catechism around such evidence and called upon readers to consider it with an open mind. He engaged in neither "idle abuse" nor immoderate praise; he needed no such devices. After all, he intoned, "The truth is everything."[1]

Lyon Tyler had been dead for sixteen years when *Tyler's Quarterly* ran his catechism. But for readers familiar with his work it was nothing new. In fact, Tyler published the first edition of his catechism in 1920 and refined it through multiple editions until his death in 1935. The one published in *Tyler's Quarterly* was a reprint of the sixth edition, representing his most detailed, unstinting defense of the Lost Cause and the American South.

The Lost Cause emerged as a distinct concept immediately after the Civil War ended, but it meant different things to different people. Assessing its role in shaping a distinct Southern culture is tricky. Confederate veterans sought to praise their military leaders. Politicians seized the Lost Cause as an opportunity to solidify their power, and Southern women formed burial societies to honor the Confederate dead as manly, heroic, and virtuous. All sought a moral high ground as they struggled to understand Confederate defeat.[2] Gaines M. Foster observes, "'Lost' acknowledged the defeat of the Confederacy; 'Cause' suggested that the South had fought less for independence than for philosophical principles that might yet triumph."[3] The Lost

Cause proved malleable, and in a scholarly context, interpreters tend to fall into two broad categories. One group sees the Lost Cause as a political tool to push for issues like states' rights and white supremacy. Others see it in more cultural terms, thus casting Southerners as "a people set apart by a special sense of mission."[4] So then, where does the Confederate catechism fit in? Tyler understood the Lost Cause in both political and cultural terms. Politically, he denounced the Civil War as an unjust invasion by the North and defended the South's right to secede from the Union. Culturally, he also venerated Confederate leaders and extolled an idealized vision of the South, one steeped in antebellum lore. Tyler invited others, young and old alike, to see his version of "truth" by using a decidedly religious form: the catechism.[5]

If anyone ever established criteria for the ideal champion of the Lost Cause, Lyon Gardiner Tyler would have exceeded their most demanding standards. He was born on August 24, 1853 to John Tyler, tenth president of the United States, and his wife, Julia Gardiner Tyler. [6] As a Tyler, he hailed from one of Virginia's most aristocratic families. As the son of a pro-Southern, pro-slavery President, he had spent his entire lifetime steeping in the "Old South way" long before there even was an "Old South."[7] He graduated from the University of Virginia with a BA and an MA. He also studied law under the capable tutelage of John Minor.[8] Tyler enjoyed a distinguished career, but he is best known for reviving the College of William and Mary. As its President, Tyler led William and Mary's transition from a private to a public institution and opened its doors to women. He led numerous building programs and he set the college on a solid financial foundation. As a scholar, he published numerous works including *The Letters and Times of the Tylers* (three volumes), and *The Encyclopedia of Virginia Biography.* He also established a scholarly journal that would become the *William and Mary Quarterly.* He wrote extensively on Virginia history and became a pioneer in records preservation and management. He led the institution until he retired in 1919.[9]

Despite his formal training as a lawyer, Tyler styled himself as a historian. One fawning admirer gushed, "The Muse of history had smiled upon him: she knew that, by his sterling honesty, his dauntless courage, and his unswerving faith, he would add lustre to her already jeweled crown."[10] This same writer described Tyler as relentless in his pursuit of truth and compared him to Robert E. Lee and Thomas J. "Stonewall" Jackson who were both fearless in the face of overwhelming odds.[11] That same admirer added, "He was like a great military strategist surveying a broad field of combat. Like a general marshalling an army, he marshalled facts and arrayed them in impregnable positions. He attacked, and he won, deserving to be ranked among as one of the greatest of all historians."[12]

Tyler might have slipped into his retirement as a distinguished, early twentieth century Southern gentleman had it not been for three things. First, his lifelong exposure to pro-Confederate rhetoric coupled with his own research into his family history instilled an exaggerated bias for his native South. Second, given his close identification with the Lost Cause and his background in regional and family history, Tyler felt compelled to answer Dixie's critics, especially those who criticized the South in national media outlets. Finally, Tyler nursed a deep-seated hatred for Abraham Lincoln. When considered together, he chose "truth," or his understanding thereof, to combat what he understood as error. His family's position in Virginia's history coupled with publications and stature as a college president furnished a certain gravitas to his thought.

Galled by what he perceived to be a misuse of American history, Tyler wanted to set the record straight. For some, Abraham Lincoln was a Christ figure who simultaneously preserved the Union and freed southern slaves, while the Confederacy claimed only rogues of the lowest order. For others, the Southern states had defended themselves against Northern aggression. For them, Lincoln was a sham at best and a tyrant at worst. Tyler believed the latter and wanted everyone to know that there was another side to America's story. By telling that story faithfully, he believed he would establish his beloved region's rightful place in the nation's conscience.

In extolling Confederate virtues, Tyler assumed a unique position in the pantheon of Lost Cause champions, but not because he defended a mythical South that never was. Rather, Tyler produced a series of catechisms grounded in a decidedly Southern reading of American history. By using catechisms, he made his views available to the public in a convenient form. Normally, one thinks of a catechism as a means of teaching religious principles through a question-and-answer format, as in the Catechism of the Catholic Church or the Westminster Shorter Catechism. Tyler used his catechisms, however, to glorify the Confederacy while vilifying the North. Tyler saved his most pointed barbs for Abraham Lincoln, who in his estimation should never have been elected.[13]

CRAFTER OF CATECHISMS

As he hammered out his Confederate catechisms, Tyler entered a phase of his post-retirement career that occupied him until his death in 1935. Between 1920 and 1935, Lyon Tyler Gardiner produced at least six editions of the catechism. In his retirement writings, he attacked "from the top down," as if in heaping scorn on Lincoln, his mythical legacy would collapse under its own weight. If he destroyed Lincoln as a symbol, he believed "the truth" of his claims would be self-evident.

Tyler conducted a two-front campaign for his version of "the truth." On one level, he met public challenges with public responses, usually in the form of booklets, letters to newspapers, and the like. Producing these works led to his second front, a more popular articulation of the Lost Cause in catechism form. Over time, the catechisms became increasingly sophisticated. For analytical purposes, the catechisms can be divided into two categories: those produced before 1930 focused on justifying secession and vilifying Lincoln, and those from 1930 on were longer and much more detailed than their predecessors.[14] In 1930 Tyler released two different catechisms, but the second marked a dramatic departure from his earlier versions. The second 1930 edition nearly tripled its predecessor, going from twenty-one questions and fifteen pages to forty-three questions and forty-three pages, and reflected a more negative assessment of the federal government in general, and Abraham Lincoln in particular. In addition to being significantly longer, this catechism carried a new subtitle: "The War for Southern Self Government." If, indeed, Clio smiled upon Lyon Tyler, World War I had summoned her.

Tyler picked up the editorial gauntlet as a personal battle to vindicate the South as the United States entered World War I. The scrum began in 1917 when an article in *The New York Times* claimed that Germany's ruling aristocrats were responsible for World War I, much like the South's aristocracy had been responsible for the Civil War. Southern slaveholders would go to any lengths to extend their empire throughout the world. "Like the leaders of the Prussian caste in Germany," the article said, "they were warlike in spirit and purpose. Haughty, resolute, subtle, and, even when desperate, unyielding, they kept the field until their land was desolate."[15] The Union had survived only by crushing the South's rebellion so thoroughly that "within a score of years from its downfall, the Southern people would not have restored it had it been in their power to do so."[16] The article predicted "that the Hohenzollern despotism for which the German people are now fighting will be destroyed to the great and lasting gain, not only of the civilized nations contending against its intolerable aggressions, but also of the misguided and mistaken people of Germany."[17]

Tyler responded to this affront by publishing two works. First, he wrote *Propaganda in History*. He did not oppose propaganda, per se, because "it signifies only a means of publicity, which, when applied properly and legitimately serves a very good purpose."[18] Tyler was disturbed, however, by what he perceived as propaganda that had become accepted as historical fact, beginning with a New England bias that filtered all American history through its northeastern states. Anyone who cared to know understood that Jamestown, not Plymouth, was American's first permanent settlement. Neither were American colonies havens of religious refuge as falsely maintained in some quarters—"The persecuted in England turned persecutors in America, and the colonial disputes with England turned upon the religious and political tyranny which Puritans enacted in New England"— and the New England states were not the cradle of America's democratic tradition.[19]

Tyler reserved most of his venom for "the wonderful hero of the North," Abraham Lincoln. In his estimation, Lincoln did not measure up to the stature of notable Southerners like Washington, Jefferson, and others. He was not an American Christ; he was too crude to be a good president—his law partner, William Herndon, said as much. He was not a great humanitarian. He was not a great emancipator. Further, the Civil War had been Lincoln's fault, not the fault of Southern aristocrats. Lincoln had been a weak, ineffective leader, enthralled to the dictates of his own cabinet. "The truth is," Tyler claimed, "there never was a war more inconsistent with principle than that waged against the Southern States in 1861."[20]

About the same time he denounced propaganda masquerading as history, Tyler published the first of his Confederate catechisms. One might describe it as a distilled version of *Propaganda in History*. In it, Tyler posed nineteen questions bearing on secession and the Civil War. Seven of the nineteen questions addressed some aspect of Lincoln's character and/or leadership. Plus, he articulated a number of familiar themes, i.e., slavery had no bearing on the Civil War, Southern states seceded from the Union out of self-determination, not treason, and the war had not been the South's fault. Of the nineteen questions, number eight is especially interesting because it is the only question answered in all capital letters:

> Question: What did the south fight for?
> Answer: IT FOUGHT TO REPEL INVASION AND FOR SELF-GOVERNMENT, JUST AS THE FATHERS OF THE AMERICAN REVOLUTION HAD DONE.[21]

The pamphlet was only eight pages long, but there, in one sentence, Tyler articulated his understanding of the Civil War. The South had been invaded by a "foreign" army and it defended itself against conquest. There had been no aristocratic meddling. It had been a war to preserve the so-called Union, but the South was a confederacy of sovereign states and had been as just to take up arms in its defense as the Patriots of the American Revolution.

Doubtless, *Propaganda in History* and the first catechism further solidified Tyler's credentials as a true son of the Old South. Still, his personal motivation to preach his version of Dixie's virtue stemmed from a series of events that affected Southerners. In 1912 Southerners had reason to believe their role in national policy was improving. Woodrow Wilson became the first Southerner to be elected president of the United States since Reconstruction, Southerners made impressive gains in the House and Senate, and farm commodity prices, especially cotton and tobacco, were rising. But in 1920 Woodrow Wilson fell from public favor as Republicans reclaimed the White House and held it until 1932. Farm commodity prices slipped significantly after 1920, thus plunging the South into economic hard times a decade ahead of the rest of the nation. Southerners may have wondered who to blame for their woes, but Lyon Tyler knew.

Most of the nation's woes could be traced back to the Civil War and its aftermath. Shifting currents in America's academic life suddenly lent credence to Tyler's understanding of history. True, numerous writers had written about the war; but by the 1920s, professional historians were taking a close look at the Civil War and Reconstruction. Tyler may not have been a trained historian, but Columbia University's William Archibald Dunning was. With Dunning at the fore, these historians began taking a more positive view of the South and legitimized their resistance to Reconstruction. They emphasized Reconstruction's "tragic" aspects and argued that Reconstruction had greatly harmed the South.[22] Dunning and his likeminded students, however, furnished the Lost Cause with an academic legitimacy that it had been missing. With titles like *Reconstruction, Political and Economic, 1865–1877* and Claude Bower's *The Tragic Era: The Revolution after Lincoln*, Lost Cause advocates could buttress their assertions by pointing to respected academicians.[23] What had the Civil War and Reconstruction really been about? Again, Tyler thought he had the answer—if he could get anyone to listen to him.

TAKING ON LINCOLN

Tyler's retirement from William and Mary coincided with another change in American culture. By 1920 most of the Civil War veterans had died, and scholars agree that a new generation faced new challenges. Earlier writers had spoken of a "New" South, but 1920 marked the end of what historian Howard N. Rabinowitz called the "First New South" and thus opened the door for a "Second New South."[24] The First World War rekindled sectional tensions and summoned a renewed Southern consciousness. Consequently, Tyler began his most spirited defense of the South as the region entered a new phase of existence. If it is true that the fortunes of the Lost Cause rose and fell based on social, cultural, and/or political circumstances, World War I and its aftermath witnessed renewed sectional animosities which, in turn, reinvigorated the Lost Cause.[25]

It is difficult to say with certainty why Tyler felt compelled to expand his catechism. Part of the story doubtless hinges on an editorial spat (dust-up) with *Time* magazine. In 1928 the Virginia House of Delegates passed a resolution honoring Abraham Lincoln. On its surface, the resolution appeared innocuous enough:

> Mr. Gordon offered the following resolution:
> Resolved, That when the House of Delegates adjourns today it adjourn in memory and honor of Abraham Lincoln, the martyred President of the United States, whose death was a distinct blow to the South, resulting in national calamity, which was agreed to.[26]

Tyler's name appeared along with other prominent Virginians requesting the House to repeal the resolution. Going one step further, Tyler expressed his displeasure in no uncertain terms. It was possible, he noted, to demonstrate excessive kindness, especially in honoring people, and Lincoln did not deserve to be honored, especially by Southerners. Worse, Tyler believed the House labored under the impression "that Lincoln would, had he lived, have prevented the horrors of reconstruction."[27] Could a man who waged the kind of war that Lincoln waged have been a benevolent peacetime leader? Would a man as vacillating/shifty as Lincoln have been trusted to extend kindness to a region he believed had betrayed the Union? "I am a believer in reconciliation and peace," Tyler claimed, "and I think every effort should be made to promote harmony and good feeling, but it does not follow that such a policy should be at the expense of historic truth and justice."[28]

The episode caught *Time* magazine's interest. On April 9, 1928 they ran a brief story titled "Tyler and Lincoln." The article acknowledged that Sergeant Giles Cook and G. W. B. Hale also supported the resolution's repeal, but they were particularly dismayed that a person of Tyler's stature would be associated with the measure, though they thought they understood why. The article referred to him dismissively as "Son Tyler" and chided, "Dr. Tyler is the oldest living son of a U. S. President. That he should join in an attack on a President beside whom his father is historically a dwarf, was not without interest." *Time* went on to describe Tyler as a marginal politician at best, who "retired from politics embittered, when his term ended, and did not appear in public life again until the days of Secession, when he championed the Southern confederacy."[29]

The article may have reminded Lyon that his father, John, had been dubbed "his Accidency" upon becoming president of the United States, or maybe any comparison whereby Abraham Lincoln bested his father was too insulting for him to bear. Either way, the *Time* article spurred Tyler into action, just as *The New York Times* article had in 1917. Tyler published *John Tyler and Abraham Lincoln: Who Was the Dwarf? A Reply to a Challenge.* He offered a spirited defense of his father's presidency and he minced no words in denouncing Lincoln. His criticisms were not especially new. Whereas his father, John Tyler, had acted from principle, Lincoln remained a crude buffoon in his way of thinking and plunged the republic into a war out of his own self-aggrandizement. Those deficiencies qualified Lincoln as a "dwarf" in Tyler's mind.[30]

In 1930 Tyler published his catechism in two editions. The first featured twenty-one questions, but the second more than doubled to forty-three questions. Moreover, this expanded catechism marked a shift away

from explaining what caused the Civil War toward casting it in more contemporary Southern terms and interests. He probably believed he had
good reason. The South's regional economy continued to languish—with
Republican Herbert Hoover at the helm, no less. Of course, for Tyler
and his fellow Southern apologists, it all seemed so clear: things would
be different had the South won the Civil War. How the rest of the nation
could buy into the "Lincoln Myth" was beyond him. The facts, he believed, spoke for themselves.

Of course, facts seldom speak for themselves. Facts need interpreters,
and Tyler's interpretation of the facts rested on his bias and a selective reading of the sources. Beginning with the fourth edition, each of the catechisms ends by asking, "If then this is a mere Northern government, how
may the old Union of the Fathers be restored?" The answer: "It may be
restored readily enough by the United States reaffirming the doctrine of
self-government, expressing sorrow for the war of conquest in 1861–65,
admitting the South into a proper share of all the functions of government,
and joining the League of Nations in banishing armies and navies and war.
The South has no vindictiveness. All it wants is truth and justice."[31] Once
again, Tyler depicted Lincoln in the most negative light possible. He believed it was imperative for others to know the difference between history
and propaganda; perhaps that is why he became embroiled in a controversy
over textbooks.

In 1931 Tyler led a crusade against Virginia's decision to replace Virginian
John H. Letane's *A History of the United States* with Harvard-trained historian
David Saville Muzzey's *An American History*. The textbook controversy likely
contributed to his catechism's final version. Miss Annie Mann, President
of the Virginia Division of the United Daughters of the Confederacy, complained that Muzzey's work "teaches that the sole cause of the War between
the States was *slavery*, and this war is spoken of as the "slavery contest."[32]
Mann was also quoted as saying that she and the Virginia UDC "would prefer no textbook at all to having Virginia children taught that their grandfa-
thers had no justification for fighting the War between the States."[33] Tyler
also registered his strong displeasure over Muzzey's text. According to one
source, "he stated that people ashamed of their past were on the road to
degeneracy. 'Don't cater to Northern tastes and be afraid to call your soul
your own,' he emphasized most emphatically, and he felt that Muzzey had
no more idea of the War between the States than he had of the moon when

he wrote the book . . . Dr. Tyler further stated that Muzzey had a tendency to whitewash such as the needless burning of the city of Columbia and Sheridan's infamous conduct, while ignoring the triumphs of men like Stuart, Forrest, and Jackson."[34]

As Tyler battled against Muzzey's textbook and its alleged misrepresentation of American history, he also considered his catechism. The final version of the catechism appeared in 1931 and offered forty-nine questions, six more than its predecessor of 1930. In refining his work, Tyler once again vindicated the Confederacy and the South's cause. But Tyler was fighting a difficult battle and in the midst of a national depression, international tension, and his own age.

The later versions of Tyler's catechisms reflect an obsession with painting Abraham Lincoln in the most negative light possible. He believed it was his duty. In its sixth edition, Tyler moved question nineteen, "Would Lincoln have saved the South from the horrors of Reconstruction if he had survived?" to question thirty-one, where it introduced a series of pointed questions regarding Lincoln:

> 32. It is often said that Lincoln, in sending armies to the South, acted only in obedience to his oath "to take care that the laws of the United States be faithfully executed." Is this true?
>
> 33. What were the main features of Lincoln's "friendship" for the South?
>
> 34. Explain more fully the course of Lincoln as to Exchanges.
>
> 35. What were the results of Lincoln's policy as to confederate prisoners?
>
> 36. What was the personal attitude of Lincoln on this policy of Grant in regard to exchanges?
>
> 37. Was Lincoln a hero?
>
> 39. Was it Lincoln's desire to preserve the Union that influenced him in violating the Constitution and resorting to barbarous methods of warfare?
>
> 41. What is Lincoln's present reputation founded upon?[35]

Tyler's version of the truth featured a clear villain, Abraham Lincoln. That villain perpetrated unspeakable evil on Southerners largely because he lacked character. Southerners took arms in self-defense. Life would be better for everyone, Northerners included, had the South won. By packaging his thought in distilled, ready reference form, Tyler armed Southerners to go on the offensive when confronted with their past. After all, according to Tyler, they had been right all along. If there was a national boogeyman it was Abraham Lincoln, not Jefferson Davis, and the entire nation suffered for it. Finding answers was as easy as asking a question.

Answering the public's questions was one thing; distributing the answers was another. Here Tyler relied on a variety of means to propagate his message. Word-of-mouth advertising proved effective and, in some cases, Tyler's admirers took the catechism's promotion upon themselves. In 1931 Mary Carter wrote, "I suppose you saw the little 'Ad.' on your Catechism—which Mr. Williams put on page 17 in Jan. 17th Southern Churchman. . . . Well, the 'Ad.' is working for I got two orders for the 'Catechism' to-day. One for two copies and one for twenty copies." Apparently Carter had placed the ad on her own initiative. She wrote, "I am hoping that this 'Ad' which Mr. Williams was good enough to put in his paper for me, will bring in many, many orders for your Catechism." If it proved effective, she planned to contact other outlets with copies of both Tyler's catechism and her ad.[36]

TYLER'S READERS RESPOND

It is impossible to gauge how many of his catechisms Tyler sold or how the public received them. Some Confederate sympathizers offered their own interpretation of the War Between the States. Others like the United Daughters of the Confederacy delighted in reading the catechism, as dozens of letters in the Tyler family correspondence attest. Many wanted the catechisms to teach their children the Confederate version of the Civil War. One letter from the Beckeley County Chapter, West Virginia, said, "Our U. D. C. chapter has a flourishing Children's Chapter—The Virginia Faulkner McSherry Chapter—who need to be educated. Therefore we are asking you to mail 4 (four) copies at 20 cts, of your fine 'Confederate Catechism' to be used at their meetings. Enclosed please find my check for .80 cents—If that is not enough for the postage, please let us know."[37] Most inquirers requested one or two copies of the catechism, but some ordered large quantities. William D. Anderson, a textile merchant from Gastonia, North Carolina informed Tyler that his order of fifty Confederate catechisms failed to arrive. He resubmitted the order and added, "I am reading with a great deal of interest Claude G. Bowers book 'The Tragic Era,' one of the best discussions of the Reconstruction period in the South that I have ever read."[38] Requests came from as far west as California and Washington to as far north as Connecticut. One can only imagine what he wanted with them, but H. L. Mencken requested fifty copies.[39]

Some professional historians took note of Tyler's work. In a letter dated January 14, 1931, Avery O. Craven thanked Tyler for sending him a copy of the catechism. While he did not specify *how* he might use it, Craven noted, "I am conducting a seminar next summer on the question of Southern secession and am delighted to put this into the hands of my students." He added that he had nearly finished a biography of Edmund Ruffin and hoped "to have it in the hands of the publisher by the beginning of the summer."[40]

Another unreconstructed soul commended Tyler for the catechism but asked that future editions warn readers about Julia Ward Howe's "Battle Hymn of the Republic." The song had "crept into the hymnals of some of our churches," and church members had no idea that "she makes the Yankee army the army of heaven and the entire Southern people as the people of the devil and about to be smitten by the vengeance of God. It is a blasphemous thing."[41]

Not everyone received Tyler's catechism with equal enthusiasm. On November 13, 1929, Frederick W. Scott of Scott and Stringfellow, Bankers and Brokers responded to Tyler's request for their financial assistance. "I have yours of the 8th," Scott said, "and also the 'Confederate catechism,' in which I am very much interested. I do not care, however, at this time to spend $250.00 distributing this Catechism. I might use that $250.00 in buying some cheap stocks."[42] A Memphis attorney, Duncan Martin, claimed the catechism contained "much food for thought," but he wished Tyler had cited his sources. "I wonder if it ever occurred to you," he asked, "that it might be of value to many of your readers if you would, as we lawyers do in our briefs, cite your authorities and comment upon them (by way of explanation)."[43]

Yet, Tyler's strongest criticism may have come from F. I. Herriott, professor of political science at Drake University. In a letter dated January 3, 1931, Herriott challenged Tyler on states' rights. He admitted that his father had served in the Union Army and he had grown up with Northern biases. While he believed that Southerners had been treated unjustly after the war, Herriott claimed that Tyler argued from a faulty premise—states' rights. Herriott maintained that the delegates to the Constitutional convention created something far greater than a loosely knit group of states. "I submit," he said, "that it was NOT A LEAGUE AND IT WAS NEITHER A CONTINUATION NOR A MODIFICATION OF THE OLD CONFEDERATION. The delegates in the celebrated convention of 1787 deliberately broke or disregarded their original instructions and designed a central government WITH POWER to effectuate its national jurisdiction in national matters per se, in interstate relationships and in all international matters."[44] He further reminded Tyler that the doctrine of states' rights had actually interfered with the Southern war effort in basic issues like supply and conscription. Herriott could not resist jabbing Tyler for comparing Civil War era soldiers to Revolutionary War patriots. With more than a tinge of irony he noted, "Does it not remind you of the many painful and crucifying experiences of Washington during the Revolution when he had to await the obstinate disinclination of the states, or colonies stoutly and selfishly asserting their 'State's Rights' before doing a thing—usually nothing!!"[45]

CONCLUSION

In one of history's ironic twists, Lyon Gardiner Tyler died on Lincoln's birthday, February 12, 1935. *The New York Times* eulogized him as a "tenacious character" who delighted in preaching Confederate virtues and venerating its leaders. "Personally," the *Times* noted, "he was one of the kindest and most genial of men. But on the subject of the Confederacy he remained 'unreconstructed' until the end of his days."[46] As an unreconstructed Southerner, Tyler was on a mission. The Civil War might be over, but the battle to convince hearts and minds that the South and its leadership was virtuous was ongoing. Anything that depicted them negatively amounted to Northern propaganda. As for Abraham Lincoln, historian Dan Monroe summed it up best by noting, "He spent much of his retirement years in a crusade to demythologize Abraham Lincoln, filling the pages of his own journal, *Tyler's Quarterly Historical and Genealogical Magazine*, with pieces highly critical of the sixteenth president."[47] He further observed, "Only Lyon Tyler could rescue truth from layers of fiction by scrupulously adhering to the truth."[48]

Yet, Tyler's catechisms did more than furnish a popularized polemical platform. In assuming their strident Lost Cause posture, the catechisms perpetuated lingering suspicion and animosity toward the federal government that quickly resurfaced at critical times—Dixiecrats in 1948, Second Reconstruction/civil rights, *Brown v. Board* and "interposition," and textbook treatment of the South in American history to name a few examples. Moreover, Tyler helped legitimize an understanding of American history that perpetuated a foundation for dissent against perceived encroachment against the rights of individual states. The catechisms promoted white solidarity, and by claiming that Southerners rejoiced in slavery's demise, it was as if everyone was absolved of their own racism. Of course, for Tyler and his ilk, it would have been better had it died at Southern hands rather than Northern bayonets.

Tyler was not the only one who battled for the truth. Even before he died, scholars had already begun to question the "Dunning School" and favorable assessments of America's post-Civil War South. While Dunning does not command the same respect that he did in the early twentieth century, Eric Foner observes that "it [the Dunning School] enjoys a remarkable staying power among the public at large."[49] The public at large represented the crowd Tyler wanted most to reach.

The Lost Cause, however, had become ensconced in the American mind long before Dunning or Tyler, and it shows no signs of dying out. Tyler did all he could to see to that. His work was especially timely for Southern apologists who celebrated the "revolt of the Dixiecrats."[50] Southern apologists met the *Brown* decision with calls for "massive resistance," interposition, and states' rights rhetoric that echoed Tyler's catechisms. He was not responsible for it and his catechisms played only a part in articulating the Lost Cause, at best. Discussions over the Civil War's causes, the legitimacy of the South's cause in general, and issues bearing on the Lost Cause and its related themes continue well into the twenty-first century, especially among historians. If issues involving white on black violence are any indication, they show no real signs of fading from the public eye.[51]

NOTES

The author would like to thank Meghan Bryant of the Special Collections at the Swem Library at William and Mary College and Johnnie Harper, inter-library loan assistant of the Southeastern Baptist Theological Seminary for their assistance in preparing this essay.

1. Lyon Gardiner Tyler, "A Confederate Catechism: The War for Southern Self-Government," in *Tyler's Quarterly Historical and Genealogical Quarterly* XXXIII, no. 2, ed. Mrs. Lyon Gardiner Tyler (October 1951): 89–106 and XXXIII, no. 3 (January 1952): 157–78.

2. See Caroline E. Janney, "Burying the Dead, but Not the Past: Ladies Memorial Associations and the Lost Cause," in *Civil War America*, ed. Gary W. Gallagher (Chapel Hill: The Univ. of North Carolina Press, 1988). See also "Remembering the Civil War: Reunion and the Limits of Reconciliation," in *The Littlefield History of the Civil War Era*, ed. Gary W. Gallagher and T. Michael Parrish (Chapel Hill: The Univ. of North Carolina Press, 2013).

3. Gaines M. Foster, "Lost Cause Myth," in *Encyclopedia of Southern Culture*, ed. Charles Reagan Wilson and William Ferris (Chapel Hill and London: The Univ. of North Carolina Press, 1989), 1134.

4. Foster, "Lost Cause Myth," 1134.

5. The literature on the Lost Cause is extensive. See Charles Reagan Wilson, *Baptized in Blood: The Religion of the Lost Cause, 1865–1920*, with a new preface (Athens and London: The Univ. of Georgia Press, 2009); Gaines M. Foster, *Ghosts of the Confederacy: Defeat, the Lost Cause and the Emergence of the New South, 1865–1913* (New York: Oxford Univ. Press, 1988).

6. For useful studies of John Tyler see Edward P. Crapol, *John Tyler: The Accidental President* (Chapel Hill: The Univ. of North Carolina Press, 2006) and Dan Monroe, *The Republican Vision of John Tyler* (College Station: Texas A & M Press, 2003). Older, yet helpful works include Oliver Perry Chitwood, *John Tyler: Champion of the Old South* (The American Historical Association, 1939; reissued New York: Russell & Russell, 1964) and Norma Lois Peterson, *The Presidencies of William Henry Harrison and John Tyler*. American Presidency Series, ed. Donald R. McCoy, Clifford S. Griffin, and Homer E. Socolofsky (Lawrence: Univ. Press of Kansas, 1989).

7. As C. Vann Woodward famously observed, "One of the most significant inventions of the New South was the 'Old South'—a new idea in the eighties, and a legend of incalculable potentialities." See *Origins of the New South, 1877–1913* (Baton Rouge: Louisiana State Univ. Press, 1971) 154–55. Woodward also observed, "The deeper the involvements in commitments to the New Order, the louder the protests of loyalty to the Old."

8. James Southall Williams, "Lyon Gardiner Tyler," *William and Mary Quarterly Historical Magazine* 15, 2nd series, no. 4, (October 1935): 319.

9. Kelly Chroninger, "Lyon Gardiner Tyler (1853–1935)," *Encyclopedia Virginia*, accessed January 30, 2018, https://www.encyclopediavirginia.org/Tyler_Lyon_Gardiner_1853 –1935#start_entry. See also James Southall Wilson, "Lyon Gardiner Tyler," *William and Mary Quarterly Historical Magazine* 15, 2nd series, no. 4 (October 1935): 319–25. The journal Tyler established later became *Tyler's Quarterly Historical and Genealogical Magazine*. See also John Lloyd Newcomb, Geo. M. Ferguson, Jr., and Robert H. Tucker, "Tribute to Dr. Lyon G. Tyler," *William and Mary Quarterly Historical Magazine* 15, no. 4 (October 1935): 344–54 and J. Gordon Bohannon, "A Tribute to the Memory of Dr. Lyon Gardiner Tyler, President of William and Mary College," *William and Mary Quarterly Historical Magazine* 15, no. 4 (October 1935): 334–43.

10. John E. Hobeika, *The Sage of the Lion's Den: An Appreciation of the Character and Career of Lyon Gardiner Tyler and His Writings on Abraham Lincoln and the War Between the States* (New York: The Exposition Press, 1948), 30.

11. Hobeika, *The Sage of the Lion's Den*, 30 passim.

12. Hobeika, *The Sage of the Lion's Den*, 35

13. Tyler's sentiments are clear throughout his catechisms. They become more detailed over time but essentially the same themes are present from one edition to the other. Catechisms have a long history as tools of instruction for the rudiments of faith, and ironically, in the antebellum era, pro-slavery writers created a variety of catechisms for enslaved people that emphasized their duty to obey God and their earthly masters. White readers were often the primary audience for most antebellum catechisms, which instructed slave owners and denominational leaders on the need and manner for efficacious evangelization and religious instruction for enslaved people. See generally, Charles Colcock

Jones, *The Religious Instruction of the Negroes in the United States* (Savannah, GA: Thomas Purse, 1842); Edward R. Crowther, *Southern Evangelicals and the Coming of the Civil War* (Lewiston, NY: Edwin Mellen Press, 2000), 57–80; and Charles F. Irons, *The Origins of Proslavery Christianity: White and Black Evangelicals in Colonial and Antebellum Virginia* (Chapel Hill: Univ. of North Carolina Press, 2008), 174–84.

14. The first catechism is dated 1920, the next two are both dated 1929, and one is dated 1930. They pose nineteen, twenty, twenty, and twenty-one questions, respectively.

15. "The Hohenzollerns and the Slave Power," *The New York Times*, April 22, 1917, E2. The First World War marked an opportune moment to rekindle smoldering Lost Cause embers. In *Burying the Dead but Not the Past: Ladies Memorial Associations and the Lost Cause*, Caroline Janney notes, "Like many other historians of the Lost Cause, I elected to end the study between 1914 and 1915. These years marked the fiftieth anniversary of the war and also the commencement of World War I. At this point, reconciliation had been firmly established between white people of the North and South and beginning at this time Memorial Days no longer exclusively celebrated Civil War soldiers." See *Burying the Dead but Not the Past*, 205, note 5.

16. Janney, *Burying the Dead but Not the Past*, 205, note 5.

17. Janney, *Burying the Dead but Not the Past*, 205, note 5.

18. Lyon G. Tyler, *Propaganda in History* (Richmond: Richmond Press, Inc. Printers, 1920).

19. Tyler, *Propaganda in History*, 4 passim.

20. Tyler, *Propaganda in History*, 10, 19.

21. Lyon Gardiner Tyler, *A Confederate Catechism: The War of 1861–1865* (n.p., n.d.) 3.

22. John David Smith and J. Vincent Lowery, eds., *The Dunning School: Historians, Race, and the Meaning of Reconstruction* (Lexington: The Univ. Press of Kentucky, 2013).

23. See William Archibald Dunning, *Reconstruction, Political and Economic, 1865–1877* (New York and London: Harper & Brothers, 1907); Claude G. Bowers, *The Tragic Era: The Revolution after Lincoln* (New York: Literary Guild of America, 1929).

24. Scholarly debate over how best to periodize the South may go on indefinitely. The point here is to note that 1920 marked a turning point in Southern history.

25. For life on the American home front during the war, see David M. Kennedy, *Over Here: The First World War and American Society* (Oxford and New York: Oxford Univ. Press, 1980).

26. *Journal of the House Delegates*, Session which Commenced at the State Capital on Wednesday, January 11, 1928 (Richmond: Davis Bottom, Superintendent of Printing, 1928), 326.

27. Lyon G. Tyler, "House Action on Lincoln Mistake Says Dr. Tyler," in *Langbourne M. Williams, Confederate Leaders and Other Citizens Request the House of Delegates to Repeal the Resolution of Respect to Abraham Lincoln, the Barbarian . . .* (Nashville: Southern Churchmen Publishing Co., 1928), 14. Tyler's brief article appeared with others written by Giles Cook and G. W. B. Hale, but Tyler apparently published his thoughts earlier in the *Richmond Times Dispatch*. Williams then pulled two other pieces together for his booklet.

28. Tyler, "House Action on Lincoln Mistake," 16.

29. *Time* magazine, April 9, 1928, vol. 11 issue 15, 13. For an excellent assessment of Tyler's attitude toward Lincoln see Dan Monroe, "Lincoln the Dwarf: Lyon Gardiner Tyler's

War on the Mythical Lincoln," *Journal of the Abraham Lincoln Association* 24, no. 1, 32–42.
See also Dan Monroe, *The Republican Vision of John Tyler* (College Station: Texas A & M Univ.
Press, 2003).

30. Lyon Gardiner Tyler, *John Tyler and Abraham Lincoln, Who was the Dwarf? A Reply to a
Challenge* (Richmond, VA: Richmond Press, Inc., 1929). Tyler responded to *Time*'s 680-word
article with a forty-one-page booklet!

31. Compare editions four, five, and six.

32. Miss Annie Mann as quoted by Mrs. John Huske Anderson, "WARNING AGAIST
UNFAIR TESTBOOKS," *Confederate Veteran* XL, April 1932, 129.

33. Miss Annie Mann as quoted by Miss Claudia M. Hagy, "U. D. C. ASSAULT ON
MUZZEY'S HISTORY," *Confederate Veteran* XL, April 1932, 129.

34. Hagy, "U. D. C. ASSAULT ON MUZZEY'S HISTORY," 129.

35. Tyler, *Confederate Catechism*; compare versions five, six, and seven. The sixth edition
features "Some Additions" under point/question forty-seven. Question thirty-eight reads,
"What importance should be placed on the statements of Rhett, Yancey and other Southern
extremists?" Question forty reads, "Were the terms of surrender granted by Grant, Sherman,
and other Federal generals anything extraordinary?"

36. Mary D. Carter to Lyon Gardiner Tyler, January 17, 1931, The Tyler Family Papers,
Group B, Box XXXIII, Folder 5.

37. Mrs. M. A. Snodgrass to Lyon Gardiner Tyler, n.d (circa 1930?), The Tyler Family
Papers, Group B, Box XXXIII, Folder 4.

38. William D. Anderson to Lyon Gardiner Tyler, March 29, 1930, The Tyler Family
Papers, Group B, Box XXXII, Folder 9.

39. H. L. Mencken to Lyon Gardiner Tyler, August 7 (1930 or 31?) The Tyler Family
Papers, Group B, Box XXXIII, Folder 4. Mencken's note reads, "Dear Sir, Will you please
send me 50 copies of your pamphlet, 'A Confederate Catechism'? I enclose my check
for $2.50. Sincerely yours (signed) H. L. Mencken." The note is on Mencken's personal
letterhead.

40. Avery O. Craven to Lyon Gardiner Tyler, January 14, 1931, The Tyler Family Papers,
Group B, Box XXXIII, Folder 5. News of a scholarly biography on Ruffin likely piqued
Tyler's interest. In 1923 he married Sue Ruffin, who, according to Dan Monroe, descended
from Edmund Ruffin. Her hatred for Abraham likely equaled that of her husband.

41. Daniel Prisman (?) to Lyon Gardiner Tyler, March 13, 1930, The Tyler Family Papers,
Group B, Box XXXII, Folder 9.

42. Frederick W. Scott to Lyon Gardiner Tyler, November 13, 1929, The Tyler Family
Papers, Group B, Box XXXII, Folder 6.

43. Duncan Martin to Lyon Gardiner Tyler, March 4, 1930, letter incomplete, The Tyler
Family Papers, Group B, Box XXXII, Folder 9.

44. F. I. Herriott to Lyon Gardiner Tyler, January 3, 1931, The Tyler Family Papers,
Group B, Box XXXIII, Folder 5. Emphasis Herriott. For biographical information on Frank
Irving Herriott see Charles Blanchard, *History of Drake University: Building for the Centuries*, vol.
1 (Des Moines: Drake Univ., 1931) 71–74.

45. Herriott to Tyler, January 3, 1931, The Tyler Family Papers.

46. "A Tenacious Character," *The New York Times*, February 12, 1935.

47. Dan Monroe, "Lincoln the Dwarf: Lyon Gardiner Tyler's War on the Mythical Lincoln," *Journal of the Abraham Lincoln Association* 24, no. 3: 33.

48. Monroe, "Lincoln the Dwarf," 41. Monroe also has a clear assessment of Tyler's career on pages 40–41.

49. Eric Foner, "Foreword," in *The Dunning School*, ed. Smith and Lowery, xii.

50. For a summary of the Dixiecrats see Edward F. Haas, "Dixiecrats," in *Encyclopedia of Southern Culture*, ed. Wilson and Ferris, 1185–86. Haas notes, "Although race was clearly their key concern, the States' Rights Democrats included, in addition to white supremacists, antiunion industrialist oil men and constitutional conservatives who abhorred civil rights and communism." David Muzzey's textbook had been criticized in part because he had been labeled a "Bolshevik." See also Kari Fredrickson, *The Dixiecrat Revolt and the End of the Solid South, 1932–1968* (Chapel Hill: The Univ. of North Carolina Press, 2001).

51. See Mathew Karp, *This Vast Southern Empire: Slaveholders at the Helm of American Foreign Policy* (Cambridge, MA and London: Harvard Univ. Press, 2016). Karp's work is not about the Confederacy, but he does credit Lincoln and the Republicans for breaking the power of base for pro-slavery policy makers.

The Black Lost Cause: African American Christians during the Post-Reconstruction and Jim Crow Era, 1877–1925

SANDY DWAYNE MARTIN

A powerful counter-narrative, the concept of the Black Lost Cause emerged at the close of Reconstruction in 1877 and continued to develop until the decline of the Marcus Garvey movement in the US around 1925. The Reverend Dr. W. Bishop Johnson, a Baptist leader, proved pivotal in articulating and shaping this movement alongside other black spokespersons, and their ideas of a Black Lost Cause theology, form another chapter in the counterpoint of Black Civil Religion. During the critical years of 1877–1925, the Black Lost Cause enjoyed a renaissance, a resurrection of an older form of theology or religious thinking from the pre-Civil War period in which many black Christians dealt with matters related to Black Civil Religion, including questions of theodicy: Why if we too are God's people does God permit us to be victims of racial suppression? Although black Christians did not believe they exclusively were God's people, they did emphasize, as others could, that they were truly and in some "unique" or special ways God's people, through which He revealed His will for all people, but especially black folk.

Black Christians continued to believe that the period encompassing the Civil War, Emancipation, and Reconstruction was one in which God had responded to generations of black people's prayers to liberate them from slavery in much the same manner as the Old Testament says that God acted in ancient Egypt to free enslaved Hebrews. Exodus for these African Americans, as with the ancient Hebrews, meant more than freedom from physical enslavement, which they now enjoyed. It also entailed living in the Promised Land or Canaan, an existence (more than a physical place) where they could enjoy all the rights and opportunities as other Americans, which had not been fully realized and now in the post-Reconstruction period seemed delayed.

When the Reconstruction era (1866–1877) gradually but surely ended, black Christians, like white Southern Christians at the conclusion of the Civil War, espoused a theology that made sense of, or reconciled the current setbacks and defeats with, the understanding of themselves as a chosen people destined for liberation. As white Southern Christians reconciled their defeat on the battlefield and their continued struggles to maintain their own identity and way of life in a reunited nation with their conviction that they were God's chosen people, so African American Christians reconciled their defeat with the demise of Reconstruction and their continued and now intensified struggle to overcome lynching, segregation, and other forms of racial oppression with their belief that they were God's people destined for freedom spiritually and temporally, as human beings and as American citizens. This essay seeks to outline some main elements of that Black Lost Cause theology.

THEORETICAL FRAMEWORK: AMERICAN, SOUTHERN, AND BLACK CIVIL RELIGION

In engaging the formation, continuation, and expression of post-Reconstruction Black Lost Cause, there are a number of important points to bear in mind. First, the Black Lost Cause is an expression of Black Civil Religion, which is analogous in many ways to American Civil Religion and Southern Civil Religion, just as the Southern white Lost Cause is an expression of Southern Civil Religion. Robert Bellah described American Civil Religion as having a religious interpretation regarding the nature, operation, and purpose of the American nation. American Civil Religion transcends any particular Christian denomination and even Christianity itself since it speaks of God and God's purposes for America in Christian (and Jewish) principles but not exclusively Christian doctrine. For example, for much of American history, there would be little in the national leaders' and spokespersons' public, civic descriptions of God's purposes for America that would prove problematic for practitioners of Judaism.[1]

Charles Reagan Wilson persuasively contends that there is a Southern Civil Religion, a civil religion focused on the American South. While the Confederacy lost to Union forces on the battlefield, the values and principles of its leaders live on and enrich the nation as a whole. Southern Civil Religion differs from American Civil Religion in that the former focuses on a particular region of the country and its memorialization of the Civil War (or as it would perhaps term the event the War for Southern Independence), has been more explicitly Christian in its formulation, and has been even more identified with the white race given its association with Confederate traditions.[2] Black Civil Religion focuses on black people, their American-ness or possibly African-ness, and their mission for the nation and/or all of humanity. Though most of Black Civil Religion focuses on African Americans' place in American life, some expressions of Black Civil Religion emphasize or include Africa or the wider world of black humanity. This essay focuses on black Christianity, but when understood in the broader sense, Black Civil Religion would include practitioners of other religions such as Judaism and Islam.[3]

American Civil Religion, Southern Civil Religion and the Lost Cause, and Black Civil Religion and the Black Lost Cause, then, all share some major themes, including a belief in the existence of a supreme being who is providential—governing and controlling history and world affairs however much they might go against the deity's will from time to time—and a chosen people concept, the conviction that a given people, whether black Americans or black people in general, have been chosen by God for some specific or combination of purposes. This sense of mission of the chosen people generally extends beyond the protection, vindication, and rewarding of the particular people, but it is a mission that is currently, and will prove to be in the future, a blessing to the entire nation and to all of humanity.

TWO MAJOR THEMES

Beyond the theoretical and methodological background, this essay has two major focuses. The first is W. Bishop Johnson, a black Maryland pastor, a leader in state and national Baptist circles, and author of the book *The Scourging of A Race*. This work examines quite closely his sermon of the same title, because among the readily available sources it comes closest to most comprehensively expressing the Black Lost Cause by its treatment of concerns such as providence, chosen people, and group mission or destiny. Second, this essay deals with major themes related to the Black Lost Cause that appear in Johnson's sermon and in the speeches and writings of his contemporaries, including Booker T. Washington, Francis J. Grimke, representatives of the Black Women's Club Movement, Marcus Garvey, and other black leaders and spokespersons. Along those lines, my definitions of black "leaders" and "spokespersons" are expansive, denoting persons or groups who speak to and for the interests of African Americans religiously, culturally, economically, or politically. They include holders of designated offices in churches and denominations but also persons who might be only slightly affiliated or even unaffiliated with a denomination or religious group. Attention to these religious and lay or "secular" leaders demonstrates the pervasiveness of elements related to the Black Lost Cause among the general black populace during the nineteenth and early twentieth centuries and indicates that it was transdenominational and even transreligious.[4]

W. BISHOP JOHNSON'S "SCOURGING OF A RACE"

William Bishop Johnson (1858–1917) was born in Toronto, Canada and went to school in Toronto, New York, and Virginia.[5] Johnson graduated valedictorian from what was then known as Wayland Seminary, later a part of Virginia Union University in Richmond, Virginia, in 1879. He earned his doctor of divinity from the State University of Kentucky and doctor of law from the Virginia Theological Seminary and College in 1888 and 1904, respectively. Johnson was ordained and became the pastor of First Baptist Church in Fredericksburg, Maryland in 1879, and about two years later, he ministered for the Northern-based American Baptist Home Mission Society (ABHMS) in Maryland; Washington, DC; West Virginia; and Virginia. For twelve years he served as professor of mathematics and political science at Wayland Seminary, and he pastored Second Baptist Church in Washington, DC beginning in 1883.

In addition to pastoring and teaching, Johnson was also active in editing and organizing on a national scale. In 1891 he helped found the National Baptist Educational Convention, which merged with two other organizations to form the National Baptist Convention (NBC) in 1895. Johnson was also associated with the Virginia Baptist State Convention—one of the earliest black state Baptist conventions organized after the Civil War—served as trustee of Virginia Baptist Seminary and College, and was director of Baptist Young People's Christian and Educational Conference. His editorial works include the *Baptist Companion* beginning in 1886, the Wayland Seminary *Alumni Journal* starting in 1890, and the *National Baptist Magazine* beginning in 1893, which after the merger that same year would continue as a major organ for the NBC. In his introduction to Johnson's book, E. M. Brawley, Baptist leader from South Carolina, referred to Johnson as among "the most eloquent orators," an "erudite scholar and a strong writer on any subject," fervently committed to the black race, and a great advocate of black enterprises and the ability of African Americans "first, last, and all the time." Whether Brawley was embellishing or not, we get a sense of his high impression of Johnson when he writes, "He excites his opponents in debate most easily; annihilates all conflicting opinions, and turns whole assemblies into . . . astonishment, admiration, and awe."[6]

Johnson's sermon, "The Scourging of A Race," sets forth the theme that the trials under which African Americans then labored were in part because God was "scourging," or permitting the "scourging," of the race so that they might be more faithful to God and to each other. Scourging and similar biblical terms such as "flogging," "beating," or figuratively, "affliction," carry the meaning of a severe punishment.[7] By using this term, Johnson was conveying that the post-Reconstruction era was a time of great ordeal for African Americans. Interestingly, Johnson's book and sermon appear in 1904, by which time segregation had been nationally enshrined as constitutional; lynching and other acts of terrorism and intimidation against blacks largely went uncontested by local, state, and national governments; and disfranchisement, perhaps the most fatal blow of all to black citizenship, was affirmed by all the states of the former Confederacy, even states of the upper and arguably more racially moderate South, Virginia and North Carolina. In other words, white "Redemption" of the states was complete; the federal government had definitively turned over the "black problem" to the South; Booker T. Washington's accommodation approach toward racial equality and justice was reigning supreme; and the method of political agitation of former leaders such as the now-deceased Frederick Douglas had receded to the background. But a renaissance was forthcoming with the founding of the Niagara Movement and the subsequent advent of the National Association for the Advancement of Colored People (NAACP).[8]

SUMMARY OF JOHNSON'S SERMON

Johnson's sermon recalls the Exodus story in the Old Testament. The ancient Hebrews had emerged from enslavement in Egypt and crossed the Red Sea, escaping from pharaoh's pursuing army. Afterwards they found themselves wandering in the wilderness because they were not ready to advance to the promised land of Canaan. They would, of course, eventually arrive in Canaan, but first they had to undergo the trial of the wilderness. Having emerged from slavery and enjoyed the freedoms brought by Emancipation and Reconstruction, African Americans, Johnson says, now found themselves in a wilderness experience, on their way to the promised land of freedom. In this sermon are found most of the elements associated with the Black Lost Cause: the love and providence of God, the chosenness and mission of African Americans, the challenge and purposes of present crises, and the eventual freedom and contributions of African Americans.

Johnson puts forth three ingredients necessary for any race of people to progress: "wealth, religion, and education."[9] The religious leader observed that black people had made tremendous success since enslavement, describing this progress as "unparalleled strides toward the meridian of the highest and best achievements." But in black people's struggle to overcome the challenges of Emancipation, they have now confronted "stronger barriers, almost insurmountable," that militate against further advancement, and find themselves fighting for the "right to live among a people, whose traditions, language, institutions, and laws are against him." In the early years of Emancipation, African Americans had sympathizers and assistance from outside the race. Now much of that support has disappeared, and black people stand almost alone in their efforts to be regarded as citizens, adults, and siblings alongside others.[10] Johnson raises the question that goes to the very heart of the Black Lost Cause: "Now, why should the Negro be scourged so unmercifully after these years of sacrifice and service, in a land he has helped to enrich, and which he still helps to beautify and maintain?" Were this a situation involving only one person facing such injustice despite all the good he or she had done, then it would be not so disconcerting. Yet in this instance, Johnson says, he is pondering this question for ten million black Americans.[11]

Citing scriptures speaking of God's care for the faithful as they face their enemies, Johnson directs attention to the importance of God's providence to make sense of human history. "Providence is the light of history and the soul of the world. It is only when we see God in history that we get at its clear significance and truth. God's providence is the golden thread that passes through the entire web of human destiny and gives it its strength and beauty and consistency." If providence is important for the individual's

understanding of his "calamities," it is even more significant for nations because of their great longevity. And what applies to nations also is appropriate to some degree for human races. "Now, when God deals with a nation or
race, and permits that race to prosper or retrograde, He has some mighty
object in view—either that of punishment or reward." God's punishment
does not always mean destruction for nations or individuals; sometimes
God allows punishment so that people will reform. If they repent or reform,
they will receive God's mercy. If they stubbornly pursue their evil ways, "God
will utterly destroy them or cut them short of their glory." Individuals face
their punishment in eternity. Nations will find their punishment temporally on Earth.[12] Thus has God dealt with Egypt, Babylon, Greece, Rome,
and particularly the Israelites. At this point Johnson very directly draws the
parallel between the ancient Hebrews wandering in the wilderness and
black Americans wandering in their social-economic-political wilderness in
post-Reconstruction America. He specifically says that "God scourged Israel
forty years"[13] because of their disobedience and "forgetfulness of God."
Only two persons of that original group, Joshua and Caleb, ultimately saw
Canaan "after forty years of toil, privation, sorrow, danger, disappointment,
death, and expectancy in the wilderness."[14]

One might surmise that these descriptions of the wildness in the Bible
are also ones that Johnson and other African Americans applied to their
own post-Reconstruction experience. Just as ancient Israel in bondage had
asked for God's deliverance, so African American forebears had prayed ear-
nestly for freedom from their bondage. Just as God delivered the biblical
Israel from bondage, so the Lord had acted in history to create an antislavery sentiment, using such historical figures as John Brown, William Lloyd
Garrison, Abraham Lincoln, Charles Sumner, and Frederick Douglass.
God's providential care for the freed people was manifested by the services
of Christians and people of good will setting up educational institutions
that provided instruction valuable for self-government and self-support.
Johnson declared an unequivocal faith that God's providential hand had
been with the race. Black people's strong, steadfast faith was such that even
prejudiced whites were impressed.

Johnson points to the concept of chosen people, that black people had
a special contribution to make to humanity. "Let no one think, we do not
figure in the divine economy, or that we are not an element, in the divine
scheme for the world's enlightenment and civilization." Despite the trials

that blacks still faced, Johnson boldly declared, "God is still with us. His sleepless eye is ever upon us. His arms, everlasting, are still around us. He is still our Sun and Shield. He still gives grace and glory. No good thing does he withhold from those who walk uprightly." But acknowledging God's love also means that the people must understand that God chastises those whom God loves. Johnson makes this key statement: "Let us look at the evils, that have overtaken us as a people in the last few years and see if God is not permitting our enemies to scourge us as he did Israel." God continues to work with races and nations as God has always done. That is, people who honor God will be rewarded, not only in eternity but in this life as well.[15]

These statements demonstrate that nineteenth and early twentieth-century African American Christians sincerely believed in the efficacy of morality and spirituality. Therefore, we should take care when employing the term "politics of respectability" in describing black Christians' insistence on morality and proper conduct. This is not a case of "politics of respectability" in the sense that black people should demonstrate their morality so that white people would respect them and say they are worthy of freedom, though that element is certainly present sometimes. Even more important and representative of their thinking, however, is the strong conviction that morals and ethics have power. Black people should be "respectable" not for respectability's sake, but because respectability is an expression of morality, ethics, self-love, and self-honor, and most importantly because God commands righteous behavior. And what if the righteous suffer? Johnson speaks about the purpose in history that God has for blacks, a purpose that is clear because there is "an inseparable connection between sacrifice, service, and suffering."[16] He seems to be pointing toward the biblical and theological concept that would be employed by Martin Luther King, Jr., a half century later: There is redemption in unearned suffering.[17]

Johnson outlines a number of "scourges" that black people face that God is using to make the people better followers. God uses race hatred and attempts by whites to debase and destroy African Americans as a scourge. For example, laws made to humiliate blacks and to vitiate their racial pride are means by which God brings black people into greater racial unity. African Americans for the most part have indeed been disfranchised, but with that disfranchisement will be the development of character and acquisition of property and lifestyles that stand in contradiction to the political nonentity status to which disfranchisement is seeking to relegate them. Because blacks have qualities of character and enterprise, as time passes people will turn against this Southern white treatment of them.

Regarding the scourge of lynching, Johnson points to the "fragrant injustice" of subjecting blacks to lawlessness even though they surrendered their lives to protect the integrity of the country when Confederates attempted to destroy it. But God is permitting such suffering to prepare blacks to triumph in that day when right will fight against wrong and the weak against the strong. We need not assume that black people will always be in such a vulnerable, weak position relative to whites. "Because a race is once backward is no sign it will always be so."[18] In a world dominated by white European military power, blacks often pointed to nonwhite governments as examples to counteract claims of white racial supremacy. Often blacks looked with pride to Haiti and Ethiopia as two independent black countries. In his sermon Johnson, as other blacks would do, called attention to Japan as a growing power that would someday surprise the world. These nations—Haiti, Ethiopia, and Japan—were concrete reminders that people once backward and suppressed could one day take their places as equals or even superiors to the current white European nations. Consider Johnson's comment regarding Japan: "Japan is an illustration of how 'a little one may become a thousand,' and how that same little one will someday surprise the world."[19]

As other black spokespersons during this period, Johnson expressed dismay not only at the injustice of lynching as it pertained to cruelty and the denial of legal due process; he also drew attention to larger, overarching problem that African Americans faced daily: discrimination and being treated as criminal despite their abiding by the law, being economically productive, or equipping themselves educationally. He sought to distinguish members of the race that were working to improve themselves versus those relatively few persons one would find in any race who were nonproductive or criminal. Contrary to the claim of some whites that education had had an adverse effect on blacks, Johnson held that education had surely helped produce better and law-abiding citizens. Even when denied opportunities, the great majority of blacks maintained the highest character and proved their resourcefulness by building churches, supporting schools, owning personal property, taking care of their homes, and dressing their children well. The bulk of black criminals did not come from the race's educated ranks; indeed, the most educated criminals were Anglo-Saxon, according to Johnson: "Is there another people, judging from grand jury indictments, and judicial decisions, who hold a more just title to outlawry, thievery, bribery, embezzlement, robbery, murder, and every other crime found in the catalogue of criminology than the white people, and do not the educated classes among them find a large representation in jails and prisons?"[20]

On one hand, we can interpret Johnson's remarks as supporting that aspect of a "politics of respectability" approach that appeals to white people to accept blacks because the latter are behaving as the former.[21] But, to reiterate, we need to take seriously that black Christians' moral and ethical standards are not borrowed concepts from whites but ones claimed and owned by faithful blacks themselves. They believed in the efficacy and the divine requirement that all people live uprightly and that God rewards those who do so in this life as well as in eternity. There is also in these words a defense of racial honor, refutation of slanders against black people. Finally, Johnson and other leaders are attempting to deprive racists of the weapon of "othering" black people, to judge them as less than American, Christian, or to compromise their humanity. In an environment characterized by lynching, disfranchisement, and economic deprivation, refusing to be marginalized in terms of citizenship, faith, or basic humanity was—in addition to a way of life and expression of honor—a tool of survival and a perceived ladder to progress.

Johnson concludes his sermon emphasizing that blacks need to turn to a stronger faith in God. All the scourges that God has permitted to fall upon blacks have been for the purpose of "provoking the Negro to a larger faith in God, and a more devout Christian life and service" that involved a march to greater temporal freedom. Throughout his sermon Johnson teaches that works must accompany faith. From the beginning he notes the critical necessity of acquiring wealth and gaining education along with practicing religion as key elements for racial progress. Therefore, in his conclusion, Johnson emphasizes the need for African Americans to live in harmony with the love, power, and providence of God. There is no question that God listens to those who endure oppression, blunts all weapons raised against the righteous, and will provide "help against the mighty; against those who fill the earth with widows and cause the orphan's heart to bleed."[22]

There is a Black Lost Cause. Of course it is not "lost" forever, but it must be reclaimed as African American Christians, having emerged from the Egypt of slavery, wander in the wilderness of the post-Reconstruction era enduring scourges that prepare them for eventual settlement in the promised land of religious and racial redemption. Johnson was hardly a solitary voice crying in the wilderness; his contemporaries articulated similar themes. Five seem especially salient: ideas related to providence, theodicy, and chosen people; racial destiny and self-help; black nationalism; pan-Africanism; and the importance of Christianity and western culture for the progress and freedom of black people. All of these elements are present or assumed in Johnson's sermon, with the possible exception of pan-Africanism, and are related to the Black Lost Cause theology during this era. Neither Johnson nor his peers expressed all of these themes, but their thoughts taken as a whole reflect the presence of a Black Lost Cause theology among the African American Christian populace from 1877 to 1925.

PROVIDENCE, CHOSEN PEOPLE, AND THEODICY

First, the themes of providence, chosen people, and theodicy raised in Johnson's sermon—ones that this essay associates with the Black Lost Cause theology—appear in communications of race spokespersons before and after the Civil War. Indeed, there is a long history among black Christians of a focus on a Black Lost Cause theology in the sense that these Christians asserted that they were special people of God despite their enslavement or racial discrimination. Therefore, the question of theodicy—Why does God permit the suffering of God's people?—surfaced in a number of pre-Civil War contexts. One answer to that question of theodicy is that slavery would not last forever—that in time God would end the practice. One early-nineteenth-century writer, Nathaniel Paul, said that he would in fact be greatly dismayed, if not be an unbeliever, if he believed that God would forever permit the existence of the slave trade and chattel slavery. In *Appeal*, first published in the late 1820s, David Walker predicted that if slavery continued there would be an upheaval in the land because God's judgment against the enslavement of African Americans was inevitable. As illustrated in a number of works, including Raboteau's classic *Slave Religion*, Black Christian slaves were convinced that continued chattel slavery was inconsistent with Christianity and therefore would one day come to an end.[23] The Civil War, Emancipation, and Reconstruction eras provided vindication that God was concerned about the liberation of African Americans and that the question of theodicy had finally been answered.

Black Christians and their white Christian supporters before and after the Civil War found in the biblical tradition abundant passages and verses to support their conviction that their destiny was in the hands of a loving providence: the exodus, Daniel in the lion's den, Jonah, and the Gospels, among others. Perhaps the most universally referenced verse pertaining to the destiny of black people faithful to God was Psalm 68:31 (KJV): "Princes shall come out of Egypt; Ethiopia shall soon stretch forth her hands unto God." This scripture played a prominent role in or related to various events in the history of black Christians: the antislavery movement, colonization, emigration, missions, and concerning beliefs about providence, chosen people, and racial destiny. Martin, Raboteau, Fulop, and others have discussed the significance of this verse read in the King James Version of the Bible as divine prophecy.[24]

According to the interpretation at the time, Psalm 68:31 pointed to the mission and destiny of the black race and reflected other portions of the Bible regarding its past greatness. A corollary of the slave trade and enslavement was the shift of attitudes among European peoples regarding the history of Africa. Egypt was separated from any association with blacks, and Africa that was connected to blacks was regarded as uncivilized and without any notable history. Saying that Africans had no history worthy of mention became a justification for classifying black peoples as uncivilized and, therefore, in need of enslavement so that they would be Christianized and civilized. And the two—Christianity and civilization—were regarded as mutually supportive: to be Christian was to become civilized. Therefore, the black-authored histories of the black race published before and after the Civil War provided factual information regarding the history of Africa and its descendants. Furthermore, these histories, including that of Rufus L. Perry, prominent black Baptist minister, were vindication of the humanity and worth of African peoples, including black Americans. These black-authored works often included two important elements. First, the writers coopted the declaration that present-day black people were descendants of the biblical Ham whose descendants included those who were the founders of some of the world's oldest civilizations. Thereby they contradicted and corrected a theological misreading of the biblical story regarding Noah's curse on Canaan (not Ham). Second and related to the first point, these histories claimed Egypt and Ethiopia as ancient lands populated by black or Negroid peoples.[25]

RACIAL DESTINY AND SELF-HELP

A second set of themes appearing in Johnson's sermon and relevant for the Black Lost Cause theology are racial destiny and self-help. Like Johnson, African American Christians believed in a brighter day ahead. But there are two important points to bear in mind: (a) they believed in being cognizant of the tremendous progress the race had thus far made, and (b) they emphasized the need for self-help and the agency of black people themselves, a theme reflected in the overall theme of Black Nationalism and pan-Africanism discussed below. An example of someone espousing these two basic themes was the Presbyterian minister Francis J. Grimke in response to the Atlanta Riot of 1906. Both points appear in this quote of his: "It is only as the race becomes *self-reliant* that it will grow strong; that it will become self-respecting; and that it will command respect from others. And because the race is becoming more and more self-reliant; because the evidences are multiplying every year of greater activity from within, we have nothing to fear from the envious and malicious spirit of the lower classes of whites in the south, in keeping us from rising, from taking an honorable place in the procession of those who are moving forward, in the onward march of progress."[26]

African Americans had already experienced tremendous political and economic setbacks between the withdrawal of federal troops from the South in the late 1870s and the early 1900s, including the United States Supreme Court's official sanctioning of racial segregation and the disfranchisement of approximately 90 percent of all black voters throughout the South by the early 1900s. And now in 1906 Grimke was responding to a vicious race riot in Atlanta during which mobs of whites attacked the black community. Black Christians and white supporters during that time had many reasons to be pessimistic, and indeed historians and others look back at this era as a "nadir" in the fortunes of the race. Yet, as Johnson's sermon illustrates, a striking element comes through many of the contemporary sermons, addresses, newspaper editorials, and other expressions of sentiments: the element of optimism based in part on the conviction that the race since Emancipation had made gigantic progress. To be sure, Grimke is realistic and shaken by the violent event in Atlanta, describing how violence was directed against all blacks, regardless of level of education or whether they had been law abiding or lawless. As other spokespersons, Grimke often complained that in occasional acts of violence as well as everyday life whites generally tended to place all blacks into the same category regardless of their individual integrity, hard work, moral uprightness, or economic success. In fact, Grimke argues that blacks that are most successful economically are a threat to a certain lower class of whites that feel envious and threatened by their achievements. But, one might say, that is the bright cloud in this storm of racial terrorism and conflict. To a degree, Grimke said, acts of white supremacy are inflicted because blacks have in fact made great progress. Many of these spokespersons retained the faith that present difficulties would be overcome and the future would be brighter.[27]

It is worth considering why these religious people had such optimism in the midst of so many setbacks and acts of violence. Clearly some of it stemmed from their deep faith that God is just and that God will not forever permit the faithful to be the downtrodden—a faith drawn from the Christian tradition regarding the providence and love of God. But this optimism was also based on reality. Because of the significant setbacks and climate of suppression during the post Reconstruction period, it was possible for observers to miss the fact that there had been great progress since Emancipation. Some examples of progress include the following facts: the black literacy rate had improved astronomically; many blacks even in the midst of Jim Crow and lynching had access to at least elementary education to secure basic skills, and smaller but still-significant numbers of African Americans were acquiring high school and collegiate training; there were still black individuals occupying political or public offices here and there that were not accessible to blacks prior to the Civil War; despite disfranchisement of the vast majority of African Americans in the South, the approximately 10 percent of blacks still voting represented a sizable increase compared to those voting during the days of slavery; there were now more black businesses, including in some places banks, insurance companies, newspapers, and hotels; and local churches and regional and national religious organizations could operate more freely than during enslavement.

It is tempting to characterize many of these developments in terms of the elites versus the masses, noting that conditions for the great majority of African Americans were not so comfortable. Still, even the masses greatly benefitted by having access to services provided by other blacks rather than having to deal always in white-controlled situations with their attendant discriminatory treatment and lack of comparable empathy and solidarity. In fact, even "elite" business owners—and all of them were certainly not "elite"—had a powerful message for young sharecroppers, a message somewhat analogous to the one an occasional free black person showed to an antebellum slave: that freedom and human equality were possible. Highlighting the positive, rather than being dismayed by the negative, was also a way of encouraging hope in what could have often been a climate of hopelessness. It was a reminder to fellow blacks of what was possible if they put forth the effort.

Grimke's second point invites elaboration. In addition to Black Nationalism, there was an urgent need for blacks to do for themselves. While African Americans should welcome the assistance from others, they must rely only on themselves. In his response to the Atlanta Riot, Grimke said the race must march "onward." The great majority of fellow blacks increasingly realized that moving forward was the appropriate theme. As black people understood that they must be the major actors in achieving "our own destiny in this country," people put forth greater effort in that regard. If blacks continued to depend on non-blacks, the race would risk "stagnation." Blacks must be "self-reliant," take control of their own destiny, and decide that it is their own efforts by which they will rise or fall; then, the power that lies within the race would come to the surface. "It is only as we come to feel, and to feel deep down in the bottom of our hearts that we 'must sink or swim; live or die; survive or perish,' through our own exertions, that the latent powers within the race itself will be awakened, and the forces necessary to lift it, to carry it forward, be generated."[28]

Marcus Garvey likewise espoused ideas akin to those of Johnson and Grimke. The leader of the UNIA who advocated emigration to Africa during the first half of the twentieth century, Garvey strongly emphasized racial self-help and self-reliance. He believed that "the Negro has for the last five hundred years been in the position of being commanded, even as the lower animals are commanded. Our race has been without a will, without a purpose of its own, for all this length of time, and because of that we have developed but few men who are able to understand the strenuousness of the age in which we live."[29] One great advantage of believing in self-reliance is that it discourages people from becoming "helpless victims" and often promotes performance over and beyond expectations so that people accomplish what were hitherto assumed to have been impossible feats. A great danger is the possibility of "blaming the victims," suggesting implicitly or explicitly that people facing oppression are mainly responsible for their situations and are perhaps unworthy of efforts taken on their behalf. Surely, related to the second point, Garvey overstated the case when asserting that the black "race has been without a will" or "purpose of its own" for the past five centuries.

BLACK NATIONALISM

Another theme reflected in Johnson's "Scourging" sermon is Black Nationalism. In terms of the Black Lost Cause, Black Nationalism, racial identity, and pan-Africanism are related to the concept of chosen people. Black Nationalism is employed here to refer most specifically to blacks in the US or in some other nation or local sphere. Black Nationalism encompasses a sense of racial pride, emphasis on black history and culture, self-assertion, community solidarity and unity, and control of resources within the black community.[30] All of the above points revolve around or are connected with the fundamental conviction that black people are a distinct people. That distinctiveness of black peoplehood is not abrogated by other factors, such as religion, gender, socio-economic status, or political ideology. White Americans' treatment of and interactions with African Americans made it very clear from the early decades of colonial American history that blacks would occupy a separate and marginalized status. Africans on the mother continent generally viewed themselves primarily from ethnic or tribal perspectives; but the experiences of the slave trade, enslavement itself, and subsequent racial segregation with all their attendant beliefs and actions clearly defined blacks, regardless of ethnicity, as distinct, a separate people from the ruling whites.

Regarding African American identity, therefore, both internal factors such as similarities in history, culture, and customs, as well as external factors such as enslavement and discrimination combined to transition Africans of different ethnic groups in the US into one single ethnic or racial group. For this separate racial group religion became one of the most universal elements of self-identity. Over the course of generations traditional African religions and Islam as distinct religious systems receded in the US and Christianity became the overwhelming religion of African Americans. The black community in the US, then, became principally one strongly characterized by Christianity, with even variant groups, including those that might be broadly characterized as black Jews or Hebrews or as black Muslims, arguably showing some influences of the black Christian tradition.[31]

This element of Black Nationalism appeared quite strong across the spectrum of the black population during the period under study. Of course, Black Nationalist sentiment from individuals such as African Methodist Episcopal Church Bishop Henry M. Turner, who advocated the relocation of blacks to Africa, comes as no surprise.[32] Yet the existence of the racial dividing line between whites and blacks coupled with the intensity of racial discrimination compelled even "integrationist"-oriented blacks to argue for some degree of racial self-identity—that is, to espouse some key elements of Black Nationalism. Consider, for example, Frederick Douglass, the noted abolitionist and indefatigable spokesperson for the full inclusion of African Americans into all sectors of American life. He did not favor racially identifiable organizations or believe that people, black or white, should view themselves in distinctly racial terms. Furthermore, he strongly opposed emigration of blacks to countries outside the US, including the African continent or even Haiti in the Caribbean. He believed that the US was home for blacks and that here they should struggle for full civil and human rights. Yet even he spoke of the need for black self-assertion, believing that there were things that blacks must do for themselves.[33]

Even issues relating to gender could not sever black women leaders from solidarity to the race. Black club women during this period found it impossible to be women first and blacks second, for example. According to Moses, these women could not focus on gender concerns apart from race. Though some club members might have wished to deal with a variety of societal issues, it was clear that race dominated their concerns, and Moses lists four major reasons for this concentration. First, even middle-class black women could not escape the impact of racism on their lives. Second, many black club women were proponents of the Tuskegee Institute's tradition of racial self-help, and the policies and prescriptions associated with this school of thought made race a definite part of their agenda within the various club organizations. Third, white feminist women were more white than feminist. Many, if not most, exhibited racism and prejudice toward their black sisters in acts such as avoiding black-white interactions and making excuses for the lynching of blacks. Fourth, a central purpose of these black women's organizations was the vindication of black women's honor in the public domain. By definition, therefore, there was an urgent need to deal with the matter of race and how racial perceptions shaped societal approaches to black women.[34]

Consequently, given the evidence, to say that Black Nationalism was a key element in black thinking during this era is not to claim that every black leader or spokesperson or even each individual discussed in this essay was strictly speaking a Black Nationalist, but to point out that even the most integrationist-minded black spokesperson saw a need to embrace some element(s) of Black Nationalism.

PAN-AFRICANISM

While the concept of pan-Africanism does not appear strongly in Johnson's sermon, it is a logical extension of Black Nationalism and often intertwined with it. Pan-Africanism asserts that all Africans and descendants of Africans in whatever lands they reside face the same fundamental problem: the struggle against racial supremacy and the battle against black subjugation and marginalization. Specific issues attendant to this overall problem may vary as we move from the US to Brazil to Puerto Rico to Nigeria to Pakistan, pan-Africanists might say. But the underlying problem of racial supremacy and black subjugation as it relates to these issues is essentially the same. Because blacks everywhere face essentially the same problem, the freedom of blacks anywhere is accordingly tied to the fortunes of blacks everywhere.[35]

Support for pan-Africanism, especially in the late eighteenth century and throughout the nineteenth century, was sometimes connected with the endorsement of colonization and emigration to lands outside the US, especially in Africa but also the Caribbean, particularly Haiti. The most support for colonization and emigration occurred during the period when about 90 percent of African Americans were slaves. Much of this advocacy receded with the advent of the Civil War and Reconstruction and that era's promise of freedom and opportunity in this country. Before the Civil War, many blacks drew a distinction between colonization—largely represented by the American Colonization Society founded in 1816–1817 and understood as a plan of whites to move blacks out of the country—and emigration—understood as the choice of blacks themselves to relocate for their own reasons to other places in the US or even outside the country in Canada, the Caribbean, or Africa.

Both colonization and emigration advocates often enunciated a theme relevant to the topic of Black Lost Cause. They, blacks and their white supporters, often spoke of the divine plan permitting slavery so that blacks could be Christianized and gain civilization. Obviously, they identified western civilization as the pinnacle of all civilizations. Also, blacks and whites generally regarded African cultures as inferior and African religions as heathenistic or idolatrous. Promoters of and participants in colonization and emigration often joined forces with the Christian missionary movement. Hence, the emigrationist Paul Cuffee, the wealthy black Quaker who provided black emigrants passage to West Africa; Lott Carey and Colin Teague, the black Baptist Virginia leaders, who in the 1820s helped lead a black group in colonization efforts in what became the Republic of Liberia; Daniel Coker, the African Methodist Episcopal minister who also in the 1820s helped lead a group to what became the nation of Sierra Leone— they all had a common goal: to spread Christianity and western civilization in Africa, uplifting the black race. While blacks and antislavery whites would not say that God willed the slave trade and chattel slavery, they did see these events as instruments that God employed to redeem the African continent and black people, both religiously and culturally.[36]

As indicated above, movements to emigrate outside the United States were more popular (as limited as that popularity was) before the Civil War and Reconstruction. With the demise of Reconstruction, however, there were renewed calls for emigration, particularly from the South to other sections of the country. Occasionally, some called for emigration to Africa. The most successful and last major emigration movement to Africa was that led by Marcus Garvey, who sought to relocate a significant number of blacks to Africa and reclaim the continent from European nations who had by and large colonized the entire area, except for Ethiopia and Liberia.[37] Originally from the Caribbean island of Jamaica, Garvey had traveled to various parts of Central and Latin America and resided for a time in England. Having a pan-African perspective, Garvey believed that the key to the future freedom and greatness of black people in the Americas and throughout the world lay in reclaiming Africa and building an empire. Like blacks in the US, African-descended peoples everywhere faced marginalization, discrimination, and relegation to the lower strata of society, according to

Garvey. Before moving to Harlem, New York in 1916, Garvey organized the Universal Negro Improvement Association and Communities League, or UNIA.

His movement received strong support from West Indian immigrants and descendants in the US, but membership actually came from all strata of society, both urban and rural, and in various sections of the nation. One might say that Garvey founded the first truly mass movement for black liberation in the US. Many blacks across the socioeconomic spectrum agreed with Garvey that the future greatness and even survival of the race lay outside the United States and other countries controlled by whites. He foresaw continued and worsening conflict between blacks and whites, including a greater competition for jobs that would result in a racial war. For some time historians and other academics treated the Garvey movement as secular enterprise, but Randall Burkett has persuasively outlined its unmistakably religious nature, illustrated by Garvey's frequent and consistent references to religion, particularly Christianity; the motto of the movement, "One Aim, One God, and One Destiny"; the religious character of many ceremonies and rituals in its meetings; the involvement of clergy and other religious leaders; and the presence of an official chaplain for the UNIA.[38]

Like black nationalists in general, Garvey emphasized the need for self-help. As a pan-Africanist, he pointed out that what was applicable to blacks in the West Indies and the United States was equally applicable to blacks around the world. This becomes clear in his discussion of the necessity of black people throughout the world, all four hundred million of them, to reach true self-understanding. Garvey was not advocating that blacks by nature were superior to whites. Rather, the problem of race revolves around proper understanding of and behavior related to anthropology or the nature of humanity in general. God did not make humans to be servants of other humans; all people have the divine command to make the most of their abilities. Indeed, at points in his rhetoric he seems to be complimenting whites for being an assertive race, a people who build and take control of their environments.

All people, including black people worldwide, must come to this true knowledge of the nature of humanity. According to Garvey: "If four hundred million Negroes can only get to know themselves, to know that in them is a sovereign power, is an authority that is absolute, then in the next twenty-four hours we would have a new race, we would have a new nation, we would have a great empire resurrected not from the will of others to see us rise, but from our own determination to rise, irrespective of what the world thinks. Men and women of the Negro race, can you not get such a determination within you?"[39]

Some African American Christians viewed racism as a problem extending beyond American shores and even beyond the duality of blacks and whites; they saw the race problem involving the relationship between whites on one hand and peoples of color on the other. One such spokesperson that saw color prejudice as a great, divisive, global problem was African Methodist Episcopal Church leader Theophilus Gould Steward, a military chaplain whose career-long assignments included service in the Philippines.[40] In his thinking whites would face either military or economic retribution from the world's peoples of color. He foresaw the day when being white in the world would be as difficult as it currently was being black in America. "Three fourths of mankind are surely awakening. The World Negro Congress is but a straw. The coming people are those of Asia and Africa. Japan has already shown what can be done; and the Filipino, Chinese, and people of India are sure to emerge, sooner or later." It was fortunate, he wrote, that African Americans had been forcibly excluded from acceptance within the white community. "This excludes [black people] from the destiny of that race and allots [them] a portion with the age to come."[41]

BLACK CHRISTIANS AND WESTERN CULTURE

Finally, Johnson and his contemporary black leaders and spokespersons saw no conflict between their advocacy for racial justice on one hand and the embrace of Christianity and western culture on the other hand. Indeed, practically across the board African American Christians believed in the value and efficacy of Christianity and western civilization, that they were vital to the elevation of the black race both spiritually and culturally. But Christianity practiced must be genuine, not an imitation of white Christianity. Fulop examines the writing of black spokesperson J. Augustus Cole during this era, "The Negro at Home and Abroad: Their Origin, Progress and Destiny."[42] Christianity, says Cole, is key to black advancement toward their destiny of greatness. But this Christianity must be the true religion, not the white version of the faith. Cole stated that black Christians must eliminate these incorrect imitations of Christianity based on white practice if they were to continue to the land of freedom (Canaan) and not regress to the land of servitude (Egypt).

Cole's distinction between white people's version of Christianity and true Christianity is central to understanding how African American Christians during the nineteenth and early twentieth centuries approached the religion. Before the Civil War black Christians differed from many white Christians in declaring slavery inconsistent with a true understanding of the faith. David Walker, who in his *Appeal* during the late 1820s issued a call to the enslaved to be willing to take up arms if necessary to secure their freedom, contrasted a true understanding of the faith with the behavior of "the Americans" who practiced or condoned slavery. During the antebellum era Frederick Douglass, the great abolitionist and race leader, distinguished between what he called the true Christianity of Christ and what he termed the slaveholding religion that dominated much of the country, North and South. Perhaps this distinction was suggested when the enslaved sang a spiritual declaring that everyone talking about heaven was not going there. White Christians continued to embrace racial prejudice and subjugation in the postwar and post-Reconstruction periods, indicating that they still practiced an inferior, caste Christianity.[43]

Nonetheless, there was a culturally interpretive connection between black and white Christians during this time in regard to western civilization. Both groups agreed that western or European civilization, especially Anglo-Saxon civilization, was the apex of human society. Clearly blacks did not believe that Anglo-Saxon culture was perfect; indeed, it had serious faults. After all, it had condoned the slave trade, enslavement, and continued racial oppression. Anglo-Saxonism had failed to embrace pure Christianity, but overall it was superior to African cultures, at least at the present time. Blacks were making a cultural connection between themselves and whites.

Booker T. Washington, the founder and leader of Tuskegee Institute, sought to highlight this interracial connection.[44] His Atlanta Exposition Address of 1895, often referred to as the Atlanta Compromise, is a very important historical document and a reflection of how many African Americans sought to make a black-white cultural connection, though most would not go as far on the road of racial accommodation as he did. This address laid out a road map for pursuing black liberation without the tools of widespread black suffrage and political agitation. It is often called a compromise because it asked for an intermediate path between the continuation of white dominance with black suffering on one hand and black political resistance to that dominance on the other. Essentially Washington says that black people should downplay political agitation and instead form a cooperative but non-politically equal relationship with Southern whites, concentrating on their economic self-advancement (although privately Washington demonstrated a more activist orientation).

Much of the Tuskegee leader's address is devoted to demonstrating to Southern whites and blacks that the two groups have much in common. Whites are reminded how loyal and trustworthy blacks have been even during the Civil War when white slaveholders journeyed to the battlefield and left their families and property in the hands of faithful slaves. Therefore, why should white Americans look to immigrant whites for labor purposes when they already have in their midst "real Americans" whom they know so very well? As for blacks, why should they devote energy pursuing what are often irrelevant classical or liberal arts studies when they could be acquiring "industrial" or vocational skills that were far more useful for their economic advancement? There is no need for blacks to agitate for social equality, to force themselves into the company of whites, or for the latter to believe the former will do so. Black and white Southerners could be as separate from each other as fingers on the hand when it comes to social interaction but could come together as a fist, as one people, when situations demand unity for common purposes. Washington exhibited traits of Black Nationalism with an emphasis on black identity, but he did not advocate black emigration outside the South or the nation. Furthermore, as we have seen, he reflects the thinking of most black leaders that the freedom of black people was consonant with Anglo-Saxon civilization, provided that civilization is tempered by the contributions of African Americans.

CONCLUSION

Examining the writings of prominent black leaders between the end of the Reconstruction in 1877 and 1925 demonstrates the powerful theme among black Christians: a theology of the Black Lost Cause. Just as military defeat on the battlefield presented a problem of theodicy for Southern white Christians, so too the challenges of post-Reconstruction America called for theological responses from African American Christians. One of the clearest and most concise statements of the Black Lost Cause was contained in W. Bishop Johnson's sermon, "The Scourging of A Race," in which he claimed that the ordeals facing African Americans—e.g., segregation and lynching—were "scourges" used by God to bring black people back to a more faithful walk with God and a stronger commitment to their racial responsibilities. Johnson's sermon reflected themes current in the larger black Christian community: the providence of God, the destiny and chosenness of black people, the relevance of Black Nationalism and pan-Africanism to the issues of chosenness and destiny, the importance of Christianity and western culture as vehicles by which African Americans reach their spiritual and temporal destinies, and the manner in which Psalm 68:31 connects the above elements.

This enterprise is significant for at least two reasons. First, it points to the strength and significance of Christianity in the community and struggles of black people during this era. Second, it reveals at least in part how two groups, blacks and whites, sharing the same religion could have such diametrically different views and interpretations of events based on their respective experiences. Whether considering the Civil War or the demise of Reconstruction, what was welcomed by one as a blessing of God was seen by the other as an ordeal or trial that God would have them endure to become a better people.

NOTES

1. See Robert N. Bellah, "Civil Religion in America," in *The Robert Bellah Reader*, ed. Robert N. Bellah and Steven M. Tipton (Durham: Duke Univ. Press, 2006), 225–45.

2. Charles Reagan Wilson, *Baptized in the Blood: The Religion of the Lost Cause, 1865–1920*, 2nd ed. (Athens: Univ. of Georgia Press, 2009).

3. For indications of a Black Civil Religion, see Albert G. Miller, *Elevating the Race: Theophilus G. Steward and the Making of an African American Civil Society, 1865–1924* (Knoxville: The Univ. of Tennessee Press, 2003); and Sandy Dwayne Martin, "Providence and the Black Christian Consensus: A Historical Essay on the African American Religious Experience," in *The Courage to Hope: From Black Suffering to Human Redemption*, ed. Quinton Hosford Dixie and Cornel West (Boston: Beacon Press, 1999), 40–60.

4. Two works provide very helpful overviews of black thought during the late nineteenth and early twentieth centuries: August Meier, *Negro Thought in America, 1880–1915: Racial Ideologies in the Age of Booker T. Washington* (Ann Arbor: The Univ. of Michigan Press, 1973); and Wilson Jeremiah Moses, *The Golden Age of Black Nationalism, 1850–1925* (New York: Oxford Univ. Press, 1978).

5. For a biosketch of W. Bishop Johnson, see E. M. Brawley's preface, "Biographical Sketch of the Author," of Johnson's *The Scourging of A Race and Other Sermons and Addresses* (Washington, DC: Beresford Printer, 1904), iii–vi; and http://www.worldcat.org/identities /lccn-n093-24263/, "Johnson, W. Bishop (William Bishop) 1858–1917."

6. Brawley, "Biographical." Quotes found on pages v and vi.

7. See, e.g., https://www.biblestudytools.com/dictionary/scourge-scourging/. See Johnson's sermon, "Scourging of A Race," in his book, *Scourging*, 1–17.

8. For an account of challenges facing blacks in the immediate decades following the end of Reconstruction, see Rayford W. Logan, *The Negro in American Life and Thought; The Nadir, 1877–1901* (New York: The Dial Press, Inc., 1954); also for a slightly longer period, see Meier, *Negro Thought.* For a concise summary of the black religion from the post-Reconstruction era to the 1930s, see Albert J. Raboteau, *Canaan Land: A Religious History of African Americans* (New York: Oxford Univ. Press, 2001), 82–103. John M. Giggie provides a look at black religion in the Mississippi Delta from 1875 to 1915 in his *After Redemption: Jim Crow and the Transformation of African American Religion in the Delta, 1875–1915* (New York: Oxford Univ. Press, 2008).

9. Johnson, "Scourging," 1.

10. Johnson, "Scourging," 2.

11. Johnson, "Scourging," 3–4.

12. Johnson, "Scourging," 4.

13. Johnson, "Scourging," 4–5; quote on page 5.

14. Johnson, "Scourging"; quotes on p. 8.

15. Johnson, "Scourging"; information and quotes from p. 9.

16. Johnson, "Scourging," 13.

17. For a superb treatment of King and his views regarding the church, see Lewis V. Baldwin, *The Voice of Conscience: The Church in the Mind of Martin Luther King, Jr.* (New York: Oxford Univ. Press, 2010). King's theology regarding nonviolence and the role of unearned suffering of course is pervasive in his sermons, speeches, and writings, including his first book that has been republished in recent years with an introduction by Clayborne Carson. See *Stride toward Freedom: The Montgomery Story* (Boston: Beacon Press, 2010); see, for example, chapter 6, "Pilgrimage to Nonviolence," 77–95.

18. Johnson, "Scourging," 14–15; quote on p. 15.

19. Johnson, "Scourging," 15–16.

20. Johnson, "Scourging," 16.

21. The "politics of respectability" appears in Evelyn Brooks Higginbotham's historical treatment of black Baptist women during this era, *Righteous Discontent: The Women's Movement in the Black Baptist Church, 1880–1920* (Cambridge: Harvard Univ. Press, 1994). There are scholars, however, who question or would modify this critique, as does this essay. For example, see Randall Kennedy's "Lifting as We Climb: A Progressive Defense of Respectability Politics," in *Harper's Magazine* (October 2015): 24, 26–34. Kennedy's essay may be found at https://harpers.org/archive/2015/10 /lifting-as-we-climb/.

22. Johnson, "Scourging," 16–17.

23. Frederick Douglass, "Slaveholding Religion and the Christianity of Christ," 102–11; Nathaniel Paul, "African Baptists Celebrate Emancipation in New York State," 185–92; and David Walker, "Our Wretchedness in Consequence of the Preachers of Religion," 193–201 in *African American Religious History: A Documentary Witness*, 2nd ed., ed. Milton C. Sernett, (Durham: Duke Univ. Press, 1999).

24. Sandy D. Martin, *Black Baptists and African Missions: The Origins of A Movement, 1880–1915* (Macon: Mercer Univ. Press, 1989/1998); Albert J. Raboteau, *Slave Religion: The "Invisible Institution" in the Antebellum South*, updated ed. (New York: Oxford Univ. Press, 2004); and Timothy E. Fulop, "'The Future Golden Day of the Race': Millennialism and Black Americans in the Nadir, 1877–1901," in *African-American Religion: Interpretive Essays in History and Culture*, ed. Timothy E. Fulop and Albert J. Raboteau (New York: Routledge, 1997), 227–54.

25. Rufus L. Perry, *The Cushite; Or, The Children of Ham (The Negro Race): As Seen by the Ancient Historians and Poets* (Springfield, MA: Willey, 1893); see a PDF copy at https://archive.org/details/cushiteorchildreooperr. Laurie Maffly-Kipp provides an in-depth look at black writers of black histories in *Setting Down the Sacred Past: African-American Race Histories* (Cambridge: Harvard Univ. Press, 2010).

26. Francis J. Grimke, *The Atlanta Riot: A Discourse by the Rev. Francis J. Grimke, Pastor of the Fifteenth Street Presbyterian Church* (n.p., October 7, 1906), 5. Available at: https://ia801005 .us.archive.org/1/items/atlantariotdiscooogrim/atlantariotdiscooogrim.pdf. Gregory Mixon and Clifford Kuhn describe and give the significance of the Atlanta Riot in "Atlanta Race Riot of 1906," *New Georgia Encyclopedia*, available at https://www.georgiaencyclopedia.org /articles/history-archaeology/atlanta-race-riot-1906, originally submitted 9/23/2005; last edited by NGE on 10/29/2015.

27. Rayford Logan refers to the 1877–1901 period as the "Nadir" in *The Negro in American Life*. Grimke, *Atlanta Riot*, 3–4.

28. Grimke, *Atlanta Riot*, 5.

29. Randall K. Burkett, *Black Redemption: Churchmen Speak for the Garvey Movement* (Philadelphia: Temple Univ. Press, 1978); quote on p. 32, in chapter 1, "Marcus Moziah Garvey," 19–42.

30. For a solid introduction to the meaning of black nationalism in the nineteenth century, see Wilson Jeremiah Moses, *The Golden Age of Black Nationalism, 1850–1925* (New York: Oxford Univ. Press, 1978), 13–31; also, John H. Bracey, Jr., August Meier, and Elliott Rudwick, eds., *Black Nationalism in America* (Indianapolis: Bobbs-Merrill, 1970).

31. These sources provide a look at some black non-Christian traditions: C. Eric Lincoln, "The Muslim Mission in the Context of American Social History," in *African American Religion*, Fulop and Raboteau, 277–94; and Rabbi Matthew, "Black Judaism in Harlem," in *African American Religious History*, Sernett, 473–77.

32. "Bishop Henry M. Turner Demands an Indemnity to Go Home to Africa," in *Black Nationalism*, Bracey, 172–76.

33. Moses, *Black Nationalism*, 86–90.

34. Moses, *Black Nationalism*, 129–30.

35. Okon Edet Uya, *Black Brotherhood: Afro-Americans and Africa* (Lexington, MA: D. C. Heath and Company, 1971) provides an examination of the tie between African Americans and Africa.

36. Miles Mark Fisher, "Lott Carey, the Colonizing Missionary," *Journal of Negro History* 7 (October 1922): 380–418; Daniel Coker, "My Soul Cleaves to Africa," 46–47 and "Paul Cuffe Calls for the Uplift of Africa," 41–44, in *Black Nationalism,* Bracey.

37. For a biosketch of Garvey, see Randall K. Burkett, *Black Redemption: Churchmen Speak for the Garvey Movement* (Philadelphia: Temple Univ. Press, 1978), 19–26.

38. Randall K. Burkett, *Garveyism as A Religious Movement: The Institutionalization of a Black Civil Religion* (Metuchen, NJ: Scarecrow Press, 1978).

39. Burkett, *Black Redemption,* 32–34; quote on p. 34.

40. For a biography of Steward, consult Albert G. Miller, *Elevating the Race: Theophilus G. Steward, Black Theology and the Making of an African American Civil Society, 1865–1924* (Knoxville: The Univ. of Tennessee Press, 2003); and Steward's *Fifty Years in the Gospel Ministry from 1864 to 1914* (Philadelphia: AME Book Concern, 1921), electronic edition at Documenting the American South, Univ. of North Carolina-Chapel Hill, at http://docsouth.unc.edu/church/steward/steward.html.

41. Steward, *Fifty Years,* 348–49.

42. Fulop, "Golden Day," 238–39.

43. Frederick Douglass, "Slaveholding Religion and the Christianity of Christ," 102–11; and David Walker, "Our Wretchedness in Consequence of the Preachers of Religion," 193–201 in *African American Religious History,* ed. Milton C. Sernett. James H. Cone, *For My People: Black Theology and the Black Church* (Maryknoll, NY: Orbis Books, 1984), 154. For a theological interpretation of black spirituals, see James H. Cone, *The Spirituals and the Blues: An Interpretation* (New York: The Seabury Press, 1972).

44. For information on the life and thought of Booker T. Washington, consult Moses, *Black Nationalism,* 93–102; August Meier, "Booker T. Washington: An Interpretation," in *Black History: A Reappraisal,* ed. Melvin Drimmer (Garden City, NY: Anchor Books/Doubleday and Company, 1968), 336–54.

The Modernization of the Lost Cause

CHARLES REAGAN WILSON

Confederate General Tennessee Flintrock Sash was 102 years old in 1951, when Flannery O'Connor's "A Late Encounter with the Enemy" takes place. Confederate veterans had been heroic figures for generations in the post-Civil War South, symbols of regional tradition, romantic and tragic figures, respected defenders of regional values. But Sash was, well, mostly just old in O'Connor's fictional representation. "His feet were completely dead now," she wrote, "his knees worked like old hinges, his kidneys functioned when they would, but his heart persisted doggedly to beat." The action of the story takes places at two quintessentially modern southern places—a college campus and a movie theater. His sixty-two-year-old granddaughter, Sally Poke Sash, is graduating college after taking summer courses for twenty years to get her degree, and she prides herself in recognition of the general as an acknowledgment that she has social status from his stature. He is thus brought out in his wheelchair the day of her graduation. He remembers, though, little from the past, not even the Civil War, although he knows he was no general but likely an enlisted man. What he does remember is wearing a Confederate general's uniform for the first time, which the promoters of the Atlanta premiere of the film *Gone with the Wind* gave to him in 1939. "They gimme this uniform and they gimme this soward and they say, 'Now General, we don't want you to start a war on us.'" They just wanted him to "march right up in that style when you're introduced tonight and answer a few questions." Sash had no use for history, though. "If we forget our past," a speaker at Sally's graduation ceremony intones, "we won't remember our future and it will be as well for us won't have one," or at least that is the jumbled reference to the past and future he hears.[1]

During the ceremony, Sash realizes a "little hole beginning to widen in the top of his head." He hears the words, "a succession of places—Chickamauga,

Shiloh, Marthasville—rushed at him as if the past were the only future now and he had to endure it." As the ceremony ends, a young boy scout pushes him in his wheelchair out the back door of the college auditorium, and the story ends "with the corpse, in the long line at the Coca-Cola machine." O'Connor's story is a sardonic tale that shows a fictional character from the Lost Cause who is a vaguely comic and pathetic figure, far from earlier portrayals of Confederate heroes. Times had changed, and the story appeared at high tide of literary modernism, reflecting the ironic sensibility associated with modernity. O'Connor was no literary modernist herself, as her religious faith prevented the skepticism and fragmentation characteristic of that genre, but she was surely a modern southern writer at a time when the region's economic development and civil rights revolution fundamentally changed its society. The Lost Cause does not hold up well in the story, as the sad figure from the Confederate past dies next to that icon of modern popular culture, a Coke machine.[2]

TRADITION AND MODERNITY IN THE LOST CAUSE

O'Connor's story is an appropriate introduction to consideration of the Lost Cause's evolving role in the modern South, of the dynamic of tradition and modernity. The relationship between modernity and the South's Lost Cause invites exploration. Modernity has not been a discrete historical event so much as a force and a process, one that has affected differing societies at different time periods. For historians, the term is sometimes periodized back to the emergence of the sovereign nation-state after the Treaty of Westphalia in 1648 and the definition of citizenship for national subjects after the French Revolution in 1789, suggesting nationalism's importance to modernity. The Enlightenment was a crucial intellectual movement that became identified with "the modern" by the late eighteenth century, nurturing a stress on knowledge, rationalism, science, and progress. Economists point to the appearance of capitalist market economies during the British Industrial Revolution, with the centrality of commercialization to the modern sensibility. Europe became the hearth of modern thought during the nineteenth century, identified as a coherent geographical and intellectual place and at the advance of global history. Scholars, and people in the past, typically juxtaposed the modern with traditional ways. Through much of the nineteenth century, this tendency promoted an appreciation of antiquity and the classical age, but by the late nineteenth century traditional increasingly seemed merely backward, primitive, or degenerate. People in advanced societies now prized newness and looked to the future. Modernity became identified with such features as free labor, universalist notions of culture, abstract ideas of equality, gender divisions, the spread of schooling and literacy, mass culture, ever-more complex media technology, centralization of power in national governments and financial capitalist institutions, long-term capital accumulation, organized leisure, secularization, and governmental monopolies on violence.[3]

One might argue that the Lost Cause was born modern, although surely with a nineteenth-century twist. By the last decade of that century, the Lost Cause movement had become well-organized and institutionalized in centralized organizations like the United Confederate Veterans, the United Daughters of the Confederacy, the Sons of Confederate Veterans, and the Children of the Confederacy, even creating bureaucracies of governance. They worked with financial institutions to raise money for extensive projects, including monuments, annual meetings, local social and cultural endeavors, educational activities, and veteran assistance work. Annual meetings took place in the region's largest cities, giving urban spaces—always a center of modernity—a key role in the movement. By the turn of the twentieth century, white supremacy had become a key feature of modernity as western civilization made it a prominent foundation for colonial efforts to civilize supposed backward societies, and state legislators throughout the South codified Jim Crow segregation, allowing the region to claim the advanced status of a modern society in terms of its racial views.[4]

Still, the modern sensibility and its material underpinnings evolved in the twentieth century, and an analysis of the Lost Cause's changing relationship with modernity in that century proves revealing. It shows that promoters of the Lost Cause, and others, could adapt the Confederate memory to the forms of modernity, but they were less successful, in the long run, in adapting the ideology of the Lost Cause to evolving modernity in the twentieth-century South.

Elements of the Lost Cause that played a role in this story included the Confederate battle flag, the song "Dixie," Confederate monuments, Confederate Memorial Day, the funerals of Confederate veterans, the religion of the Lost Cause, the rebel yell, the term "rebels," historic sites identified with the Confederacy, and similar symbolic and ritualistic elements.

The Lost Cause became a popular movement in the early twentieth century, a cultural revitalization effort, teaching white southerners to retain the southern identity that defeat in the war had seemingly threatened. Yet the vitality of the movement had begun to wane by World War I. The war helped reincorporate the South back into the nation, as southerners fought for the nation and began embracing the national Memorial Day. The Confederate veterans themselves had been a constant reminder not to forget the past, but as their ranks thinned out, white southerners had less reinforcement for remembering the earlier war. Lost Cause activities less often evoked the spiritual feelings that had undergirded the religion of the Lost Cause in the late nineteenth century. The pattern of life in the South had changed, and the issues the war addressed no longer seemed as urgent as they had once been. Lost Cause events less frequently engaged communities. Confederate Memorial Day is still on the southern calendar and members of Confederate heritage groups still take part in its activities, but the Fourth of July has long since been the more important social and community event. Robert E. Lee's birthday is still a holiday, but newspapers rarely publish editorials about it and its combination in some states with the Martin Luther King, Jr. national holiday seems to please few of those honoring the Confederate general.[5]

THE AGRARIANS

The 1920s had been a landmark in the quickened pace of modernization in the South, with increased industrialization, urbanization, and commercialization apparent and troubling to many native white southerners who advanced the values of a traditional society in the face of social change. The writers who became the Vanderbilt Agrarians and published *I'll Take My Stand* in 1930 stood at a moment in time in the South and represented a conservative effort to assert boldly a traditional vision of the region's culture that would be relevant in a modernizing society. They were middle-class white male southerners, mostly townsmen and mostly from the hill country yeoman South. They had grown up at a particular time in southern history, hearing stories of the Civil War and noble Confederate ancestors from respected elder family members. They also grew up in a world of not only a Lost Cause outlook but also the New South ideology that embraced material progress, an increasing North-South regional convergence, southern racial separatism, and violence. The 1920s were a transition, though, with increased regional prosperity, the growth of modernist ideas and modernizing influences on society, and escalating external and internal criticisms of southern ways. The perception of increasing industrialization would be especially important to the Agrarians who would offer a new sharp focus on the southern way of life that was agrarian in values.[6]

This outlook reflected a changed regional consciousness, as the modern industrial economy and accompanying ethos entered the South with increasing force after World War I, producing a cultural shock to a more or less closed and static society. The 1930 book by the Agrarians brought together essays by twelve southern writers and intellectuals, exploring the conservative values they associated with earlier western civilization and which they saw as distinct from the American way of life that they identified as industrial society. Before they became the Agrarians, many of these intellectuals were Fugitive poets, seeing themselves as part of modernist literature and disclaiming what had become a sentimentalized Lost Cause ideology best represented by what they saw as the bad poetry of the United Daughters of the Confederacy. They dismissed the literature celebrating the Confederacy—think Thomas Nelson Page—as romanticized, feminized, downright exploitive of the South, and intended for northern audiences feasting on southern nostalgia. Instead, they saw moral issues as central to their time of transition in the South. They were still practitioners of a Southern Civil Religion, fashioning, as historian Mark Malvasi notes, "an image of the South as the good society, which could provide a moral if not always a concrete social and political alternative to the modern world." To take the South seriously, they had to debunk the romanticized South that had defined Southern tradition to Page and others in the post-Reconstruction South. Hoop-skirted Southern belles, chivalric Southern gentlemen, and happy darkies loyally devoted to their masters and mistresses defined that South, a plantation idyll that Margaret Mitchell would simultaneously support and complicate in the 1930s.[7]

The emerging Agrarians of the late 1920s turned to the Southern past, though, especially the Civil War, for inspiration in creating narratives of a traditional agrarian society that could sustain a sensibility suitable to the new modernist age. Donald Davidson had heard stories from his grandmother about the heroic Confederates and the postwar federal occupation and supposed black rule during Reconstruction. In the 1920s he turned from the classical poems he had been writing to explore regional history in his epic poem "The Tall Men" about Tennessee's frontier heritage. John Crowe Ransom made a crucial distinction between an anti-materialist Lost Cause and a sentimental Lost Cause, admitting the unreconstructed white Southerner had "a fierce devotion to a lost cause," although he noted that even his contemporary Southerners thought it was indeed lost and condescendingly offered the true believer only "a little petting" in indulging such whimsy as taking the past seriously. He ridiculed the sentimental Lost Cause, noting that some people in effect tarnished the legacy of the Confederate war effort, making the South "the nearest available locus for the scenes of their sentimental songs," snipping at popular culture's expressions of the South in the process. Ransom disdained simple nostalgia for the Old South, as when white Southerners sorrowfully agreed "to abandon an old home, an old provincial setting, or an old way of living to which we had become habituated." The Agrarians dismissed such nostalgic leanings, hoping to revitalize a dynamic southern tradition.[8]

Allen Tate perhaps best embodied the quandary of the Agrarian writers' efforts to use the Lost Cause in a time of modernist ideology. Born in Winchester, Kentucky, Tate attended Vanderbilt University and came away a self-conscious intellectual, firmly aware of and committed to the latest modernist literary outlook and assumptions. He moved to New York City and enjoyed its sophisticated Greenwich Village scene. But eventually he came to reassess his southern heritage. In the fall of 1926 he began work on "Ode to the Confederate Dead," which showed the frustration of a modern young white southerner pausing at the gate of a Confederate cemetery. He thinks of the "inscrutable infantry rising" and of the battles fought, jealous of the Confederates' confidence in their beliefs for which they fought. The narrator confesses that the modern southerner has too complicated a worldview for simple convictions, doubting and questioning in typical modernist ways, unable to gain the faith and wholeness that once characterized the past.[9]

Tate began an intense study of the Confederacy in the hope that knowledge of the Lost Cause could lead him to a traditional southern faith. His biography of Stonewall Jackson led to his embrace of a "neo-Confederate" identity, and he soon challenged a critic to a duel. Further cementing his obsession with the sectional crisis was his 1928 biography of Jefferson Davis, in which he dramatically portrayed the North's brutality toward the South. He studied genealogy, toured battlefields, bought an antebellum home with columns and porches, and kept a loaded rifle and Confederate flag over his mantelpiece. His obsession with the Lost Cause was not an engagement with the memory of Confederate defeat, with the tragic history that had such a pronounced role in the rhetoric and rituals of the late nineteenth century. Rather, Tate embraced the Lost Cause because it offered a vision of southern crusaders, a chosen people, battling for a way of life in which they believed.[10]

In spite of Tate's passionate interest in it, by the 1920s the Lost Cause lacked the popular enthusiasm that had once animated the white South. He and his literary colleagues were largely without influence with the masses of the southern people themselves. In the modern South, most white southerners seemed to prefer to forget the tragic lessons of the Civil War and to think in more upbeat ways. Tate went to a Confederate memorial service in Clarksville, Tennessee, and a local Baptist minister told him that Confederate defeat was simply God's ordained way to bring about the industrial development that would bring progress to the South. Factories in Clarksville—that was what the war had been about. A conventional understanding of the war's results for many southerners in the 1920s, it was a frustrating view for Tate and other neo-Confederate writers who themselves were caught between the traditionalism and modernism that would thereafter characterize the role of the Lost Cause in the twentieth century.[11]

RADIO AND FILM

Literary modernism rested uncomfortably with the Agrarians' efforts to forge a new traditionalist understanding of the Lost Cause as a crusading model for a South in time of transition. Radio represented a new form of media in the same years that the Agrarians were writing, and it also represented a dynamic between modernity and traditionalism in the South, with technology offering the potential of new centralization of social thought. Regulators issued the first licenses to radio stations in the South in 1922, but the region was slower than elsewhere in establishing local stations. It soon became clear that broadcasting could accommodate many ideological perspectives. William Kennon Henderson broadcast on clear-channel KWKH in Shreveport, Louisiana, across much of the South, becoming known as the "Bolshevik of Radio" for his crusade against retail chain stores destroying local department stores and blaming the new chains as "damnable thieves from Wall Street." Radio was a boon to the spread of traditional southern musical forms through Nashville's WSM and its Grand Ole Opry in the 1930s and afterwards, and Memphis's WDIA that later helped popularize black music and early rock and roll. In terms of the Lost Cause, local radio included the activities of the United Daughters of the Confederacy and other latter-day Civil War groups in their coverage of community events, keeping the rituals and discourse of the Lost Cause alive even as society was changing.[12]

Douglas Southall Freeman was the acclaimed and popular author of a four-volume biography of Robert E. Lee in the Depression years, a classic restatement of the romance and tragedy that had defined the Lost Cause in the late nineteenth century. Also the editor of the *Richmond Times-Dispatch*, Freeman was a community leader with a radio show, which he used to extend his traditional Lost Cause sensibility into the interwar era. In a radio address, "How a Great Leader Met Adversary," Freeman compared Lee's career after Appomattox with Americans suffering through the financial hardships of the Depression, reassuring them that the message of Lee and the post-Civil War South was that it was possible to overcome loss and still retain hope for the future. The 1940s national broadcast show "Cavalcade of America" eulogized Lee as the epitome of the romance and tragedy of the Lost Cause, showing the continued appeal of the Lost Cause narrative over a new technology of communication.[13]

Film, like radio, was a new media that flourished in the interwar years and became a carrier for the Lost Cause into the new world of technological communications. *Birth of a Nation* (1915) showed the power of film to dramatize the Confederate memory; President Woodrow Wilson observed that the film was "like writing history with lightning." Writer Thomas Dixon, Jr. had shown the popularity of his stories about the war and Reconstruction, including *The Leopard's Spots* (1902) and *The Clansman* (1905), upon which Kentuckian D. W. Griffith based his film. Using such modern film techniques as the long shot, close-up, flashback, and montage, Griffith harnessed emotional depth that cultivated excitement and tension in audiences across the nation. In the film, former wartime enemies came together through a romantic story of a northern and southern couple and their families, resulting in—according to the subtitles—"defense of their Aryan birthright." The rising national racism after the turn of the twentieth century found a ready support in the film, which portrayed African Americans as either loyal, submissive slaves or bestial freedmen who threatened pure white women's sexuality. Here, the Lost Cause received an outlandish racial taint, reinforced through modern communications. The second Ku Klux Klan took inspiration from the film as it launched its campaigns for white supremacy outside Atlanta near the time the film premiered there.[14]

Margaret Mitchell's *Gone with the Wind* (1936) was an even more popular film than *Birth of a Nation*, a national phenomenon that fit the mood of the Depression years. A nation disillusioned by its experience in World War I and economic disaster became intrigued by the comparison with southern failure in the past. Some sixty Civil War novels appeared during the 1930s, with Mitchell's best-selling story only the most prominent. The enormous response to the novel and the 1939 film based upon it suggested how popular culture could use the Lost Cause to provide escape and solace for a disheartened national, and even international, audience. Mitchell's romantic image of the Confederacy reflected the traditions of late-nineteenth-century southern novelists, telling of a superior antebellum life overrun in wartime by tawdry industrial society. The book depicted a land of happy servants, fine horses, and beautiful lands. Mitchell, to be sure, went beyond existing Southern stereotypes in her portrayal of high-spirited Scarlet O'Hara as a "new southern woman" who was not a shrinking violet; but overall, she effectively employed the Southern cavalier imagery as well. Premiering in Atlanta in December 1939, the film touched off celebrations in the South wherever it showed. A parade in the city drew three hundred thousand to observe it, and Confederate battle flags and the song "Dixie" gained a renewed currency throughout the region.[15]

COLLEGE FOOTBALL

Sports was another modern form of popular culture, and one version of spectator sports, college football, is also revealing of how some Southerners adopted the Lost Cause for this newly popular venue in the early twentieth century. The sport had begun in the late nineteenth century in the Northeast and spread only slowly through the Southern states. As historian Andrew Doyle notes, early college football in the region was "an amalgamation of innovation and tradition." Evangelicals opposed this Northern sport, which they saw as a brutal one, but supporters of college football in the region overcame such opposition by imbuing the sport with a regional identity. They did so by connecting it to the South's martial tradition, in-cluding the Lost Cause, as fans sang "Dixie" at the games, compared cheers to the Rebel yell, waved the Confederate battle flag, and compared coaches and players to Confederate soldiers. By the 1920s, urban middle-class white southerners had become enthusiastic supporters of the game, spending ris-ing levels of income to support this commercialized entertainment.[16]

The 1920s had seen rising sectional tensions as the national image of the South became that of a benighted region, with lynchings, Ku Klux Klan ac-tivity, religious fundamentalism, and other regional expressions souring na-tional sentiments on the region. Business and industrial growth increased notably in the decade, and southerners both embraced these aspects of mo-dernity while also showing signs of anxiety at social change. Southern col-lege football teams began having success in the decade, becoming a point of pride in victories over nationally ranked teams. The turning point in the popularity of college football in the South was the University of Alabama's victory over the University of Washington in the 1926 Rose Bowl game, as well as the Crimson Tide's invitation to play in the bowl again the follow-ing year. After that year's team tied Stanford University, Alabama Governor Bibb Graves declared, "The hearts of all of Dixie are beating with exultant pride." He insisted the Tide "upheld the honor of the Southland and came back to us undefeated." Graves's words showed how intersectional competi-tion could unite the South around football triumphs. The same sentiment appeared in an *Atlanta Journal* story, which noted that "the Crimson Tide no longer belongs to Tuscaloosa and the state of Alabama. It belongs to the whole South just like the Stone Mountain Memorial," referring to the carved monument to Lost Cause heroes on the side of a granite mountain east of Atlanta.[17]

Doyle notes that supporters of college football throughout the South now saw the region's football success as meaning "the region was every bit as modern and progressive as the rest of the nation." Newspaper editorialists, business people, and politicians used college football success as the basis for a booster campaign to appeal to national financial interests and invest in a region of growing modern values. Still, the Lost Cause's backward-looking ethos and embrace of a heritage of loss worked against a modern, future-oriented outlook. The rhetoric around college football in the South was flexible enough, though, to combine the Lost Cause martial and honor value system with a progressive vision of an expanding southern future.

Alabama newspaper editor John Temple Graves was a business progressive who also loved college football. He put the importance of the sport to the region in perspective when he noted in 1941 that "for all the last stands, all the lost causes and sacrificings in vain, the South had a heart. And a tradition." He saw college football as a new tradition for the South, one based in survival and embrace of victory. "It had come from the football fields. It had come from those mighty afternoons in the Rose Bowl at Pasadena, when Alabama's Crimson Tide had rolled to glory." His conclusion was that "the South had come by way of football to think at last in terms of causes won, not lost."[18]

TOURISM, POPULAR CULTURE, AND THE LOST CAUSE

The interwar period saw not only southern triumphs in football; national respect for Confederate heroes, the seeming national acquiescence to white racial dominance in the South, and economic interaction all promoted continued regional reconciliation through the 1930s, seen in the popular image of the Lost Cause as part of what Jack Temple Kirby called "the Grand Old South." The nationalist component of modernity could thus easily incorporate Southern consciousness, and one aspect of economic development, tourism, showed in the interwar period how the South took advantage of the marketing of the Lost Cause to attract visitors to historic sites and refurbish the Confederate memory for modern times. One key ingredient in this development was paved roads, with more than sixteen thousand roads reaching across the South by 1933 and twelve well-promoted interstate highways connecting the region to the rest of the nation. They bore names from the South's past, including the Dixie Highway, the Andrew Jackson, the Robert E. Lee, and the Jefferson Davis.[19]

By the mid-1930s the routes south had "become a commercial enterprise," according to *The New York Times*, and the partners were "hotels, restaurants, oil and garage companies, ferry operators, amusement concessions, roadside stand and overnight cabin owners, city societies and everyone who has any reason to welcome visitors along the wayside." This commercial landmark was a modern one, seen in terms of the extension of modern civilization into the region. One Georgian wrote in a 1927 letter to the Savannah paper that the Atlantic Coastal Highway's "ribbon of concrete has brought to your doors civilization which you hardly realized was in existence." Some cities, such as Richmond, drew most directly from Civil War sites, with travel brochures emphasizing Confederate monuments and parades of the Richmond howitzers with the Confederate battle flag prominent. Charleston was in the forefront of using the South's historical imagery to market itself to tourists seeking the romantic southern way of life, establishing early on tourist hotels, brochures, advertisements in popular magazines, film and radio spots, and a permanent tourist bureau to coordinate its efforts. The colonial era was one aspect of the city's tourism, but it also embraced a romantic Old South, with slavery a prominent feature.[20]

Natchez, Mississippi was also in the forefront of using the older South to project a vanished civilization for tourists. The Natchez Pilgrimage began in the early 1930s, hosted by two competing garden clubs. Their purpose was civic improvement, especially preserving local architecture. It allowed people from all over the nation to see, as historian Karen Cox notes, "the Old South that they had envisioned from music, radio, and other forms of popular culture." Hoop-skirted white women and African Americans clothed in servant outfits welcomed visitors to historic antebellum mansions. The Confederate Pageant was the highlight, with organizers assigning demeaning roles to black servants, donning them in tattered garb of cotton pickers and having them sing spirituals in the pageant. The southern business world thus exploited the Lost Cause memory, which remained vibrant even in the changing times of the interwar years. Still, the content of the Lost Cause memory changed little in essence, even if adapted to new ways of marketing it.[21]

The marketing of the Lost Cause also appeared in other aspects of popular culture in the interwar years. Regional brands like Maxwell House Coffee and Avon cosmetics projected imagery from the Southern past, showing a romanticized, pre-modern, unchanging Southern society. This image appealed to white middle-class women across the nation, who bought items (such as Aunt Jemima's products) that would symbolically be like having a black servant in their house to help them with meals. National advertising embraced the Old South and the Lost Cause with new enthusiasm. One advertisement in the 1930s featured "Hams from Ole Virginia," noting they were "as good as though you went to the plantation and had Mammy cook it." Liquor advertisements especially loved to embrace the appeals of the Old South. Richmond's Dixie Belle gin used the South's patriotic song to sell its liquor. A Four Roses whiskey advertisement in 1934 had text that said it was "soft as Southern moonlight," with a color picture of Confederate generals sipping their mint juleps. In 1934 the Illinois Central Railroad advertised tours of the Deep South in language that linked racism to the appeal of the Lost Cause. "Land O' Lee where the 'white man's burden' can be laid down in the Sunny South."[22]

The 1940s saw another outbreak of Lost Cause imagery and ritual as it became a national fad of sorts, seen especially on college campuses where the flag became more prominent than ever. Kappa Alpha (KA), a southern college fraternity founded at Washington College in Lexington, Virginia in December 1865, had long preserved what an early history of the group called "the southern ideal of character—that of the chivalrous warrior of Christ, the Knight who loves God and country, honors and protects pure womanhood, practices courtesy and magnanimity of spirit and prefers self-respect to ill-gotten wealth." By the 1920s, KA chapters across the South held Dixie Dances, or Old South balls, which included Confederate uniforms, Civil War-era dresses, mint juleps, and often Confederate battle flags. Students at some campuses had increasingly displayed the flag at football games in the 1930s, a trend that increased after World War II.[23]

POLITICIZATION OF THE LOST CAUSE

This popular culture display of the flag coincided with the political use of the flag and the song "Dixie" in support of the Dixiecrat political movement in 1948. At the Democratic National Convention that year, students and others protested President Harry S. Truman's civil rights program, using the Lost Cause to stir emotions. "There are yells and the rebel flag is working overtime," reported the *Christian Science Monitor.* "Cowbells ring. Waved back at them are the Truman placards of other states." A band from one of the southern states began playing "Dixie" to add to the pandemonium. The Dixiecrat convention met in Birmingham on July 16 with Strom Thurmond marching to the podium, accompanied by the American flag and the Confederate battle flag, to accept the party's presidential nomination. Among convention delegates were students from Alabama College, Alabama Polytechnic, Birmingham-Southern College, Cumberland University, Georgia Tech, Howard College, Loyola of the South, Mississippi State University, the University of Alabama, and the University of Virginia. The University of Mississippi counted the largest number of students to the convention, and news reports credited them with bringing the Confederate flag into the convention hall—as well as wearing Colonel Rebel black hats.[24]

College students had by then long waved the flag at football games and fraternity parties, but the 1948 events in Birmingham signaled a new ideological use of the Lost Cause as protest against racial change. University of Mississippi students told a reporter that their presence at the convention was "serious business," and they were not there "as college students on a lark." University of Alabama students added, "We're just here to protest," noting that "every fraternity at Tuscaloosa is flying a Confederate flag from the roof today." African American newspapers emphasized this Lost Cause presence and the emotions that it seemed to generate among white southerners. "Screaming, frenzied, frightened and comical," reported the *Pittsburg Courier*, "Dixie ran up the Confederate flag again here Saturday, eighty-three years after Lee hauled it down and handed it over to Grant at Appomattox . . . and those frantic Democrats bellowed their resistance to civil rights and their allegiance to the principles of the KKK."[25]

Resistance to the civil rights movement would indeed become a late-twentieth-century use of the Lost Cause, with Confederate symbolism figuring prominently in the segregationist Lost Cause, a popular movement in the 1950s and 1960s in response to the civil rights movement and one which left the Lost Cause with a harsher racial meaning. Whether at Central High School in Little Rock in 1957, at the University of Mississippi in 1962, or at Selma in 1965, segregationists displayed the Confederate battle flag and played "Dixie." After the integration of Central High School at bayonet point, a local official in Forest, Mississippi told the high school band there to play "Dixie" before football games instead of the "Star-Spangled Banner." During the riot in Oxford in 1962, students pulled down the Stars and Stripes from the flagpole and raised the Confederate flag. This was powerful symbolism a hundred years after the Civil War. The Ku Klux Klan had made that Confederate flag a central symbol in the early twentieth century, the White Citizens' Councils used it in the 1950s, and in the minds of many Americans that became its prime association. The Citizens' Councils saw its cause as preserving traditional racial views in a modern society, and they used modern media to produce television films justifying segregation that television stations across the nation showed.[26]

Still, the national and international consensus on white supremacy that had dominated the early twentieth century had long vanished by the 1950s, and the southern white resistance seemed to reinforce the Lost Cause image as part of a backward South, out of touch with modern American racial attitudes that were now more tolerant. Writer Walker Percy explained the historic shift in meaning of Confederate symbolism, pointing out in 1961 that "racism is no sectional monopoly. Nor was the Confederate flag a racist symbol. But it is apt to be now. The symbol is the same, but the referent has changed. Now when the Stars and Bars flies over a convertible or speedboat or a citizen's meeting, what it signifies is not a theory of government but a certain attitude toward the Negro." Alabama's attorney general Richmond Flowers wrote in *Look* magazine in 1966 that "today the flag for which my grandfather fought is desecrated." Arguing that the Confederate flag "should be a thing of honor," he saw a South where racists flaunted the flag, making it "mean one thing: hate." He insisted that the flag deserved a better place in history than on car bumpers or on the bloody robes of the killers, floggers and night riders who call themselves the Ku Klux Klan." Flowers thus linked the popular culture display of the flag on cars and elsewhere with the use of the flag to resist desegregation.[27]

The civil rights movement, and resistance to it, paralleled the economic development of the South, as industry and business came to surpass agriculture as the basis of the Southern economy and commercial values increasingly predominated. The sale of such souvenirs as bumper stickers of the Old South and the Confederacy represented a commodification of the Lost Cause in the 1950s and afterwards, the triumph of modern capitalist attitudes that easily exploited the Confederate memory for profit. In the late 1940s, sales of Confederate flags and other Lost Cause items at novelty shops and roadside stands increased during football season and before Memorial Day and other Confederate holidays. In this period of the flag fad, even the NAACP's magazine *The Crisis* claimed that "the waving of the Confederate battle flag is just a fad like carrying foxtails on cars, or the increasing use of skull and cross-bones on flags, t-shirts, caps, and cuff links." Confederate heritage groups campaigned against the commercialization of the flag and other Lost Cause items, with the South Carolina legislature even passing a resolution condemning William D. Hartman, an executive with a company that sponsored "Dixie beach towels" bearing the Confederate battle flag. The resolution noted that Hartman was "an unworthy American" whose sales project "constitutes a veiled attack, parading in the garb of legitimate advertisement, on the valor, courage and sacrifice of the Men in Gray who followed the immortal Robert E. Lee." South Carolina's Confederate War Centennial Commission's handbook pointed to the variety of souvenirs being marketed in the early 1960s, noting that "the use of the Confederate flag as a design on jackets, underwear, handkerchiefs, paper plates, napkins, and receptacles is generally to be deplored."[28]

The Civil War centennial in the early 1960s itself became a national fad of sorts, a modern American event that advertisers used to sell everything from automobiles to razor blades. One trade magazine effused that "the Civil War Centennial is one of the most mouth-watering marketing situations to come along in years." One could buy "turncoats" (blue on one side, gray on the other) for dogs; neckties with American and Confederate flags on them; flag-embossed music boxes that played "Dixie"; and miniature statues of a reconstructed white Southerner saying "Forget Hell." Newspapers printed editorials, magazines did stories on the blue and the gray, and genealogists displayed their knowledge of family legacies. The centennial became an occasion for social activities, something that William Faulkner had anticipated. In *Requiem for a Nun* (1951), he wrote that "the old deathless Lost Cause had become a faded (though still select) social club or caste."[29]

Some observers noted the connection between the centennial and the civil rights movement. Writer Robert Penn Warren (one of the Vanderbilt Agrarians in 1930) wrote in *The Legacy of the Civil War: Meditations on the Centennial* (1961) that "any common lyncher becomes a defender of the southern tradition, and any rabble-rouser the gallant leader of a thin gray line of heroes." He saw the modern white southerner's protest against racial change as "an obscene parody of his history." He confessed that he could not imagine Robert E. Lee even willing to shake hands with Orval Faubus, the Arkansas governor who defied the national government with opposition to the integration of schools in Little Rock. Walker Percy made the same point about the modern South. "When Lee and the Army of Northern Virginia laid down the Confederate flag in 1865, no flag had ever been defended by better men. But when the same flag is picked up by men like Ross Barnet and Jimmy Davis, nothing remains but to make panties and pillowcases with it," touching again on the commodification of the Lost Cause as linked to its role in racial protest. In both cases, the trivialization of the Confederate memory had drained away any noble meaning earlier attributed to the Lost Cause.[30]

The political uses of the Lost Cause in this era left it with an ideological meaning that would remain ever after. Georgia, Alabama, and South Carolina added the battle flag onto their state flags, a symbolic assertion of the whites-only Confederate memory in the face of the African American challenge to it. Southern states had considered not participating in the federally sanctioned centennial, but they did so to make use of it in advertising their states and to win support for southern states' rights. Virginia Governor J. Lindsay Almond saw the centennial as the chance to emphasize "the basic underlying principles in defense of which the war was fought," by which he meant opposition to the federal government. Mississippi Governor Ross Barnett looked forward to the event attracting "the kind of people who can and will come South," and he added that "I don't mean 'freedom riders.'" Barnett added that the centennial would bring attention to a South that was now modern but that also preserved its "precious heritage of local self-government."[31]

After the 1960s, the Lost Cause appeared embedded in national entertainment, much of it downright silly. *Dukes of Hazzard* of television, for example, included a souped-up automobile called the General Lee, with a Confederate flag in its roof. But southerners themselves made the Lost Cause symbolism part of a cultural revitalization movement in the late 1970s and 1980s. One saw it again in sports, especially college football. The god of southern football is a tribal god, and when Alabama played Notre Dame in the 1970s, southerners from many states waved the Confederate flag and rooted for their legions against the Yankee. In his last years, Bear Bryant was as close to a southern saint as the modern South had produced, with frequent comparisons to General Lee. Bryant's role in recruiting African American athletes to his Southeastern Conference team pointed to this new post-Jim Crow South as a biracial one, making college football in touch with national ideals now of inclusion. One also saw a renewed Southern spirit in country music, where Charlie Daniels consciously evoked the image of a Rebel and used Confederate symbols as he sang "The South's Gonna Do It Again"; Hank Williams Jr. sang "If Heaven Ain't a Lot Like Dixie, Then I Don't Want to Go"; and the group Alabama displayed the Confederate flag on virtually every record album, and one of their songs was "If It Ain't Dixie, It Won't Do." Bob McDill's song "Good Ole Boys," recorded by Don Williams, evoked Southern images, recalling his youth when a picture of Stonewall Jackson hung above his bed at night. Southern rock music drew from African American blues and earlier rhythm and blues, as well as country music, suggesting a new biracial cultural synthesis. But Lynyrd Skynyrd, one of the most popular band's in this genre, consciously asserted a rough Southern masculine ethos, using display of the Confederate flag to point to that sensibility. Elvis Presley's performance of "American Trilogy" in the 1970s was a slow, dirge-like effort to assert a new unifying cultural synthesis in which the Lost Cause was one ingredient of Southern symbolism, but no longer the dominant one. The song included "Dixie," an African American spiritual, and "The Battle Hymn of the Republic."[32]

This brief survey of ways that the Lost Cause intertwined with modern cultural and intellectual forms suggests the ability of promoters of the Confederate memory to combine it with other elements of evolving American culture. In the early twentieth century, writers, sports enthusiasts, film makers, and radio broadcasters showed that they could use new cultural forms to project Lost Cause ideas and symbols into the modern world. This was an uneasy alliance, in some cases, and tensions would remain between the traditional southern and the modern. The 1960s was a turning point in the evolution of ideas about modernity, particularly in regard to race, with more voices for inclusion, diversity, and tolerance for racial differences becoming a new norm in the modern world. The Lost Cause after that could be a popular culture projection, sometimes silly but sometimes allowing for a biracial southernism that might include the Confederate memory along with African American cultural features, as with music. The rise of a neo-Confederate ideology in the 1980s and its alliance with conservative and religious political movements brought renewed attention to the inevitable problems of asserting a Lost Cause that had associations with both slavery and resistance to racial integration, making it seem part of a resistance ideology to modern attitudes. In the twenty-first century, this tension would lead to new efforts to purge the South of not only the public display of the Confederate flag and the playing of "Dixie," but also the removal of Confederate monuments, many of which were in that prime landscape of modernity: the city.

NOTES

1. Flannery O'Connor, "A Late Encounter with the Enemy," in *Old Glory and the Stars and Bars: Stories of the Civil War*, ed. George William Koon (Columbia: Univ. of South Carolina Press, 1995), 216, 218, 220–21.

2. O'Connor, "A Late Encounter with the Enemy," 222, 224.

3. Chandon Reddy, "Modern," in *Keywords for American Cultural Studies*, ed. Bruce Burgett and Glenn Hendler (New York: New York Univ. Press, 2000), 160–61. See also Elizabeth Fox-Genovese, "The Anxiety of History: The Southern Confrontation with Modernity," *Southern Cultures* 1 (1993): 65–82.

4. David Blight, *Race and Reunion: The Civil War in American Memory* (Cambridge, MA: The Belknap Press of Harvard Univ. Press, 2001), 290–94, 352.

5. Charles Reagan Wilson, *Baptized in Blood: The Religion of the Lost Cause, 1865–1920* (Athens: Univ. of Georgia Press, 1980); Charles Reagan Wilson, "God's Project: The Southern Civil Religion, 1920–1980," in *Judgment and Grace in Dixie: Southern Faiths from Faulkner to Elvis* (Athens: Univ. of Georgia Press, 1996), 19–22. See also Blight, *Race and Reunion*, 172.

6.Paul K. Conkin, *The Southern Agrarians* (Knoxville: The Univ. of Tennessee Press, 1988), chapters 2 and 3.

7. Mark G. Malvasi, *The Unregenerate South: The Agrarian Thought of John Crowe Ransom, Allen Tate, and Donald Davidson* (Baton Rouge: Louisiana State Univ. Press, 1997), 8. See also "Introduction" in *I'll Take My Stand: The South and the Agrarian Tradition*, Twelve Southerners (1930; reprint Baton Rouge: Louisiana State Univ. Press, 2006).

8. Twelve Southerners, *I'll Take My Stand*, 2, 6.

9. Allen Tate, "Ode to the Confederate Dead," in *Poems: 1928–1931* (New York: Charles Scribner's, 1932), 50.

10. Daniel Joseph Singal, *The War Within: From Victorian to Modernist Thought in the South, 1919–1945* (Chapel Hill: Univ. of North Carolina Press, 1982), 232–60.

11. Singal, *The War Within*, 245–46.

12. C. Joseph Pusateri, "Radio Industry, Early," in *The New Encyclopedia of Southern Culture* 18, ed. Allison Graham, Sharon Monteith, and Charels Reagan Wilson (Chapel Hill: Univ. of North Carolina Press, 2011): 157–60.

13. Thomas L. Connelly and Barbara L. Bellows, *God and General Longstreet: The Lost Cause and the Southern Mind* (Baton Rouge: Louisiana State Univ. Press, 1982), 125, 127.

14. Joan L. Silverman, "The Birth of a Nation," in *The New Encyclopedia of Southern Culture* 18: 199–201.

15. Darden Asbury Pyron and Helen Taylor, "Gone with the Wind," in *The New Encyclopedia of Southern Culture* 18, ed. Graham, Monteith, and Wilson, 256–59.

16. Andrew Doyle, "Turning the Tide: College Football and Southern Progressivism," *Southern Cultures* 3, no. 3: 228–51.

17. Doyle, "Turning the Tide," 36–37.

18. Doyle, "Turning the Tide," 45, 48.

19. Jack Temple Kirby, *Media-Made Dixie: The South in the American Imagination* (Baton Rouge: Louisiana State Univ. Press, 1978), 64–78; W. Fitzhugh Brundage, *The Southern Past: A Clash of Race and Memory* (Cambridge, MA: The Belknap Press of Harvard Univ. Press, 2005), 192, 196.

20. "To Florida: Many Routes South for Motorists," *The New York Times*, December 20, 1936; A. A. Ainsworth to Editor, *Savannah Morning News*, October 27, 1927, quoted in Karen L. Cox, *Dreaming of Dixie: How the South was Created in American Popular Culture* (Chapel Hill: Univ. of North Carolina Press, 1948), 146.

21. Cox, *Dreaming of Dixie*, 155. See also Brundage, *The Southern Past*, 322.

22. Kirby, *Media-Made Dixie*, 74–76, quote 75; Cox, *Dreaming of Dixie*, 47–57.

23. Paul Murrill, comp., *Catalogue of the Kappa Alpha Fraternity 1865–1906* (Charlotte, NC: Kappa Alpha, 1906), 3.

24. Quote in John M. Coski, *The Confederate Battle Flag: America's Most Embattled Emblem* (Cambridge, MA: The Belknap Press of Harvard Univ. Press, 2005), 100–101.

25. Dean DuBois, "Fifty-Five Ole Miss Students Attend States' Right Meeting," *The Mississippian*, July 22, 1948; Gene Wortman, "There's An Auditorium Full of Suspense before Opening," *Birmingham Post*, July 17, 1948; "Dixie Rebs Say U.S. Can't Stop Segregation," *Pittsburg Courier*, July 24, 1948.

26. Walker Percy, "Red, White and Blue-Gray," *Commonweal*, December 22, 1961, 338; Walter Lord, *The Past that Would Not Die* (New York: Pocket Books, 1967), 31, 63, 134, 137, 178; James W. Silver, *Mississippi: The Closed Society* (New York: Harcourt Brace and World, 1964), 5; Connelly and Bellows, *God and General Longstreet*, 117–19; Numan V. Bartley, *The Rise and Fall of Massive Resistance: Race and Politics in the South during the 1950s* (Baton Rouge: Louisiana State Univ. Press, 1969), third illustration.

27. Walker Percy, "Red, White and Blue-Gray," *Commonweal*, December 22, 1961, 338; Richmond Flowers, "Southern Plain Talk about the Ku Klux Klan, *Look* 30 (May 3, 1966): 36.

28. Coski, *Confederate Battle Flag*, 112 (first quote). "Those Confederate Beach Towels," *Richmond Times-Dispatch*, March 3, 1958 (second quote); K. Michael Prince, *Rally Round the Flag, Boys!: South Carolina and the Confederate Flag* (Columbia: Univ. of South Carolina Press, 2004), 38 (third quote).

29. "The Civil War Marketing Marches On," *Sales Management* 86, March 17, 1961, 38 (first quote); William Faulkner, *Requiem for a Nun* (1951, reprint New York: Vintage Books, 1975) (second quote).

30. Robert Penn Warren, *The Legacy of the Civil War: Meditations on the Centennial* (New York: Random House, 1961), 54, 57; Percy, "Red, White and Blue-Gray," 338.

31. Minutes of Virginia Civil War Centennial Commission, August 4, 1958, in Minute Book 1958–1965, Records of the Virginia Civil War Centennial Commission, Library of Virginia, Richmond, Record Group 71 (first quote); Barnett quote in speech, November 3, 1961, Civil War Centennial Files, National Archives and Records Administration, Washington, DC (second quote).

32. John Shelton Reed, *Southerners: The Social Psychology of Sectionalism* (Chapel Hill: Univ. of North Carolina Press, 86–87; Connelly and Bellows, *God and General Longstreet*, 137–48; Thomas L. Connelly, *Will Campbell and the Soul of the South* (New York: Continuum, 1982); Charles Reagan Wilson, "The Death of Bear Bryant: Myth and Ritual in the Modern South," *South Atlantic Quarterly* 86 (Summer 1987), 282–95; J. Michael Martinez, William D. Richardson, and Ron McNinch-Su, eds., *Confederate Symbols in the Contemporary South* (Gainesville: Univ. of Florida Press, 2000), 57–60; Will Kaufman, *The Civil War in American Culture* (Edinburgh: Edinburgh Univ. Press, 2006), 80–84.

"Old Times There Are Not Forgotten": Confederate Commemoration, Protest, and Debate at the University of Mississippi, 1865–2017

LEIGH McWHITE

In April 1861, a large number of University of Mississippi students mustered into the Confederate Army as "the University Greys." As Company A of the 11th Mississippi Regiment of Volunteer Infantry, they received commendations for their actions on the field and fought in numerous battles including First Manassas, Seven Pines, Second Manassas, Antietam, and Gettysburg. In the latter battle, it was the Greys who reached the "high water mark" of the Confederacy, advancing farthest into Union lines and suffering 100 percent casualties.[1]

While the university may have closed during the war as an educational facility, the doors remained open as a state-funded Confederate military hospital that saw numerous casualties, particularly after the Battle of Shiloh. More than seven hundred patients lie buried in a cemetery on campus. Later generations commonly referred to the small brick building adapted into a morgue as "The Dead House" until the university disassembled it in 1958 in order to extend a modern building.[2]

The dead may not haunt the campus as ghostly apparitions, but the Civil War certainly has. In the aftermath of hostilities, Confederate commemorative activities tended to follow a timeline and pattern typical across the South. As racial tensions in the region over civil rights began to increase in the mid-twentieth century, the University of Mississippi adopted symbols of the Confederate past that became entrenched in the traditions of the institution. When African Americans enrolled and their presence on campus grew, the symbols of the Lost Cause became the subject of challenge and debate—a discourse that continues to this day.[3]

THE UNIVERSITY ACCUMULATES SYMBOLS

After hostilities ended in 1865, Chancellor John Waddel conferred honorary bachelor of arts degrees on all members of the 1861 class. Following this ceremony, the Alumni Association expressed a determination to erect a monument "to memorialize those who died in service."[4] Although several decades passed before this structure appeared, the sentiment was typical of commemorative activities that emphasized bereavement in the immediate postwar era.

One of the first ritualistic activities undertaken by white southerners was Decoration Day, a time for the community to mourn the Confederate dead. Typically scheduled in the spring, a procession would wind its way to the site of local burials, women and children would "decorate" the graves with flowers and wreaths, and men would offer prayers and orations recalling the noble sacrifice of the deceased heroes, defending the righteousness of their cause, and anticipating a future that would vindicate the past. The campus cemetery hosted many such occasions. In 1877, more than a thousand people assembled to pay tribute to the dead on the anniversary of General Stonewall Jackson's death.[5]

The few Confederate memorials erected in the South during the three decades after the war exemplified this focus on mourning the dead. During this period, communities tended to erect monuments in cemeteries or churchyards; designs reflected the Victorian preference for obelisks and other funerary forms such as urns; and (most importantly) inscriptions were brief and exclusively referenced the dead. The first Confederate memorial on campus certainly reflected this latter emphasis in its inscription, but it also incorporated the second memorial phase's focus on instructing future generations about the legitimacy of the Confederate cause. During the 1870s, the Delta Gamma sorority at a local female academy decided to raise money to memorialize the university's Civil War dead. Assisted by donations from the class of 1877 and the Alumni Association, by 1890 funds had increased enough to install a $506.50 Tiffany window on the stair landing of the newly constructed campus library.[6] In the right-hand panel, a Confederate formation drills before a civilian audience in front of the campus observatory, while the middle section portrays the two opposing forces fighting with sabers. The left panel represents Lee's surrender at Appomattox. The main inscription reads, "In honor of those who, with ardent valor and patriotic devotion in the Civil War, sacrificed their lives in defense of principles inherited from their fathers and strengthened by the teaching of their Alma Mater, this memorial is lovingly dedicated."[7]

In the aftermath of the war, living veterans demonstrated little inclination to gather together in any organized fashion. The few Confederate groups operating during that era were ladies' memorial societies dedicated to the dead. Veterans on both sides appeared more interested in the present than the past, in rejuvenating their prewar careers or forging new vocations, and reconnecting with their families and society. Yet the Confederate past retained a significant presence in the South. At the university, many of the administrators and faculty were former veterans, and former Confederate soldiers occupied almost all of Mississippi's elected offices even as late as 1900.[8]

By the late 1880s, the former soldiers began to wax nostalgic about their service, and local veterans associations became common. In 1889, a regional organization known as the United Confederate Veterans (UCV) formed with objectives "social, literary, historical, and benevolent." Membership grew rapidly. By 1900, Mississippi possessed eighty UCV camps out of 1,277 organized nationwide. The local Lafayette County Camp No. 752 became active in 1896. Reunions at the local, state, and national levels were the primary inducement for membership where large gatherings attended by all generations and both sexes featured oratory, parades, memorial services, and entertainments.

In addition to their enthusiasm for social activities, the national UCV also evinced a strong interest in molding interpretations of the war that would encourage future generations to venerate the actions of their forebears. For example, the UCV monitored all available history textbooks and commended volumes deemed accurate and appropriate to southern school boards. In 1906 one Mississippi veteran, John W. Odom of Desoto County, gave the university $2,000 to encourage the perpetuation of this history: the best annual student essay or oration defending the constitutional and legal rights of the Southern states to secede would receive a monetary award.[9]

In light of their inevitable mortality, the aging veterans transferred this historical burden to the next generation, which in turn created auxiliary associations such as the United Daughters of the Confederacy (UDC) and the Sons of Confederate Veterans (SCV). In Oxford, the Albert Sidney Johnson chapter of the UDC organized in 1900, and the women spent several years raising funds for another Confederate memorial on campus.[10]

Monuments built in the last few years of the nineteenth century and first few decades of the twentieth reflected a desire to protect the reputation of former Confederates. In this second phase of memorialization, monuments appeared in public spaces like courthouse grounds or busy intersections where their placement ensured greater visibility. Inscriptions became more elaborate. The chiseled words not only mourned the dead but also lauded those soldiers who had survived and began to mention or at least imply that present and future generations were a target audience. Written messages praised not only the glory won by the soldiers but also remarked upon the righteousness of their cause. The monument at the county courthouse in Oxford, for instance, asserts that "they gave their lives in a just and holy cause," a core concept of the Lost Cause.

These inscriptions sought to ensure the transmission of the "true story" of the Confederacy to subsequent generations. The transition from funereal designs to figural sculptures suggests further evidence of this intent. The typical monument from this era is a single Confederate soldier at rest atop a marble shaft. These silent sentinels serve not only as symbolic representations for entire lost legions but also as totemic guards of a community's Confederate heritage. One popular variation even depicts the soldier shading his eyes to prevent the sun from obscuring his watchful gaze—the monument on the university's campus is a representative sample of this type. Of course, a more pragmatic reason for the sentinel design was the democratic gesture. Selecting a common soldier rather than a more highly ranked officer ensured widespread support and enthusiasm for fundraising endeavors.

In 1906, the local UDC chapter reported to the Mississippi division that "on May 10th, God willing, we shall unveil, on the University campus, a monument to the men, living and dead, who wore the gray. Standing on the beautiful campus of our State university we feel that this monument will not only be a silent reminder of our love for and our devotion for those who gallantly preserved untarnished the cause of Southern honor, *but will be a potent factor in the education of the noble sons of our proud old commonwealth who gather here from year to year from all parts of the State.*"[11] A grand occasion, the monument unveiling began with a procession from the Oxford courthouse square to the monument site, followed by music, a presentation of flowers, several speeches, and an armed salute by the veterans.[12]

The campus memorial reflects the more learned nature of its intended academic audience. While the east side on the base simply reads, "To Our Confederate Dead 1861–1865," and the west states, "To the Heroes of Lafayette County Whose Valor and Devotion Made Glorious Many a Battlefield," the south side offers a stanza from Lord Byron's poem "The Siege of Corinth" about the massacre of six hundred Venetians defending their city from Ottoman Turks in 1715. The Greek inscription facing north is identical to that on an ancient monument honoring the three hundred Spartans who fell at Thermopylae defending Greece against the Persians. The English translation (not provided on the statue) reads, "Tell them in Lakedaimon, passer-by. That here obedient to their word we lie."[13] In both cases, the historical analogies equate the Confederates to glorious, sacrificial heroes of past civilizations.

A segment of the local UDC chapter was unhappy over the placement of the monument on campus, fearing it did not pay proper tribute to the county's Confederate contribution. These women worked with the local veterans to erect yet another memorial the following year, this time on the grounds of the county courthouse.[14] Afterwards, the local UDC devoted their interests on campus to the Confederate cemetery. In 1907 or 1908, they erected a small marker with the simple inscription "Our Heroes, 1861–65."[15] Several decades later in 1927, the group erected a stone archway at the entrance. The UDC also enclosed the site in 1939 with bricks and stones and then installed a granite stone marker with an inscribed bronze tablet bearing 132 known names of the seven hundred-plus soldiers buried there.[16]

All of these totems are physical manifestations of the Civil War on campus. But it is important to note that more intangible, symbolic reminders of the past developed as well. One of these is the name "Ole Miss" itself. Many people assume the phrase derives from "Mississippi," although the origins are quite different. In 1897, at a time when the South was solidifying segregation with Jim Crow laws, Emma Meek won a yearbook staff contest to name the new university annual. Her suggestion—"Ole Miss"—was the traditional title of respect used by slaves for the mistress of the plantation.[17] Very quickly, the phrase became the adopted nickname for the university itself. Hence, the bastion of higher education for whites in the state was known familiarly by a phrase from slave dialect.

The name "Ole Miss" is not an anomaly when one takes into consideration a popular category of literature and oral tradition from this era. While white southerners tended to ignore the role of African Americans in the war between the Blue and the Gray in their reminiscences, the one exception was a subgenre of "Faithful Slave" anecdotes that honored the loyalty of those servants who marched with the Confederate Army or stayed behind on the plantation to protect the white women and children instead of escaping to the enemy camp. Several monuments to faithful slaves are scattered across the South, and Mississippi even granted Confederate pensions to African American soldiers. Stories of faithful slaves were common in Southern journals, and the popularity of this particular theme indicated a nostalgic need among white southerners of the racially troubled New South to recall the presumed harmony of the Old South. During this same period, black dialect tales written by white authors, like the Uncle Remus stories, became prevalent in literature.[18]

In 1936, the university held a contest to select a new name for the football team, known at the time as the "Mississippi Flood." The winning entry was "Rebels." Ironically, the first game under the new title occurred against Union University, an occasion described by the campus newspaper as a re-enactment of the Civil War.[19] The mascot became Colonel Rebel, depicted as an older Southern gentleman in civilian attire using a cane, perhaps an allusion to a disabled Confederate veteran. His image appeared on the yearbook in 1937, cheerleader uniforms possessed the emblem by 1942, and by the 1950s Colonel Rebel was a widely acknowledged symbol of Ole Miss.[20]

By 1948, a number of white southerners upset with President Harry S. Truman's integrationist policies bolted from the national Democratic Party to form their own States' Rights Party. Commonly referred to as "Dixiecrats," these staunch segregationists held their own nominating convention in Birmingham. The University of Mississippi contributed the largest delegation with fifty-five students. Several of them appeared in published photographs wearing their Colonel Rebel hats and posed in front of a large Confederate battle flag.[21] This image marks the origin of the university's association with the Rebel flag.[22]

The year 1948 was also significant as the centennial celebration of the university's origin. Among the festivities were reenactments of the University Greys by ROTC units in Confederate uniforms and bearing the Confederate battle flag. Their appearance in the homecoming parade fueled the flag's popularity, and soon cheerleaders and fans waved the standard with great enthusiasm at football games. The band also added "Dixie" to their repertoire. By 1953, halftime featured the band's display of a massive Confederate battle flag measuring sixty by ninety feet. Three years later, band members received new uniforms designed to resemble the Confederate dress uniform for officers, and the group changed its name to "the Band of the South."[23]

The executive council of the student body inaugurated the tradition of Dixie Week in 1950, celebrating the antebellum South and the Confederacy. At the beginning of the week, ROTC students lowered the United States flag and replaced it with the Confederate battle flag. The student body president would then read an order of secession. In 1958, the proclamation read, "The time has come when we, the people of the Soverign [sic] State of the University of Mississippi, can no longer tolerate the suppression of our beliefs and most cherished ideals, by the governing powers of the Union. In the past, we have tried to live peacefully according to the genteel tradition of the Old South, but constant intervention on the part of Union supporters has made the prospect of our continuing this life dubious. Therefore, we must take positive action against this aggression toward our great cause."[24]

Events during the week included Confederate balls, University Grey reenactments, memorial tributes to the dead, mint julep parties, drafting male students into the Confederate Army, beard growing contests, and a mock slave auction selling cheerleaders to the highest bidders. The week culminated in a home football game, when the football coach was designated "Chairman of the War Department" and ordered to defend the stadium from invasion.[25]

In 1954, Chancellor J. D. Williams commissioned an opera about the University Greys from a professor in the music department. The work featured a fictional student marching off to war only to die in the campus hospital after saying farewell to his bride. After two performances at the university, a condensed version aired on a local Memphis television station.[26] The opera would have a revival in 1961 as part of the university's Civil War Centennial activities.[27]

Congress formed a Civil War Centennial Commission to plan national remembrances during the historic anniversary. Federal officials viewed the occasion as an opportunity to educate Americans about the valiant struggles of the two opposing forces and to promote a sense of unity across the nation. Needless to say, southern states participated eagerly albeit with a slightly different perspective, viewing the anniversary as an excellent opportunity to rally the regional loyalties of white southerners and potentially as a tool for swaying some of the northern public to greater sympathy.[28]

The Mississippi Commission on the War Between the States organized a grand parade in the capital to commemorate the one hundredth anniversary of the state's secession from the Union. Communities created reenactment units to march in the capital parade and appear at other centennial events in their local area. Nearly one hundred male students organized as the University Greys. The Band of the South and their famously large Confederate flag appeared third in the parade order in Jackson, and the Greys marched at the head of all the other Confederate-clad groups. Later that day, participants watched a reenactment of the Secession Convention and attended Confederate balls.[29]

The University Greys (both historic and contemporary) certainly played a central role in the centennial activities on campus. In addition to a reprisal of the opera scheduled to coincide with the anniversary of the Greys' departure from Oxford, the day also featured a grand ceremony in which the reenactors represented their namesakes. After a service of music, poetry recitations, speeches, and memorial tributes, the reenactors marched away as if to war.[30]

CONFEDERATE SYMBOLS AND INTEGRATION

A year later, a real battle transpired on campus when a white southern mob attacked US Marshals protecting the right of the first African American to enroll in classes at the University of Mississippi. Symbolic and rhetorical references to the Civil War pervaded Mississippi and the university campus during this crisis and the following synopsis offers a mere sampling of these allusions.[31]

When the federal courts ordered the university to admit James Meredith on September 13, 1962, Governor Ross Barnett gave a radio and television broadcast to the state in which he claimed, "I speak to you now in the moment of our greatest crisis since the War Between the States."[32] Seven days later when Meredith arrived on campus to enroll, students gathered in front of the antebellum administrative building and began to chant, "Glory, glory, segregation, the South will rise again." A few students even rushed the flagpole with a Confederate banner and attempted to haul down the

American flag. A campus leader managed to stop the insurrectionists, re-turning the Stars and Stripes to its proper height.[33] Later that day, the governor formally barred Meredith's admission to the university.

On September 25, more than two thousand people gathered outside a state office building in the capital where the federal government made yet another registration attempt, and the governor again refused to admit Meredith. The assembled crowd, listening to a live broadcast of the confrontation, burst into a chorus of "Dixie" while one man waved a huge Confederate flag from the steps of the building.[34]

During the tense week that followed, cars throughout the state flew Confederate banners and "Dixie" frequently blared over the radio. On September 28, a legislator offered a petition in the chamber to sever relations between the United States and the state of Mississippi—an action derailed only by expedient calls for lunch.[35] National media began making comparisons between the governor's defiance of federal court orders and similar states' rights posturing a century earlier.[36] A mother of an Ole Miss student wrote her son, "Your great-grandfather set out to fight the federals from Ole Miss with the University Greys . . . nearly a hundred years ago—He didn't accomplish a thing! See that you don't get involved!"[37]

As the US Marshals cordoned off the antebellum administrative building on the afternoon of September 30, students, locals, outsiders, and newsmen gathered. Two youths in Confederate uniforms circulated through the crowd, and a bugler began blowing cavalry charges.[38] A group of students replaced the American flag with a Confederate one, succeeding in a task that others had failed to accomplish nine days earlier.[39] When the riot finally broke out, the Confederate monument became a significant point of orientation and rallies for the mob. In the end, two bystanders died, 166 US marshals and forty federalized National Guard soldiers received injuries, and authorities arrested two hundred individuals.[40] Combined with the federal-state nature of the conflict over racial equality, the Civil War Centennial in progress, and the rioter's use of Confederate symbols, comparisons and allusions to the Civil War came naturally to commentators then and years later as they attempted to explain the events on campus that night.

Watching the riot unfold through his office window, G. Ray Kercui, an assistant professor of art, abandoned his usual focus on quiet landscapes in favor of the brash modernist style of Jasper Johns. But instead of portraying the American flag, Kerciu painted the Confederate version. On one such banner, he superimposed typical segregationist slogans including "Yankee Go Home," "Kennedy Koon Keepers," "Never," and "Would You Want Your Daughter to Marry One?" He labeled another "Sovereign State of Mississippi" with the "S's" written backwards. Of all the shapes and color combinations the artist could have utilized to depict his horror at the events surrounding the riot, Kerciu determined that the rebel flag best represented the action. Five of these paintings appeared in the spring art exhibition the following year. When the Citizen Council and others protested, the university provost ordered the artwork removed from the show.[41]

Reflecting on the riot seventeen years later, a former student body president told a newspaper journalist, "It was like watching the last battle of the Civil War."[42] In 1982, during the twenty-year anniversary, the mayor of Oxford used identical phrasing in his address.[43] Reporting on the anniversary for *Time*, noted Mississippi author Willie Morris wrote, "It was the last battle of the Civil War, the last direct constitutional crisis between national and state authority."[44]

In the context of the civil rights movement, the struggle at Oxford was relatively unique, and not just because of the violence, for violence and death were nothing new and persisted for several more years. The distinctive characteristic of the riot lay in the mass white-on-white nature of the aggression. For the first time since 1865, southern whites directed their racial rage in a large-scale physical encounter not at African Americans but at federal authorities. The use of Confederate symbols and rhetoric reinforced the historical parallels even further, giving the allegorical allusions greater credence.

AFRICAN AMERICAN CHALLENGES TO SYMBOLS

The historical record has thus far provided no clear indication that African Americans had ever attacked a Confederate symbol in Mississippi before 1966. Yet in his autobiography, James Meredith infers that an earlier generation of black men had successfully seized an opportunity to erase one such Confederate emblem on the University of Mississippi campus. These comments come in the midst of describing a game of golf. Surrounded on the ground by troops and accompanied by a few of the professors who would interact socially with him, Meredith set out to play a round on the university course. As he recalled, "The very first drive I hit sent a contingent of soldiers scurrying for safety in the graveyard of the Confederate soldiers killed a hundred years before. The ball was lost in the cemetery and I never found it. . . . I noticed that there were no headstones, monuments, or other normal signs of a cemetery. I inquired about this strange appearance, and the story goes that a work detail of Negroes was ordered to clean up the graveyard and that was exactly what they did, without exception."[45]

This story about the absence of the grave markers appears numerous times throughout the years in various descriptions of the cemetery, yet no other author ever seemed to speculate that the action of the groundskeepers might be deliberate. Instead, the accounts by whites tend to blame black intellectual inferiority in misunderstanding a simple set of directions.[46] Meredith's assessment hints, quite to the contrary, that the work crew utilized the persona of slow-witted, shuffling blacks to protect themselves while they perpetrated an attack against the dead who had fought to preserve slavery. Meredith penetrated the mask of docile obedience related in the anecdote to suggest the potentially subversive implications in the incident.

Under the glare of the protection provided by national publicity in 1966, civil rights activists in Mississippi began to publicly make physical, rhetorical, and symbolic assaults against Confederate emblems. Such episodes did not occur often, but the advent of these public demonstrations are noteworthy after a hundred years of nearly complete quiescence. The first verifiable example at the University of Mississippi occurred in 1970 when the black student population rose to two hundred and the newly organized Black Student Union began a dialogue with the administration over their concerns. On February 24, seventy-five African American students in the cafeteria began to protest racism on campus by dancing on the tables to the blues music of B.B. King and burning a Confederate flag.[47] Arrests occurred on the following day when eighty-nine African American students raised their fists in the manner of black nationalists and chanted black power slogans during an Up with People concert.[48]

In March, the Black Student Union (BSU) published a list of demands that included ending discrimination in the hiring of administrators, faculty, coaches, staff, and student workers; improvement of black representation in various student organizations; and development of a black studies program. Included in the list was a demand to curtail use of the Confederate flag as a campus symbol.[49] A month later, African American students burned a large rebel flag outside a board of trustees meeting. The following day during a biracial parade and sit-in condemning the board, campus security, and racism, black students brought out a Confederate flag, walked on it, and then burned the banner. Security officers prevented a crowd of three to four hundred spectators from descending upon the small group.[50]

The tactics adopted by these protestors emerged from a context of "Black Power." Whatever the depth of their intellectual attachment to the philosophical concept, a number of African American students on campus felt some degree of allegiance to its ideas, as evidenced by the calls for a black studies program and as demonstrated in their use of its slogans and symbols. In fact, one mimeographed black student publication illustrated the confrontation between "Black Power" and the Lost Cause perfectly by superimposing a raised black fist over the battle flag of the Confederacy.[51]

DEBATING SYMBOLS

While the university administration acquiesced to a number of the goals outlined by the BSU, Confederate flags continued to wave to the tune of "Dixie" during athletic contests. Although flag burnings declined by the end of the 1970s along with sit-ins, public confrontations on the issue continued over the following decades. Most significantly, the disputes on campus sparked debate. People from both camps felt so strongly about the issue of Confederate symbols in contemporary life that they put pen to paper, writing letters to the campus newspaper, the *Daily Mississippian.* Representatives from the entire community—local townspeople, administrators, faculty, staff, alumni, and students—commented on the subject. And a debate it definitely was, as most contributors not only offered their own points for consideration but attempted to counter those given by opponents. Many individuals even wrote in direct response to statements that had appeared in previously published letters or editorials. It was not a dispassionate exchange of views. And the division was not simply one between two races, as self-identified whites joined the debate opposing the use of Confederate symbols on campus.[52]

Those opposing the rebel flag marshaled just a few simple arguments in their favor. Almost all involved a denunciation of the emblem as racist. The most popular justification for this characterization cited the adoption of the banner by the Ku Klux Klan and other extremist groups as well as its more general use by segregationists during the civil rights movement.

"Anyone who still does not understand why the so-called "Rebel" flag is offensive," wrote a columnist in 1993, "has only to ponder why the Ku Klux Klan marched on this campus in November of 1982 in defense of its use here. Its symbolism goes far beyond mere regionalism. Even European Nazis wave it, because it is an international symbol of white supremacy. Displaying it thus communicates racial ideas, like it or not."[53]

The typical anti-Confederate flag argument often delved deeper into the past by condemning its Civil War usage. To these authors, the emblem was a reminder of slavery and a Confederate cause to preserve that institution: "The men who fought under the Confederate (Rebel) flag risked their lives to maintain a way of life that favored the enslavement of my people. Do you honestly expect me to be proud of this history and pay tribute to it? Are you mad?"[54]

Anti-flag advocates also offered a pragmatic reason for surrendering the banner, highlighting the damage caused to the university by its close association with the rebel flag. An English professor questioned if those who waved the flag considered that however unintentional the racist implication, the action "hurts the recruitment of students, of athletes both black and white, and of faculty who, together, might make this an even greater university?"[55]

Other authors simply touted a progressive impulse to disregard the past in favor of the present and the future. As one editorialist wrote, "We must all work together for a brighter future. That may mean giving up time held traditions in the name of progress, but it must be done."[56] Finally, those who supported changes suggested that school symbols should represent all students, not create divisions among them. A Southern studies graduate student asserted that "all Mississippians should benefit equally, and that includes an equal sense of sharing in and belonging to the symbols of the institution."[57]

For proponents of the rebel flag, the charge of racism was too central to the issue to ignore. Several writers acknowledged the use of the flag by groups with a racist agenda but then asserted that such was not the intent of those who waved the emblem at Ole Miss. In 1983, the Associated Student Body passed a resolution approving retention of the university's Confederate symbols, stating, "All wrongful connotations and stigmas attached to this flag have been caused by racist organizations despised by all decent Southerners, regardless of their race, and . . . the Confederate flag is no more a symbol of racism than is the American flag which is carried around in marches by the KKK, Nazi Party, and Communist Party and flew for almost ninety years over a nation that allowed slavery."[58] Some flag supporters denied any personal responsibility for past injuries, such as one freshman in 1983: "I have never uprooted an African from his homeland. I have never stripped anyone of their culture, black or white. I have never chained anyone in the name of tradition or the great southern heritage. I did not pass the Jim Crow laws. And there's no one living today who did."[59]

A more common approach concentrated on the historical origins of the flag, rejecting the importance of slavery as a cause of the Civil War. One writer stated, "The War for Southern Independence was not an organized uprising to perpetuate racism. It represented many things to many people, among these, a striving for Southern nationhood, resistance against a brutal invading army, and an attempt to prevent the unwarranted growth of the federal government at the expense of the sovereign states."[60]

Several flag proponents described an expanded understanding of the flag's symbolic meaning, often using the term "heritage" to incorporate traditional southern values and culture: "When we think of the Confederate flag, we think of that wonderful place where you can still wave to your neighbor or a stranger as you pass them, where everyone can take the time to enjoy a sunny afternoon, and where everyone takes pride in their home and their heritage. That's what we think of, not slavery."[61] In this sense, the Confederate battle flag represented the South and everything positive that distinguished that region from all other locales.

A smaller number of flag supporters denied that the banner held any special associations other than that of school spirit and tradition. One student claimed, "It seems ignorant, even to the point of udder [sic] stupidity, that anyone would waste his/her valuable time complaining about how the confederate flag brings forth images of racism. The flag has no meaning what-so-ever, except for pride at Ole Miss."[62]

As advocates for change became increasingly successful in their removal of the university's Lost Cause symbols, proponents for the past began to articulate a minority rights defense. In 2014, for example, a Sons of Confederate Veterans attorney complained in an interview that in an effort to promote inclusivity the administration was ignoring "Mississippians that care about their Southern heritage. Why don't we get to figure into this diversity?"[63]

The very presence of a debate where none previously existed denotes an environment in flux. Sensing that the collapse of a segregated, Southern way of life had left previously unassailable symbols vulnerable, avid admirers of Confederate commemoration rushed to shore up the breaches. Meanwhile, opponents of these same symbols, perceiving the weakness of their adversaries, went on the offensive. This debate at the University of Mississippi that began in 1979 and continues into the twenty-first century constitutes the longest-running dialogue on Confederate symbols in the nation.

PERSISTENCE AND PROTESTS

Engaging in more than a mere war of words, both sides on the issue participated in public protests and demonstrations. This time, consistent with the urge to persuade, those attacking the rebel flag refrained from any physical desecration such as flag burnings, which would only incite or insult those whites who might possibly be convinced to acknowledge the justness of their cause. Instead, opponents to such symbols tended to utilize passive resistance tactics such as refusing to participate in school traditions that perpetuated references to the Confederacy.

In 1982, the university's first black cheerleader, John Hawkins, told *The New York Times* that he would not join the other cheerleaders in waving the rebel flag, stating, "While I'm an Ole Miss cheerleader, I'm still a black man. In my household, I wasn't told to hate the flag, but I did have history classes and know what my ancestors went through and what the Rebel flag represents."[64] That year was also the twentieth anniversary of the school's integration. During a speech at the commemorative ceremony, James Meredith asserted that "there is no difference between these symbols and the segregation signs of 20 years ago."[65] Soon afterwards, the Ku Klux Klan entered the picture, holding a "public awareness march" in Oxford to support the rebel flag.[66]

For several years, various members of the faculty and coaching staff had privately touted the need for change, complaining that the Confederate symbols damaged the institution's national image and inhibited recruitment of quality students, athletes, and faculty.[67] In March 1983, Chancellor Porter L. Fortune announced that he had asked several different advisory groups to consider discontinuing use of the flag and that he would respond with a decision in May.[68] Both sides of the debate sought to influence the outcome. The ASB passed a resolution that stated, "The Confederate flag, Colonel Rebel, and 'Dixie' remain our endeared traditions until the stones crumble from the buildings and Ole Miss is a mere whisper in history."[69] At a grassroots level, students conducted a petition to urge the chancellor not to abandon the flag.[70] On the opposing side, the BSU organized a demonstration where black students waved the red, green, and black flag of African nationalism and presented demands to the visiting governor and board of trustees president that included a request to remove all Confederate symbols.[71] Rumors that the BSU planned to burn copies of the yearbook that included photographs of the KKK march sparked a rally of fifteen hundred white students on April 18. Chanting "hell no, the flag won't go," protestors gathered in front of the main administrative building waving flags. The group eventually ended up at a black fraternity house shouting racial epithets until dispersing.[72]

On April 20, the chancellor announced a new policy restricting official representatives, such as cheerleaders and band members, from using unregistered symbols of the university, including the Confederate battle flag. To prevent infringement upon freedom of expression, fans would still be permitted to wave the emblem. He also directed the campus bookstore to stop selling rebel flags and merchandise depicting its image.[73] The Faculty Senate quickly passed resolutions supporting the decision. The mayor of Oxford and the current president of the Alumni Association concurred, although other alumni spoke out against the measure.[74] The BSU, too, complained that the chancellor had not gone far enough with regard to retaining the mascot and "Dixie."[75] Although the bookstore purchased red, white, and blue flags with "Ole Miss" printed on them, the new banners flopped, as became evident at the very first pep rally when spectators waved even greater numbers of rebel flags.[76] Chancellor Fortune retired that spring, and reflecting upon his tenure acknowledged the recent flag controversy as "one of the most emotional issues I have dealt with since I have been here," stating, "I think the major conflict has been resolved."[77]

But these expectations proved incorrect. In 1985, a *Daily Mississippian* article implied that Chancellor Gerald Turner had requested the band to play "Dixie" less often.[78] From this point on, the controversy surrounding Confederate symbols, commonly referred to as "the flag issue," reemerged on an annual basis—sometimes reignited by nothing more than the start of the football season. In 1989, the senior class sold a new flag based upon their own design. Named the "Battle M" in reference to its design of a large blue block "M" containing white stars that rested in the center of a red field, the seniors sold two thousand and the administration officially adopted the emblem.[79] Although seniors asserted that they offered the Battle M only as an alternative and not as a replacement for the rebel flag, the new standard faced some opposition.[80] However, it gradually joined the rebel flag as a much junior partner among the ranks of Ole Miss sports fans.

In 1991, both the Alumni Association and the Faculty Senate passed resolutions requesting fans not to bring rebel flags to university athletic events.[81] Perhaps bolstered by this support, the administration banned flags larger than twelve by eighteen inches, purportedly for safety and convenience reasons. Not surprisingly, loyal supporters of the Confederate flag believed themselves the target of the new ruling, and a student filed a complaint in court alleging that the university banned freedom of speech and expression.[82]

The "flag issue" expanded into demonstrations and boycotts in the spring of 1993 when four black members of the band silently protested "Dixie" by refusing to play the tune during basketball games.[83] The BSU exhibited support by wearing light blue ribbons and turning their backs to the court when the tune was played.[84] T-shirts appeared on campus reading, "Play Dixie, Damnit!" The ASB held a forum on the subject, and soon afterwards a twenty-two to eleven vote passed a resolution endorsing the band's continued use of the song "to instill honor, pride and the spirit of aggression in the hearts and minds of everyone who hears it."[85] The BSU responded with an eight-day boycott of food outlets on campus and encouraged individuals to show visible support by wearing black ribbons during a football weekend.[86] While the university administration actually possessed the authority to eliminate "Dixie" from the band's repertoire, they declined to take the step. Chancellor Turner told a campus reporter, "Until there's a call by alumni, faculty, staff and students that there should be a change, you continue on with what you have."[87]

In 1996, the university introduced a version of the Battle M that reversed the colors (red M on a blue field) and eliminated the stars.[88] The campus newspaper surmised that the similarity of the first Battle M to the Rebel flag when viewed at a distance on television prompted the alteration.[89] The following February, the BSU resurrected complaints against the campus

Confederate symbols, and Chancellor Khayat disclosed that he had hired an independent marketing firm to conduct an image review of Ole Miss. The announcement sparked a firestorm, since everyone implicitly understood that the university's symbols posed the major impediment to an improved national image.[90] Student and outside organizations protested this threat to campus traditions.[91] In the end, the image survey results proved anticlimactic, as the marketing firm had eliminated all questions mentioning the symbols purportedly to prevent bias. Of the 1,450 interviewed, only fifty-six voluntarily brought up the issue of symbols, leading the report to claim that "symbols have no significant impact on academic perception."[92] Chancellor Khayat stated that the popularity of symbols depended on students and alumni and that "we have symbols now that will go through an evolutionary process. It's in the hands of the community."[93]

In the fall of 1997, the head football coach publicly asked fans to leave their rebel flags at home.[94] Over the following weeks, momentum slowly built within the ASB to support the request and resulted in a resolution asking the administration to ban flag sticks from the stadium. The administration worked quickly to implement the measure.[95] Although a faithful contingent continued to wave rebel banners, the number of supporters shrunk. Gradually, the balance of opinion shifted against the use of the rebel flag as a university symbol.[96] In 2003, the university announced that it would no longer use Colonel Rebel as a mascot at sporting events. For several years, athletic events proceeded without a mascot until a multi-year, student-led initiative to find a replacement began in 2009. Rebel the Black Bear made its debut in 2011 after winning a poll of students, faculty, staff, alumni, and season ticket-holders.[97]

A year later, a racially charged political confrontation occurred between some students on the night of President Barack Obama's reelection. Exaggerated reports of rioting appeared on social media and in early mainstream news coverage. Later analysis by a columnist in the campus newspaper suggested that white protestors felt marginalized and wanted to defend a Confederate heritage whose symbols were slowly disappearing from campus.[98] This episode led the university's Sensitivity and Respect Committee to suggest twelve recommendations for improving the racial climate and inclusivity. Among the suggestions was a review of divisive campus symbols such as the Confederate monument, Dixie, and the Rebels name.[99] The university hired consultants, two of whom focused on issues related to symbols. In August 2014, Chancellor Dan Jones issued an action plan based upon their work that included the goal of "putting the past into context" without removing existing memorials or renaming structures.[100] Four months earlier, another incident had garnered national attention when a small group of students placed a noose and a Confederate flag on the campus civil rights memorial depicting James Meredith.[101]

In the wake of the tragic church killings in South Carolina that ignited a national conversation about the Confederate flag, Mississippi's state flag came under fire for its representation of the controversial emblem in the upper left corner. While the campus attempted to preserve civil discourse on the matter, hate groups showed up to sling racial slurs at an anti-flag rally.[102] In October 2015, Acting Chancellor Morris H. Stocks issued a statement with the support of the ASB and Faculty Senate announcing the removal of the banner, stating, "The University of Mississippi community came to the realization years ago that the confederate battle flag did not represent many of our core values such as civility and respect for others. Since that time, we have become a stronger and better university."[103] Proponents of the flag demonstrated their objections visually by wearing stickers and flying the banner on campus while tailgating.[104]

The debate over the Mississippi flag reignited objections to other symbols that remained on campus, including the Confederate statue. These issues also coincided with a national movement among colleges and universities to confront their institutional history of slavery and racism. In the process, administrators in higher education faced decisions on buildings named after now-disgraced donors and other offensive memorials. Among the options were removal or renaming. [105] The University of Mississippi largely opted to take the route of contextualization, which did neither.

In March 2016, Chancellor Jeffrey Vitter announced the installation of a plaque in front of the monument which would provide "context" through a brief recitation of its history. Developed by an appointed four-man committee, the text elicited protest from the university NAACP chapter because it failed to reference slavery as a cause of the Civil War. Others, including the history and English faculty, concurred and urged the chancellor to revise the plaque.[106] The history department held two forums on the issue, circulated a national petition, and produced a comprehensive report on the monument with suggestions for a revised plaque.[107] In June 2016, Vitter announced a new text for the marker that referenced slavery and stated,

"This historic statue is a reminder of the university's divisive past. Today the University of Mississippi draws from the past a continuing commitment to open its hallowed halls to all who seek truth, knowledge, and wisdom."[108] However, one proponent for the statue's removal complained about contextualization: "It pleases nostalgic fans of cherry-picked sanitized history and guilty white 'liberals' alike. The former remains satisfied with their symbols standing tall, while the latter seem content with a little paragraph to ease their guilt. . . . Some could argue that contextualization is a step in the right direction, that at least we're not letting divisive symbols stand unchallenged. But couldn't it be that contextualization is just a way to legitimize and preserve those same symbols?"[109] In the fall of 2016, Vitter charged the fourteen members of the newly established Chancellor's Advisory Committee on History and Context (CACHC) to seek community input while using their professional expertise to recommend further sites for contextualization.[110] He made it clear that the university "will continue to use the terms Ole Miss and Rebels as endearing nicknames for the university," claiming that the former was a positive brand with widespread national recognition and the latter has evolved "to indicate someone who bucks the status quo, an entrepreneur, a trendsetter, a leader." [111] Meanwhile, the athletic director announced at the start of the 2016–17 football season that "Dixie" would no longer be part of the university's sporting events.[112] Among the sites CACHC eventually suggested for an explanatory plaque in their June 2017 report was the stained glass window in Ventress Hall. The committee also proposed that the university place headstones in the Confederate Cemetery as well as a memorial recognizing the service of US Colored Troops from northern Mississippi in the Civil War.[113] Meanwhile, reappraisal of the institution's Confederate legacy continues.

CONCLUSION

In 1964, George B. Tindall suggested that southern mythology was a field ripe for exploration, since "a myth itself becomes one of the realities of history, significantly influencing the course of human action, for good or ill."[114] The first generation of historians in the 1970s and 1980s to examine the Lost Cause concentrated on the creation of Confederate memorial efforts, never expanding their analysis much beyond World War I.[115] Citing a variety of indicators that range from veterans' mortality rates to national reconciliation, these historians assumed that the Lost Cause became increasingly irrelevant in southern society. Yet veteran organizations and their auxiliaries had put a tremendous effort into constructing a historical interpretation that would vindicate their actions to future generations. Clearly, the use of Confederate symbols and rhetoric by segregationists rallying support against civil rights during the mid-twentieth century and the national debates and protests surrounding the battle flag and monuments of more recent decades indicate that the Lost Cause had established a strong foothold in southern memory. By the 1990s, historians began to consider how Confederate commemoration continued into the twentieth century and the impact these accumulated historical endeavors had on the region.[116]

The University of Mississippi's relationship with the Lost Cause is, in one sense, a microcosm of the South in general. Prolonged identification with the Confederacy and its symbols makes the institution a prism for concentrated examination of the components. Initially, the campus became the venue for several traditional commemorative activities such as Decoration Day and physical memorials. By the mid-twentieth century, the institution adopted a number of emblems that tied it even closer to a Confederate past during a period when the civil rights movement began to challenge racial precepts. The events surrounding the university's integration highlight the strong allure and relevance this past held for contemporary participants. When African Americans began to acquire a presence on campus that extended beyond housekeeping and maintenance staff, public confrontations and discussion over Lost Cause symbols arose, analogous to similar disputes in the larger region as African Americans gained greater sociopolitical power.

And yet, the University of Mississippi is atypical. Since 1979, the campus community has participated in an extended debate over Confederate symbols and their place in contemporary society. This protracted conversation, as well as the accompanying protests, is in part reflective of an environment in a constant state of flux as students and even faculty and administrators cycle through the institution at a rate exceeding most non-university communities. Each generation reengaged with university traditions and emblems existing on campus at that time. Initial challenges focused on several symbols adopted in the mid-twentieth century with a prolific presence on campus—the flag, the song, and the mascot. The pace of change was slow, demonstrating the overwhelming strength of the opposition in both size and devotion to a Confederate legacy. In addition, the university administration during this period never attempted to eliminate more than a single contested symbol at a time. With a historical link to a number of Confederate tokens, the institution faced a lengthy discourse that also included natural ebbs and flows as issues faded to reignite at a later time.

Until the late 1990s, the student government's participation in the debates mirrored the sentiments of a white majority student population that objected to the elimination of Lost Cause symbols on campus. The 1997 vote by the ASB to endorse the stick ban at athletic events was the first of several occasions that had the organization demonstrating a generational shift in the attitudes of white southerners with regard to their Confederate past. However, adherents to these historical representations remain among a portion of the students, and off-campus groups such as the Ku Klux Klan and the Sons of Confederate Veterans continue to lodge protests in deeds and words. While the administration seeks to improve the national image of the university, it also wrestles with a need to retain the allegiance of older alumni with a traditional view of the past whose financial support is essential in augmenting the declining contributions of the state.

The university's current contested debate revolves around the presence and interpretation of physical manifestations on campus of the Confederacy. Echoing the national conversation, the primary focus is on the monument that occupies a prominent location in the landscape, although other subjects such as the stained glass memorial and the cemetery are under consideration as well. Given the institution's history, it would be disingenuous to assume that contextualization will prevent future challenges to these sites or that the terms "Rebels" and "Ole Miss" will not face further scrutiny and possible evolution.

Over the last thirty years, the University of Mississippi has acknowledged its historical legacy of racial intolerance. It has sought not just to transcend its past, but also to become a central forum for open dialogue on the subject of race relations. Confrontations over the university's Confederate symbols are part of this story as well . . . and should not be forgotten.

NOTES

1. Maud Morrow Brown, *The University Greys: Company A, Eleventh Mississippi Regiment, Army of Northern Virginia* (Richmond: Garrett and Massie, [1940]); Michael Alan Upton, "'Keeping the Faith with the University Greys': Ole Miss as lieu de memoire" (MA thesis, Univ. of Mississippi, 2002); and Steven H. Stubbs, *Duty-Honor-Valor: The Story of the Eleventh Mississippi Regiment* (Philadelphia, MS: Dancing Rabbit Press, 2000).

2. Jemmy Grant Johnson, "The University War Hospital," *Publications of the Mississippi Historical Society* 12 (1912): 94–106; R.W. Jones, "Confederate Cemeteries and Monuments in Mississippi, *Publications of the Mississippi Historical Society* 8 (1904): 87–119; and Manuscript "Partial List of Men Buried in University Cemetery" Univ. Small Manuscripts, Box 49, Folder 4, Archives and Special Collections, Univ. of Mississippi (hereafter the repository and institution cited as UM). A few Union soldiers from General Grant's occupation of the community ended up buried in a corner of the cemetery until the federal government eventually removed these Union bodies to the new Corinth National Cemetery. For the Dead House, see Gerald Walton Collection, Box 3, Folder 12, UM; and Buildings and Grounds Collection, Box 1, Folder "Dead House," UM.

3. For more detail on the university and Confederate commemoration up to 1962, see Upton, "Keeping the Faith." Sally Leigh McWhite, "Echoes of the Lost Cause: Civil War Reverberations in Mississippi, 1865–2001" (PhD diss., Univ. of Mississippi, 2003) contains several chapters offering a closer examination of the Lost Cause and the university between 1962 and 2001. See also scattered references to the university in John M. Coski, *The Confederate Battle Flag: America's Most Embattled Emblem* (Cambridge: Harvard Univ. Press, 2005). Recent scholarly works on the Lost Cause and other educational institutions include the following: Jon D. Bohland, "Look Away, Look Away, Look Away to Lexington: Struggles over Neo-Confederate Nationalism, Memory, and Masculinity in a Small Virginia Town," *Southeastern Geographer* 53, no. 3 (Fall 2013): 267–95; C. Richard King, "Preoccupations and Prejudices: Reflections on the Study of Sports Imagery," *Anthropologica; Waterloo* 46, no. 1 (2004): 29–36; Pamela H. Simpson, "The Great Lee Chapel Controversy and the 'Little Group of Willful Women' Who Saved the Shrine of the South," in *Monuments to the Lost Cause: Women, Art, and the Landscapes of Southern Memory*, ed. Cynthia Mills and Pamela H. Simpson (Knoxville: The Univ. of Tennessee Press, 2003), 84–99; Christopher C. Nehis, "Flag-Waving Wahoos: Confederate Symbols at the University of Virginia, 1941–51," *Virginia Magazine of History & Biography* 110, no. 4 (2002): 461–89; and Kathleen Riley, "The Long Shadow of the Confederacy in America's Schools: State-Sponsored Use of Confederate Symbols in the Wake of *Brown V. Board*," *William & Mary Bill of Rights Journal* 10, no. 2 (2002): 525–49.

4. Franklin E. Moak, *A History of the Alumni Association of the University of Mississippi 1852–1986* (University, MS: Alumni Association of the Univ. of Mississippi, 1986), 29–31.

5. "Decoration Day in Oxford," *Mississippi University Magazine* 2, no. 6 (May 1877): 182.

6. Jones, "Confederate Cemeteries," 97; manuscript by Mrs. T. O. Gilbert, "The Memorial Window to 'The University Grays,'" Univ. Small Manuscripts Box 49, Folder 12, UM; letter from Edward Colegate to John Wesley Johnson dated April 12, 1989, Chancellors Papers: Robert Burwell Fulton, Box 19, Folder 9, UM; *Mississippi University Magazine* 2 (May 1877): 184–85, 189; "An Appeal in Behalf of the University Grays," *Mississippi University*

Magazine 3 (December 1877): 52–53; *Mississippi University Magazine* 3 (June 1878): 255; Upton, "Keeping the Faith," 37–41.

7. The window is in the main stairwell of Ventress Hall, which currently houses the administrative offices of the School of Liberal Arts.

8. William W. White, "Mississippi Confederate Veterans in Public Office, 1875–1900," *Journal of Mississippi History* 20, no. 3 (July 1958): 147–55; William B. Hesseltine and Larry Gara, "Mississippi's Confederate Leaders after the War," *Journal of Mississippi History* 8, no. 2 (April 8, 1951): 88–100.

9. Manuscript "John W. Odom Award," Univ. Small Manuscripts, Box 47, Folder 23, UM; Letters from J.W. Odom to Robert B. Fulton dated February 23, 1906 and June 30, 1906, Chancellors Collection: Robert Burwell Fulton, Box 2, Folder 5, UM; Upton, "Keeping the Faith," 54–56.

10. Mississippi Division, United Daughters of the Confederacy Minutes (1900), 33. SCV dates and membership size are difficult to ascertain as the group failed to consistently publish centralized records. However, one report indicates the presence of a camp in Oxford by 1914. "List of S.C.V. Camps in Good Standing November 15, 1914," *Confederate Veteran* 23, no. 1 (January 1915): 37.

11. Emphasis added. Mississippi Division, United Daughters of the Confederacy Minutes (1906), 44; Mrs. N.D. Deupree, "Confederate Monument at Oxford, Miss.," *Confederate Veteran* 14, no. 7 (July 1906): 306–7.

12. "Dedication of the Monument to the Departed Confederate Soldiers," *Oxford Eagle* (Oxford, MS), May 17, 1906.

13. David Moore Robinson, "A Simonidean Epitaph at Mississippi," *Classical Bulletin* 27 (February 1951): 37–40.

14. J.L. Shinault, "Monument at Oxford, Miss.," *Confederate Veteran* 16, no. 2 (February 1908): 59.

15. Minutes of the Annual Convention of the Mississippi Division, United Daughters of the Confederacy (1908), 41; Johnson, "University War Hospital," 106.

16. See the following *Minutes of the Annual Convention of the Mississippi Division, United Daughters of the Confederacy*: (1901), 29; (1903), 36; (1905), 45; (1908), 41; (1937), 59; (1938), 67; (1939), 93–97. "Beautiful Arch Adorns Entrance to Old Cemetery," *Our Heritage* 17, no. 4 (December 1927): 4; and manuscript "Presentation of Monument, United Daughters of the Confederacy, May 1939," Univ. Small Manuscripts, Box 50, Folder 8, UM. Gerald Walton Collection, Box 3, Folder 6, UM.

17. *The Ole Miss* 39 (1935): 182; Univ. of Mississippi press release "Ole Miss Origin," dated October 39, 1947, Univ. Small Manuscripts, Box 25, Folder 8, UM. The staff dedicated the first yearbook to the University Greys. *The Ole Miss* 1 (1897): 7.

18. McWhite, "Echoes of the Lost Cause," 145–50.

19. "'Ole Miss Rebels'—It's Permanent," *Mississippian* (Univ. of Mississippi, hereafter location omitted), September 19, 1936; Upton, "Keeping the Faith," 64–65.

20. Upton, "Keeping the Faith," 66–69.

21. Dean DuBois, "Fifty-five Ole Miss Students Attend States' Rights Meeting," *Mississippian*, July 22, 1948. See also Richard C. Etheridge, "Mississippi's Role in the Dixiecrat Movement" (MA thesis, Mississippi State Univ., 1971); Richard D. Chesteen,

"'Mississippi Is Gone Home!': A Study of the 1948 Mississippi State's Rights Bolt," *Journal of Mississippi History* 32, no. 1 (February 1970): 43–59.

22. While cognizant that correct terminology for the flag discussed in this article is "Confederate battle flag," the university community and sports fans will often use the phrase "rebel flag" or "Confederate flag" and the text of this chapter reflects this popular nomenclature.

23. Upton, "Keeping the Faith," 82–85.

24. "Proclamation of Secession," *Mississippi Hi Ya'll* (Univ. of Mississippi), November 26, 1958, Vertical Files Folder: "University—Dixie Week," UM.

25. Upton, "Keeping the Faith," 86–91.

26. Arthur Kreutz, *University Greys* (New York: Independent Music Publishers, 1954). Programs, correspondence, and clippings in Arthur Kreutz Collection, Box 10, Folder 11, UM.

27. Arthur Kreutz, *The University Greys: An Opera in 2 Acts* (New York: Ricordi, 1961).

28. Robert J. Cook, *Troubled Commemoration: The American Civil War Centennial* (Baton Rouge: Louisiana State Univ. Press, 2007).

29. McWhite, "Echoes of the Lost Cause," 188–90. See also Alyssa D. Warrick, "'Mississippi's Greatest Hour': The Mississippi Civil War Centennial and Southern Resistance," *Southern Cultures* 19, no. 3 (2013): 95–112.

30. Material in Civil War Centennial Collection, Box 1, UM.

31. The Civil War references during this civil rights episode are explored at greater length in McWhite, "Echoes of the Lost Cause," 239–76.

32. Ross R. Barnett, "Mississippi Still Says 'Never!' and 'Victory at Oxford: An Official Expression of Opinion by the Citizens' Council Concerning the Old Miss Invasion" (Jackson, MS: Citizens' Council, c. 1962), 1–2, 4.

33. Walter Lord, *The Past that Would Not Die* (New York: Harper & Row, 1965), 156. Other accounts of the episode appear in Russell H. Barrett, *Integration at Ole Miss* (Quadrangle Books, 1965), 106; Michael Dorman, *We Shall Overcome: A Reporter's Eyewitness Account of the Year of Racial Strife and Triumph* (New York: Dial Press, 1964), 14; "To Ole Miss Students," *Mississippian* (September 21, 1962): 1.

34. William B. Street, "Meredith Walks Aisle of Jeers," *Commercial Appeal* (Memphis, TN), September 26, 1962.

35. Lord, *The Past that Would Not Die*, 167, 174–75.

36. Claude Sitton described the crisis as "the most serious clash between state and Federal authority in a century" in "Meredith Rebuffed Again Despite Restraining Order," *The New York Times*, September 26, 1962.

37. Lord, *The Past that Would Not Die*, 191; Curtis Wilkie, *Dixie: A Personal Odyssey through Events that Shaped the Modern South* (New York: Scribner, 2001), 103–4.

38. For mention of the Confederate uniforms, see Lord, *The Past that Would Not Die*, 202; Barrett, *Integration*, 139; and letter dated October 2, 1962 from [James Silver] to Betty Silver, James Silver Collection, Box 7, Folder 3, UM. Lord also comments on the bugle.

39. Lord, *The Past that Would Not Die*, 202.

40. Nadine Cohodas, *The Band Played Dixie: Race and the Liberal Conscience at Ole Miss* (New York: Free Press, 1997), 86–87; Lord, *The Past that Would Not Die*, 197–231; Russell

H. Barrett, *Integration at Ole Miss* (Quadrangle Books, 1965), 144–62; William Doyle, *An American Insurrection: James Meredith and the Battle of Oxford, Mississippi, 1962* (New York: Anchor Books, 2003), 131–255; and Charles W. Eagles, *The Price of Defiance: James Meredith and the Integration of Ole Miss* (Chapel Hill: Univ. of North Carolina Press, 2009), 340–70.

41. Cohodas, *The Band Played Dixie*, 103–4; James W. Silver, *Mississippi: The Closed Society* (New York: Harcourt, Brace & World, 1964), 222–27; "Obscene and Indecent," *Time* 81, no. 16 (April 19, 1963): 76–77; James M. Ward, "Objectionable Painter and 'Art,'" *Jackson Daily News* (Jackson, MS), April 11, 1963; clipping "Charge Is Filed: Statements Issued in Removal of Art," James W. Silver Collection, Box 2, Folder 6, UM. The University of Mississippi possesses one of Kerciu's controversial paintings entitled "Ignore the Nigger . . ." in its University Museums holdings. J. Adrian Fox, "Political University Art Collection Stirs Debate," *Daily Mississippian*, February 5, 1987.

42. Lynn Watkins, "Ole Miss Alumni Reflect on a Historic Day at School," *Clarion Ledger* (Jackson, MS), September 20, 1979.

43. Manuscript by John O. Leslie, "Inspiration to Achieve," dated September 30, 1982, Verner Holmes Collection, Box 4, Folder 6, UM.

44. Willie Morris, "At Ole Miss," *Time* 120, no. 14 (October 4, 1982): 8. Constance Baker Motley, James Meredith's attorney, also used the phrase "last battle of the Civil War" in her memoir *Equal Justice—Under Law: An Autobiography* (New York: Farrar, Straus and Giroux, 1998), 191.

45. James Meredith, *Three Years in Mississippi* (Bloomington: Indiana Univ. Press, 1966), 283. Meredith apparently did not notice nor care to remark upon the small monument that the local UDC chapter had erected in 1939.

46. Minnie Holt Smith, *Oxford, Mississippi* (n.p., 1935), 26; Johnson, "The University War Hospital," 106. Johnson dated the "clean up" incident during the employment of Dr. M.W. Phillips as proctor of the university, which narrows the episode to 1876–1880. The fact that more permanent stone markers had yet to replace the temporary wooden ones would have facilitated the ease with which the groundskeepers "tidied" the cemetery. Another possible attack on symbols might have occurred in 1954 when unknown vandals smeared tar on the Confederate monument at the Greenwood, Mississippi courthouse. For further discussion, see McWhite, "Echoes of the Lost Cause," 278–79.

47. Tin Kriehn, "Tensions Flair, Blacks Protest," *Daily Mississippian*, February 25, 1970. The first documented Confederate flag burning in the state occurred on June 26, 1966 when a member of the Student Nonviolent Coordinating Committee torched one during the March against Fear (or Meredith March) at the capitol in Jackson. Gene Roberts, "Meredith Hailed at Rally at Mississippi's Capitol," *The New York Times*, June 27, 1966.

48. Tim Kriehn, "Forty-Nine Blacks Arrested," *Daily Mississippian*, February 26, 1970, 1.

49. "The Black Demands," *Daily Mississippian*, March 6, 1970.

50. "Racial Flare-ups See Charges Filed," *Daily Mississippian*, April 29, 1970; "Students Protest Incidents Minor," *Daily Mississippian*, May 1, 1970. Michael Welch describes flag desecrations of the 1960s and 1970s as part of the era's social movement of protest in *Flag Burning: Moral Panic and the Criminalization of Protest* (New York: Aldine de Gruyter, 2000), 47–52.

51. Untitled publication by black students at the University of Mississippi in 1970, Race Relations Collection, Box 1, Folder 18, UM. See also Donald Cunnigen, "Malcom X's

Influence on the Black Nationalist Movement of Southern College States," *Western Journal of Black Studies* 17, no. 1 (Spring 1993): 32–43. Reactions to the flag burnings included the following letters to the editor of the campus newspaper that vilified and supported the protests; a student government resolution condemning the actions; and a campus security announcement that the Mississippi statute prohibiting abuse of American, state, or Confederate flags would be enforced in the future. McWhite, "Echoes of the Lost Cause," 302–4.

52. For more extensive examination of the campus Confederate symbol debate and protests, see McWhite, "Echoes of the Lost Cause," 307–43.

53. Ricky Baldwin, "Dixie Symbol of 'Abominable' Ideology," *Daily Mississippian*, April 16, 1993.

54. Charles Brown, [Letter to the Editor], *Daily Mississippian*, February 17, 1997.

55. Amanda Byrd, "Ignorance Hurts UM," *Daily Mississippian*, October 21, 1997.

56. Patrick Hopkins and Perry Stevens, "Flag Issue—History; No Kudos for Column," *Daily Mississippian*, September 4, 1985.

57. Charlene E. Dye, "Letters to the Editor," *Daily Mississippian*, March 26, 1997.

58. "ASB Flag Bill," *Daily Mississippian*, April 12, 1983.

59. David Powell, "Students Comment," *Daily Mississippian*, April 18, 1983.

60. Danny Toma, "Letters to the Editor," *Daily Mississippian*, September 12, 1983.

61. Jason S. Comfort, "Letters to the Editor," *Daily Mississippian*, September 8, 1994.

62. Michael Kennedy, "Letters to the Editor," *Daily Mississippian*, November 4, 1991.

63. Lacey Russe, "Sons of Confederate Veterans Files Petition against UM," *Daily Mississippian*, September 30, 2014.

64. Wendell Rawls, "Black Cheerleader Balks at Waving Rebel Banner," *The New York Times*, September 4, 1982; Kitty Dumas, "Hawkins Responds to Press," *Daily Mississippian*, September 2, 1982; Stephanie Hall, "Spragin Says Idea for Flag Not Viable," *Daily Mississippian*, September 13, 1982; and Kate McGandy, "Hawkins Carries His Own Flag at Game," *Daily Mississippian*, September 21, 1982.

65. James H. Meredith, manuscript "Speech for the University of Mississippi—30 September 1982," Chancellors Collection: Porter Fortune, Box 155, Folder "Meredith Admission—20th Anniversary," UM; and Stephanie Hall, "Meredith Talk Sparks Praise and Criticism," *Daily Mississippian*, October 1, 1982.

66. Associated Press, "KKK Rally Allowed in Oxford on Oct. 23," *Daily Mississippian*, October 14, 1982; Diane Rado, "Anger Vented over Permission for Klan Flag March," *Commercial Appeal* (Memphis, TN), October 15, 1982; Lee Freeland, "Klan Rally: Leader Says Flag Key Issue," *Daily Mississippian*, October 19, 1982; "Ole Miss, City, Klan Concerned by March," *Commercial Appeal* (Memphis, TN), October 23, 1982; Mary Ann Connell, *An Unforeseen Life: A Memoir* (Oxford, MS: Nautilus Publishing Company, 2017), 153–55; Patti Patterson, "Klan Demonstrates Calm," *Daily Mississippian*, October 25, 1982; Glenn Montgomery and Lee Freeland, "Ku Klux Klan Attracts Curiosity, Protests," *Daily Mississippian*, October 25, 1982; and Samuel Prestridge, "Notes from the Laughing Factory," in *Mississippi Writers: Reflections of Childhood and Youth*, ed. Dorothy Abbott, vol. 2 (Jackson: Univ. Press of Mississippi, 1986), 522–31.

67. For example, see letter from James D. Minor and Ardessa H. Minor to Dr. Porter L. Fortune dated October 27, 1982, Chancellor Collection: Porter L. Fortune, Box 145, Folder "Student Activities for Minority Affairs," UM.

68. Lee Freeland, "Fortune Considers Issue: May Flag Decision," *Daily Mississippian*, March 9, 1982.

69. Terry R. Cassreino, "State Flag Bill Is Defeated in Senate," *Daily Mississippian*, April 13, 1982.

70. Lee Freeland, "Save the Flag," *Daily Mississippian*, April 11, 1983; Terry R. Cassreino, "Flag Stirs Petitions," *Daily Mississippian*, April 12, 1983; and Dan Turner, "3,000 Sign Petitions: Support Increasing," *Daily Mississippian*, April 15, 1983.

71. Lee Freeland, "Officials Hear Black Demands," *Daily Mississippian*, April 18, 1983.

72. "Rumors Stir Protest," *Daily Mississippian*, April 19, 1983.

73. Dan Turner, "Rebel Flag: Half-Mast," *Daily Mississippian*, April 21, 1983. See also, "Chancellor's Statement to the Press, April 20, 1983," and "Chancellor's Response to Issues Raised by the Black Student Union April, 1983," *The Monday Report* in George Street Collection, Accretion 95–34, Box 19, Folders "UM v. MS," UM; Connell, *An Unforeseen Life*, 159–60.

74. "Reaction," *Daily Mississippian*, April 21, 1983; and "Resolution, Faculty Senate," *Daily Mississippian*, April 25, 1983.

75. Clara Bibbs and Terry R. Cassreino, "Spragin Says 'Not Enough,'" *Daily Mississippian*, April 21, 1983; and Mary Nettleton, "Flag Verdict Rejected," *Daily Mississippian*, April 22, 1983.

76. Marry Nettleton, "Bookstore Selling New Flags," *Daily Mississippian*, April 24, 1983; flag photograph, *Daily Mississippian*, April 24, 1983; and Lynda Tullos, "Reb Flags Wave at Pep Rally," *Daily Mississippian*, September 2, 1983.

77. Susan Teasley, "Fortune Reflects on Ole Miss Years, *Daily Mississippian*, September 7, 1983.

78. Todd Fullam, "Look Away . . . Look Away, Dixieland . . . : Critics Object to Playing 'Dixie' a Lot," *Daily Mississippian*, September 18, 1985.

79. Amy Vincent, "Senior Class Raises $2,200 Selling Flag in Grove," *Daily Mississippian*, October 20, 1989; Bob Yarbrough, "Battle M May Become Official Flag," *Daily Mississippian*, December 5, 1989; and Christina Cannon, "M-Flag, Rebel Flag Controversy Continues," *Daily Mississippian*, October 19, 1990.

80. Christine Cannon, "M-Flag, Rebel Flag, Controversy Continues," *Daily Mississippian*, October 19, 1990.

81. Associated Press, "Alumni Association Supports Flag Ban," *Daily Mississippian*, May 1, 1991; and Olen Anderson, "Faculty Senate Passes Rebel Flag Resolution," *Daily Mississippian*, June 17, 1991.

82. Associated Press, "New Flag Ruling Angers Some," *Daily Mississippian*, September 19, 1991.

83. Nicole V. House and Stephen Rosamond, "Band Members Protest Playing Dixie," *Daily Mississippian*, February 25, 1993. See also Douglas Lederman, "Old Times Not Forgotten: A Battle over Symbols Obscures U. of Mississippi's Racial Changes," *Chronicle*

of Higher Education 40, no. 9 (October 20, 1993): A51–A52; Marilyn M. Thomas-Houston, "Stoney the Road: A Look at Political Participation in an African American Community" (PhD diss., New York Univ., 1997), 116–18.

84. Stephen Rosamond, "Black Student Union Backs Protesters," *Daily Mississippian*, March 4, 1993.

85. Chris Allen Baker, "ASB Senate Passes 'Dixie' Resolution," *Daily Mississippian*, April 7, 1993.

86. Larue Roberts, "Black Student Union Considers Boycott," *Daily Mississippian*, April 8, 1993; and Michael Saunte McLendon, "BSU Extends Food Services Boycott," *Daily Mississippian*, April 20, 1993.

87. Chris Allen Baker, "BSU Plans Protest at Red-Blue Weekend," *Daily Mississippian*, April 23, 1993.

88. Amanda Byrd, "New M-Flag Introduction Is Set for This Saturday," *Daily Mississippian*, September 6, 1996.

89. Melanie Simpson, "The New Flag," *Daily Mississippian*, September 10, 1996.

90. Jenny Dodson, "Several University Symbols up for Image Review," *Daily Mississippian*, February 27, 1997; and Robert Khayat, *The Education of a Lifetime* (Oxford, MS: Nautilus Publishing Company, 2013), 11–12, 153–75.

91. Connell, *An Unforeseen Life*, 240–41.

92. Jenny Dodson, "Khayat Symbols Expected to 'Evolve' over Time," *Daily Mississippian*, July 18, 1997.

93. Dodson, "Khayat Symbols," July 18, 1997.

94. Tommy Tuberville, "Making a Decision," *Daily Mississippian*, September 26, 1997.

95. Allison Pruitt, "Senator Pleads for ASB to Take Action on Flag," *Daily Mississippian*, October 8, 1997; "ASB Resolution 97–17," *Daily Mississippian*, October 16, 1997; Jenny Dodson, "ASB Senate to Vote on Banning Sticks from Games," *Daily Mississippian*, October 16, 1997; Jenny Dodson, "Senators Renege on Banning Sticks from Vaught," *Daily Mississippian*, October 17, 1997; *Daily Mississippian* staff, "Nix the Sticks," *Daily Mississippian*, October 17, 1997; "Revised ASB Resolution," *Daily Mississippian*, October 17, 1997; Jenny Dodson, "Separate ASB Resolution Asks to Keep Sticks out of Stadium," *Daily Mississippian*, October 21, 1997; Jenny Dodson, "Students Take Stand Against Flag," *Daily Mississippian*, October 22, 1997; and Khayat, *The Education of a Lifetime*, 199–200.

96. Connell, *An Unforeseen Life*, 240–41; and Khayat, *The Education of a Lifetime*, 215–17.

97. Leah Cayson, "Ole Miss Fans' Reception of Rebel Black Bear Mixed," *Daily Mississippian*, September 11, 2011. Despite winning the poll, the bear never became a popular mascot. In 2017, the university replaced it with the landshark. Slade Rand, "Chancellor Announces Plan for Official Mascot Switch," *Daily Mississippian*, October 9, 2017.

98. Meghan Holmes, "Our Campus and Its Symbols," *Daily Mississippian*, November 14, 2012. Civil War references by university students also occurred on social media following Obama's election in 2008. Leslie Banahan and K.B. Melear, "The University of Mississippi Incident Review Committee Public Report," January 25, 2013, 7, History Department, Univ. of Mississippi, history.olemiss.edu/wp-content/uploads/sites/6/2016/07/IRCPublic Report-Jan252013.pdf.

99. "The University of Mississippi Report, Findings and Recommendations of the Extended Sensitivity and Respect Committee," 2013, 11, History Department, Univ. of Mississippi, history/olemiss.edu/wp-content/uploads/sites/6/2016/07/SR-Committee -Report-and-Response.pdf; and Hawley Martin, "Racial Climate Report Released," *Daily Mississippian*, October 9, 2013.

100. However, the university did rename the street "Confederate Drive" to "Chapel Lane." Dan Jones, "Action Plan on Consultant Reports and Update on the Work of the Sensitivity and Respect Committee," August 1, 2014, Office of the Chancellor, Univ. of Mississippi, chancellor.wp.olemiss.edu/wp-content/uploads/sites/17/2013/08/2014 -ActionPlanonConsultantReportandUpdateontheWorkoftheSensitivityandRespect Committee/pdf.

101. Adam Ganucheau, "UPD Investigating Discovery of Noose and Flag on Meredith Statue," *Daily Mississippian*, February 18, 2013.

102. Logan Kirkland, "Tensions Build after Protest, Rally on Friday," *Daily Mississippian*, October 19, 2015.

103. "UM Takes down State Flag," October 26, 2015, Univ. of Mississippi, https://news .olemiss.edu/um-takes-state-flag/; Lana Ferguson, "Faculty Senate to Discuss State Flag," *Daily Mississippian*, October 22, 2015; and Lana Ferguson, "Faculty Senate Adopts Resolution 41–1," *Daily Mississippian*, October 23, 2015.

104. Francisco Hernandez, "Don't Let Tailgating Become a Confederate Monument," *Daily Mississippian*, September 8, 2017; and Clara Turnage, "Confederate Symbols Conversation Comes to the Grove," *Daily Mississippian*, October 12, 2015.

105. Marc Parry, "Stained by Slavery," *Chronicle of Higher Education* 63, no. 27 (March 10, 2017): B6–B9; Lawrence Biemiller, "Reckoning with History," *Chronicle of Higher Education* 63, no. 26 (March 3, 2017): B32–B34; and Peter A. Galuszka, "Shadows of the Past," *Chronicle of Higher Education, Supplement Convergence Diversity & Inclusion* 62 (March 18, 2016): 10–15. While the University of Mississippi had several decades of experience acknowledging its experience with discrimination, links with slavery had gone largely unexplored. The effort at the University of Mississippi began in 2014 with the creation of a campus-wide "Reading Group on Slavery and the University" and a speaking invitation to Craig Steven Wilder, author of *Ebony and Ivy: Race, Slavery, and the Troubled History of America's Universities*. Later that year, the University of Mississippi Slavery Research Group (UMSRG) organized with administrative support to examine the institution's history with slavery through research, instruction, and community outreach. "UMSRG History, 2013–2016," Univ. of Mississippi Slavery Research Group, http://slaveryresearchgroup. olemiss.edu/history/. One member of UMSRG, Jeff Jackson, has conducted research on the slaveholding status of the University Greys and shared the results. Allen Coon, "The University Greys: Students, Soldiers, and Slaveholders," *Daily Mississippian*, October 20, 2017.

106. "UM Begins Installing Plaque Offering Context for Confederate Statue," March 11, 2016, Univ. of Mississippi, https://olemiss.edu/um-begins-installing-plaque-offering -context-confederate-statue/; Lana Ferguson, "Contextual Plaque Faces Criticism," *Daily Mississippian*, March 21, 2016; "University of Mississippi History Faculty Statement," *Daily Mississippian*, April 4, 2016; and "Statement from Members of the University of Mississippi

Department of English on the Plaque Recently Installed in Front of the Confederate Memorial on Campus," *Daily Mississippian*, April 7, 2016.

107. An overview of these efforts as well as links to further documents are available on the University of Mississippi History Department website, "History & Context at UM," at http://history.olemiss.edu/history-context-at-um/.

108. Lyndy Berryhill, "Oxford Reacts to Updated Confederate Memorial Plaque Language," *Daily Mississippian*, June 16, 2016. The university installed the revised marker in October 2017.

109. Francisco Hernandez, "Why Contextualization Doesn't Work," *Daily Mississippian*, October 30, 2017.

110. "History, Context, Identity," June 10, 2016, Office of the Chancellor, Univ. of Mississippi, http://chancellor.olemiss.edu/history-context-identity/; and "Charge to CACHC," August 16, 2016, Office of the Chancellor, Univ. of Mississippi, http://chancellor .olemiss.edu/charge-to-cachc/.

111. "History, Context, Identity," June 10, 2016, Office of the Chancellor, Univ. of Mississippi, http://chancellor.olemiss.edu/history-context-identity/; and "Charge to CACHC," August 16, 2016, Office of the Chancellor, Univ. of Mississippi, http://chancellor .olemiss.edu/charge-to-cachc/.

112. Morgan Walker, "UM Reacts to Removal of 'Dixie' from Sporting Events," *Daily Mississippian*, August 2016.

113. "Final Report Chancellor's Advisory Committee on History and Contextualization," June 16, 2017, Univ. of Mississippi, context.olemiss.edu/wp-content /uploads/sites/89/2017/07/ChancellorAdvisoryCommitteeFinalReport.pdf; "Chancellor's Advisory Committee on History and Context Final Report," July 6, 2017, Office of the Chancellor, Univ. of Mississippi, http://chancellor.olemiss.edu/chancellors-advisory -committee-on-history-and-context-final-report/.

114. George B. Tindall, "Mythology: A New Frontier in Southern History," in *The Idea of the South: Pursuit of a Central Theme*, ed. Frank E. Vandiver (Chicago: Univ. of Chicago Press, 1964), 2.

115. C. Vann Woodward first applied the phrase "the Lost Cause" to postbellum Confederate commemorative activities that he briefly described in *Origins of the New South, 1877–1913* (Baton Rouge: Louisiana State Univ. Press, 1951), 155–57. The primary works in the 1970s and 1980s providing general overviews of the Lost Cause include Susan Speare Durant, "The Gently Furled Banner: The Development of the Myth of the Lost Cause" (PhD diss., Univ. of North Carolina, 1972); Rollin G. Osterweis, *The Myth of the Lost Cause, 1865–1900* (Hamden, CN: Archon Books, 1973); Lloyd Arthur Hunter, "The Sacred South: Postwar Confederates and the Sacralization of Southern Culture" (PhD diss., St. Louis Univ., 1978); Charles Reagan Wilson, *Baptized in Blood: The Religion of the Lost Cause, 1865–1920* (Athens: Univ. of Georgia Press, 1980); and Gaines M. Foster, *Ghosts of the Confederacy: Defeat, the Lost Cause, and the Emergence of the New South, 1865–1913* (New York: Oxford Univ. Press, 1987).

116. For examples of recent literature, see David W. Blight, *American Oracle: The Civil War in the Civil Rights Era* (Cambridge: Harvard Univ. Press, 2011); Coski, *The Confederate*

Battle Flag; W. Fitzhugh Brundage, *The Southern Past: A Clash of Race and Memory* (Cambridge: Harvard Univ. Press, 2005); K. Michael Prince, *Rally 'Round the Flag, Boys!: South Carolina and the Confederate Flag* (Columbia: Univ. of South Carolina Press, 2004); J. Michael Martinez, William D. Richardson, and Ron McNinch-Su, eds., *Confederate Symbols in the Contemporary South* (Gainesville: Univ. Press of Florida, 2000). Most recently, historians have engaged the general public during the national debate on Confederate monuments. "Historians on the Confederate Monument Debate," American Historical Association, https://www .historians.org/news-and-advocacy/everything-has-a-history/historians-on-the-confederate -monument-debate.

Subverting the Myth: Lost Cause Gender and the Cold War

ALAN SCOT WILLIS

The Lost Cause echoed across the Cold War South, its message firmly enshrined in stone and bronze throughout the region. Victory in the Good War and the South's participation in the postwar economic boom changed the South dramatically, but the Lost Cause proved a malleable myth. The rhetoric once fired against the ignoble North was now aimed at atheistic Communists and outside agitators. The South found no shortage of threats to its identity and culture, and the Lost Cause provided a comfortable myth despite its increasingly uneasy fit with the realities of Southern society. In its rhetoric and rituals, the Lost Cause cemented Southern ideals of masculinity and femininity that formed the bedrocks of faith and family, ideals which shaped the Southern religious response to the challenges of the Cold War at the same time that the Southern response to those challenges undermined the myth itself.

Charles Reagan Wilson provided the touchstone text for studying the Lost Cause in *Baptized in Blood: The Religion of the Lost Cause, 1865–1920*. Numerous scholars have followed Wilson's pathbreaking analysis, but none wove gender into their analysis so much as David Goldfield in *Still Fighting the Civil War*. Central to Goldfield's analysis is the idea that "Southern white men could not live with failure and dishonor, so they manufactured a past that obviated both and returned their pride, dignity, and above all their control." White men's control of their society extended not only to blacks but also to white women. In the Cold War, that control meshed with the need to contain Communism, both at home and abroad; indeed, traditional gender roles would serve to contain in the home. Yet, as Goldfield shows, certain aspects of the Lost Cause, particularly the forming of women's memorial societies and the United Daughters of the Confederacy, spurred an increase in women's organizing and public activism that, eventually, served to undermine traditional gender roles and men's control.[1] Perhaps ironically, the leadership of the South's dominant religious and cultural organization—the Southern Baptist Convention—similarly aided the undermining of the gendered Lost Cause.

MANLINESS AND THE LOST CAUSE

The Lost Cause, Wilson argued, provided a response to Northern insults, a critique of a corrupt and materialist New South, and a promise of redemption if the youth of the South emulated the virtues of the Confederate generation. Each aspect was thoroughly gendered. Boys would emulate the martial spirit of the virtuous Christian warrior and girls the sacrifice of luxury while honoring the men who had fought to defend their homes and families. Girls would follow their mothers in honoring the dead through Confederate Memorial Day services and preserving the Lost Cause through the education of the South's youth. As a closed system, the Lost Cause offered a Southern myth of the "noble knight fighting for the sexual purity of fair damsels" and created the blueprint for refined Southern white masculinity and femininity.[2]

Stonewall Jackson provided the cornerstone for martial masculinity and the "myth of the Crusading Christian Confederate." As Wilson noted, "To Southern ministers, Stonewall Jackson was like a stern Old Testament prophet-warrior."[3] Other scholars have agreed with Wilson's interpretation. In *Enduring Legacy* W. Stuart Towns cited Moses Drury Hodge's oration at the dedication of the Jackson memorial in Richmond when he told the crowd that people could hardly think of Jackson without "associating the prowess of the general with the piety of the man," making Jackson a "soldier of the cross."[4] Christopher Lawton provides a more complicated picture of Jackson's religious life, noting that he had little interest in religion prior to the Mexico campaign in 1848 but by the Civil War piety had become one of Jackson's defining characteristics.[5] Lawton points to the effort of Jackson's nineteenth-century biographer-mythmakers in highlighting his inauspicious beginnings, helping to make the demigod "Stonewall Jackson" of the Lost Cause into an everyman of humble origins.

Jackson became—and remains—one the touchstones of the Lost Cause devotion to the Christian warrior. Undoubtedly, some of this resulted from nineteenth-century efforts. For example, Mary L. Williamson intended her

1899 biography, *The Life of Thomas J. Jackson ('Stonewall') in Easy Words for the Young*, to inspire young readers with Jackson's Christian virtues and military genius. As Gary W. Gallagher pointed out, modern artwork far outpaces the art of the late nineteenth century in showing the religious devotion of Confederate leaders, and art depicting Jackson leads all Confederate themed artwork in sales by a wide margin.[6]

Heroism spread beyond the ranks of the General Corps. The common soldiers were, in Edward Crowther's phrase, transformed into "knights errant."[7] As Towns notes, "Many of the orators of the Lost Cause devoted their speeches not to the Lees and the Jacksons but to the private soldier, whose praise they lifted to the heavens. Always, the soldiers fought against overwhelming odds and their heroism would live forever in the hearts and minds of liberty-loving people everywhere."[8]

Indeed, it was those overwhelming odds, the manpower and machinery of the materially rich North, that lie at the heart of the Southern defeat on the battlefield. The South may have lost, but no one doubted that the Confederates had been the "better men" on the battlefield. That idea, according to James Cobb, began with Edward Pollard's first writings of the Lost Cause barely a year after the war had ended. The myth was clear: Southern soldiers had suffered, but the North had plentiful, even luxuriant, supplies. Northern men "were coarse and inferior in comparison with the aristocracy and chivalry of the South."[9] In *The Culture of Defeat*, Wolfgang Schivelbusch cast the Lost Cause in the context of two other defeats: France after the Franco-Prussian War and Germany after World War I. In each case, Schivelbusch claims, the defeated held up their men as the better soldiers who would have won in a "fair fight." The enemy won not only because of sheer numerical superiority and the exhaustion of the defeated, but also because they refused to fight honorably.[10] At the outset of the Civil War, Schivelbusch argues, defeat at the hands of the North had been incomprehensible given Southern martial superiority. After the war, Southerners convinced themselves that they had exhausted their resources in their victories only to succumb to a "reprehensible perversion" of total-war tactics that "compensated for the weakness of a mercantilist culture incapable of fighting a true soldierly war."[11] The North, it might be said, had fought as a military machine, not as *men*.

The ideas of "better men" and of the Christian soldier's fighting for right above might provided the foundation of Southern masculinity and a model for Southern youth to emulate. It created a mythic past that could be mobilized against any threat to Southern mores or identity which was preserved through a variety of institutions, including Southern military academies. Rod Andrew's examination of the Southern military academies in *Long Grey Lines* follows Wilson with a clear delineation of how the martial and Christian merged into a particular Southern masculinity. For Andrew, the military colleges tempered the Southern propensity toward violent masculinity by providing it with the discipline of soldiering and balancing it with evangelical morality. As Andrew explained: "The perceived philosophical connections between piety and military service made it only natural for the southern military school cadets to receive heavy doses of Protestant evangelical Christianity. While high-spirited cadets rarely resembled devout choirboys, the machinery of discipline encouraged and enforced outward signs of piety."[12]

By the outbreak of the Spanish-American War, Andrew argues that the soldier and veteran came to epitomize patriotism in an increasingly gendered vision of citizenship.[13] Here Andrew built upon what Wilson laid out in *Baptized in Blood*. Wilson saw the Spanish-American War and World War I as offering Southern ministers an opportunity to reconcile the Confederate past with the current union. In valorizing the next generation's participation in martial manhood, Lost Cause celebrants updated the myth and "articulated their interpretation of the South's part in the nation; in particular, they explained how their region was the most American of all areas of the country. They revealed their view of what the American civil religion should be, and what the Lost Cause values and traditions should contribute to it."[14] Andrew fleshes out how that happened:

> Northern veterans abandoned their earlier interpretation of the war as a patriotic struggle for racial equality and began to hail ex-Confederate soldiers as heroes rather than traitors and rebels. Northerners forgot the wartime call for racial justice, and popular memory instead regarded the Civil War as a gallant struggle between brothers. It was possible for this to occur, however, only as Americans, particularly veterans, redefined patriotism as "male warrior heroism" or "battlefield valor." This definition gradually superseded the meaning of patriotism as civic virtue or respect for racial equality. The Spanish-American war consolidated this reconciliation and redefinition of patriotism.[15]

By 1900, then, the Lost Cause resonated beyond the South and permeated American ideas about masculinity.

Confederate memorialization continued apace as Lee and Jackson became symbols of masculinity beyond the old Confederacy. As J. Vincent

Lowery noted, the promoters for the Stone Mountain Confederate Memorial Association "believed that the monument's inspiration would stretch beyond the South, offering an unrivaled representation of manhood and service for future generations." Apparently, New York Mayor James J. Walker agreed. He attended the unveiling of the model in 1928 and declared that it would "serve as a beacon of light to the youth of the nation," but the Depression interfered. By the middle of the 1960s, Stone Mountain offered visitors a reconstructed southern plantation complete with slave cabins and the claim that Georgia's plantation owners "as a rule" treated their slaves well. The massive sculpture of Confederate heroes was finally dedicated 1970. The ties to gender ideology persisted. Lowery explained, "After the Civil War, the Plantation South offered a preferable model of manhood for many northern whites, and whites of both regions consumed the fiction of Joel Chandler Harris, preferring his accounts of loyal slaves and benevolent masters to the New Negro and the lynch mob. Now Stone Mountain Park permitted visitors to physically experience this lost world, transferring to generations with no personal recollections of the Plantation South memories of their own from which to interpret contemporary challenges."[16] Playing in the sanitized Old South at Stone Mountain also reinforced the interpretation of a Southern history led by benevolent, virtuous men.

Stone Mountain's colossal tribute to the Lost Cause took shape during the Cold War, yet the Southern experiences in the Civil War and World War II, and their respective postwar eras, were almost unimaginably different. Despite victory and prosperity, instead of defeat and destitution, the similarities were enough to preserve the myth: the cause had been fundamentally noble, Southern men had fought bravely, the sacrifices had been great, and the disruptions in social norms dramatic.

Mississippi Governor Ross Barnett drew the legacy of the Revolution, the Civil War, World War II and the Korean conflict into the *mentalité* of the Lost Cause while speaking against the desegregation of Ole Miss. Barnette declared: "Generations [have] defended their liberties with blood and sweat and tears at Valley Forge, at Shiloh and at Vicksburg, in the Argonne, at Guadalcanal and on the Heartbreak Hills of Korea." Barnett, undoubtedly, had in mind the sacrifice of white soldiers, not of the United States Colored Troops of the Civil War nor of Air Force veteran James Meredith, the very man he was trying to keep out of the university. Some Southern whites,

however, recognized that if honor and manhood were earned through courage and action, then Meredith had achieved them. Duncan Gray, the rector
of St. Peter's Church in Oxford, counseled accepting Meredith and argued
that "Oxford's Christian men had an opportunity to show how Christian
brotherhood could produce a better world."[17] For Gray, the Christian religion had parted ways with the white South's civil religion; the test of manhood could be passed by black as well as white men, and Christian brotherhood could break the region's racial barriers.

GENDERED PRESCRIPTIONS IN THE COLD WAR ERA

The Cold War and racial change in the South helped create a vision of "the
world as on the edge of disorder," which Dickson and Emily Bruce suggest
calls forth the courage at the heart of manhood and reinforces the imper-
atives of manly honor.[18] In the Cold War, Southern Baptist leaders saw dangers everywhere. G. Kearnie Keegen was hardly alone when he told readers
of *The Baptist Student* that "the United States of America is now in one of
the most critical periods of her history," claiming "there is no denying that
we are confronted with the most menacing external enemy of all time—
Communism."[19] With the Soviet Union and the United States "engaged in
what is called a cold war," John Hill admitted "peace seems a long way off."[20]
Communism and its irrepressible conflict with Christianity created a tense
world. For Walter Judd, it was "a total conflict—unresolvable."[21]

Trouble brewed at home, too, and not just because Communism could
infiltrate American society. According to Joe Burton, editor of the Southern
Baptist publication *Home Life*, "Within our national border, organized labor and management continue their titanic struggles; race prejudice
strikes terror in the souls of minorities and majorities alike; murder and
rapine, drunkenness and destruction, lawlessness almost from infancy stalk
through the land almost without restraint. Where is there hope for victory
over entrenched iniquity in our wicked world? How can the world ever be
redeemed?"[22]

America's opportunity to lead worldwide redemption depended on a
morally sound nation, and this included martial masculinity. Through the
Cold War the Soviet Union provided the obvious negative referent, and
Soviet women were presented as mannish, Soviet men as emasculated.
Against that reversal of supposed natural gender roles, America "could be

defined, its moral superiority imagined, its order and civility restored."[23] Yet this demanded that masculine men be in charge of the nation. When the scandalous *Washington Confidential* broke in 1951 supposedly offering proof about overly feminized men and mannish women in the bureaucracy, America's gendered superiority was suddenly in question.[24]

Redemption often meant maintaining traditions. K. A. Cuordileone argued that anti-Communism meshed with opposing change in United States— it was a defense against America's "self-indulgence, its godlessness, its laxity and apathy, its lack of boundaries, its creeping sexual modernism—which could be so readily wedded to family values and sexual containment."[25] Sex provided a meeting point for the defense of American traditional values and defense against Communism in part because of the belief that Communists used sex to lure people into membership. Most provocatively, and most directly tied to the myths of the Lost Cause, anti-Communists alleged that the party "encouraged white women to offer themselves to black men" as a way of recruiting African American men.[26]

Political and popular resistance to change drew directly upon the symbols of the Lost Cause. The battle flag of the Army of Northern Virginia became *the* Confederate flag, and its political use in defense of segregation revived quickly after the 1948 Dixiecrat Convention.[27] By the early 1960s, increasingly belligerent and aggressive confederate-themed merchandising represented a "ratcheting up of the heat."[28] For many Southerners, their society was Christian and, ipso facto, their traditions were Christian. As Wilson noted, Southerners' self-image as God's chosen people left little room for self-criticism. His claim, however, is perhaps paradoxically the least true for the region's most religious people. While Baptist mission leaders clearly believed that America was "'God's chosen vessel' for bringing peace and Christianity to the troubled world," they also worried that America was not up to the task.[29] Thus, while Southern Baptist leaders looked to shore up American traditions, like many who opposed Communism, they called for soul-searching introspection and Christian brotherhood that would lead the nation and world into a changing future.

The religious revival following World War II contained two intertwined but distinct strands. The revival was undoubtedly sincerely religious as many people came to an abiding faith in God; it was also social as the devotion to a national civil religion transcended faiths and, sometimes, obscured traditional beliefs. The Southern Baptist Convention blended the streams more tightly, perhaps, than any other religious organization. No one in the

Convention doubted that America had a Christian mission in the world, and the South had a Christian mission in America. And yet, it would be difficult indeed to find a group more anxious about the region's readiness to carry out that mission or more unsure about the region's dedication to Christianity than the Southern Baptist leadership.

J. B. Lawrence headed the Home Mission Board and worried that America could not provide Christian leadership to the world. He pointed to "twenty-seven million youths under twenty-one years of age . . . growing up in America with no religious training of any kind—growing up to join the already large army of adult pagans." Cal Guy agreed, telling his young readers that only 10 percent of people in the average Southern town attended church regularly, then asking, "Does this show that God has first place" in the lives of Southerners? Courts Redford, who followed Lawrence as head of the Home Mission Board, lamented that "for many, religion is a sort of adjunct to life that gives some measure of social acceptance and self-respect," and that it was roughly on the same level as property, security, and happiness—all purchasable with money. Materialism had infected Southern society during the postwar economic boom. One writer lamented, "Materialism and secularism have brought a let down in our reverence for things once sacred."[30] The echo of the Lost Cause was profound. Its early prophets had warned "Southerners of their decline from past virtues," and more remarkably, "even during the poverty-stricken Reconstruction years, the prophets of the Lost Cause anticipated the dangers of materialism and worldliness."[31]

Gender ideology permeated the cry against materialism. For the Lost Cause prophet Robert Lewis Dabney, wealth weakened manhood "with costly pomps and luxuries." Southerners should look to the sacrifice of the Confederate soldiers who were "forever a warning against this spirit."[32] This laid a deep responsibility at the feet of women. Lost Cause ministers, Wilson noted, "viewed woman as virtuous because she was the symbol of home and family."[33] The family was the bulwark against the corruptions of the world. The home, after all, affected the future generation day and night, while church attendance—though important—was at most a few hours a week. Moreover, the Christian home was itself a missionary activity, affecting not only the children raised in it but the entire community. The idea was pervasive, and clearly encapsulated in Jean A. McSween of Tennessee's contribution to *The Window*, "Homemaking is My Mission."[34]

The Christian home and concern for the family represented a key separation between the Christian and Communist worlds. Communists, dedicated to atheism and materialism, attempted to undermine the family by demanding primal loyalty to the state.[35] Indeed, the idea that the Bolshevik revolution had made women's sexuality and labor a state asset, and that it arranged and broke marriages and promoted sexual chaos including homosexuality and miscegenation, stretched back to the first Red Scare of the 1920s.[36] Kenneth Chafin told Baptist boys that "communism does not have a place for strong home ties" and noted that Hitler, too, had "tried to do away with the home." He reminded the boys of a constant theme in Baptist literature: "no nation lasts long that fails to realize the importance of the home."[37]

The reality was unsettled. The home, Southern Baptists feared, was being battered from all sides, with alcoholism, unclean literature, and divorce being among its enemies. Southern Baptists recognized changing roles for women and the changes in home life they necessarily brought about. That recognition fit uneasily with their espousal of an eternally unchanging, biblically based family, though both strands of thought found their way into *Home Life* and other Baptist publications.[38] David Goldfield traces changes in women's roles directly to the Lost Cause: women organized the memorialization of the Confederate dead, founded and ran the United Daughters of the Confederacy, and, most importantly, defended the region's honor. Most historians agree upon this much. Goldfield, however, takes the argument further, noting that clubwomen and churchwomen became increasingly active, joining forces with such organizations as the Women's Christian Temperance Union. The clubwomen of the New South, he argues, "questioned their surroundings, believed in the new science, and took steps to change the immutable features of their society."[39] Within the Convention, Southern Baptist women created, and continued to run independently, the highly influential Woman's Missionary Union. These activities did not directly cause, or even necessitate, changes in southern home life, but they did help create the conditions under which those changes could take place.

Southern Baptist leaders clearly believed family life in America was changing and launched *Home Life* to promote their vision of the Christian home. Its editor, Joe Burton, and other writers like H. C. Brearley and David R. Mace, recognized that the "new woman" meant new arrangements within marriage were inevitable. Identifying the "new woman" as educated and independent, Brearley noted, "The new woman has in turn changed the pattern of family life in America. In the first place, she has demanded an end to the semipatriarchial family." While Mace asserted that "today we have the concept of men and women in marriage as partners, as equals," his admission that this was not the case throughout the world belied the fact that it was hardly the case throughout the United States.[40] Indeed, it belied the fact that many conservative anti-Communists in the United States tied their anti-Communism to defense of the patriarchal family and the social structures that supported it.[41]

Baptist leaders were clearly ambivalent to these changes. What Mace considered "the easy blueprint" for roles for husbands and wives had disappeared. The new arrangements "brought equality and cooperation" but also, at least sometimes, confusion. The uncertainty led to conflict and sometimes divorce. As Brearley noted, "Once we in the South thought that divorce was something sinful Yankees and westerns had and that we didn't have much of it," but, he admitted, the South had roughly twice the divorce rate of the Northeast, though still only half the divorce rate of the West.[42] Confusion in the home was a serious problem during the Cold War. Joe Burton reminded Baptists that "it is in the home that young lives are schooled for the battles of life."[43]

Amid chronic worries about the rising divorce rate and unstable homes, Southern Baptists actively encouraged young women to think seriously about both marriage and attending college. *The Window*, the official publication of the Young Women's Auxiliary, sounded both themes throughout the Cold War. While Margaret Perry simply assumed, "Young women, are you dreaming of marriage and Christian homemaking? Of course you are," Edith Huckabee could advise a reader named Peggy on the choice between college and marriage, saying, "My advice is to choose college." Huckabee did reassure her readers that attending college did not consign a woman to spinsterhood. She admitted, "I can't guarantee that you'll end up with the same husband after college as you would not," but insisted, "I think I can safely say that the one you'll find was worth waiting for."[44]

The mixed messages could be difficult to decode. John McClanahan considered thinking about college primarily in terms of dating to be "superficial," but he also considered that it was likely a woman would meet her husband at college. As a result, he suggested that "a girl should choose a college where she will have an opportunity to meet the kind of boy she may later want to marry," but in the end, he advised that "marriage should not, however, be the primary factor in choosing a college. The college woman should seek first a place where she can most fully equip herself to meet the demands of mid-twentieth century living as a mature, poised Christian citizen."[45]

Boys and girls got different messages. In *The Window*, girls were reminded that a housewife could be a heroine because "it takes real courage for a girl to be as good a housewife as she expects her husband to be a breadwinner." In a Christian home, the wife must be a good steward and assure her husband that "she will not squander her husband's money or the leisure he may provide for her."[46] To be sure, *Ambassador Life*, which targeted boys, carried stories on the vital importance of Christian homes. Cal Guy minced no words when he told Baptist boys, "A nation can be Christian only if it is made of Christian individuals in Christian Homes," but he and other authors for *Ambassador Life* said far less about preparing boys for marriage.[47] When S. J. Watson wrote "Girls are People, Too" he focused primarily on Christian behavior during dating, decrying the low moral standard set by Hollywood movies. He did tell boys it was important to know girls as friends so they would know what personality type suited them "when you choose the girl who will become your wife."[48] *Ambassador Life* articles, however, rarely discussed and never glorified husbandly duties.

Family and masculine honor could be reconciled in a man's obtaining dependents, but the modern marriage emasculated men by empowering women in the home, making them partners rather than dependents.[49] Popular images of marriage distressed Southern Baptists. Laurella Owens lamented comic strips in her "Viewpoints" column for *The Window*. She noted, "If a couple is pictured dating, the man is tall and aggressive, the girl charming and a bit coy. When married couples are shown, the man usually has shrunk, his shortness suggesting that he is weaker than his wife."[50] Joe Burton worried that men had abdicated their role as strong fathers to "aggressive mothers," allowing mothers to take the place of fathers as symbols of authority. This formed a part of what Suzanne Clark called a form of "disciplinary domesticity" guided by the work of Dr. Benjamin Spock. She considered it an oppressive world that contained women and children and from which only men could escape.[51] For Burton, however, men should not have sought escape; they should have been deeply involved in their families. After reviewing survey data revealing that the vast majority of adult men were both married and had children, he decided the situation was not as dire as some feared. Burton wrote, "The overall picture then is of steadfast commitment to family life as the accepted and deliberate pattern in American social organization—of husbands devoted to their wives, of parents rearing their children, of men at work for their families. It is a good picture of purpose, of deliberate diligence in relation to man's basic duty and need, the home." They were indeed being the providers manhood demanded of them.[52] Such a glimmer of hope amid the broad anxiety about the Christian home suggested that the home, that critical bulwark against Communism, was holding fast.

America, after all, had to face down the Communist threat to liberty whether or not it was fully ready to do so. No Baptist would have challenged Charles A. Well's assessment of the Cold War when he said, "No peace effort can go far without facing the threat of communism to human liberty and human rights which is a historic cause of war."[53] In the early twentieth century, and certainly by the onset of World War I, Wilson argues, the Lost Cause myth had promoted "liberty" to the central cause of the Civil War. World War I, he argued, provided the South's young men the opportunity to prove their valor on the battlefield and "vindicated the Lost Cause . . . because American participation in it had validated the same principles the Confederacy had fought for: belief in liberty and Democracy."[54] The Cold War merely continued the fight the Confederates had taken up from their Revolutionary forefathers.

If wars offered young men an opportunity to prove their valor on the battlefield, atomic warfare changed the equation—mutual annihilation was no way to prove valor in a Christian world. Southern Baptist leaders called for ideological war, not a military war, against Communism. Strength of character and a willingness to stand tall for Christian values would now constitute the essence of the crusading Christian, fighting Communism soul by soul. The battle, however changed, was imperative. Baptist leaders recognized two intriguing similarities between Christianity and Communism. John E. Saunders explained, "World conquest is the goal of communism. World conquest is also the goal of Christianity." Additionally, as noted by Robert L. Lynn, "The truth is that Christianity and communism are both forms of revolution." Indeed, for Lynn, Christianity was the more radically revolutionary of the two.[55]

True Christians, then, were both revolutionaries and counter-revolutionaries in the battle for world conquest. Foy Valentine, then at the Texas Christian Life Commission, sounded the call when he declared, "This is not the time for hollow professions of loyalty to Christ and his teaching. Our age of crisis demands that the Christian match his profession with practices, his attitudes with action, and his faith with works." Such an existential crisis demanded that Christians be "warrior converts, commissioned to proclaim the gospel in such power as to enable God, through them, to change the world!" Christianity was, after all, the "greatest social revolution in history" compared to which Communism "pale[d] into insignificance."[56]

Just such a conviction had come to Karen Elvgren, a student who had entered college an agnostic but became a Christian after learning of the "anti-God darkness" of Communism. She lamented that "Communists have succeeded because they have prevented us from developing fully the one weapon which could conceivably halt them. This weapon is a living, breathing, fighting faith as dynamic as communism and offering the world what communism seeks to provide: a reason to live and a reason to die." For Elvgren, the time was now to "renew our vow to our Lord and ask him to teach us what we must do in order to be effective Christian soldiers. We must let him put us into the battle."[57]

If Karen Elvgren saw herself a Christian soldier in the battle against Communism, Baptist leaders undoubtedly welcomed her. She had stared into the darkness of Communism and come forth as Valentine's "warrior-convert." Olive Alice Jeanfreau was also ready for the challenge. Defending her generation in her essay "We're not *All* Delinquents," she announced that her generation found the world challenging and inspiring. She assured the readers of *Home Life* that "for every delinquent in a reform school, there are many Christian teenagers ready to meet the challenge of real living." Even younger children felt the call. Nancy Lou Story, a member of the Girl's Auxiliary in Houston, wrote, "Although I am just a junior girl, in a city of over one million people, if my life is wholly dedicated unto, I can surely have a part in making my community Christian."[58] Elvgren, Jeanfreau, and Story were just the types of young people Christian leaders looked to with hope for the world's future. All three were female. The shifting theater of engagement allowed the mantle of masculinity, Christian warriorhood, to be claimed by women.

Women like Elvgren, who claimed the masculine mantle of Christian warriorhood, did it out of true Christian conviction, not out of an effort to subvert the region's gender roles. Still, they broke out of the containment that marginalized women's work in Cold War years by making their work central to the world's Christianization and victory over Communism. It is possible that they never realized their actions' gendered implications. Yet the sum of such actions had broad implications. In 1963, the Convention passed a resolution allowing the ordination of women. Twenty years later, when Southern Baptist Women in Ministry organized prior to the Pittsburgh convention, the women counted 175 ordained clergywomen and claimed hundreds more were awaiting ordination. In response, according to David T. Morgan, "The convention made an attempt to pay tribute to Southern Baptist women by adopting a resolution that expressed gratitude for contributions made by women in various forms of ministry and praised them as homemakers."[59] The Convention's mixed messages reflected internal confusion and failed to provide guidance on an issue dividing Southern Baptists.

After the Pittsburg meeting in 1983, the Convention began to bend back toward more conservative gender ideologies. While the Southern Baptists leadership never renewed its devotion to the Lost Cause vision of race relations, the mythic gender ideologies reemerged as a central theme. Conservatives gained the upper hand in the Southern Baptist Convention and began their efforts to slay the "two-headed dragon of feminism and homosexuality," at least inside their churches.[60] Barry Hankins notes: "The Southern Baptist conservative subculture has placed its prohibition against ordained women pastors at the center of its theological-cultural program," adding, "This was merely one aspect of an overall theology of gender that carves out separate roles for men and women, both in churches and in families." The Convention proclaimed women were to be submissive in their marriages and, after thirty-seven years, specifically barred women from becoming pastors in 2000.[61]

TOWARD THE NEW MILLENNIUM

For Hankins, it was clear that across the 1980s and 1990s "the gender issue [had] moved to center stage in the SBC conservative drama." Indeed, Landon Storrs's conservatism from the 1920s through the 1980s often included the "defense of white, Christian, heterosexual, *patriarchal,* family" as a "driving concern."[62] A lot had changed since the prophets of the Lost Cause took up the issues of manhood and womanhood, and now the Convention's "countercultural" resistance to changing gender roles in

America ran against the norms of society. Southern Baptists would be true counter-revolutionaries in the name of Christianity. It was not quite so simple. Despite their claims, Hankins suggests, "denying women full equality within their churches and insisting that they submit to the authority of their husbands within the family" had far more recent origins than the writing of the Bible. He notes, "For Southern Baptists . . . recent history has been an experience of cultural change that must be met head on with conservative countercultural positions based on traditional, some would say outdated, readings of scripture."[63] Nevertheless, their views resonated through conservative sectors of the South, even where the Lost Cause position on race no longer found support.

Conservative Baptists' attempted counter-revolution faced long odds in changing American society. Still, other aspects of Southern masculinity, though unacceptable among the religious leadership, seemed to survive: alcohol and violence. While Bertram Wyatt-Brown, among others, has shown violence and alcohol to be key aspects of Southern masculinity and honor, they were incompatible with Southern religious institutions' conception of manhood. Lee, Wilson had noted, was both "a bold military man" and "supremely gentle," with his known tenderness toward children and storied nursing of his mother late in her life as proof of his saintliness.[64] Indeed, A. L. Crabb held Lee up to Southern Baptist students as "one of the Greatest Characters in History," specifically indicating that "he never sulked or flew into a rage when frustrated. He never spoke profanely." Furthermore, in the battle against alcohol, Lee and Jackson again stood as models for Christian manhood in the South as Jackson had reportedly said, "I am more afraid of King Alcohol than of all the bullets of the enemy."[65] Crabb pointed to Lee, claiming he had led a "pure life" and "never drank whiskey or used tobacco." The relevance was clear. Ben Browne looked at a world divided between Christianity and Communism and lamented that "the twenty stiff vodka toasts (not to mention champagne and Martinis) which our generals have admitted to drinking at the Yalta Conference with Stalin now come in for the dizzy-headed reckoning."[66]

One of the gravest concerns Cold War Southern Baptists expressed was the possibility of women's drinking. According to Patsy Ann Norwood, "Young people often drink because of parental influence. With so many parents engaging in drinking in their home bars, one can easily understand the increase in juvenile delinquency as the youths." It was not just father, either. Though she pointed outside the South for her evidence, Norwood concluded that "more than 60% of the juvenile delinquents in Boston, Massachusetts, have drinking mothers."[67]

Vigilante violence, with deep roots in masculinity, proliferated during the racial upheavals of the Cold War, which, Estes has argued, "galvanized southern white men with ideals of whiteness, honor, and manhood."[68] Such fit solidly with Cold War masculinity when, according to Cuordileone, political cultures "put a new premium on hard masculine toughness and rendered anything less than that soft and feminine and, as such, a real or potential threat to the security of the nation."[69] Martial masculinity was tough on Communism, but its toughness could not always be contained and directed; this, too, drew upon the Lost Cause. As Wilson pointed out, "the Klan, in truth, was a vital organization of the religion of the Lost Cause. Southerners romanticized it as a chivalrous extension of the Confederacy."[70] It was not, however, the Lost Cause of Robert E. Lee; it was instead the Lost Cause of Nathan Bedford Forrest.

While Wilson notes that Lost Cause advocates stretched the idea of Christian warriors to include the impious, Forrest's legacy changed as the South changed and he came to symbolize a more reckless, violent masculinity than Lee and Jackson.[71] Court Carney notes that the general and first KKK grand wizard offered an "archetype of violent, white Southern Masculinity."[72] Perhaps as importantly, Forrest represented, at least according to his agrarian biographer Andrew Lytle, the plain people of the South. In his view, Forrest was more of a clan patriarch than a planter.[73] During and after the Cold War, Forrest stood for a violent, masculine resistance to change, not coincidentally because his leadership of the KKK during Reconstruction had turned him into the warrior who never gave up—Lytle's "last ruler of the South."[74] Carney argues that "Forrest emerged from the 1960s an embattled icon as white admirers countered race related attacks on their hero with appeals to Southern manhood and honor."[75]

Forrest has not fared as well in historical memory as Lee and Jackson. In *God and General Longstreet,* Thomas Connelly and Barbara Bellows suggest his reputation had faded so far that, in 1979, a sizable percentage of incoming students at a Southern university could not even identify him. Yet his brand of masculinity certainly survived and, as Alan T. Nolan has suggested, Forrest has risen to prominence among neo-Confederates. It is possible that what Connelly and Bellows missed when they quipped that it was "no surprise" that so many Southern college students could not identify Forrest was the class divide in the Lost Cause. Though Forrest was certainly wealthy, and his wealth had derived from slave trading, his particular brand of violence-laden masculinity was shunned by the Southern clergy who spoke for the region's more refined culture. He appealed instead to those Southerners derided as "white trash." Forrest's brand of masculinity found expression in popular culture, often in Southern rock.[76]

Forrest's emergence as a symbol of violent masculinity and southern rock's rise to popularity on the backs of songs about violence and alcohol abuse offer a view of deeply discordant strands of masculinity in the late-Cold-War South.[77] There was continuity, of course, as J. Michael Butler noted when he pointed out that "all southern rock bands emphasized evangelical themes in their music and demonstrated primarily through their lyrics, album art, and interviews that they recognized the tension between their lifestyles and their spiritual worldviews."[78] Nevertheless, the class conflict is clear. Southern rock celebrated what Jason T. Eastman and Douglas P. Schrock called "white trash manhood," which, they argued, allowed middle- and upper-class Southern men to deflect anxieties about their own masculinity by pointing to "white trash" men as "philandering wife-beaters."[79]

Southern rockers themselves certainly saw "hot-rod cars, drinking, debauchery" as inspirations for the music they created. They tended to perceive wives and girlfriends as threats to their independence and celebrate fleeting sexual encounters while viewing women primarily as property who provided domestic labor, but they tended not to see their claim to Southern masculinity as laced with privilege. They could, as Eastman and Schrock note, wave Confederate flags and present women primarily as property without demonstrating any concern for those people they offended.[80] That privilege, it would seem, was only possible if their vision struck a chord with the region's myths, which still held some resonance for the broader society.

Even here, though, women claimed the mantle of honor and masculinity. If Dickson and Emily Bruce are correct, and "the idea of violent self-defense as a moral act also figures strongly in the links between conservative arguments for gun ownership and honor's demands for independence and self-determination," Southern rock came to celebrate women's usurpation of masculinity. Carrie Underwood's popular "Before He Cheats" celebrates violence against property. After carving her name into the leather seats of the man's car, the same unnamed heroine "took a Louisville slugger to both headlights" and "slashed a hole in all four tires" in the belief that "maybe next time he'll think before he cheats." The Louisville slugger is swung by a woman defending her own honor who makes it clear that "the next that he cheats, oh, you know it won't be on me." Property damage is only one kind of revenge, though. The Dixie Chicks' "Goodbye Earl" tells the story of two friends, Mary Ann and Wanda, who murdered Wanda's abusive husband, Earl, and disposed of his body. Earl turned out to be "a missing person nobody missed at all," and the women's revenge murder simply faded from anyone's mind. By killing Earl the women provide Wanda with the protection and security male society had failed to provide. Such revenge violence is clearly masculine.[81]

CONCLUSION

In his study of Southern identity, James Cobb noted that Scarlett O'Hara, the heroine of the quintessential Lost Couse film *Gone With the Wind*, unsexed herself and began "conducting her affairs in a masculine way." [82] However much white women after the Civil War wanted to return to the tranquility and safety of home and family, destruction had simply made that an impossible hope for many of them. World War II certainly left many women widows, but its aftermath brought unprecedented prosperity to the region, and the Cold War years have long been romanticized as an era of ideal family life in America. Yet some women—sometimes purposefully, sometimes unwittingly—continued to unsex themselves and claim the mantle of masculinity. Indeed, in calling all Christians, men and women alike, to join the battle against Communism as Christian soldiers, the Southern Baptist Convention helped undermine the gendered ideologies of the Lost Cause myths. Finally, the Convention had had enough of the unintended consequences of its own actions and declared that women could not be pastors and should submit to their husbands. The broader American, and even Southern, society had left the myth behind. The rearguard action against women's full participation in American life may well be a lost cause; women, after all, have breached even the walls of the Citadel, the quintessential Southern military school, and in the views on "defender," "the only vestige of the old Confederacy we have left."[83]

NOTES

1. David Goldfield, *Still Fighting the Civil War: The American South and Southern History* (Baton Rouge: Louisiana State Univ. Press, 2002), 2.

2. Charles Reagan Wilson, *Baptized in Blood* (Athens: Univ. of Georgia Press, 1980), 47.

3. Wilson, *Baptized in Blood*, 51.

4. W. Stuart Towns, *Enduring Legacy: Rhetoric and Ritual of the Lost Cause* (Tuscaloosa: Univ. of Alabama Press, 2012), 82.

5. Christopher R. Lawton, "'The Pilgrim's Progress': Thomas J. Jackson's Journey Toward Civility and Citizenship," *The Virginia Magazine of History and Biography* 116, no. 1 (2008): 2–41. See also Wallace Hettle, "A Romantic's Civil War: John Esteon Cook, Stonewall Jackson, and the Ideal of 'Individual Genius,'" *The Historian* (Fall 2005).

6. Gary W. Gallagher, *Causes Won, Lost, and Forgotten: How Hollywood & Popular Art Shape What We Know About the Civil War* (Chapel Hill: Univ. of North Carolina Press, 2008), 136, 146, 157. See also Will Kaufman, *The Civil War in American Culture* (Edinburgh: Univ. of Edinburgh Press, 2006), 48–49, 53.

7. Edward R. Crowther, "Iron Chests: Honor and Manhood in Southern Evangelicalism," in *The Field of Honor: Essays on Southern Character and American Identity*, John Mayfield and Todd Hagstette (Columbia: Univ. of South Carolina Press, 2017), 280.

8. Towns, *Enduring Legacy*, 68.

9. Wilson, *Baptized in Blood*, 69. James C. Cobb, *Away Down South: A History of Southern Identity* (New York: Oxford Univ. Press, 2005), 64.

10. Wolfgang Shivelbusch, *The Culture of Defeat: On National Trauma, Mourning, and Recovery*, trans. Jefferson Chase (New York: Metropolitan Books of Henry Holt and Company, 2001), 16–17.

11. Shivelbusch, *The Culture of Defeat*, 61–62.

12. Rod Andrew, Jr., *Long Grey Lines: The Southern Military School Tradition, 1839–1915* (Chapel Hill: Univ. of North Carolina Press, 2002), 47–50; quotation from page 50.

13. Andrew, *Long Grey Lines*, 105–6.

14. Wilson, *Baptized in Blood*, 161–64, quotation from 164.

15. Andrew, *Long Grey Lines*, 108.

16. J. Vincent Lowery, "A Monument to Many Souths: Tourists Experience Southern Distinctiveness at Stone Mountain," in *Destination Dixie: Tourism and Southern History*, ed. Karen L. Cox (Gainesville: Univ. Press of Florida, 2012), 229, 233.

17. Towns, *Enduring Legacy*, 122–23.

18. Dickson D. Bruce, Jr., and Emily S. Bruce, "Honor and the Rhetoric of Conservatism in Twenty-First-Century America," in *The Field of Honor*, Mayfield and Hagstette, 293.

19. G. Kearnie Keegen, "United Under God," *The Baptist Student* (February 1955), 1.

20. John L. Hill, "Lord Make Us Thinkful," *The Baptist Student* (November 1950), 3.

21. Walter Judd, "A World in Conflict," *The Baptist Student* (February 1956), 2.

22. Joe Burton, "The Home Can Change the World," *Home Life* (October 1959), 50.

23. K. A. Cuordileone, "'Politics in an Age of Anxiety': Cold War Political Culture and the Crisis in American Masculinity, 1949–1960," *The Journal of American History* 87, no. 2 (Sept. 2000): 538.

24. Landon R. Y. Storrs, "Attacking the Washington 'Femmocracy': Antifeminism in the Cold War Campaign against 'Communists in Government,'" *Feminist Studies* 33, no. 1 (Spring 2007): 118–52.

25. Cuordileone, "Politics," 538.

26. Stoors, "Attacking," 131.

27. Cobb, *Away Down South*, 290.

28. Kaufman, *The Civil War in American Culture*, 88.

29. Willis, *All According to God's Plan: Southern Baptist Missions and Race, 1945–1970* (Lexington: Univ. Press of Kentucky, 2005), 93.

30. Willis, *All According to God's Plan*, 93–100.

31. Wilson, *Baptized in Blood*, 11, 81.

32. Wilson, *Baptized in Blood*, 86.

33. Wilson, *Baptized in Blood*, 46.

34. Willis, *All According to God's Plan*, 108; Sandra Burr and Alan Scot Willis, "Policing Parents: Children's Moral Vigilance in Southern Baptist Instructional Literature, 1945–1963," *Interjuli Internationale* (February 2012), 59–72. Jean A. McSween, "Homemaking is My Mission," *The Window* (June 1958), 7–9.

35. Joe Burton, "Function of the Family," *Home Life* (June 1964), 4.

36. Storrs, "Attacking," 129.

37. Kenneth L. Chafin, "The Importance of Christian Homes," *Ambassador Life* (May 1957), 15.

38. Burr and Willis, "Policing Parents," 62–65.

39. Goldfield, *Still Fighting the Civil War*, 138, 144.

40. H. C. Brearley, "New Roles of Women and Children," *Home Life* (July 1955), 6–7; David R. Mace, "Equality in Marriage," *Home Life* (August 1959), 7.

41. Storrs, "Attacking," 120.

42. H. C. Brearley, "Internal Conflicts in Family Life," *Home Life* (August 1955), 17; Mace, "Equality in Marriage," 8.

43. Burton, "The Home Can Change the World," 50.

44. Margaret C. Perry, "When You Marry," *The Window* (May 1950), 4; Edith Huckabee, "Ask Edith," *The Window* (June 1958), 23.

45. John H McLanahan, "College for You?" *The Window* (May 1962), 6. Winni Breines offers an extended look at the mixed messages young women received in the 1950s, particularly between pursuing an education and getting married, in *Young, White and Miserable: Growing up Female in the Fifties* (Chicago: Univ. of Chicago Press, 1992).

46. "Happy Commencement," *The Window* (May 1952), 3; Eva Berry, "The Ideal Home-Maker," *The Window* (March 1948), 21.

47. Cal Guy, "How Christian is America," *Ambassador Life* (February 1950), 15.

48. "Happy Commencement," *The Window* (May 1952), 3; Eva Berry, "Your YWA Programs, Second Week: The Ideal Home-Maker," *The Window* (March 1948), 21; S. J. Watson, "Girls are People, Too," *Ambassador Life* (September 1962), 19.

49. Bruce and Bruce, "Honor and the Rhetoric of Conservatism," in *The Field of Honor*, ed. Mayfield and Hagstette, 295.

50. Laurella Ownes, "Viewpoints," *The Window* (June 1963), 7.

51. Suzanne Clark, *Cold Warriors: Manliness on Trial in the Rhetoric of the West* (Carbondale: Southern Illinois Univ. Press, 2000), 56.

52. Joe Burton, "Of Abdicated Fathers and Aggressive Mothers," *Home Life* (April 1959), 48; Joe Burton, "Men at Home," *Home Life* (January 1957), 48; Crowther, "Iron Chests," 283–86.

53. Charles A. Wells, "Trends," *The Baptist Student* (March 1950), inside cover.

54. Wilson, *Baptized in Blood*, 175.

55. John E Saunders, "I Will Do My Best . . . To Have a Christlike Concern for All People," *Ambassador Life* (November 1962), 4; Robert L. Lynn, "Religion's War in Europe," *Ambassador Life* (November 1961), 19.

56. G. Kearnie Keegen, "United Under God," *The Baptist Student* (February 1955), 1; Foy Valentine, "Whetting Your Social Conscience," *The Baptist Student* (June 1954), 13–14.

57. Karen Elvgren, "A Coed Looks at Communism," *The Baptist Student* (May 1961), 43–44.

58. Nancy Lou Story, "My Part in Leading My Community to Be Cristian," *Tell* (March 1956), 6.

59. David T. Morgan, *The New Crusades, The New Holy Land: Conflict in the Southern Baptist Convention, 1969–1991* (Tuscaloosa: Univ. of Alabama Press, 1996), 155.

60. Goldfield, *Still Fighting the Civil War*, 85; Crowther, "Iron Chests," 284.

61. Barry Hankins, *Uneasy in Babylon: Southern Baptist Conservatives and American Culture* (Tuscaloosa: Univ. of Alabama Press, 2003), 201. For a thorough and insightful study of gender and church roles, see Elizabeth Flowers, *Into the Pulpit: Southern Baptist Women and Power since WWII* (Chapel Hill: Univ. of North Carolina Press, 2012).

62. Storrs, "Attacking," 120.

63. Hankins, *Uneasy in Babylon*, 238–39.

64. Wilson, *Baptized in Blood*, 49.

65. Wilson, *Baptized in Blood*, 87.

66. Ben Browne, "Conviviality With Communists," *The Window* (July 1951), 1.

67. Patsy Ann Norwood, "You're Too Smart to Fall for That," *The Window* (January 1950), 15–16.

68. Estes, "A Question of Honor," 86.

69. Cuordileone, "Politics," 516.

70. Wilson, *Baptized in Blood*, 111.

71. Wilson, *Baptized in Blood*, 57.

72. Court Carney, "The Most Man in the World: Nathan Bedford Forrest and the Cult of Southern Masculinity," in *White Masculinity in the Recent South*, ed. Trent Watts, 139.

73. Carney, "The Most Man in the World," 141.

74. Carney, "The Most Man in the World."

75. Carney, "The Most Man in the World," 144.

76. Connelly and Bellows, *God and General Longstreet*, 117; Alan T. Nolan, "The Anatomy of the Myth," 19.

77. Ted Ownby, "Church Camping and White Southern Masculinity: Evangelical Males and Christian Primitivism, 1920s–1970s," in *White Masculinity in the Recent South*, ed. Watts, 40.

78. J. Michael Butler, "'Lord, Have Mercy on My Soul': Sin, Salvation, and Southern Rock," *Southern Cultures* 9, no. 4 (Winter 2003): 74.

79. Jason T. Eastman and Douglas P. Schrock, "Southern Rock Musicians' Construction of White Trash," *Race, Gender & Class* 15, no. 1/2 (2008): 207.

80. Eastman and Schrock, "Southern Rock," 210–11, 214.

81. Carrie Underwood, "Before He Cheats," lyrics available at https://genius.com /Carrie-underwood-before-he-cheats-lyrics. Accessed January 25, 2018. Dixie Chicks, "Goodbye Earl," lyrics available at https://genius.com/Dixie-chicks-goodbye-earl-lyrics. Accessed January 25, 2018.

82. Cobb, *Away Down South*, 135.

83. Goldfield, *Still Fighting the Civil War*, 181–82.

Black and White and Red All Over: Mississippi's Religious Red Scare

CAROLYN DUPONT

On a late July night in 1962, excitement percolated at downtown Jackson's King Edward Hotel as three hundred people gathered to hear a debate on the Communist threat in Methodist churches. An eager press extended the audience; every important Mississippi paper covered the spectacle and the Citizens' Council broadcast the action live on its Rebel Radio Network. One of the disputants, Myers Lowman of Cincinnati, Ohio, enjoyed an established reputation with Mississippi audiences as an expert on Communism in religious life. His opponent, the youthful Reverend Gerald Trigg, lacked Lowman's name recognition. Yet Trigg's parishioners believed he would shine in this setting, so a group of them drove three hours from the gulf coast town of Pascagoula to show support.[1]

In the course of the debate, Lowman pounded his well-worn theme that Communism had so deeply infiltrated the Methodist Church as to render it a dangerous institution. He heightened listeners' sense of imminent peril by claiming, "Mississippi is one of the most communist-exploited states in the nation." Lowman denounced Trigg as naïve, misinformed, and too ingenuous to understand the deeply subversive nature of the Church and its programs. At one point, he waved a copy of the 1908 Social Creed of the Methodist Church, on which he had super-imposed a picture of Lenin.[2] For his part, Trigg accepted the Cold War's basic axioms and never questioned the reality of a Communist menace in Mississippi; neither did he challenge the validity of fighting Communists as an important activity for Mississippi Methodists. He opened, in fact, by stating, "The church of Jesus Christ faces a communist conspiracy—the greatest threat to its nearly twenty centuries of existence." He disagreed with Lowman, however, about who really constituted this threat, insisting that those who made "innuendoes, half-truths and sow[ed] seeds of suspicion against the Church and

her leaders aid[ed] the Communist conspiracy rather than hinder[ed] it."
Trigg went on to characterize Lowman as just this kind of irresponsible
purveyor of fear and suspicion, a witch hunter who incited gullible people
to hysteria. Church members, Trigg cautioned, needed to understand and
recognize *true* Communism so that they would not fall prey to traducers of
Lowman's sort.[3]

A bit tragicomically only weeks before a riot engulfed Ole Miss over the
admission of a black student, Mississippi's white evangelicals preoccupied
themselves with the precise nature and depth of Communist influence in
their religious institutions. Yet this debate—beginning years before this July
1962 event and continuing well after—spoke more to the state's convul-
sions over black equality than it first appears. Its language and references
helped southerners frame segregation as deeply Christian, profoundly
American, and crucial to the global struggle against evil.

Indeed, Mississippi's religious red scare performed cultural work similar
to the ideology of the Lost Cause. By the years of high-profile civil rights
activity, the Lost Cause had lost much of its salience as a civil-religious belief
system. Sacralization of the Confederate defeat no longer spoke effectively
to white southerners in the context of attenuating regional identities and
new geopolitical realities. Yet as the fight to end segregation garnered the
authority of many American faith leaders and institutions, white southerners heard the moral judgement of other Americans on their racial arrangements and, once again, felt themselves spiritual pariahs within the nation.
Reminiscent of the Lost Cause, they reinvigorated the notion of a special
destiny for their region, one that endowed their diminished stature with
meaning and that understood their own brand of evangelical Protestantism
as the purest form of Christianity. Only this pure southern Christianity—not
the northern liberal sort—could redeem a nation threatened internationally by Communism and domestically by racial integration. Just as the Lost
Cause had conferred purpose and meaning on the Confederate defeat, the
religious red scare gave new and cosmic purpose to white Mississippians'
struggle to preserve segregation and elevated their role in the narrative of
American destiny.

The use of anti-Communism to thwart black equality has received substantial scholarly elaboration, but the religious dimensions of this discourse
have attracted far less attention. Anti-Communism had a special meaning,
use, and trajectory in religious circles. There it functioned as more than the

laughable misconception of right-wing nut jobs and served purposes beyond the simple smear. As employed by mid-twentieth-century Christians,
anti-Communism advanced specific understandings of the Gospel and its
implications for the political and economic system. In an America where
the political allegiances of the religious remained fluid, the language of
the Cold War helped Christians of differing theological persuasions identify and describe their political and economic affinities.[4] In particular, anti-Communist discourse baptized political and economic conservatism as
godly ideologies. Somewhat contradictorily, this extraordinarily malleable
language also helped theological moderates and liberals to articulate resistance to far-right principles and commitments to different political and
economic principles.

In Mississippi, the religious and racial uses of anti-Communism braided
themselves together in an ideological chord that evoked deep commitments to evangelical faith, segregation, and laissez-faire economics. In the
midst of a battle they would soon lose, at least in the legal sense, the affinities captured by religiously based anti-Communism helped Mississippians
present their rejection of black equality as deeply Christian and profoundly
American.

Mississippi's religious red scare worked profoundly on the racial struggle
and Mississippi's religious life in the midst of it. The religious red scare
thwarted the religious argument for racial equality, helped shape attitudes
toward outside religious intervention long before it arrived, and deeply dis-
rupted religious life.

THE PINK FRINGE OF AMERICAN RELIGION

Cold War language rang rich with religious overtones. Many Americans believed that the struggle between the West and the Soviet Union, though
manifested in military, economic, and political conflict, rested on deeper,
spiritual dimensions. The contest for spheres of influence transcended
mere geography and politics; it resembled a cosmic struggle between two
forces whose spiritual natures pervaded their entire systems. No less than
President Eisenhower advanced such an understanding in his well-known
query, "What is our battle against communism if it is not a fight between
anti-God and a belief in the Almighty? [Communists] . . . have to eliminate
God from their system. When God comes, Communism has to go."[5]

Communism appeared to display religious characteristics that rendered it Christianity's—rather than democracy's—sinister counterpart. Communists believed in both sin and salvation of sorts: "Communism sees the source of evil outside of man—in the economic system—and the source of salvation within man—in communism. Christianity finds the source of evil within man himself and the source of salvation outside of man—in God," explained the National Council of Churches' handbook on Communism. Communist leaders had expressed their vision to spread the Marxist faith to the entire world in decidedly evangelical terms. The Marxist/Stalinist dogma required "the kind of absolute allegiance and dedication with passion from its followers that Christians can give only to God." Communism, then, did not ask for mere superficial assent to its tenets. Rather, as a diabolical spiritual force, it seemed to vie with Christianity for the possession of men's souls.[6]

This view of Communism as a primarily spiritual force encouraged a renewed conflation of Christian and American identity, as the patriotic duty to fight Communism seemed to require Christian faith as never before. Indeed, both politicians and preachers promoted religion as essential to America's political traditions. A Mississippi layman explained, "Our citizens must realize that democracy is rooted in, and depends for its life upon, the religion of the Holy Bible." Thus, America's national security interests augmented the urgency of Christian conversion: "The whole scheme of our present government . . . IS TOTALLY UNWORKABLE EXCEPT AMONG A PEOPLE THE MAJORITY OF WHOM HOLD CHRISTIAN BELIEVES [sic]"[7] (emphasis in original). Indeed, the fundamental role that religious faith played in sustaining democracy increasingly seemed self-evident: the nations that "fell" to Communism often had little or no Christian—particularly Protestant—tradition. Postwar Americans sought to combat the red menace with an orgy of church-going, and denominational memberships soared.

In spite of widespread consensus about the Cold War's essentially spiritual foundations, Americans disagreed about exactly what *kind* of Christianity best countered the Communist threat; here the religious construction of Communism took on distinct theological and political dimensions. Many Americans accepted the association between Christianity and democracy in the vague fashion described by another oft-quoted Eisenhower assertion: "Our government makes no sense unless it is founded on a deeply religious faith—and I don't care what it is."[8] Others, however, articulated this connection in more specific terms. No less a figure than the evangelist Billy Graham described the best antidote to Communism not as religious faith in general, but as "conservative and Evangelical Christianity," by which he meant "a personal faith in God, a belief in the Bible as the rule of faith and practice and an experience of the regenerating grace of God, which transforms character."[9] For many evangelicals, the *real* bulwark against the red menace came only from *real* Christianity—in their understanding, a faith that emphasized personal salvation, pursued evangelism as its primary mission, hewed to literal or quasi-literal Biblical interpretation, and disavowed political involvement. In this view, liberal Christianity—which might include religious perspectives ranging from the much-maligned social gospel to modernist or neo-orthodox theologies—did not offer an alternative faith to Communism; to the contrary, such faiths represented a first step on the path toward red domination. In particular, those who identified a biblical mandate to encourage economic and social equality by championing greater market regulation or by empowering labor seemed to teeter dangerously close to "statism" and "totalitarianism," aiming to "force equality." In the starkly dichotomized language of the Cold War, liberal ministers "play[ed] left guard on the Communist-front teams," and socially activist forms of Christianity joined the ranks of suspected "fifth columns" in American life.[10]

In conservative religious circles then, "Communism" often functioned as code for liberal Christianity, and Cold War discourse helped strengthen the working alliance between religious, political, and economic conservatism. L. Nelson Bell, former medical missionary, father-in-law to evangelist Billy Graham, and editor of the *Southern Presbyterian Journal*, exemplified these associations. Bell explained why evangelical Christianity, with its emphasis on individual conversion, fit organically with a conservative political philosophy that favored protection of property rights, small government, and unrestrained free enterprise. Bell affirmed his own Presbyterian tradition that had long advocated a "non-political" mission for the church, but apparently he believed he was merely explaining the Bible, not advocating a specific politics, when he lauded the virtues of untrammeled markets. In his understanding, the Bible's answer to social injustice contained "no suggestion that the government was to institute a 'Welfare State'" or any other sort of ameliorative or redistributive effort. In fact, the Old Testament prophets, in Bell's interpretation, dealt with economic inequities by strengthening the hand of property owners who would then give generously to their less fortunate fellows, not by systemic reform or by guarantees of equal access to economic opportunity: "Laws were given [in the Old Testament] to protect the property rights of individuals. Men were to acquire wealth by hard work and were to be strictly honest in their dealings with their fellowmen. . . . Those in need were to be cared for and treated with kindness." In Bell's skillful rendering, ancient Israel offered an exquisite model of laissez-faire capitalism: "If God had wanted Communism or Socialism, he would have set up such a system when His people began their life in Canaan. . . . Free enterprise, where Christian principles are practiced, is nearer the ideal."[11]

Evangelicals blessed unrestrained free enterprise as the most biblical economic system and feared that Communism inspired Christian efforts to check capitalism's abuses. A Christianity that challenged the social and economic order seemed clearly unfit for Americans, and this truth reverberated from powerful political voices. The House Un-American Activities Committee (HUAC) made the subversive proclivities of religion a special concern. In its pamphlet series published in 1948 and 1949, "One Hundred Things You Should Know about Communism," HUAC identified the church as a favorite Communist haunt. In their crude question-and-answer format, the pamphlets cautioned: *"Where can a Communist be found in everyday American life?* Look for him in your school, your labor union, your church, or your civic club."[12] HUAC even made Communism and religion the focus of its own "One Hundred Things" pamphlet. The piece endeavored to demonstrate Communist disregard for personal spiritual devotion, to highlight Moscow's willingness to use the clergy as a mouthpiece, and to widen the cast of potentially suspicious organizations to include para-church organizations like the YMCA, the YWCA, and the Epworth League.[13] Presumably, clerical wolves in sheeps' clothing would betray themselves by their embrace of a Christianity that advocated redistributions of wealth and power.

The FBI under the leadership of J. Edgar Hoover also adopted this concern. A proud booster of church attendance and Sunday school training as vital for creating robust young Americans, Hoover charged that "communists [were] able to secure ministers of the gospel to promote their evil work," and the FBI singled out for surveillance ministers who critiqued America's social and economic system.[14] The agency conducted an ongoing investigation, for example, of the Methodist Reverend Harry F. Ward from 1941 until his death in 1965, producing a dossier of eight hundred pages. The file described Ward as a "suspicious character," because while he "should be . . . saving . . . souls," he focused more on critiquing America's capitalistic economic system as inimical to the Christian Gospel. Other ministers who pursued a brand of socially activist or politically leftist Christianity that warranted FBI dossiers included Methodist theologian, pacifist, and social activist Georgia Harkness, Princeton Theological Seminary professor Edler Hawkins, Episcopalian social action leader and editor William B. Spofford, and Methodist pastor and labor advocate Henry Hitt Crane.[15]

Thus, a struggle over the meanings of faith and their implications for social, economic, and political life drove the debate over whether the red menace had seized the soul of American Christianity. In the mid-twentieth century, no political party had yet captured the powerful cultural authority of religion. The controversy over which branch of the faith really bolstered Communism—and consequently which form best suited Americans—raged most furiously within religious communities themselves. Not surprisingly, traditions with the greatest theological diversity seemed to fret and argue most about the presence of Communists among them. At mid-century, no Protestant denomination harbored a more richly heterogeneous constituency than the Methodist Church. Drawing from every American region, ethnic group, and social class, Methodism attracted fundamentalists like Californian "Fightin' Bob" Shuler, theological radicals the likes of which staffed the Methodist Federation for Social Action, and everything in between.

Increasing its vulnerability as the target of reds, Methodism came closer than any other tradition to claiming the mantle of "America's church." Certainly its national scope and diversity contributed to this impression, as did its stature as the largest single Protestant denomination in the United States, but even its history read like a micro-tale of the American past. Brought from England by a disciple of John Wesley, American Methodism severed its trans-Atlantic bonds to form a denomination independent of its mother. The American Methodist Church quickly outstripped its English counterpart both in numbers and vitality, and by 1844 it had secured preeminence as the largest denomination in the nation, surpassing the nearest contender by nearly 50 percent. Though antebellum Methodists—like the nation—split over slavery, the Church reunited in 1939, quickly becoming a superpower among churches. Thus embodying a distinctively American constituency, history, and outlook, Methodism seemed, perhaps more than any other faith tradition, uniquely charged with guarding the nation's democratic institutions. This church lacked only a firm commitment to a distinctively American theology.

Not coincidentally then, just as the Communist menace appeared most aggressive internationally and most pernicious domestically, its threat to and within American Methodism seemed to grow dramatically. In March 1950—when Communist revolutionaries had just completed their ouster of the American-backed nationalist regime in China, only weeks after the British physicist Klaus Fuchs's espionage confession and Alger Hiss's perjury conviction, and as Joseph McCarthy's infamous "205 communists in the state department" speech of February still rang in the public's ears—*Reader's Digest* published an article that purported to identify "Methodism's Pink Fringe." Authored by the journalist Stanley High, himself the son of a Methodist minister, the article articulated the conservative conflation of laissez-faire economics, American democracy, and evangelical Christianity, along with corollary associations among state management of the economy, Communism, and liberal Christianity. The piece aimed primarily to "expose" the Methodist Federation for Social Action (MFSA) as a breeding ground of Communist influence. An unofficial agency of the church that rented space in the denomination's New York office building, the MFSA maintained that greater socioeconomic planning might provide for a more equitable distribution of wealth in America. High suggested the agency's economic critiques called its political loyalties into question. Employing the kind of loose reasoning that became standard fare among McCarthyites, High found the MFSA officers' economic and social appraisals sufficient to brand these leaders as Communists, while never offering to document actual party membership for any of these prominent Methodist pastors, seminary professors, bishops, and editors. He implied that an essentially weak and naïve Methodist leadership enabled a fundamentally dishonest and sneaky MFSA: "That such a left-wing minority is officially tolerated is, in itself, an indication of the success of their tactics in concealing their real aims behind a humanitarian façade." Finally, High relied on the conflation of evangelical Christianity and democracy to advocate the extirpation of liberal Christianity as crucial to American strength: "For those of that church to fail to reassert their faith against this growing, aggressive minority will be to fail both America and the church."[16]

In spite of the piece's lack of documentation, the circularity of its argument, and its reliance on innuendo, the *Reader's Digest* article stirred up a
maelstrom of suspicion, fear, and paranoia among American Methodists,
rousing dedicated churchmen to identify fellow travelers in their midst.
Accusations against Methodist leaders multiplied, and Methodists rushed
to put their disavowal of Communism on record. A spate of "vigilante"
groups organized themselves to fight "the insidious and undercover efforts that are being made in many quarters to undermine the fundamental
principles upon which free democracy is builded[AU: *sic?*]," commitments
they expressed through theological and social conservatism. While many of
these groups had only a local constituency, others, like Circuit Riders, Inc.,
founded by thirty-three well-known conservative Methodists from various
states, claimed national interest.[17]

Yet another ordeal darkened the clouds of suspicion over the Methodist
Church, providing further evidence of the suspect political proclivities of
liberal Protestants. In July 1953, HUAC launched an investigation of ministers, with Methodist Bishop G. Bromley Oxnam of Washington, DC, at
its center. Oxnam's disdain for unchecked capitalism and his embrace
of the social gospel as the very essence of Christianity opened him to the
charge that he "served God on Sunday and the Communist front the rest
of the week." He spent ten hours on the witness stand, but little substance
came from his appearance. The committee summarily concluded that few
churchmen actually embraced Communism; Oxnam and HUAC Chairman
Harold Velde closed the ordeal on a friendly note by shaking hands for
photographers.[18] Nonetheless, in an era in which "under investigation by
HUAC" signaled immediate incrimination, Oxnam struggled for the rest
of his life to shake the label of "communist," a charge he deflected with
good humor: "There are some among us who will soon declare that Moses
must have studied Marx . . . [and] Amos must have read the Communist
Manifesto."[19]

American Presbyterians suffered similar assaults on their left flank. The
two regionally based and internally diverse Presbyterian denominations
had struggled to reunite after a century on separate trajectories, and this
endeavor brought their differences into direct confrontation, while at the
same time strengthening their identities as part of the same "reformed family." As in the case of Methodism, the popular conservative press stoked concerns that a red stain threatened Presbyterianism purity. In the July 1953

issue of *American Mercury*, professional red-baiter J.B. Matthews identified Dr. John Mackay as foremost among the "at least 7,000 Protestant clergymen who were Communist Party members, fellow travelers, espionage agents, party-line adherents, and unwitting dupes."[20] Other conservative organs joined the chorus against Mackay, newly elected as moderator of the (northern) Presbyterian Church and president of Princeton Theological Seminary.[21] Presbyterian leaders' response, a "Letter to Presbyterians" that denounced careless and indiscriminate anti-Communism, provoked a flood of both approbation and censure. The mainstream press, including *The New York Times* and *The Washington Post*, applauded Presbyterian leaders' reasoned position, but conservative pundits—religious and secular—added to the symphony of detractors.[22] The *Christian Herald*'s editor Dr. Daniel Poling cited the letter as proof of Protestant ministers' naïve failure to understand Communist tactics.[23] L. Nelson Bell argued that Presbyterian leaders "played into the hands of the communists." Bell went on to identify Mackay as one of the "many men who had permitted their social passion to lead them into associations, where any attempt to expose communist infiltration would find them in the limelight."[24]

Importantly, concerns about the Communist leanings of their leaders troubled Southern Baptists far less than other denominations. The SBC remained too thoroughly evangelical and too monolithically conservative for such struggles to make sense. Even members of the small Baptist left tended to advance social action as a by-product of evangelical faith rather than as Christianity's essence. In any case, Southern Baptists' socially conscious cadre remained largely confined to its seminaries and to leaders who worked cautiously in denominational agencies. Yet Southern Baptists did not remain entirely untouched. They spawned their own professional Christian anti-Communist in the colorful ex-Air-Force-officer-turned-minister, Edgar C. Bundy, founder of the Church League of America and author of *Collectivism in the Churches*.[25]

Conservatives from all denominations launched perhaps their most shrill and consistent assaults on liberal Christianity in a sustained campaign against the National Council of Churches (NCC). The NCC had succeeded the Federal Council of Churches (FCC) in 1950 as the leading representative body of mainstream Protestantism. Representing thirty-one American religious bodies (notable non-joiners included the Catholic Church, the Southern Baptist Convention, and the Lutheran Church, Missouri Synod), the organization worked to coordinate efforts among Protestant denominations and para-church organizations. Hardly radical, the NCC enjoyed considerable prestige in an America where mainstream Protestantism functioned as the informal national religious establishment. The enthusiastic participation of several members of the Eisenhower administration, perhaps most notably Secretary of State John Foster Dulles, strengthened the organization's establishment character. For the most conservative evangelicals, however, the NCC represented the prime example of Communism's insidious influence in American religion. Far-right religious conservatives like Bundy, Carl McIntyre, Vernon Kaub, and Billy James Hargis, all of whom made careers of identifying Communists among American protestant ministers, devoted much of their energy to "exposing" the NCC and its subversive activities. In 1960, for example, an allegation that Communist ideology influenced the NCC found its way into the Air Force Manual, and McIntyre appeared the source of the charges.[26] The claims of these far-right leaders often received amplification even from more moderate conservatives who, in the Cold War context that made anti-Communism the highest American virtue, also believed that the NCC's slightly left theological and political orientation rendered it a source of red influence. By 1964, when the bestselling anti-Communist exposé, *None Dare Call it Treason*, included a chapter on the NCC entitled "Subverting Our Religious Heritage," the author's contention that red influences dominated the NCC had become a mantra among conservatives and something of a tired trope to liberals.[27]

Thus, the argument about the influence of Communism in American faith institutions represented two political perspectives battling for the imprimatur of religion. "Anti-Communism" evoked a specific interpretation of the Gospel and its implications for politics and the economy, which varied according to the user. Mississippi-born NCC executive Francis Stuart Harmon advanced exactly this interpretation of the hunt for Communists in American religious institutions: "All of this talk about the NCC being subversive and communistic is a smoke screen thrown out by half a dozen persons who [proclaim] that they are the only true and faithful, 'Bible believing Christians' and [denounce] all liberals in religion or in economics as 'red apostates' serving Satan and the Soviet Union."[28] Indeed, while some Christians emphasized Jesus as defender of the underprivileged, oppressed, and forsaken, many others understood the Son of God as an ardent and unapologetic capitalist.

ANTI-COMMUNISM AND THE RACE STRUGGLE

In addition to its usefulness in damaging liberal Christianity, the language of anti-Communism conveyed a variety of other meanings. Extraordinarily multifaceted and malleable, this language expressed fears ranging from the loss of male control over female sexuality to the possibility that rogue scientists with esoteric knowledge might destroy the world. Not surprisingly, anti-Communism wreaked havoc in many different communities; academic, artistic, and scientific circles, for example, each suffered their own tailor-made red scares. Anti-Communism enjoyed an especially destructive career among the advocates of black equality.[29]

Nationally, fears of a domestic Communist threat had already played out to dramatic effect by 1954, but after the *Brown* decision of that year, Dixie adopted the rhetoric, language, and tactics of McCarthyism with renewed vigor. Though the notion that Communists drove the quest for black equality had a decades-old history, the presence, strength, and apparent credibility of this argument increased exponentially in the wake of the High Court's announcement. Segregationists from every southern state perpetuated the belief that civil rights initiatives originated in a Soviet plot to weaken America, but Mississippians occupied the vanguard of this effort.

The Communist Party's long-standing advocacy for black Americans strengthened the perceived connections between the bid for equal rights and red influence, and segregationists fully exploited these historic ties. Even in Mississippi, these links had sufficient factual basis to lend a faint ring of viability to false accusations. The Communist Party had garnered national and even international attention for the plight of Willie McGee, a black Mississippian accused in 1945 of raping a white woman. Due in part to the party's efforts, petitions poured in from all over the world to ask for clemency for McGee, some bearing the signatures of luminaries like Josephine Baker, Jean-Paul Sartre, and Albert Einstein. Such celebrity notwithstanding, McGee's case wended its way through three trials before he died in Mississippi's portable electric chair in 1951. Many Mississippians in the post-*Brown* era would also remember the trials of the Scottsboro Boys in neighboring Alabama, where lawyers supplied by the Communist Party had defended nine young black men accused of rape in a decade-long saga that began in 1931.[30]

Mississippi's US Senator James O. Eastland helped launch the southern race-related red scare and nourished it during its ruinous career. As the ranking Democrat on the Senate Internal Security Subcommittee (SISS), counterpart to the better-known HUAC, Eastland occupied a powerful post from which to wield this weapon. An ardent segregationist and nearly equally zealous anti-Communist, the Mississippi senator publicly linked racial equality with Communism in the spring of 1954. As the *Brown* case loomed, he held a series of hearings that attempted to show the Communist associations of five white liberals who had worked for the Southern Conference Educational Fund (SCEF), an organization dedicated to eliminating racial discrimination, particularly in southern education. Though by most assessments the hearings degenerated into a fiasco that failed to prove Communist associations for any of the accused, the Eastland subcommittee's account of it suggested otherwise. Segregationists used the trial itself as evidence of the Communist origins of civil rights initiatives for years to come. Thanks to the efforts of the likes of Eastland, "those who flunked [the test of white supremacy] were dyed an unacceptable shade of pink, and that was that."[31]

Many other Mississippians cultivated the myth that a Communist plot to weaken America lay behind efforts at integration. Mississippi circuit court judge Thomas Brady's infamous *Black Monday* pamphlet, widely circulated as a diatribe against the *Brown* decision, described the entire civil rights movement as a Soviet initiative: "Communist Russia's aim is the establishment of a beachhead through the Negro in the United States. To alienate racial groups against racial groups . . . Negro against white, is what Russia desires."[32] As "the loudest and most influential voice linking the black revolution to a Communist conspiracy in the South," the Citizens' Council also made this argument. At its first statewide convention in December 1955, Senator Eastland endorsed both the organization and the message, identifying integration as "a radical, pro-Communist political movement in this country."[33] These beginnings well adumbrated both the tactics and the content of Citizens' Council literature for the coming decade and a half.

While this particular use of anti-Communism did not necessarily rely on religious elements, in Mississippi and other southern states, segregationists braided it into the religiously framed anti-Communism running at full tilt in America's religious institutions. The anti-Communism that linked black equality to a plot hatched in Moscow meshed quite well with the strain that described links between liberal religion and liberal economics. The resulting three-ply chord united Mississippians' religious, racial, and political concerns in one effective framework. This race-baiting religious red scare, like the ideology of the Lost Cause, articulated the notion of a special destiny for America and in particular, for white southerners' own version of evangelical faith.

MISSISSIPPI'S RELIGIOUS RED SCARE

Mississippi's evangelicals met the challenge of black equality in the context of national debates about the meaning and nature of Christianity in which the language of Communism played a defining role. Because most white Magnolia State evangelicals had long since settled the meaning of their faith, the summons to purge their religious institutions of Communist influence found abundant resonance there. In their zealous adoption of anti-Communism, they articulated their conviction that faith placed them on the side of an anti-labor, anti-union, low-tax, small-government, and anti-black agenda. Yet the political allegiances of their denominations remained in flux, and as Mississippians articulated a position in opposition to their national leaders, they joined the chorus denouncing the red menace that threatened their faith institutions.

Mississippi's religious red scare added an additional element. There, evangelicals amplified the national religious strain of anti-Communism with the southern race-related red scare, a strategy that seemed to strengthen the perceived spiritual evil attendant upon racial integration. Mississippians' anti-Communist discourse captured all elements of its long-standing orthodoxy: their devotion to evangelical faith, to conservative politics, and to black subordination. The fight to preserve the one became a struggle to preserve the others, and in their Herculean effort to thwart black equality, they sealed the perceived alliance between these forces.

Not surprisingly, Mississippi's religious red scare tore most malevolently through the denominations already wracked by anti-Communism at the national level. Deeply ambivalent about their communions' openness to heresies like the social gospel, economic planning, and racial equality, Methodists and Presbyterians in Mississippi elaborated the notion that only an apostate faith would champion the racial struggle. Methodists began braiding the race-related red scare into concerns about the church's "liberalism" early in the Cold War era. Local groups registered complaints about church literature describing material such as an article titled "Many Races . . . One Brotherhood" as "communistic in trend."[34] Tellingly, some of the complaints included Methodist advocacy of the Fair Employment Practices Committee and other "liberal" policy positions. Mississippians' analysis of this literature identified it as part of a trend "in direct contradiction to the traditions and principles held by the vast majority of Southern Methodists."[35] An elderly layman described it even more darkly. Methodism had entered, he thought, "days of rank apostasy and even treason in the most holy places."[36]

Mississippi Methodists continued to identify the advocates of racial equality in their denomination as Communists, or—only slightly less evil on the slippery slope—socialists. In the wake of the 1950 "Pink Fringe" article in *Reader's Digest*, both Mississippi Conferences passed motions condemning the "communistic and atheistic program" of the Methodist Federation for Social Action.[37] Once the Methodist Church endorsed the *Brown* decision in 1954, however, the facile lashing of religious liberalism to Communism reached a fever pitch and remained there for a decade. A group of the state's ministers and laymen formed an organization for the express purpose of fighting integration in the Methodist Church. These conservative leaders of the Mississippi Association of Methodists Ministers and Laymen (MAMML)—many of them business elites like John Satterfield and John Wright—played a pivotal role in weaving Mississippi Methodists' concerns into a crackling discursive whip.

MAMML's segregationist and anti-Communist gospel spun out of its crudely written monthly newsletter, whose rather dispassionate title, *Information Bulletin*, belied the inflammatory rhetoric within. The *Information Bulletin* followed the pattern of other anti-Communist publications that borrowed and recycled material from a rather small pool, relying primarily on reprints of works by other far-right conservatives. The writings of Tom Anderson, a John Birch Society member and editor of *Farm and Ranch* magazine, provided useful material for MAMML's anti-Communist, anti-NCC, and anti-Methodist tirades. A Methodist layman, Anderson impugned his denomination with an insider's credibility. "Criticizing a person's church is even less rewarding than criticizing a person's children," opened an Anderson piece. "So perhaps it is just as well that the church which appears to be most 'liberal,' most Socialistic, most Communistic, most open to criticism, is my own."[38] The *Information Bulletin* repeated charges of red influence among important Methodist leaders like Reverend Harry Ward, Bishop Oxnam, and even the revered missionary E. Stanley Jones, as well as leaders in the National Council of Churches, including United Church of Christ spokesman Robert Spike and the prominent Presbyterian Eugene Carson Blake. MAMML spokesmen also recommended and cited other strident anti-Communist literature, including the writings of Carl McIntyre. In typical radical right fashion, MAMML circulated reports without attribution and with no investigation of their accuracy. Exemplary of this practice, the oft-cited "Report to the Vestry of St. Marks Episcopal Church, Shreveport, Louisiana, on the National Council of the Churches of Christ in the United States of America," claiming to document the "harmful and highly dangerous" aspects of the NCC, occupied nearly an entire issue of the *Information Bulletin* in 1961.[39] The *Information Bulletin* also borrowed work from conservative publications of less extreme stripes, such as *Christianity Today*, though that magazine's claim that "liberal Christianity and the social gospel have shared so many of Marxism's suppositions and taken it so seriously as a religion that one must criticize them together in the same terms" made it hardly distinguishable from the extremists.[40]

Perhaps most important to its struggle to keep Mississippi Methodists wedded to a tri-partite right-wing racial, political, and theological ideology, MAMML sponsored a series of speaking tours by Myers Lowman, the professional Methodist anti-Communist and leader of Circuit Riders, Inc., the Ohio-based one-man vigilante group that aimed to expose the Communist associations of the Methodist Church. Lowman provided information about subversive organizations to a variety of groups (including HUAC, SISS, the Citizens' Council, and the Mississippi State Sovereignty Commission), and Mississippians seemed to have an insatiable appetite for his message. Already a widely recognized name in the state by his 1962 face-off with Gerald Trigg—an event sponsored by MAMML and the Sovereignty Commission—Lowman appeared on Citizens' Council radio and television programs, peddling self-published polemics that purported to reveal the "public records" of Methodist leaders. By 1964, when MAMML conducted him on a seven-city speaking tour, he claimed to have spoken more than one hundred times in the state.[41]

MAMML's strident anti-Communism did more than simply discredit the advocates of racial equality—though it served this purpose splendidly. It married the concept of racial equality to a kind of religion most Mississippians regarded as inauthentic and apostate. The group clearly cared most about stopping integration of the Methodist Church and silencing it as a voice for black civil rights. However, branding the religious champions of racial equality as Communists—who could not be real Christians—endowed the quest for continued segregation with a greater spiritual urgency and wound the racial hierarchy tightly to conservative religion. To six hundred MAMML members who had gathered in Jackson to learn how to save their church from integration, John Satterfield repeated the familiar assertion that only a conservative religion offered a safeguard against Communism: "Jesus Christ spent his years on earth in saving souls of sinners . . . and that is what we must return to if our country is to . . . save the world from Communism."[42] MAMML rhetoric constantly affirmed the centrality of the Bible and of traditional interpretations of it, describing "faith in the Bible as the infallible, inspired, and authoritative Word of God" as central tenets on its letterhead.[43] A Jackson gathering of the group expressed its goal "to insure that the Commandments of God, the Teachings of Our Lord and Saviour, Jesus Christ, and the Apostles' Creed be adhered to without equivocation."[44] Perhaps particularly telling, an especially noxious wave of anti-Communist hysteria hit Mississippi Methodists in 1952 and again in 1960, with the Revised Standard Version of the Bible at the center. Rumors that "32 clergyman with communist front associations" had worked on the new translation ran so rampant that in 1960 the *Mississippi Methodist Advocate* used space in three separate issues to carefully refute it.[45] If the Citizens' Council wrapped its commitment to "racial integrity" in the high-sounding language of "states' rights," its religious counterpart connected commitments to segregation with devotion to the traditional, evangelical Christianity many believed was endangered in their own communion.

Methodists networked with Presbyterians who shared the conviction that American churches lay in the grip of a dangerous "socialistic and political drift." Members of both communions understood that the relationship of Southern Evangelicalism to conservative politics and white supremacy stood under imminent threat. If Methodists had MAMML and John Satterfield as religious race-and-red-baiting spokesmen, Presbyterians had their own anti-Communist champion in the Hattiesburg businessman L.E. Faulkner. Ranking as one of Hattiesburg's most successful and eminent citizens,

Faulkner presided over the Mississippi Central Railroad after climbing upward through the ranks. With an energy and civic-consciousness comparable to Satterfield's, his business interests and activities extended to a network of related enterprises. Most importantly, as a Sunday school superintendent, deacon, and elder, Faulkner labored to preserve a Presbyterian faith he regarded as threatened by theological liberalism, political and social activism, and doctrines of racial equality. He loaded these religious, political, and racial concerns together, training his rhetorical guns on the NCC and carrying forward a long-standing Southern Presbyterian animosity to that organization under the anti-Communist banner.

Faulkner's invectives elaborated on the notion that liberal or social gospel theology, government attempts to foster economic justice, and the quest for black equality all flowed from the same diabolical font. In an artless and rambling pamphlet, self-published in 1951 as *Reasons Why the Presbyterian Church in the United States should Withdraw from the National Council of Churches of Christ in the U.S.A.*, Faulkner identified the NCC as spiritually apostate, claiming that its "acts, objectives and policies [were] contrary to the Constitution of the Southern Presbyterian Church—yes, contrary to the commands of the Head of the Church, our Lord Jesus." Prefacing the pamphlet, a series of quotes presented without commentary strongly intimated that Communism lay behind all critiques of free enterprise. The bulk of the pamphlet focused on the NCC's endorsement of racial equality, arguing that "the so-called 'race-question' that Communists and some of our politicians . . . emphasize for selfish reasons [is] harmful to both races." Faulkner especially criticized the NCC's endorsement of President Truman's proposal to establish the Fair Employment Practices Commission (FEPC)—the wartime measure designed to eliminate racial discrimination in defense industries—on a permanent basis.[46]

Mississippians' avid interest in religion and Faulkner's status as a prominent and philanthropic businessman helped him garner an audience beyond the conservative enthusiasts that dominated many of the state's presbyteries. Early in 1951, he expounded his charges against the NCC in a month-long series in the *Hattiesburg American*. In these essays, Faulkner again united conservative economics and politics with conservative religion, sliding easily from attacks on NCC leaders as "enemies of the free enterprise system and our present form of government" to concern that these same leaders "are not believers in supernatural religion—the Christian religion.

Some of the prominent leaders of the National Council of Churches . . . have gone on record as not believing in the virgin birth, the death and resurrection of our Lord Jesus. . . ." Faulkner found especially self-incriminating a 1942 document that the Council described as principles "the Churches should stand for." Particularly disturbing to Faulkner, the document advocated the "application of the Christian principle of social well-being to the acquisition and use of wealth, subordination of speculation and the profit motive to the creative and cooperative spirit. . . a wider and fairer distribution of wealth; a living wage, as a minimum and above this a just share for the worker in the product of industry and agriculture." In short, Faulkner's concerns about the NCC extended beyond its spiritual failings and focused as much on its economic philosophy which, if put into effect, would make the "free enterprise system . . . a thing of the past."[47]

Prominent business elites like MAMML's leaders and Faulkner, who would have significant interests in preserving religious support for a conservative racial and economic program, promulgated this anti-Communist and segregationist gospel. Their business, civic, and religious leadership rendered them too influential to warrant dismissal as mere "crackpots." Yet, whether they fueled or merely reflected such sentiments among Mississippi's religious folk, Mississippians routinely demonstrated how widely they shared the belief that the religious argument for racial equality stemmed from the influence of Communism in American faith traditions. At Forrest Methodist Church, Dr. Gilbert Oliver assured his congregation that the quest for racial equality stemmed from "soap box orators" among the clergy who were "paid by Russian Communists to divide the people of this country."[48] A Presbyterian pastor from Columbus, Mississippi believed that "those who are committed to a program of racial integration are . . . promoting the very thing they sometimes deny: communism. It has been common knowledge for a long time . . . that some of the 'big mouth' church leaders of the East during the past several decades are fellow-travelers with communists."[49] The Central Mississippi District (Methodist) Laymen's Fellowship "blasted" the NCC for its "liberalism and communism," and a Vicksburg woman warned Bishop Franklin that most American denominations "under the leadership of the National Council of Churches refuse to believe that the Communists have infiltrated the clergy."[50] A woman at Galloway Memorial Methodist in Jackson left the church because its policies "definitely support[ed] communism."[51]

Anti-Communism seemed strongest among Methodists and Presbyterians, whose exploitable internal divisions rendered them vulnerable. But Mississippians of all denominations believed that the red menace threatened their conservative faith and promoted integration. Though Southern Baptist polity ostensibly tolerated theological differences and the denomination remained exempt from damning associations with the NCC, Baptists still frequently framed their religious concerns about race in the language of anti-Communism. Like their coreligionists in other traditions, they often used Communism to describe theologically progressive elements in the SBC. Members of the First Baptist Church of Grenada included a disavowal of Communism when they condemned their denomination for endorsing the *Brown* decision in 1954: "This Church [will] vote against . . . anything that smacks of . . . communism."[52] Baptist churches in Sunflower County responded to the Meredith crisis by resolving "that we do all we can to keep communism from infiltrating the churches and schools of our county."[53] Louis Hollis railed against Brooks Hays, a past president of the SBC and former Arkansas Congressman, for making a trip to Moscow with another "subversive minister."[54] When Mississippi Baptists learned that the SBC's Christian Life Commission (CLC) had accepted substantial grant monies from a progressive source, news traveled rapidly that the source was directed by "a radical integrationist, [who] contributes huge sums to such organizations as the NAACP and the Urban League."[55] Even First Baptist's polished pastor, Reverend Douglas Hudgins, argued the agency should return money so compromised by a "decided 'pinkish' tinge."[56]

COMMUNISM IN ACTION: THE DELTA MINISTRY

By 1964, when the National Council of Churches sent a ministry team to work with black citizens in the Delta region, the state's white religious folk had feared and fought a politically subversive and spiritually apostate form of faith that they believed threatened their churches from within for a decade and a half. In the Delta Ministry, their fears seemed to have materialized, and they believed the cancer of Communism had bred a large and aggressive tumor right in their state. Though many American Christians outside the state applauded the Delta Ministry, Mississippians decried it with near unanimity. Their objections demonstrate how their Gospel included not only evangelical faith, but also an economic and political philosophy that maintained the privileges of whites. In every respect, the Delta Ministry represented a Christianity in opposition to the one Mississippians widely espoused. Challenging all three elements of the state's orthodoxy, the Ministry embraced a faith more social than evangelical, an economics that empowered workers rather than augmented capital, and a political ethic rooted in racial equality. Not surprisingly, white Mississippians summed up their objections to the Delta Ministry in one phrase: Communism in action.[57]

For social and economic deprivation, no region in the United States matched the Delta, usually described as the football-shaped area comprising eighteen counties along the Mississippi River, beginning just below Memphis and extending south to above Vicksburg. Here the economic dimensions of white supremacy displayed themselves most vividly. In a grossly exploitative arrangement, white landowners had grown wealthy on the backs of slavery's descendants. African American families labored in the fields, earning little more for this service than shelter in dilapidated shacks that lacked even basic plumbing. Poverty-related health problems like infant mortality far exceeded national averages. The school systems tailored the academic year to the planting and harvesting needs of landowners, and literacy rates remained correspondingly low. The region's benighted status grew steadily worse in the 1950s as the area increasingly mechanized—among the last parts of the South to do so. Turned off the plantations in increasing numbers, young blacks who migrated out left behind a destitute population of the very old and the very young.[58]

As an outreach of the National Council of Churches' (NCC) Commission on Religion and Race, the Delta Ministry aimed to address the plight of this population. The project looked nothing like Baptists' limited and paternalistic Department of Negro Work, the sort of interracial ministry Mississippians typically applauded. Neither did the Delta Ministry resemble the heavily evangelistic endeavors Mississippians favored. To the contrary, this program offered little to address the classically defined "spiritual needs" of Delta blacks—it conducted no Bible classes or worship services, and it did not promote personal salvation as the solution for this dispossessed people's woes. However, the ministry did fill important humanitarian needs. It provided immediate relief in the form of food and clothing distribution, and in 1966 it erected a tent city to provide housing for sharecroppers who had been evicted from the plantations for their political activity. The Ministry placed itself even more firmly in opposition to the economic and political interests of white evangelicals in its unabashed and open support of civil rights initiatives and economic empowerment. Its programs of voter registration, adult education, and economic development all directly challenged white supremacy. Yet perhaps the Delta Ministry offended white Mississippians most grievously by supporting black workers in labor organization and strike activity. With the encouragement and backing of Ministry staff, Delta blacks picketed a carpet manufacturing plant in Greenville, joined a newly formed agricultural union, and occupied the Greenville Air Force Base. In short, the Delta Ministry sided with the victims of white supremacy and dared to support them in efforts to seize the economic and political rights necessary to secure a place of human dignity. In a real sense and practical sense, the project offered the imprimatur of the Christian faith for a redistribution of economic and political power.[59]

Mississippians' pervasive and longstanding hostility to the NCC guaranteed a cold reception for the Delta Ministry even before it began. For more than fifteen years, Magnolia State congregations had denounced the organization with rhythmic regularity—they drafted resolutions of opposition, cancelled their financial contributions, and asked their denominations to withdraw membership. Yet this opposition came mostly from layfolk, like Satterfield, Faulkner, and others, and a few ordinary pastors. Until the advent of the Delta Ministry, many prominent religious leaders ignored the battle against the NCC as much as they could, regarding the chorus of antagonism as merely the annoying carping of a reactionary constituency. Some moderate leaders even defended it.[60] Yet when the NCC launched the Delta Ministry, even these moderates joined the detractors.

Though many civil rights initiatives had elicited divided responses from Mississippi Christians, the Delta Ministry seemed abominable to all. New moderate Methodist leaders, Bishop Edward Pendergrass and *Advocate* editor Roy Lawrence, worked to deprive the Ministry of Methodist funds. Owen Cooper, possibly the state's most prominent Baptist layman, spoke against it. All three of these leaders would provide powerful voices of moderation, especially in the second half of the 1960s. They decried segregationist violence, supported the public schools during integration, and participated in sustained interracial dialogue. Yet even as they participated in such initiatives, their Christian moderation foundered on the rocks of an alternate

Gospel—one that championed the rights of the black poor against the privileged economic position of Mississippi whites.[61]

Mississippians' critique of the Delta Ministry underscores their conviction that the empowerment of the oppressed sprang from an alien faith. When Bishop Pendergrass and his cabinet of twelve district superintendents raised objections to the use of $70,000 from the church's National Board, their displeasure focused on the Ministry's political and economic efforts among impoverished black Deltans. The bishop and his cabinet regarded the endeavor as "more political in nature and civil rights in allegiance than Christian in context." The bishop's statement complained that "the activities of the staff have been directed toward building the 'poor Negro community' into a politically powerful pressure group."[62] A Methodist from Leland regarded such activities as "of a highly controversial political and economic nature."[63] When the Pace Methodist Church drafted a resolution in opposition to the Delta Ministry, the congregation complained it taught "socialistic ideas as against basic American concepts" and had no "religious emphases or purposes."[64]

In fact, however, the Delta Ministry and the evangelical faith of Mississippians represented two radically different kinds of Christianity—competing and mutually exclusive interpretations of the Gospel—that warred against one another. The contradictory understandings of the faith that warred at the national level carried their fight straight into the Mississippi Delta. Local evangelicals cut to the heart of the matter, dispensing with side issues about the attitudes of Delta Ministry staff and the lack of cooperation among local leaders. A Methodist from Greenville who observed the picketing at the Carpet Mill thought that the whole project stemmed from a misguided faith. The NCC, she argued, "had accepted too many into its folds without being born again." She worried that Methodist contributions to this endeavor would ultimately "leav[e] us a churchless and godless people, which is exactly what the Communists said they would make of us."[65] Even secular sources honed in on the Ministry's failure to pursue a program of personal salvation. An editorial in the Leland Progress argued that "the ministers who came here with the Delta Ministry did not come south to win souls."[66] Even though Southern Baptists had no connection to the NCC, Baptist Record editor Joe Odle assured his readership that their monies did not support the Delta Ministry, because "[Mississippi Baptists would] have no part in any programs which give emphasis to theological liberalism, ecumenism, and the social gospel."[67] The Christianity represented by the Delta Ministry, it seems, was no Christianity at all.

In fact, the Mississippians who identified the roots of the Delta Ministry in a different Gospel were exactly right. Although the staffers of the program came to it from positions of ministry and understood their work among Mississippi's poor in terms of their faith, this kind of Christianity did not highlight the need for individual salvation. Rather, it took the life of Christ as a model and advocated the direct amelioration of worldly conditions as part of the Gospel. The project's director, Art Thomas, explained that such work fit the example of "the Man who blest and fed the poor."[68] For Thomas and other project staffers, work in the Delta represented an opportunity to carry out the ministry of Jesus as revealed in his life and teachings.

This outlook entirely failed to resonate with many Mississippians, whose evangelical faith structured their perception so that the utter depravation in the Delta continued to appear to be the fault of blacks themselves, not the result of systemic exploitation. As Mississippians expounded their frustration with the Delta Ministry, one Methodist explained simply that poverty arose from individual, not systemic, causes: "There are two things that keep a person poor: (I) A feeling that he is too good to do manual labor when he hasn't the ability to do other work [and] (II) Spending money unwisely."[69] White Mississippians clearly saw the morality of their economic system, where power and privilege accrued to those who deserved and earned it. They little understood that, in actual fact, such blessings flowed to a racially defined group who had created unfair advantages for themselves. Inevitably, a faith-based effort to redistribute power to the dispossessed could only meet utter rejection from those who believed the Gospel favored the already privileged.

"SCATTERING SEEDS OF DISCORD"

As an outgrowth of the civil rights years, Mississippi's religious red scare proved extraordinarily destructive, not only to the religious argument for racial equality, but to religious life in the state. The state's once-vibrant Methodist communities, perhaps more than any other, passed the civil rights years in profound disorientation and disarray. Formerly large and thriving congregations like Galloway and Capitol Street Methodist in Jackson devolved into conflict-ridden bastions of tension and intrigue.

Spiritual leaders expended inordinate time and energy defending their denominations against the tirades of detractors. Young Methodist ministers left the state in such proportions that Bishop Franklin appointed a commission to investigate the causes of this brain-drain. The fractures in an already contentious Presbyterian community grew wider, readying that body for massive defections in the 1970s and 80s. In all the confusion, few clarion voices on behalf of black equality emerged from white religious communities. To most Mississippi evangelicals, the civil rights cause seemed a murky and dirty business rather than the clear moral mandate it appears in retrospect.

Yet importantly, in the midst of such chaos, evangelical moderates appropriated anti-Communism to separate themselves from their more zealously segregationist coreligionists. In the tumult of the 1960s, such moderates increasingly objected to the state's strategy of do-or-die resistance and to the atmosphere it created. Though still often tepid in their commitments to black equality, many moderates maintained intense loyalty to their denominations and expressed a willingness to follow the racial policies enacted at the highest echelons of religious leadership. They wielded anti-Communism in defense of the national church and against the divisive tactics of the far right. These moderates adopted the same essential starting point as arch-conservatives, indeed, as most Americans: democracy relied on Christianity for its existence and thus no institution had greater significance than the church in the fight against Communism. Yet moderates' reasoning turned the attacks of the red baiters back on them. To weaken the church, this great bulwark of democracy, by criticizing it and creating confusion, indiscriminate red baiters aided and abetted the red menace far more effectively than the theological liberals they so decried, moderates argued. Democracy, then, had no greater foe than Mississippi's own home-grown superpatriots: MAMML, Faulkner, and the Citizens' Council. Gerald Trigg made exactly this argument in his debate with Myers Lowman in 1962, suggesting that Lowman "play[ed] into the hands of communism" by "sowing seeds of suspicion."[70] Sam Ashmore of the *Advocate* described such traducers, who undermined layfolks' confidence in their leaders, as the most effective handmaids to Communism: "The only way Communism can succeed in America is to undermine Christian teachings and divide the churches. . . . The infiltration is taking place among the careless, indifferent and the unwary. They are being influenced by organized pressure groups."[71] In 1962, the North Mississippi Conference of the Methodist church condemned the Citizens' Council as "an extremist organization which has had the audacity to list the Methodist Church as an enemy of the people in this area in which we live."[72]

Indeed, in attacking the institutional church so ruthlessly, right-wing detractors ultimately overplayed their hand. The religious red scare pitted Mississippians' conservative religious, racial, and political commitments against their loyalties to the church. Many Mississippians accepted the radicals' assessments and joined robust Methodist and Presbyterian breakaway movements. Yet others, even though they valued segregation, greatly resented these attacks on institutions to which they had such attachments and that they regarded as so important to personal and public religious life. A layman who responded to "the loud voices of hate" within the church admonished, "we have taken sacred vows of fealty to our church which we must not forget. We who are Methodists in Mississippi are members of and a part of that great fellowship of over ten million Methodists which we call our Church . . . it is our duty and responsibility to respect the . . . decisions of our church."[73] Though this sort of institutional loyalty often garnered criticism, it ultimately preserved a voice of moderation in the state. Commitments to the institutional church helped attenuate devotion to the racial hierarchy.

Thus, though religion bolstered the ideological elements in the fight against black equality, it also provided a strong cultural tether to countervailing trends within American life. In a Mississippi struggling desperately to hang on to its most defining southern characteristic, such connections proved powerful and important. When MAMML created a new denomination that pulled members from many Mississippi Methodist Churches, the massive defections that they had predicted failed to materialize. Even John Satterfield ultimately could not forsake the institutional church, though his commitments to segregation remained as firm as ever. Just as the Lost Cause permitted white southerners to accept political reunion with the United States, anti-Communism provided Mississippi evangelicals a path to continued denomination unity, even amid the racial maelstrom of the 1950s and 1960s.

NOTES

1. *Mississippi Methodist Advocate* (hereafter *MMA*), August 8, 1962; *Jackson Clarion Ledger* (hereafter *CL*), July 31, 1962.

2. *MMA*, Aug. 8, 1962.

3. *CL*, July 31, 1962; *MMA*, Aug. 8, 1962.

4. Three of the most important works on anti-Communism in the South are Jeff Woods, *Black Struggle, Red Scare: Segregation and Anti-communism in the South, 1948–1968* (Baton Rouge: Louisiana State Univ. Press, 2004); George Lewis, *The White South and the Red Menace: Segregationists, Anticommunism, and Massive Resistance, 1945–1965* (Gainesville: Univ. Press of Florida, 2004); and Cate Fosl, *Subversive Southerner: Anne Braden and the Struggle for Racial Justice in the Cold War South* (Lexington: Univ. Press of Kentucky, 2006). For the Christian dimensions of anti-Communism, see Angela M. Lahr, *Millennial Dreams and Apocalyptic Nightmares: the Cold War Origins of Political Evangelicalism* (New York: Oxford Univ. Press, 2007) and older works that include Mark Silk, *Spiritual Politics: Religion and America since World War II* (New York: Simon and Schuster, 1988); Stephen J. Whitfield, *The Culture of the Cold War*, 2nd ed. (Baltimore: Johns Hopkins Univ. Press, 1996); and on an earlier period, Leo P. Ribuffo, *The Old Christian Right: The Protestant Far Right from the Great Depression to the Cold War* (Philadelphia: Temple Univ. Press, 1988).

5. *Religious Herald*, Jan. 25, 1952, quoted in Andrew Michael Manis, *Southern Civil Religions in Conflict: Black and White Baptists and Civil Rights, 1947–1957* (Athens: Univ. of Georgia Press, 1987), 43. On the Christian dimensions of the Cold War, see William Inboden, *Religion and American Foreign Policy: the Soul of Containment, 1945–1960* (New York: Cambridge Univ. Press, 2010).

6. *A Christian's Handbook on Communism* (New York: National Council of Churches of Christ in the U.S.A., 1962), 22, 23.

7. *MMA*, July 13, 1955; Nov. 7, 1962.

8. Dwight D. Eisenhower, Address at the Freedoms Foundation, Waldorf-Astoria, New York City, New York, Dec. 22, 1952, http://www.eisenhower.archives.gov/all_about_ike /quotes.html (accessed April 19, 2012).

9. Reverend Billy Graham, "Satan's Religion," *American Mercury*, 1954.

10. Quote from Howard Rushmore, "Dr. Daniel A. Poling: Preaching Fullback," *American Mercury*, Feb. 1954, 89–92.

11. L. Nelson Bell, "Amos Condemns Social Injustice," *Southern Presbyterian Journal* 12, no. 4 (May 26, 1954): 12.

12. House Committee on Un-american Activities, "One Hundred Things you should Know about Communism," Washington, DC: US Government, 1949.

13. House Committee on Un-american Activities, "One Hundred Things You Should Know about Communism and Religion," Washington, DC: US Government, 1948.

14. Testimony before the House Committee on Un-American Activities, March 26, 1947, quoted in J.B. Matthews, "Reds and Our Churches," *American Mercury*, July 1953.

15. Quotes from FBI Dossier of Harry F. Ward, in George D. McClain, "Social Ministry and Surveillance: Harry F. Ward and the Federal Bureau of Investigation," in *Rethinking*

Methodist History: A Bicentennial Historical Consultation (Nashville: Kingswood Books, 1983). See also David Nelson Duke, *In the Trenches with Jesus and Marx: Harry F. Ward and the Struggle for Social Justice* (Tuscaloosa: Univ. of Alabama Press, 2003).

16. Stanley High, "Methodism's Pink Fringe," *Reader's Digest*, March 1950, 134–38. The author also thanks Morris L. Davis for sharing his unpublished paper, "The Pink Fringe of Methodism," that advances an analysis of this piece similar to the one offered here.

17. Ray Ellis Branch, "Born of Conviction: Racial Conflict and Change in Mississippi Methodism, 1945–1983" (PhD diss., Mississippi State Univ., 1984), describes Circuit Riders' Mississippi Connections, 31. Another description of the group may be found in Don E. Carleton, *Red Scare! Right-wing Hysteria, Fifties Fanaticism, and their Legacy in Texas* (Austin: Texas Monthly Press, 1985), 110. See a mainstream Methodist perspective in Ralph Lord Roy, *Apostles of Discord: A Study of Organized Bigotry and Disruption on the Fringes of Protestantism* (Boston: Beacon Press, 1957).

18. This description is taken from Oxnam's own account of this ordeal, Garfield Bromley Oxnam, *I Protest*, (New York: Harper Books, 1954).

19. *MMA*, Sept. 15, 1954. For more on Oxnam, see the biography by Robert Moats Miller, *Bishop G. Bromley Oxnam: Paladin of Liberal Protestantism* (Nashville: Abingdon Press, 1990).

20. Matthews, "Reds and Our Churches."

21. See the response of Dr. Daniel Poling as described in Howard Rushmore, "Dr. Daniel A. Poling: Preaching Fullback," *American Mercury*, Feb. 1954, 89–92.

22. See for example *The New York Times* [AU: check that this is what NYT stood for here], July 12, 1953. Among the detractors, see the comments of Carl McIntyre in *The New York Times*, Nov. 5, 1953.

23. *The New York Times*, Sept. 14, 1953. See also J.B. Matthews, "America is Losing the War Against Communism," *American Mercury*, Jan. 1954, 3–8.

24. L. Nelson Bell, "A Strange Pronouncement," in *Southern Presbyterian Journal*, Nov. 18, 1953, 3–4. A thorough and well-contextualized treatment of this affair is offered in Rick Nutt, "For Truth and Liberty: Presbyterians and McCarthyism," in *Journal of Presbyterian History* 78, no. 1 (Spring 2000): 51–66.

25. Edgar C. Bundy, *Collectivism in the Churches* (Wheaton: Church League of America, 1960). Bundy authored other anti-Communist treatises that included *Apostles of Deceit* (Wheaton: Church League of America, 1966) and *How the Communists Use Religion* (New York: Devin-Adair Co., 1966).

26. *MMA*, Mar. 23, 1960.

27. John Stormer, *None Dare Call it Treason* (Florissant, MO: Liberty Bell Press, 1964).

28. *MMA*, July 8, 1960.

29. The literature on McCarthyism, as this phenomenon is often called, is too immense to detail here. Works that focus on the red scare in specific communities include Larry Ceplair and Steven Englund, *The Inquisition in Hollywood: Politics in the Film Community, 1930–1960* (Garden City, NY: Anchor Press/Doubleday, 1979); Victor Navasky, *Naming Names* (New York: Viking, 1980); Ellen W. Schrecker, *No Ivory Tower: McCarthyism and the Universities* (New York: Oxford Univ. Press, 1986); Jane Sanders, *Cold War on the Campus: Academic Freedom at*

the University of Washington (Seattle: Univ. of Washington Press, 1979); Jessica Wang, *American Science in an Age of Anxiety: Scientists, Anticommunism, and the Cold War* (Chapel Hill: Univ. of North Carolina Press, 1999); and Walter Gellhorn, *Security, Loyalty and Science* (Ithaca: Cornell Univ. Press, 1950).

30. On the Willie McGhee case, see Alex Heard, *The Eyes of Willie McGee: A Tragedy of Race, Sex, and Secrets in the Jim Crow South* (New York: Harper Collins, 2010). For the classic treatment of the Scottsboro case, see Dan T. Carter, *Scottsboro: A Tragedy of the American South*, rev. ed. (Baton Rouge: Louisiana State Univ. Press, 2007). On connections between the Communist Party and black activism, see Robin D.G. Kelley, *Hammer and Hoe: Alabama Communists During the Great Depression* (Chapel Hill: Univ. of North Carolina Press, 1990); Cedric Robinson, *Black Marxism: The Making of the Black Radical Tradition* (Chapel Hill: Univ. of North Carolina Press, 2000); William J. Maxwell, *New Negro, Old Left: African American Writing and Communism Between the Wars* (New York: Columbia Univ. Press, 1999); and Gerald Horne, *Black Liberation/Red Scare: Ben Davis and the Communist Party* (Newark: Univ. of Delaware Press, 1994).

31. The hearings are described in Woods, *Black Struggle, Red Scare*, 45–47 and also in John Egerton, *Speak Now Against the Day: The Generation Before the Civil Rights Movement* (New York: Alfred A. Knopf, 1994), 561, 569–71.

32. Judge Thomas Brady, *Black Monday* (Winona, MS: Association of Citizens' Councils, 1955).

33. Woods, *Black Struggle, Red Scare*, 143.

34. *Jackson Daily News*, June 26, 1946.

35. *Jackson Daily News*, June 4, 1946.

36. Victor Scanlan to Dr. Bob Schuler, May 28, 1951, L.E. Faulkner Papers, Box 51, Folder 9, McCain Library and Archives, USM.

37. Branch, "Born of Conviction," 31–32.

38. *Information Bulletin*, September 1960, in Paul Johnson Papers, Box 22, Folder 13, McCain Library and Archives, USM.

39. *Information Bulletin*, August 1961, in Paul Johnson Papers, Box 22, Folder 13, McCain Library and Archives, USM.

40. Cited in *Information Bulletin*, March 1961, in Reverend Jack Troutman, personal papers. The author thanks Dr. Joe Reiff of Emory and Henry College for sharing these materials from his research collection.

41. Information about Myers Lowman and his extensive work in Mississippi is available from a variety of sources. Woods describes his work as a professional anti-Communist, but his work in Mississippi can easily be discovered in the Sovereignty Commission Files at http://mdah.state.ms.us/arrec/digital_archives. See also *Information Bulletin*, March 1961 in Jack Troutman private papers, and June 1964 in Reverend Jack Napier private papers. The author thanks Dr. Joe Reiff of Emory and Henry College for sharing these materials from his research collection.

42. *Information Bulletin*, April 1963, in Dr. Maxie Dunnam private papers. The author thanks Dr. Joe Reiff of Emory and Henry College for sharing these materials from his research collection.

43. See letterhead, John R. Wright to Mississippi Methodists, February 7, 1964, A.E. Cox Collection, Box 1-B, Folder 49, Mitchell Memorial Library, Mississippi State University.

44. "A Resolution Urging Preservation of the Methodist Church and Recommending Specific Action by each Local Church in Mississippi Toward that End," in Rev. Ned Kellar personal papers. The author thanks Dr. Joe Reiff of Emory and Henry College for sharing these materials from his research collection.

45. *MMA*, April 6, April 20, June 29, 1960.

46. "Reasons Why the Presbyterian Church in the United States should Withdraw From the National Council of Churches of Christ in the U.S.A." in L.E. Faulkner Papers, Box 37, Folder 16.

47. *Hattiesburg American*, Feb. 17, 1951. The *Hattiesburg American* ran the other installments in Faulkner's series on Feb. 10, 24, March 3, 10.

48. *Scott County Times*, October 2, 1957.

49. Horace Villee to Rev. Malcolm P. Calhoun, DD, March 26, 1959 in Division of Christian Relations of the PCUS, RG 986.1 (unprocessed collection), Box 2, PHS.

50. Resolution, March 22, 1962, Bishops Office Papers (hereafter BOP); *Jackson Clarion-Ledger*, March 3, 1963; Mrs. Orley Hood to Bishop Marvin Franklin, January 5, 1963, BOP, Box 1, Folder 19.

51. Kathryn McInnis to My dear friends, August 25, 1965, W.J. Cunningham/ Galloway Methodist Church Collection, Folder 2, Small Manuscripts, Archives and Special Collections, J.D. Williams Library, The University of Mississippi.

52. *The Baptist Record*, June 17, 1954. Copy of resolution also in Christian Life Commission Papers, Box 1, Folder 8, Southern Baptist Historical Library and Archives (SBHLA).

53. Minutes, 42 Annual Session, Sunflower County Baptist Association of Mississippi.

54. Attachment with Doug Hudgins to Dr. Porter Routh, April 23, 1959, Executive Committee Records, Box 57, Folder 21, SBHLA.

55. The source was the Fund for the Republic, an agency of the Ford Foundation. This New York-based philanthropic endeavor evidently elicited these charges because of its participation in the Southern Regional Council's Consultative Conference on Desegregation.

56. Doug Hudgins to Porter Routh, February 18, 1958, Executive Committee Records, Box 57, Folder 21, SBHLA.

57. See Joseph Crespino's treatment of Mississippi evangelicals' response to the Delta Ministry in *In Search of Another Country: Mississippi and the Conservative Counterrevolution* (Princeton: Princeton Univ. Press, 2007), chapter five.

58. For a history of the Delta region, see James C. Cobb, *The Most Southern Place on Earth: The Mississippi Delta and the Roots of Regional Identity* (New York: Oxford Univ. Press, 1994).

59. Mark C. Newman, *Divine Agitators: The Delta Ministry and Civil Rights in Mississippi* (Athens: Univ. of Georgia Press, 2004) is a thorough treatment of the work of the Delta Ministry.

60. See for example the resolution adopted by the Mississippi Conference of the Methodist Church printed in the *MMA*, June 22, 1960, as well as the Report of the Committee to Investigate the National Council of Churches, BOP, Box 3, Folder 11.

61. Episcopal Bishop John N. Allin, another important moderate, also condemned the Delta Ministry. See Crespino, *In Search of Another Country*, 159.

62. *MMA*, Oct. 5, 1966. See also *JDN*, Oct. 1, 1966.

63. B.F. Smith to Bishop Edward J. Pendergrass, May 20, 1965, BOP Box 2, Folder 5.

64. Resolution in BOP, Box 3, Folder 11.

65. Hattye H. Eiland to Bishop Edw. J. Pendergrasss, Jan. 27, 1965, in BOP, Box 2, Folder 5.

66. *Leland Progress*, n.d. (c. May 1965), attached to B.F. Smith to Bishop Edward J. Pendergrass, May 20, 1965, in BOP, Box 2, Folder 5.

67. *BR*, 1964. The SBC's one tenuous connection to the NCC lay in a very small royalty—inconsequential really, in the context of the SBC's huge coffers—that the SBC Sunday School Board paid for use of a uniform lesson plan.

68. Thomas quoted in Crespino, *In Search of Another Country*, 163.

69. *MMA*, Nov. 9, 1966.

70. *CL*, July 30, 1962.

71. *MMA*, March 2, 1960.

72. Journal of the North Mississippi Conference, 1963, 143, cited in Branch, "Born of Conviction," 93.

73. *MMA*, Feb 24, 1965.

"May Their Gallant Souls . . . be Honored and Glorified": Civil War Reenacting and the Lost Cause

BRADLEY KEEFER

On July 3, 2013 nearly two hundred Union reenactors stood among thousands of spectators along the stone wall leading to "The Angle" at the Gettysburg National Military Park. Across the way, an even larger number of spectators assisted several hundred Confederate reenactors and flag-carrying NPS personnel in recreating the great charge that took place 150 years before. As the Confederate throng solemnly approached the nearly silent Union line, the rebel yell broke out as "the moment was temporarily ruined by a small handful of Confederate reenactors who childishly insisted on storming the stonewall [sic] despite the pleas of park rangers who urged they stop." By the time the spearhead reached the sacred angle, it became clear that the repulse of the charge was not what was on display; rather, it was the celebration of the failed 1863 attempt that dominated the event. While the impromptu rush to the wall was not part of the NPS plan, one can understand why this group of reenactors thought it was appropriate, since it was not the first time it had been done. The official Park Service sesquicentennial event was the latest in a string of recreations on or near the actual ground since 1863 commemorating one of the war's climactic moments when, despite the courage and devotion of the Army of Northern Virginia's soldiers, the Lost Cause was probably lost.[1]

Nearly four years later, some of the same Union reenactors fell back before a line of Confederate infantry at the New Market Battlefield in Virginia's Shenandoah Valley. The occasion was the annual reenactment of the May 15, 1864 Battle of New Market, where a small Confederate Army defeated a slightly larger Union force during the early stages of General Ulysses S. Grant's Overland Campaign. The highlight of the engagement was the triumphant charge of the Virginia Military Institute Cadets, whose assault broke the Union force and sealed the victory for the Southern army. Whether warranted or not, the job of the hapless Union force was to yield the field to the VMI's sweeping charge. Like Pickett's attack at Gettysburg, the charge of the VMI cadets at New Market is an annual Lost Cause ritual that reminds all who experience it of the devotion and immortal valor of Virginia's sons, many who fell in both memorable attacks.[2]

Ample records and experience demonstrate the persistence of the Lost Cause in Civil War reenacting. Inspired by the accounts written by the veterans that extoled the virtues of comradeship, the nobility of their opponents, and the commonality of the military experience, reenactors function in the mythical, non-political world of the "common soldier." Immersed in the minutiae of food, lifestyles, drill, tactics, and equipment, they strive to educate the public, amuse themselves, and if possible, walk in the shoes of the "old boys" for a few weekends a year. Their admiration for the Civil War veterans and the history of the war as they understand it is real and sincere, despite the many historical and interpretive flaws in their knowledge and understanding of the period. All of this favors a Lost Cause interpretation of the war, which emphasizes the heroic nature of the soldiers and obscures the influence of slavery on the causes, conduct, or outcome of the conflict. While it is not surprising that Confederate reenactors subscribe to this point of view, those portraying Union soldiers often readily buy into the program. Not only does this mean allowing the Confederates their battlefield triumphs, both real and pyrrhic, but it requires the adoption and acceptance of many well-established Lost Cause tenets.[3]

THE LOST CAUSE AND CIVIL WAR REENACTING

Ironically, the Lost Cause developed and thrived along with other elements and interests promoting a common nationalism. The impulse toward reunion—and to a lesser extent, reconciliation—helped Americans promote the Lost Cause without choosing sides. The rhetoric of reunion dominated the dedication of the jointly constructed Chickamauga-Chattanooga National Military Park, where during the Spanish-American War, northern and southern soldiers served together against a common foe. While the outcome of the War with Spain did not generate the lasting memories that the Civil War created, the outpouring of national unity triggered another round of monument building on battlefields and public places around the country, where the image of the standing soldier became ubiquitous in hundreds of parks, village greens, and cemeteries during the early twentieth century.[4]

This focus on the experience of common soldiers by some scholars and many lay authors of Civil War history created a reenactor historiography, which emphasized the similarities and differences of common soldiers, and, at least on the surface, seems free of obvious Lost Cause themes. However, their acceptance of Confederate myths and focus on the military rank-and-file fueled the interest of a whole generation of future reenactors, whose visions of banjo-playing cavaliers, shoeless rebels, stolid immigrant Yankees, and the comradery of camp, march, and battle left a lasting impression on the ways they recreate the Civil War experience.[5] In many ways, reenactors strive to connect with the soldiers they know from the stories, letters, books, and photographs they grew up with. As the central point in United States history, the Civil War and its veterans became a larger-than-life symbol of manhood, courage, and sacrifice that segments of our society continue to hold in high regard.

For the baby boomers who make up the bulk of the aging reenactor armies, the actual veterans of the war were tantalizingly out of reach, with the last of them dying in the 1950s. Lacking direct approbation from the "old boys," Civil War reenactors search for that connection by portraying soldiers and civilians in camp and combat, while simultaneously serving as the unofficial guardians of the battlefields, monuments, symbols, and cemeteries that represent their heroic sacrifices. As proxies for the actual participants in the war, reenactors feel that they are responsible for telling the "real" story of the conflict that does not require a discussion of slavery, abolition, or reconstruction as key elements. Using the uniforms and equipment as vestments, camps and battles as rituals, and the battlefields and monuments as sacred sites, the reenacting community functions with a common goal: to keep alive the memory of the war and the idealized men and women who fought, and defend them from modern elements that threaten to obscure them. As such, they straddle the ground between the interpreters of history and keepers of heritage.[6]

As the veterans grew older and their recollections began to fade, the rituals and ceremonies that commemorated their service became more important in determining how they are remembered. Eventually, the facts of the conflict, its stories and legends, and the recollections of its participants

became intertwined as part of the "imagined" history of the nation's struggle. Although the construction of historical narratives often includes elements of memory, some of the most evocative memories become more of
a community's *heritage* (its mythical, imagined past) than its actual *history*.[7]
Within this quest to preserve important memories, groups frequently memorialize or "sanctify" the physical sites of dramatic, significant past events.
Not all sites are sanctified. Some are used in multiple ways while others
fade away and become forgotten or obliterated, along with the memories
they represent. By preserving and protecting the physical landscapes (battlefields) and carrying out rituals like reenactments on or near them, both
veterans and reenactors can emphasize the importance of the events that
took place on that sacred ground and reinforce the common, national values represented there.[8]

Commemoration also plays a role in the ways reenactors preserve the
Civil War past. According to John Connerton, the repetition of "commemorative ceremonies and bodily practices" is the primary means by which
"the memories of groups [are] conveyed and sustained." These activities
serve as "representations or constructions of reality" that involve "an active,
ongoing process of ordering the past."[9] One of the most effective ways to
transmit and preserve these memories is to engage in ritual ceremonies
that anchor them in time and space. Thus, the annual reunions of the war's
veterans, regular celebrations of Memorial Days, living histories, and battle reenactments (particularly on key anniversaries) serve the same general purpose by actively involving members of the group—or their modern
descendants or reenactment proxies—in remembering the past. By holding encampments, parades, rallies, and ceremonies in public places or on
the sites of their heroic deeds, Civil War veterans placed themselves both
physically and spiritually as close as possible to the past, thus keeping the
memory "alive" for themselves and others. The task of the reenactors is to
replicate and repeat this process on behalf of the veterans and the values
they represented then and now.[10]

Not surprisingly, the Lost Cause serves as a dominant collective memory of
the war, influencing much of what follows. Reverence for Confederate symbols and the replication of the lifestyles and battles of the war's veterans reinforce a Southern heritage that encompasses individualism, Protestantism,
a distrust of federal authority, and pride in the region's role as underdogs.
For Union reenactors, the Lost Cause becomes part of a national heritage,

since protecting the sites and memories of their victory celebrates the common values shared by all reunified, patriotic Americans. The threat of destruction by commercial developers that hangs over many battlefields and
the widely held opinion that the Civil War is no longer taught (or taught
correctly) to the current generation of students adds urgency to the maintenance of Lost Cause memories and traditions. In times of change or conflict, such as the controversies involving racism and Confederate symbols,
reenactors representing both sides see themselves as leaders in the preservation of sacred ground, traditional values, and patriotic ideals.[11]

Civil War reenacting recreates the lifestyle, military activities, and other
aspects of Civil War soldiers and civilians for commemorative, entertainment, and/or educational purposes. The men, women, and children who
participate in this hobby are amateur "weekend warriors" who often travel
to partake in events ranging from school visits and living history encampments to battle reenactments. While many are active in local history organizations, they should be distinguished from costumed docents, craftspeople,
non-military living history groups, or first-person interpreters often found
at historical sites like Colonial Williamsburg. Unlike uniformed, costumed,
professional entertainers; actors portraying famous people; and vendors
selling their wares, reenactors are rarely paid and usually have lives and
jobs outside the hobby.[12]

As part of his journey to discover the Lost Cause, author Tony Horwitz
spent time with Robert Lee Hodge, a reenactor obsessed with authenticity
and dismayed by the commercialism of most battle reenactments. Hodge
and his Southern Guard devoted themselves to recreating the feels, smells,
and misery of the soldier experience by sleeping on battlefields without
tents, eating hardtack, and immersing themselves in a ritual that Hodge
termed "the Civil Wargasm." Hodge rejected the notion that he was glorifying a slaveholding Confederacy and considered what he was doing educational and beneficial. He took pride in exposing the public to his tattered,
gray uniform while promoting the hardships and heroism of the common
soldiers. In short, he was one of many communicants in what Charles
Reagan Wilson describes as the "civic religion" of the Lost Cause.[13]

THE CULTURE OF REENACTING

Various forms of battle reenacting began shortly after the Civil War, evolving throughout the twentieth century from the veterans themselves to their descendants, collectors, competitive shooters, and living history demonstrators. Over time, the mythic and mythical have become central to reenacting, including an intense devotion to companies and regiments via painstaking displays of insignia and accoutrements, along with sanctifying rituals that seemingly equate consuming vintage hardtack with the communion wafer of a religious sacrament. Reenactors often debate the degrees of authenticity required of the faithful, including whether proper reenacting permits sleeping in modern tents, wearing incorrect eyewear, or eating inauthentic food. While "hardcores" like Hodge act out their version of the war in muddy, odiferous splendor, the seemingly clueless "farbs" break the rules with impunity. Most reenactors exist somewhere in the middle, but all agree on the centrality of the soldiers' experiences, the ritual of camp life, and preparation for and participation in battles that preserve at their essence a vital piece of the Lost Cause.[14]

The heart of this interpretation argues that the war can be remembered as a strictly military contest, thus separating its veterans and their reenactor descendants from the larger issues of the war. The obsession with authenticity is part of that single-mindedness. Leigh Clemons explains why the debates within the reenactor community over the historical accuracy of uniforms and equipment "is . . . the core issue for battle reenacting." Since hardcores cannot fight in real battles with real bullets, they "prefer to focus on drilling, forced marches, and details of the soldier's life that occurred outside of fighting." In response to academic criticisms of reenactors as bad interpreters of the past, Civil War blogger Rob Baker reminds the critics that "reenactors are not there to interpret. They are not there to discuss the racial tensions of the Civil War, or broaden the understanding of the Civil War beyond that of visual simulations of appearance and battle. They provide, primarily, a military visual narrative of the war." Divorcing their primary activities from the larger issues of history makes it easy for reenactors to deny or ignore that the war was about slavery, even if most historians agree that it was. Ultimately, "reenactments may purport to serve an educational purpose, but their primary goal is commemoration, either of a specific battle or the life of the common soldier." Having dedicated themselves to honoring and remembering the soldiers and their experiences, reenactors are under-standably confused when criticized for not doing more.[15]

Many reenactors have personal libraries filled with memoirs, biographies, and campaign/battle studies. However, new scholarly interpretations on the war (or Reconstruction) rarely penetrate embedded Reconciliationist memories. Having read many books insisting that the average Union and Confederate soldiers did not care about slavery, they are unlikely to accept Chandra Manning's evidence that "rescues slavery from the periphery of soldiers' mental worlds . . . and returns it to the rightful place at the center of soldiers' view of the struggle." Nor will they absorb Caroline Janney's ar-gument that "deep bitterness and a refusal to cast aside judgements about the worthiness of the two causes remained throughout the lives of the gen-eration that had survived the war." Many Lost Cause ideas are held equally by reenactors on both sides. During a discussion of the Union emancipa-tion narrative with the women of the 66th Ohio, the matriarch of the camp interrupted the conversation to point out that "we have two card-carrying members of the UDC under this fly," illustrating that even in the friendly confines of a federal camp, Reconciliationist thinking retains its hold.[16]

Drill was important to Civil War soldiers, and most reenactor units at-tempt to achieve a modest level of proficiency. As Earl Hess explains in *Civil War Infantry Tactics*, the skill with which regimental and brigade command-ers could utilize and improvise standard tactics often made a significant dif-ference on the battlefield. Whereas actual soldiers drilled daily, reenactors usually only get a handful of opportunities during a year of activities. Most work on the School of the Soldier and School of the Company, where basic movements are repeated until they can be done without error. Although most reenactors would disagree with Hess's exposition on the relative in-effectiveness of the rifled musket, they embrace his emphasis on the im-portance of drill to make Civil War armies tactically effective.[17] To maintain unity and effectiveness, many company-sized reenactment units combine into larger, geographically oriented organizations made up of companies that hold to similar standards of authenticity. At large reenactments, these units conduct battalion-level drills that give reenactors a sense of what regimental maneuvers would have been like for the soldiers themselves. Ultimately, the thing that all participants strive for is to recreate the drama and spectacle of Civil War combat that includes hearing the guns, smelling the smoke, and moving in large formations at a big battle reenactment.[18]

THE GROWTH OF REENACTING

There are some disputes over what constituted the first Civil War reenactment, but most accounts suggest that the earliest semi-modern reenactments—what looks like reenacting to contemporary observers—appeared
in conjunction with the Civil War Centennial. The primary participants con-
sisted of members of the North-South Skirmish Association (N-SSA), who
had been doing shooting demonstrations and skirmishes at state and local
events for some time leading up to the national reenactment at Manassas,
Virginia. They were joined during the centennial by a collection of other
participants wearing a variety of gear and toting a vast array of period and
non-period weaponry, including actual Civil War ordinance. Early events
held in places like Missouri and western New York reveal the limitations
of the N-SSA units for carrying out ambitious recreations. In May 1961,
a reenactment of the Battle of Lexington, Missouri "us[ed] bales of hay
to illustrate use of 500 lb. hemp bales at the same spot 100 years ago." In
New York, the "skirmish would be the first act in a pageantry of parade,
dramatization, and dedication celebrating the region's part in the war's
centennial."[19]

The first large mock battle on the Manassas National Military Park in
1961 featured N-SSA infantry, cavalry, and artillery units, required numerous rehearsals, and was ultimately deemed by its "chief stage director" to
have been "very realistic." However, another participant later recalled that
"the uniforms only looked good from a distance" and the fighting was stag-
nant because "nobody knew Civil War drill," concluding that "it was a farb-
fest but it sure was fun!" While deemed a success, the civilian casualties
from heat stroke outnumbered those on the battlefield, and some members
of the Centennial Commission were so unimpressed that they denounced
reenactments as inappropriate and "an affront to good taste and an abuse
to history."[20]

Undeterred, the National Park Service (NPS) and Department of Defense
presented several more reenactments and living histories, highlighted by
a huge event at the Antietam National Military Park in September 1962.
Typical of the units on the field was the 19th Ohio Light Artillery, whose
number two gun crew included a thirty-eight-year-old mom, her ten-year-
old daughter, and their son's teenage fiancé. Aided by a "spirited narrative

broadcast over loudspeakers" the crowd was treated to "a sweep of colorful uniforms, the smoke of muskets and cannons, the charge of wheeling
horses, and a tangled profusion of falling bodies." Although spectator
injuries again outnumbered those of the reenactors, one writer declared
that it was a "festive and satisfying day." Following a Gettysburg event on
the battlefield in July 1963 that featured a piped-in soundtrack and culminated in a unifying patriotic display, the Centennial Commission noted
that subsequent "sham battles . . . were solely the production of state and
local organizations." The NPS's subsequent prohibition on reenactments
on National Park lands lasted almost thirty years and drove an unfortunate
wedge between the living history community and the officials who managed
and interpreted the battlefields.[21]

In the two and a half decades between the centennial and the war's next
major anniversary, the reenacting hobby grew and evolved. Since the N-SSA
participants continued to prefer live shoots, a new group of participants began to improve their authentic appearance and focus on battle scenarios that
included maneuvering, casualties, and opposing fire.[22] In addition to these
activities and the patriotic celebrations of the nation's bicentennial, annual
Civil War reenactments held on state battlefields in Virginia, Kentucky, and
Florida provided the growing number of reenactors with authentic places to
march, camp, and fight. However, the national hobby of reenacting would
not really take off until the war's 125th anniversary.[23]

Whereas some early reenactments were connected with official commemorative activities on National Park lands and state battlefields, the
large events that began in 1985 were conducted on private property and
sponsored by non-government entities. The reenactment community en-
thusiastically supported 125th events held in both the Eastern and Western
theaters,[24] while the widely circulated *Camp Chase Gazette* printed letters,
advertisements, and articles that encouraged its readers to recount their
participation in both large and small reenactments. A Maryland company
called *Classic Images* produced high-quality (VHS) videos of the major battles that included enhanced sound, maps, narration, period photographs,
music, reenactors portraying famous characters, and professional camera
work and editing.[25]

The combination of videos, word of mouth, and local and national
media coverage resulted in a huge boom in the numbers and quality of
Civil War reenactors, merchants, and civilian participants.[26] The 125th

reenactment at Gettysburg drew more than ten thousand participants and even greater numbers of spectators, and it was followed by a series of reenacted battles at Chickamauga, Spotsylvania, Atlanta, Franklin, Bentonville, and Sailor's Creek, culminating with a surrender ceremony on the NPS site at Appomattox Court House, Virginia. By the end of the anniversary sequence, much of the heritage community had embraced reenactments as the centerpiece of its efforts to remember, relive, and commemorate the Civil War. The annual Remembrance Day celebration at Gettysburg on the anniversary of Lincoln's speech served as another formal recognition of the reenactors' role as living embodiments of the veterans who created the parks and monuments in the 1890s.[27]

This surge of interest in the Civil War was augmented by an outpouring of films, books, and television shows that appeared in conjunction with the 125th anniversary.[28] Ken Burns's epic *The Civil War*, which ran on PBS in 1989, featured no live action, but its visual grandeur, dramatic readings, moving music, and compelling historical characters made a powerful impression on reenactors and the public. Southern writer Shelby Foote channeled the Lost Cause by praising Confederate courage, exalting the military virtues of KKK founder Nathan Bedford Forrest, and claiming that "the North won that war with one hand tied behind its back." His languid drawl overwhelmed the sensible Emancipationist voice of historian Barbara Fields, who emphasized a meaning of the war beyond the battlefield that extended to the ongoing struggle for civil rights.

Burns also highlighted the way the veterans remembered the war. Joshua Lawrence Chamberlin, one of the film's featured characters, remarks wistfully that "the pageant has passed. The day is over. But we linger, loath to think we shall see them no more together—these men, these horses, these colors afield." The eleven-hour film ended amidst scenes of aging veterans marching and posing for photographers while Foote recited a long quote from a former Confederate who wished to "meet again in the old quarters," noting that after reliving the thrill of battle "the slain and wounded will arise and all meet together under the old flags, sound and well" and ask one another "did it not seem real?" Not surprisingly, immediately after every battle reenactment, the casualties rise, remove their headgear, and stand together in silence as a bugler plays "Taps." One can picture such a scene as the film's last line asks on behalf of its fading veterans, "Was it not as it was in the old days?"[29]

Although Edward Zwick's *Glory* (1989) offered a counter-narrative to the persistent Lost Cause in popular culture, its story of the 54th Massachusetts did not alter the tactical-centered reenactor narrative.[30] At about the same time, developers' efforts to build theme parks, shopping malls, and casinos adjacent to battlefields strengthened the cultural and political clout of the reenactor community. This credibility was well represented by versatile historian Brian Pohanka, commander of the colorful 5th New York Zouaves, who served as a technical advisor on several high-profile, big budget Civil War movies and appeared as one of the prominent historical commentators on A&E's *Civil War Journal.* Pohanka, a founding member of the Association for the Preservation of Civil War Sites (APCWS), was a preservation "true believer" who, after the 2001 September 11 attacks, led a fundraising effort for New York's fire fighters, noting that the original 5th New York was partially made up of firemen. In 1999, he praised the Civil War veterans' "sublime amalgam of patriotism, duty, devotion, acceptance of self-sacrifice . . . idealism [and] . . . devotion to ideals they cherished more than life itself." He continued, "I bless and revere them—both North and South alike—heroes to me forever," and concluded, "may their gallant souls rest in peace, and be honored and glorified, to the last pulse of this country's existence." At the time of his death in 2005, Pohanka was a respected historian who wore the mantle of reenacting with class and dignity.[31]

Beginning with the 130th Bull Run in 1991, reenactors expanded their footprint during a five-year pattern of reenactments on the anniversaries of major battles. The very successful 135th Antietam was sponsored by the APCWS and heavily promoted as an "educational event." A year later, the massive 135th Battle of Gettysburg reenactment nearly doubled the numbers of participants from the 125th and claimed to be "the largest ever held in the United States."[32] State-run battlefields at Cedar Creek and Perryville hosted annual reenactments that served as fundraisers for the local park foundations.[33] By the end of this ten-year sequence (1991–2001), the National Park Service's long-standing reluctance to use reenactors for living history demonstrations that included firing finally crumbled, leading to ongoing programs featuring both Union and Confederate reenactors on the Gettysburg, Chickamauga, Spotsylvania, and Antietam battlefields that included the 2013 NPS/reenactor event described at the beginning of this essay.[34]

REENACTING PICKETT'S CHARGE

If there is a single moment, time, and place that represents the Lost Cause, it is Pickett's Charge at Gettysburg. As Carol Reardon pointed out, the third day's frontal assault on Cemetery Ridge became the most remembered moment of the war thanks to the press, the public, and the battle's veterans. With the help of park designer John Batchelder, the repulse of Lee's Virginians by the Army of the Potomac's 2nd Army Corps was exalted as the nadir of the Confederacy. The creation of the National Cemetery and Abraham Lincoln's immortal speech in November 1863 sanctified both the ground and the men who fought and died on it. The entire battle was "like a conscious work of art"—an epic tale of boldness, lost opportunities, blunders, and unlikely heroes. The final scene in any Gettysburg pageant always includes a massive artillery barrage, the methodical advance of three Confederate divisions across the wide open plain, and the final push to the "copse of trees," where they are repelled by an extraordinary effort from the heroes behind the wall. All the Lost Cause elements are present: mutual heroism, great sacrifice, glorious spectacle, and the devotion of the veterans who returned decades later to mark the fields with monuments and remember fallen comrades.[35]

The somewhat tainted sesquicentennial version of Pickett's Charge was not the first time the seminal attack had been recreated on the National Park's sacred ground. During the fiftieth and seventy-fifth anniversary reunions in 1913 and 1938, Civil War veterans had conducted ritualized assaults that contained all the key elements of a "commemorative ceremony and bodily practice." Both occasions passed the test of authenticity by providing the public with the spectacle of the aging veterans advancing across the field for the express purpose of remembering the original bloody event and shaking hands in the spirit of national healing. More than any other moment, this sentimental portrait of the Civil War generation left a space in the thread of authenticity and reconciliation that the modern reenactors strive to fill.[36]

Reenactors are drawn to both the battle and its commemorative rituals. J. Christian Spielvogel notes, "Ironically, the site of the Union's most famous victory seems more hospitable to the Confederate Lost Cause interpretation of the war." Union reenactors are content to play a secondary role in the spectacle, since the outcome is a foregone conclusion. While the attack's failure is fixed in both history and memory, the Confederate "what ifs" are endlessly tantalizing, as illustrated by William Faulkner's famous passage from *Intruder in the Dust*: "For every Southern boy fourteen years old . . . there is the instant when it's not yet two o'clock on that July afternoon in 1863 . . . it's all in the balance, it hasn't happened yet . . . but there is still time for it not to begin against that position . . . maybe this time with all this much to lose and all this much to gain . . . [a] desperate and unbelievable victory." For Confederate reenactors, the promise of success lies at the end of whatever space has been designated for the charge; for Yankees, it is a chance to see their foes fall in droves under their relentless fire.[37] Sadly, most modern reenactors will never get a chance to follow in the veterans' footsteps and recreate this epic assault on the sacred ground at Gettysburg National Military Park. Besides the scene in 2013, the charge has only been done a handful of times before and after the veterans made the final walk in 1938: in 1922 courtesy of five thousand United States Marines, several times around the centennial and 125th anniversaries, and once more thanks to Civil War buff and media mogul Ted Turner, whose efforts further demonstrated the power of Pickett's Charge to perpetuate Lost Cause themes in popular culture.[38]

In 1991, Turner and director Ron Maxwell teamed up to make a film version of Michael Shaara's 1974 novel *The Killer Angels* that drew extensively on reenactors for props, expertise, and a literal cast of thousands for the battle scenes. Maxwell wrote of the reenactors, "It's not just the uniform and the musket. It's the feeling. These people are living and breathing the Civil War." Putting large numbers of amateurs in scenes with A-list actors was a huge boost for the visibility and credibility of the weekend warriors who made up the bulk of the extras. Martin Sheen, who played Robert E. Lee, remarked that the reenactors "are here because of their commitment and love of what they do." Sam Elliott, who was featured as the grizzled John Buford observed that "they are taking this all very seriously and paying tribute to the people who died here" and added, as several of the actors had, "[We] couldn't be making this picture without them."[39]

Reenactors established military camps like those at major reenactments, despite not being required to maintain authenticity when "off the clock." Unless being transported to the park for filming on the battlefield, the troops marched to and from the camps in military columns, where the

Confederates were often greeted by Stephen Lang's Pickett, who later wrote, "The men are here to be inspired . . . there is a richness to the feeling, a depth to the emotion." All the combat scenes were filmed on nearby ground that bore a striking resemblance to the actual battlefield landscape. The battle sequences were exciting and intense, with the struggle at The Angle featuring reenactors engaged in mock hand-to-hand combat. Some units played both sides over the course of the week, which led to the odd moment where they could see themselves on one side shooting at themselves on the other. [40]

In Maxwell's hands, *Killer Angels* took on a distinctly Lost Cause feel. From the fatalistic Lee, hoping to win the decisive victory with God's help, to the bombastic, glory-seeking Pickett, to the sentimental story of friends Hancock and Armistead pitted against one another, *Gettysburg* suggests that all that separated the two sides were "different dreams." Its Virginia-centric bias makes Tom Berringer's Longstreet a disgruntled outsider, whose defensive philosophy counters Lee's desire to end the war with one offensive blow. Even Chamberlain, the New England abolitionist, can only conclude that "what we are fighting for is each other" before saving the day at Little Round Top. There was little in the final film that contradicted the Reconciliationist view of the war and its outcome. Hood regrets not "going around to the right," Pickett declares, "I have no division," to a distraught Lee, who after declaring that "it was all my fault" reassures Longstreet that "we will do better another time." When the film debuted in theaters, many reenactors turned out in uniform to soak in the experience of being, for at least a few days, movie stars. [41]

Thanks to Turner's machinations, parts of Pickett's Charge were filmed on the sacred ground inside the National Military Park. Brian Pohanka wrote, "The participation of Civil War reenactors in the filming made possible a dramatic and *literal* retelling of Pickett's Charge." Gary Gallagher observes that as "a centerpiece of Lost Cause celebrations of Confederate gallantry and manhood, the Pickett-Pettigrew assault unfolds in a sequence that lasts about as long as it took Lee's infantry to traverse the undulation ground between Seminary Ridge and Cemetery Ridge on July 3." Minor damage to the grounds, an unauthorized assault on the Emmitsburg Road (followed by a somber, emotional retreat), and ghostly rumors aside, the movie reaffirmed the bond that reenactors felt with the battlefield, its veterans, and the national values they fought for.[42] In exchange for the reenactors' participation, TNT donated $100,000 toward battlefield preservation. The popularity of *Gettysburg* solidified the status of reenactors as valid historical interpreters and served as a significant catalyst for the partnership between the living history, NPS, and preservation communities.[43]

Since the centennial, there have been plenty of recreations of Pickett's Charge held on private ground. The standard for all such reenactments was established at the 125th event in 1988, where the charge was immortalized in a *Classic Images* video. As the camera panned the mess of the advancing Confederates, the narrator intoned Frank Haskell's 1863 description: "More than half a mile their front extends; more than a thousand yards the dull gray masses deploy, man touching man, rank pressing rank, and line supporting line. The red flags wave, their horsemen gallop up and down; the arms of eighteen thousand men, barrel and bayonet, gleam in the sun, a sloping forest of flashing steel. Right on they move, as with one soul, in perfect order, without impediment of ditch, or wall or stream, over ridge and slope, through orchard and meadow, and cornfield, magnificent, grim, irresistible."[44] Although from the perspective of the defender, this quote describes the qualities and spectacle that every Pickett's Charge reenactment must contain. Whether Union or Confederate, male or female, young or old, participation in Pickett's Charge is a mandatory act of devotion in honor of the veterans who made the original attack, placed the monuments, and attended the reunions on that sacred landscape. [45]

Two-thousand thirteen may be last time that Confederate reenactors will be able to carry their battle flags across the Gettysburg battlefield. Although still a heritage mecca for reenactors in many ways, the NPS continues to alter both the ground and its interpretation of the battle in ways that counter the reconciliation narrative. The visitor center contains displays that tell the story of the war and battle in the context of slavery and abolition, while paid living history interpreters tell stories of civilians and townspeople. The observation tower, cyclorama, and many trees and structures that covered the battlefield during past commemorations are gone, restoring the landscape to its 1863 appearance. While the park still invites reenactment units to hold living histories on the battlefield, its willingness to play host to another large-scale Lost Cause exercise is open to question.[46]

The final observation on Gettysburg and its connection to reenactors comes in a book hyperbolically titled *Gettysburg 1863—Seething Hell: The Epic Battle of the Civil War in the Soldiers' Own Words*. In its introduction, the author

extolls the lost generation of heroes and the "thousands of . . . original letters and journal entries" they left behind. Renouncing the "axes to grind,
reputations to denigrate or bolster, personal pandering to gain political
favor, scores to settle, losing blame to ladle out, winning credit to grab,
grandiose hymns of heroism to sing, [and] a 'Lost Cause' to create and
mythologize," he vows to focus on the "rank and file soldiers" who fought
the battle. The book consists of transcribed letters, images of original artifacts, period CDVs, and hundreds of photos of reenactors sleeping, eating,
marching, fighting, and falling "dead" in battle, all seamlessly arranged and
juxtaposed on oversized pages. There are no slaves, Black troops, politicians, women, or civilians—only images of brave "soldiers" engaged in battle surrounded by reminders of their legacy and purpose.[47]

REENACTING THE LOST CAUSE AT NEW MARKET

If Gettysburg is the golden hour in the construction of Lost Cause memory,
the charge of the VMI cadets at the Battle of New Market is one of the war's
micro-moments of heroic glory. Where the July 3, 1863 attack at Gettysburg
was a sweeping pageant that covered a mile of open ground, the climactic assault at New Market in May 1864 took place on a stretch of rolling
landscape not much longer than a couple of football fields. What makes
this small battle important is the confluence of Lost Cause elements: the
defense of home and hearth, the heroic sacrifice of youth, the creation of
burials and sacred icons, and a tiny but symbolic Southern victory. Add to
that an annual battle reenactment (a ritualized remembrance claiming to
be one of the oldest in the country) that skillfully folds its participants into
the master narrative.

Unlike the battle in Pennsylvania that turned the tide of the war, the
Battle of New Market maintains a low profile in the conflict's overall history.
The author of a recent study admits, "It was the participation of the young
men from VMI that catapulted the battle into the popular imagination of
the public at large and has given New Market a stature in Southern folk-
lore that arguably exceeds its military significance."[48] The impact of this
encounter stems from its direct connection to VMI, itself an iconic Virginia
landmark. Home to a growing number of military heroes, the institute was
already sanctified during the war after its luminous faculty alumni Thomas
"Stonewall" Jackson was killed at the 1863 Battle of Chancellorsville and

buried in a Lexington cemetery. Above and beyond the need to defend the Valley and its people, the teenage boys who marched to glory on May 15, 1864 carried the weight of the Confederacy, their home state, and the vaunted institute on their shoulders.[49]

Much had happened since the climactic moment at Gettysburg. The war had turned more brutal, conscription and desertion were rampant, and Grant had begun a relentless campaign against Lee's army in the Virginia wilderness, making the Shenandoah Valley tangential to Union strategy in the east. The undersized federal force of nine thousand men was commanded by an inept political general, while the opposing five thousand Confederates were led by Kentuckian John C. Breckinridge. As one of the opening acts of the conflict's final twelve months, it was dwarfed by the carnage of Spotsylvania and Cold Harbor, trench warfare around Petersburg and Atlanta, and the eventual destruction of the South's infrastructure. Yet for one day in the valley, the flower of Virginia's manhood made a bold charge that drove the dreaded Yankees away. One former Union soldier was quoted as saying, "I don't believe the history of war contains a deed more chivalrous, more daring, or more honorable, than the charge of those boys to a victory which veterans might well boast."[50]

The battle was a simple affair, with the Union force taking advantage of its superior numbers and driving the Confederates south toward New Market. As the story goes, Breckinridge reluctantly sent the boys into the fight when the tide of battle required their participation. The Cadets advanced past the Bushong Farm and led a sweeping countercharge "of the entire Confederate line . . . across a rain-soaked wheat field," driving the federals back and capturing several guns of a Union battery. The mud had sucked the footwear off many of the boys, thus creating "the field of lost shoes" in the legendary telling of the encounter. The Cadets had suffered five killed, five mortally wounded, and forty-seven wounded out of the 257 engaged.[51] Like the charge at Gettysburg, the advance of the Cadets drew admiring comments from their enemy: "I never witnessed a more gallant advance and final charge than was given these brave boys on that field." Their heroics resulted in a visit to Richmond to meet President Jefferson Davis, but by the time they returned to Lexington, another Union force had burned much of VMI to the ground.[52]

The commemorative rituals began almost immediately following the end of the war. Every year on the anniversary of the battle, the Corps conducts a roll call in which cadets representing those killed reply "fallen on the field of honor." In the chapel/museum on the VMI campus—Jackson Memorial Hall—a gigantic painting that depicts "the cadet charge, and the shoeless field," by a VMI alumni, hangs behind the pulpit, flanked by portraits of Lee and Jackson. Reburials of the martyred cadets, annual ceremonies, and monument dedications attended by Confederate organizations, VMI alumni, dignitaries, and veterans of the battle occurred frequently during the late nineteenth and early twentieth centuries. Other rituals specifically commemorating the Battle of New Market, including a reenactment in 1914, continued the thread connecting Virginia, Southern military valor, and VMI to the Lost Cause. Just as at Gettysburg, the US Marines recreated the key moments of the battle in 1923, and like Gettysburg's centennial, the 1964 commemoration of the Battle of New Market included the trappings of modern reenacting. With the creation of the New Market Battlefield Historical Park in 1967, all the reenactments held on the site repeated consistent Lost Cause themes, but on a smaller, localized scale.[53]

The charge is now carried out by regular Confederate reenactors, with only a color guard made up of actual VMI cadets. In a video on the Virginia Civil War Museum website, Institute historian Col. Keith Gibson reminds the viewer that "the cadets never carried the Confederate flag during the war" and that the annual ceremony recognizes the heroism and sacrifice of the three hundred-plus VMI alumni killed in the service of the United States. The entrance to the Hall of Honor celebrating these heroic alumni is lined with photographs of recent battle reenactments. Like the big Gettysburg book, the juxtaposition of reenactor photos with artifacts, period material, and a sacred space places the living historians and their activities in nearly the same company as the original participants.[54]

CONTEMPORARY ISSUES IN REENACTING

Although the history/memory/reenactment dynamic functions with relative harmony at New Market, controversy surrounds Civil War reenacting for a variety of reasons. Some people have been critical of the battles, claiming that they promote war and violence. Others find it silly that grown men and women would pretend to be from another time, while a few accuse reenactors of escapism, since "reenactors sense the modern world fading away when facing the enemy . . . or feeling the thunder of cannon fire in

their bones." More substantive criticisms suggest that reenactors misrep-
resent the war to the public and contradict their role as educators. Leigh
Clemons observes that "while war is not beautiful, battle reenacting does
try to craft narratives for visitors that appeal as much to their emotions as
to their intellect, often by downplaying war's brutality." This was certainly
true during the marine reenactment at New Market, where "thousands of
spectators set up a yell that could have been heard for miles" when the cadets made their final attack. Yet the experience of war is an emotional one,
so reenactors can argue that they are simply conveying something that their
Civil War ancestors would recognize.[55]

On the eve of the Gettysburg sesquicentennial, Gettysburg Institute director Peter Carmichael opined that battle reenactments were "an unfortunate distraction" to a clear understanding of the conflict. He suggested
that reenacting fell short as an educational tool since it did not tell the
whole story of the war. This brought a rebuttal penned by Donald Gilliland,
who had embedded himself with the National Regiment during the three
days at the GMP. Describing the debate between academics and reenactors
as "eggheads versus interlopers," he characterized professional historians
as "the establishment" while the reenactors were "literally the unwashed
masses." In Carmichael's view, living historians were preferable to battle
reenactments, and licensed battlefield guides were superior to both in what
Gilliland called "the hierarchy of respectability outside the lecture hall."
One reenactor criticized media for drawing its negative characterizations
from "the yahoos and goons—the ones with crossed bandoliers and feath-
ers in their hats." For reenactors, it ultimately comes down to the visceral
experiences—the cold, the heat, the mud, sleeping on the ground, sore
feet, bug bites, rashes, and other forms of discomfort—that put them a little
closer to the old boys. Echoing Hodge's "Wargasm," Gilliland wrote that "in
some odd, unspoken way, it seemed like the re-enactors' suffering—though
not literally religious—was an homage to the men who fought and died in
the Civil War."[56]

The inauthentic farbs and "yahoos" can be more than just an embarrass-
ment; in their worst form, they appear as racist, unrepentant secessionists
who put an ugly face on the Lost Cause. Unfortunately, some operate as
chapters of the Sons of Confederate Veterans, a once-respected organization that offered a dignified (if not equally misguided) presentation of the
Lost Cause for public consumption. In the cruder, modern version, the

war was not about slavery, blacks fought for the Confederacy, Lincoln was a tyrant, and the battle flag "does not stand for racism or hate." While not usually living historians, their presence at public events often makes reen-actors guilty by association.[57]

Apart from academic matters, a more serious challenge to reenactors comes from people who believe that honoring, remembering, and reenact-ing soldiers who fought a war to defend slavery is a terrible idea. At its most benign, this leads to head-shaking scorn at the naiveté of the reenactment participants; at its most vitriolic, it brands reenactors as racists and white supremacists. The problem usually starts with the ubiquitous Confederate battle flag, which means different things to different groups in American society. To reenactors on both sides, it was the authentic banner carried into combat by brave American soldiers at places like Gettysburg and New Market. To generations of tourists and Civil War buffs, it was a souvenir purchased on the battlefield. During the contentious civil rights era in the 1950s and 60s, it became a Southern symbol of defiance against federal laws mandating desegregation and the dismantling of Jim Crow (the fact most often ignored by flag defenders). For African Americans and twenty-first-century social justice activists, it is a maddeningly persistent symbol of a racist perspective that flies in the face of modern human rights. In the Reconciliationist world of Civil War reenacting, the first view overwhelm-ingly prevails, leading to denial of the third and outright hostility towards the fourth.[58]

Like it had during the 125th, the Civil War sesquicentennial wound down with reenactments at Wilderness/Spotsylvania, Atlanta, Fort Harrison/New Market Heights, and Franklin, Tennessee in 2014 and ended with the sur-render of Lee's army at Appomattox Court House National Historical Park in April 2015. Featuring nearly 750 Union and Confederate reenactors and several dozen African Americans depicting the freed men and women, the event on NPS property included a rare, real-time, opposing-fire battle sce-nario. The surrender was the standard Reconciliationist version repeated multiple times over the long weekend, with reenactors from the nearby battle event invited to participate in the last ceremony. For the aging re-enactor population, it was a time to consider retirement, migrating to a Grand Army of the Republic or United Confederate Veterans impression, or simply anticipating the start of the 155th cycle. For some Union units, including United States Colored Troops who had been excluded the first time, there was a Grand Review in Washington, DC to conclude the 150th sequence.[59]

Everything changed on June 17, 2015 when a white supremacist named Dylann Roof killed nine African Americans at the Emanuel African Methodist Episcopal Church in Charleston, South Carolina. Roof's crime penetrated deep into the historical and reenacting communities because he had deliberately chosen Charleston for its Confederate connections and appeared in photographs brandishing racist symbols, including a Confederate battle flag. For social justice activists, this was the last straw. They denounced the flag and all who carried it as racists, or at the very least, racist enablers. The easy targets were flags at the South Carolina statehouse and similar government buildings in the South. Within weeks, Confederate flags in stores, on toys, and those flying at other public places, including NPS sites, also came under scrutiny.[60]

The reenactor community responded with the only argument it could draw on: "The Confederate battle flag is a necessary part of history and it's . . . important to clarify history and not fall into some politically correct retelling." Other reenactors repeated the orthodoxy that that "many Southern soldiers did carry square Confederate battle flags like the one flying in front of Charleston's state house, but very few of those soldiers were slave owners and for many of them, the battle was more about other issues, including states' rights." Many felt that removing the banner from a government building was probably a good idea but feared that this would be the tip of the iceberg. After pointing out that the flag was "about heritage not hate," another commenter added, "but if this symbol is successfully toppled, what's next?"[61]

The situation escalated after Republican Donald Trump's election as president of the United States in November 2016. Trump's pro-law enforcement, anti-immigration, America-first rhetoric appealed to many conservatives but horrified social justice activists, who vowed to oppose what they saw as racist thinking. Groups like Black Lives Matter and their allies renewed attacks on Confederate symbols, particularly monuments located in public places and near government facilities. After a riot between defenders of the Lee statue in Charlottesville, Virginia and members of left-wing "antifascist" groups resulted in the death of a demonstrator, the issue dominated the national media for weeks. For the defenders of Lost Cause memory, Charlottesville was a disaster: they had allied themselves with the worst neo-Nazi groups in the country to protect a Confederate statue, people had been injured and killed, and photos and news footage showed dozens of Confederate flags mixed with swastikas and Aryan Nation symbols throughout the crowd.[62]

The backlash was rapid and brutal. Confederate statues and monuments were vandalized or toppled in several places as towns, cities, and colleges scrambled to distance themselves from Confederate symbols under their jurisdictions. Reenacting was seen by some as "an attempt to fantasize about living in a bygone world of white supremacy" and condemned for celebrating slavery and those who fought for it. The impulse to wipe out all vestiges of the Old South led critics to conclude that "the gulf between these backward-looking fantasies and the modern moment . . . has made America . . . an ugly and angry place." The threat of violence caused the organizers of the annual Second Battle of Manassas commemoration to cancel the event, generating concern among reenactors across the country. At the bi-annual reenactment in Zoar, Ohio a few weeks later, the only Confederate battle flags were those displayed by spectators, while Southern units carried regimental or early-war banners into battle. There were no protests or incidents and the atmosphere was surprisingly relaxed. [63]

Defenders of reenacting rose to the occasion. An author in *The Federalist* pointed out that "it is a tremendous mistake to refuse to examine the complexities of history in the name of social justice." She pointed out the "pitfalls of postmodernism" in a world in which "all beliefs are essentially the same" and accused the reenacting's critics of erroneously drawing a straight line from slavery to Jim Crow to civil rights violence to Confederate reenactors and declaring that since some of these things are wrong, anyone honoring Confederate veterans is evil. She claims that "much of the history taught to American students is highly negative . . . [and] tends to kill student interest," whereas "reenactors help nurture a community of ordinary people who recognize that history is cool, and who communicate the message to others." Admitting that they don't have the last word on the whole history of the Civil War, reenactors reminded their critics that their task was to emulate the veterans themselves, noting that the fiftieth reunion at Gettysburg "was marked by repeated acts of Union and Confederate camaraderie. There were no signs of unpleasant differences, such as we saw at Charlottesville this past weekend."[64]

One popular annual event attended by many reenactors is the mid-October weekend commemorating the 1864 Battle of Cedar Creek, where a Confederate force launched a bold, daybreak, surprise attack against the encamped federal army. The assault fell apart when Union commander Philip Sheridan rallied his divisions and drove Jubal Early's forces out of the Shenandoah Valley. The Cedar Creek Battlefield Foundation (CCBF) shares the site with the NPS's Belle Grove Plantation and hosts the annual anniversary reenactment to benefit the park's preservation and maintenance. On October 6, 2017 the CCBF received a letter warning of possible "bodily harm" to reenactment participants, which it communicated to reenactors, merchants, and spectators via its website. After a successful battle on Saturday, October 15, "events were suddenly cut short when a 'suspicious device'—rumored to be a pipe bomb—was found on site." This incident led many in the reenactment community to "increasingly worry that living history will become the next casualty of America's culture war."[65]

After the Confederate reenactors were evacuated, the Union commanders "ordered the entire Federal army to conduct an immediate and thorough search of the camp . . . [where] every tent, every box, [and] every container" underwent inspection. Law enforcement officials allowed the Union Army to remain and assist the Confederates when they returned to their camps. Although Sunday's spectator battle was officially cancelled, the CCBF gave the reenactors permission to stage a skirmish the next morning. After some firing and maneuvering, the Union Army "charged the enemy not to engage it, but rather to embrace their brothers in arms." Darrell Markijohn confessed that "it was one of the most emotional moments I have ever experienced." Like their predecessors at the Gettysburg centennial fifty-three years before, the mixed armies stood while the federal band "struck up the Star-Spangled Banner" while "EVERYONE placed their hands over the hearts and SANG." Thus, amidst a traumatic experience, reenactors found unifying, patriotic inspiration.[66]

Reenactors were not the only ones horrified by this occurrence. A writer for the *National Review* speculated that "the simplest and most logical explanation is that this is a new, violent extension of the effort to remove Confederate statues," adding "but to terrorize or threaten a Civil War reenactment is completely different; this marks an indisputable attack on America's history." The reporter for *The Washington Post* observed that the reenactors' display of unity reflected "not just their sense of patriotism, but the umbrage many felt at having their hobby dragged into the national debate over race and Confederate-era symbolism." When asked why they persisted with the Sunday battle despite having been threatened, evacuated, searched, and inconvenienced, one reenactor replied, "We wanted to show the US that we are not going to let some terrorist . . . stop the event," adding, "I was never prouder of people in our hobby."[67] Markijohn echoed this sense of pride in his after-action report—"I have never seen the hobby more UNITED than I did this past Sunday"—and declared that the perpetrators "have only strengthened the resolve of every person present to continue the mission of reenacting the history of our country." He ended with a familiar and steadfast refrain: "Civil War reenactors tell military history stories and there is no place for political movements inconsistent with this respectable objective, let alone ones premised on violence." [68]

The unity on display at Cedar Creek was not surprising to anyone in the hobby. After more than a half-century of emulating the Civil War veterans, reenactors have built a legacy that they are extremely proud of. Many are the same ages as the veterans when they built the monuments on the battlefields, held reunions, and watched their comrades fade away one by one. Unlike the old boys, reenactors can replenish their ranks as they continue to interact with the public and find kindred spirits who also feel the connection to the past. There are more women in the hobby than ever, portraying soldiers, nurses, laundresses, widows, Christian Commission workers, and serving as "ice angels" on the battlefield. While academic historians uncover more evidence that the war was about slavery, that abolition was the primary goal of many Union soldiers, that some white veterans suffered from trauma and violently repressed black citizens, and that the Lost Cause cloaked the evils of Jim Crow in a sentimental haze, reenactors will continue to tell the only story they feel qualified to share. They will stick to the premise that sectional reunion and national reconciliation were good things and that reenacting helps "remember those who fought, and the causes they fought for [and] remember the bad causes in order to avoid them." Another reenactor pointed out that in addition to "illustrating the horror of war, we show what can happen when Americans turn on Americans." Rather than see themselves as out of touch with the present, reenactors feel that they are performing a necessary educational and civic duty. Their focus on the lives of ordinary soldiers demonstrates the persistence of both reconciliation and the Lost Cause in United States culture, even as the rituals and symbols they employ become embroiled in contemporary disputes.[69]

NOTES

1.   The Union soldiers were members of the National Regiment who camped behind the Pennsylvania Monument and served as NPS volunteers for the duration of the three-day anniversary. An equal number of Confederates were bivouacked in Pitzer's Woods. One suspects that the renegade rebels were not the sanctioned NPS reenactors, but had come from the BGA reenactment and joined the massive crowd. An unsanctioned Confederate charge had also taken place during the 125th anniversary in 1988; the latest scholarly work on the battlefield fails to mention the recreated charge on July 3. Jennifer M. Murray, *On a Great Battlefield: The Making, Management, and Memory of Gettysburg National Military Park, 1933–2013* (Knoxville: The Univ. of Tennessee Press, 2014), 199–200; quote from Jared Frederick ,"Reenactors: Educators or Entertainers?" *History Matters: The Historical Musings of Jared Frederick,* July 17, 2013, http://jaredfrederick.blogspot.com/2013/07/reenactors -educators-or-entertainers.html.

2.   The National Regiment was one of the Union units on the field at New Market; "The Reenactment," Virginia Museum of the Civil War, Virginia Military Institute, http://www.vmi .edu/museums-and-archives/virginia-museum-of-the-civil-war/the-reenactment/.

3.   General characteristics of reenactors can be found in Mark Elson and Jeannine Stein, *Battlefields of Honor: American Civil War Reenactors* (London: Merrell Publishers, 2012), 7–19; other works that explain the various elements of the Lost Cause include Gary Gallagher and Alan T. Nolan, eds., *The Myth of the Lost Cause and Civil War History* (Bloomington: Indiana Univ. Press, 2000); Edward H. Bonekemper III, *The Myth of the Lost Cause: Why the South Fought the Civil War and Why the North Won* (Washington, D. C.: Regnery History, 2015); and William C. Davis, *The Cause Lost: Myths and Realities of the Confederacy* (Lawrence: Univ. Press of Kansas, 1996).

4.   Nina Silber, "The Romance of Reunion: Northerners and the South, 1865–1900," in *Civil War America,* ed. Gary Gallagher (Chapel Hill: Univ. of North Carolina Press, 1993); J. Kurt Piehler, *Remembering War the American Way* (Washington: Smithsonian Books, 1995), 71–73; Bradley S. Keefer, *Conflicting Memories of the River of Death: The Chickamauga Battlefield and the Spanish-American War, 1863–1933* (Kent State Univ. Press, 2013), 125–27; Timothy B. Smith, *A Chickamauga Memorial: The Establishment of America's First Civil War National Military Park* (Knoxville: The Univ. of Tennessee Press, 2009); Kirk Savage, *Standing Soldiers, Kneeling Slaves: Race, War, and Monument in Nineteenth-century America* (Princeton: Princeton Univ. Press, 1997), 162–87.

5.   Leading writers of this type include Bruce Catton, Shelby Foote, Bell Irvin Wiley, and Douglass Southall Freeman. Examples include Bruce Catton, *The Centennial History of the Civil War Trilogy* (New York: Doubleday & Co., 1965); one reviewer called Catton's *Terrible Swift Sword* "a masterpiece of historical writing." Dr. John R. Slater, "A Masterpiece of Historical Writing," undated clipping in third volume of the Rochester (NY) *Democrat-Chronicle* scrapbook "This Was the Civil War," which is a mix of clippings collected by readers of the newspaper from 1961 through 1963, when the paper quit publishing the special centennial sections. The three scrapbooks are in the possession of the author from the collection of the late Barton Nolan of Ashtabula, Ohio and will be subsequently cited as *Chronicle* "Civil War"

followed by the scrapbook number; Catton's contribution to memory is discussed in Robert
J. Cook, *Civil War Memories: Contesting the Past in the United States Since 1865* (Baltimore: Johns
Hopkins Univ. Press, 2017), 161–63; see also Shelby Foote, *The Civil War*, 3 vols. (New York:
Vintage Books Ed., 1989); Bell Irvin Wiley, *The Life of Billy Yank and The Life of Johnny Reb*, 2
vols (Garden City, NY: Doubleday, 1971); and Douglass Southall Freeman, *Lee' Lieutenants: A
Study in Command* (New York: Scribner, 1944).

6. Frederick, "Reenactors: Educators or Entertainers?" *History Matters.*

7. For a general discussion of memory and tradition, see Eric Hobsbawm, "Introduction:
Inventing Traditions," in *The Invention of Tradition*, ed. Eric Hobsbawm and Terrence Ranger
(Cambridge, 1984); W. Fitzhugh Brundage, "No Deed But Memory," in *Where These Memories
Grow: History, Memory, and Southern Identity*, ed. W. Fitzhugh Brundage (Chapel Hill: Univ.
of North Carolina Press, 2000), 1–28; Anthony Molho and Gordon S. Wood, eds., *Imagined
Histories: American Historians Interpret the Past* (Princeton: Princeton Univ. Press, 1998), 16–18;
David Lowenthal, *Possessed By The Past: The Heritage Crusade and the Spoils of History* (New York:
The Free Press, 1996).

8. The notion of "sacred ground" is described in Edward Linenthal, *Sacred Ground:
Americans and their Battlefields* (Chicago: Univ. of Illinois Press, paperback ed., 1993), 1–7;
J. Christian Spielvogel, *Interpreting Sacred Ground: The Rhetoric of National Civil War Parks and
Battlefields* (Tuscaloosa: Univ. of Alabama Press, 2013); Kenneth Foote, *Shadowed Ground:
America's Landscapes of Violence and Tragedy* (Austin: Univ. of Texas Press, 1997) 10–44.

9. Paul Connerton, *How Societies Remember* (New York: Cambridge Univ. Press, 1898), 4,
40; John R. Gillis, ed., *Commemorations: The Politics of National Identity* (Princeton: Princeton
Univ. Press, 1994), 3; Brundage, *Where These Memories Grow*, 5.

10. John Bodnar, *Remaking America: Public Memory, Commemoration, and Patriotism in the
20th Century* (Princeton: Princeton Univ. Press, 1993) discusses commemorative events
in cities, 78–109; in National Parks, 169–205; and during the American centennial and
bicentennials, 206–244; for a discussion of Memorial Days, see Ellen M. Litwicki, *America's
Public Holidays, 1865–1920* (Washington, DC: Smithsonian Institution Press, 2000), 9–49;
on the role of place in commemoration, see Linenthal, *Sacred Ground*, 1–6. Marita Sturken,
Tangled Memories: The Vietnam War, the AIDS Epidemic, and the Politics of Remembering (Berkeley:
Univ. of California Press, 1997) argues that "memory is a narrative rather than a replica of an
experience that can be retrieved and relived," and points out that "the production of cultural
memory . . . is thus historically situated and specific," 7, 15. Her study includes photographs,
film, television, and objects like the AIDS quilt along with more traditional symbols as
sources of memory construction.

11. Jenny Thompson, *War Games: Inside the World of 20th Century Reenactors* (Washington:
Smithsonian Press, 2004), 34–39.

12. "Many reenactors have a mythical bent towards the hobby . . . [and] cling to their
units and uniforms in mythical ways." Lee Haddon, *Reliving the Civil War: The Reenactor's
Handbook* (Mechanicsburg, PA: Stackpole Books, 1996), 2; Jay Anderson, *The Living History
Sourcebook* (Nashville: American Association of State and Local History, 1985); W. C. Smith
III, "Reenacting the War Between the States," in *The Civil War Reenactor's Encyclopedia*, ed.
William C. Davis (Guilford, CT: Lyons Press, 2002); the host of this popular show allows

reenactors to sample actual hardtack from the war, which they regard as a spiritual moment, *Bizarre Foods with Andrew Zimmern,* http://www.imdb.com/title/tt6497782/ (Feb. 2018).

13. Tony Horwitz, *Confederates in the Attic: Dispatches from the Unfinished Civil War* (New York: Pantheon Books, 1998), 7–8, "wargasm" 209. Charles Reagan Wilson, *Baptized in Blood: The Religion of the Lost Cause, 1865–1920,* with a new preface (Athens: Univ. of Georgia Press, 1980, 2009); see also Gaines Foster, *Ghosts of the Confederacy: Defeat, the Lost Cause, and the Emergence of the New South* (New York: Oxford Univ. Press, 1987)

14. Horwitz describes farbs as a separate category along with mainstreamers and hardcores, Horwitz, *Confederates in the Attic,* 7–17, 209–81, although in many cases, "farb" is a way of being rather than a defined group of reenactors. Jenny Thompson notes that "farb is a label that reenactors rarely, if ever, bestow on themselves" in *War Games,* 215–16; Leigh Clemons, "Present Enacting Past: The Functions of Battle Reenacting in Historical Representation" in *Enacting History,* ed. Scott Magelssen and Rhona Justice-Malloy (Tuscaloosa: Univ. of Alabama Press, 2011), 11; according to Rob Baker, the three groups are mainstreamers, progressives, and hardcores, "Reenactors vs Historians vs Historians, part 1," in *Civil War Memory,* July 17, 2013, https://historicstruggle.wordpress.com/2013/07/18/re-enactors-vs-historians-vs-historians/.

15. Clemons, "Functions of Battle Reenacting," 11–12, last quote 17; Baker, "Reenactors vs Historians vs Historians, part 1," in *Civil War Memory,* July 17, 2013, https://historicstruggle.wordpress.com/2013/07/18/re-enactors-vs-historians-vs-historians/.

16. Chandra Manning, *What This Cruel War Was Over: Soldiers, Slavery, and the Civil War* (New York: Alfred A Knopf, 2007), 11; Caroline Janney, *Remembering the Civil War: Reunion and the Limits of Reconciliation* (Chapel Hill: Univ. of North Carolina Press, 2013), 6; UDC stands for United Daughters of the Confederacy; the 66th OVI is a mainstreamer unit with farb tendencies since the women slept on modern cots in A-tents and served as cooks for the entire company.

17. Earl Hess, *Civil War Infantry Tactics: Training, Combat, and Small-unit Effectiveness* (Baton Rouge: Louisiana State Univ. Press, 2015) emphasizes the importance of the various drill manuals utilized by both original and reenacting officers, 176–77; rifles, 202–3. Following a conversation about drill at the SHA in Tampa, I sent Hess a video from the Battle of Crampton's Gap where the NR executed a left-wheel from a column of companies into line. He replied via e-mail: "I especially enjoy seeing the wheeling by companies. It all seems more sophisticated than what I have normally seen re-enactors do, which are simple line forward and back, and moving by the flank movements." Earl Hess to Brad Keefer, October 12, 2017; see also Hess, *The Rifled Musket in Civil War Combat: Reality and Myth* (Lawrence: Univ. of Kansas Press, 2008) where he argues in more detail that the rifled musket did not increase accuracy or casualties on most Civil War battlefields; the National Regiment holds an annual Officers/NCO school in Gettysburg each year, featuring topics like "Learn how to teach drill" and "Role of staff in support of combat operations," National Regiment 2004 School of the Officer and NCO, in author's collection.

18. Union groups include The National Regiment (NR), United States Volunteers (USV), Birney's Division, Vincent's Brigade, Cumberland Guard, Mifflin Guard, Army of the Ohio

(AO), and Army of the Pacific (AOP). Major Confederate organizations predictably include Longstreet's Corps, Jackson's Corps, Army of the Shenandoah, Cleburne's Division, and the Army of Northern Virginia (ANV); many have online presence to enhance recruiting, http://www.nationalregiment.com/; this is only a partial list, and includes overseas units, http://civilwar-reenacting.com/reenactment-units/regional-national-international.

19. Robert J. Cook, *Troubled Commemoration: The American Civil War Centennial, 1961–1965* (Baton Rouge: Louisiana State Univ. Press, 2007); founded in 1950, a history of the N-SSA was introduced in a 1995 issue of *The Skirmish Line: Magazine of the North-South Skirmish Association*, 40, no. 3 (May–June 1995) and continued for three consecutive bimonthly issues; Nicky Hughes, "Taking Aim for the Civil War: The N-SSA Approach," *Civil War Historian* 4, no. 1 (January/February 2008): 20–25; "What? Fighting it all Over Again?" *Rochester Times-Union*, May 21, 1961 and "2 Battles Loom—Guns and Dollars for Fishers" both in *Chronicle* 1; Smith, "Reenacting the War Between the States," 19; the makeshift hemp bales were based on a sketch that appeared in Colonel James A. Milligan, "The Siege of Lexington, Missouri," in *Battles and Leaders of the Civil War* 1, 3 vols, ed. Robert Underwood Johnson and Clarence Clough Buel (New York: Thomas Yoseloff, 1956): 307; "balloon" quote, Anderson, *Time Machines*, 138; Jennifer Murray documents reenactments on the Pickett's Charge field using N-SSA units in 1959 and 1960, which predate the more highly promoted centennial "Unity" event in 1963, *On A Great Battlefield*, 91.

20. The usual participants were augmented by members of the Sons of Union Veterans Reserve, the uniformed representative of the SUV, http://suvcw.org/svr/svrhist.htm; other reenactment sites included New Market, Perryville, Antietam, and Gettysburg, but the last reenactment of the centennial was at Palmito Hill, Texas on May 15, 1965 when "eleven Confederate buffs attacked one Yankee," Anderson, *Time Machines*, 138, 141–43; "Large Crowd at Battlefield—Civilian Casualties Exceed Armies at Bull Run," Rochester *Democrat and Chronicle*, July 23, 1961, clipping in *Chronicle* "Civil War" 1; participant account in Snell, *My Gettysburg*, 164–65; Murray, *On A Great Battlefield*, 99–100.

21. Quoted in US Civil War Centennial Commission, *The Civil War Centennial: A Report to Congress* (Washington, DC: The US Civil War Centennial Commission, 1968), 13–14, 32, 44–45; see also Michael Kammen, *Mystic Chords of Memory: The Transformation of Tradition in American Culture* (New York: Alfred Knopf, 1991), 590–610; photos of the centennial appear in "Commemorating the Civil War," The Center for Civil War Photography, Page from the Past, *Hallowed Ground* 10, no. 3 (Fall 2009): 34–35; see also Jon Weiner, "Civil War, Cold War, Civil Rights: The Civil War Centennial in Context, 1960–1965," in *The Memory of the Civil War in American Culture*, ed. Alice Fahs and Joan Waugh, from Civil War American Series, ed. Gary Gallagher (Chapel Hill: Univ. of North Carolina Press, 2004), 237–57; clipping, "20,000 Spectators at Historic Site See Battle of Antietam Fought again," City Life, *The Washington Post*, September 16, 1962, and undated clipping, "After 100 Years—Antietam Battle Is Fought Again," both in *Chronicle* "Civil War" 2.

22. Anderson defines *living history* as "simulation of life in another time" and a *reenactment* as "a living history event that simulates a particular historic event," *Living History Sourcebook*, 459–61; D. A. Saguto, "Reflections on Reenacting: Seeking an Authentic Past in a Specious Present," *Colonial Williamsburg, the Journal of the Colonial Williamsburg Foundation* 33, no. 1

(Winter 2011): 76–81; see also William T. Alderson and Shirley Payne Low, *Interpretation of Historic Sites*, 2nd ed., rev. (Nashville: American Association for State and Local History, 1985), 23–70.

23. Anderson, *Living History Sourcebook*, 165–67; from the beginning, N-SSA and reenactors differed on standards of authenticity, as one N-SSA member complained in a 1990 article about recruiting, "the NSSA's biggest problem is the large numbers of regulations demanding extremely authentic uniforms," adding that "the N-SSA is a shooting organization, not a warped reenactment group." Michael L. McDaniel, "Recruiting and Authenticity: Myth and Reality," *The Skirmish Line: Magazine of the North-South Skirmish Association* 37, no. 3 (May–June 1990), 12.

24. An example of a 125th event can be found in American Civil War Commemorative Committee, Inc., "The 125th Anniversary Reenactments of Sheridan's Richmond Raid and Stuart's Pursuit, Wilderness, Yellow Tavern, Laurel Hill, Trevillian Station, and Spotsylvania and The Heritage Weekend Memorial Parade—Update Package Number One," *8th O.V.I, The Gibraltar Brigade's Finest* (April 1989), author's collection; and "North Carolina—the South's Last Stand," sponsored by the Bentonville Battleground Historical Association, *Reenactor's Journal* (February 1990); the 125th Gettysburg was sponsored by a group called Napoleonic Tactics, Inc., Jim Weeks, *Gettysburg: Memory, Market, and American Shrine* (Princeton: Princeton Univ. Press, 2003), 171–72; descriptions of the organization of Civil War reenactment units can be found in Rory Turner, "Bloodless Battles: The Civil War Reenacted," *TDR* 34, no. 4 (Winter 1990): 123–36, JSTOR; and Reid Mitchell, "Theater of War: History Comes Alive as Weekend Warriors Recreate the Conditions and Reenact the Battles of the Civil War," *Philip Morris Magazine* (May–June, 1990), 28–31.

25. Examples of postings for 1988 events, letters reviewing the 125th Chancellorsville, and an ad for *Classic Images* can be found in "Upcoming Events" and "Camp Gossip," *The Camp Chase Gazette* 15, no. 8 (July 1988): 7–12, 20–21, and on the last page, where *Classic Images* offered videos of First Manassas, Shiloh, and Cedar Mountain with prices of $29.99 for thirty minutes and $39.99 for one hour. The company's VHS videos of 125th Gettysburg, Spotsylvania, Franklin, and Appomattox are in the author's collection.

26. Turner, "Bloodless Battles," 125–27; for example, *The Quartermaster Shop: Quality Reproduction 1855–1884 Military Uniforms and Men's Clothing Since 1975*, paper catalog dated 6/01 or www.quartermastershop.com; an outdated list of sutlers and suppliers appears in Anderson, *Living History Sourcebook*, 306–38.

27. Linenthal, *Sacred Ground*, 100–103; Weeks, *Gettysburg Memory*, 171–72; Turner did much of her research at the 125th Gettysburg, "Bloodless Battles"; footage from this event also found its way into the opening scenes of the film *Glory* (see note 30).

28. The most influential was James McPherson's Pulitzer Prize winning *Battle Cry of Freedom: the Civil War Era*, Oxford History of the United States series (Oxford Univ. Press, 1988); well-received television mini-series, *The Blue and Gray* (1982) and *North and South* (1986–1995), followed fictional characters through various parts of the war and featured prominent actors and actresses and utilized reenactors in key battle scenes. *The Blue and the Gray* http://www.imdb.com/title/tt0083387/; *North and South*, http://www.imdb.com/title/tt0088583/ (Jan. 2017).

29. Chamberlin quote, Geoffrey C. Ward, Ric Burns & Ken Burns, *The Civil War: An Illustrated History* (New York: Alfred A. Knopf, 1991), 394; film clip, "The Civil War: Was it Not as in the old days?" https://www.youtube.com/watch?v=mumPcoIZa_I (Jan. 2018); see also Gary Edgerton, *Ken Burns's America* (New York: Palgrave for St. Martin's Press, 2001), 1–26; Eric Foner, "Ken Burns and the Romance of Reunion," *Who Owns History? Rethinking the Past in a Changing World* (New York: Hill and Wang, 2002), 189–204; other commentary can be found in Robert B. Toplin, ed., *Ken Burns's "The Civil War": Historians Respond* (New York, 1996); Gary Gallagher excludes TV productions in his analysis, including *The Blue and the Gray, North and South,* and the Burns epic, *Causes Won, Lost, and Forgotten: How Hollywood and Popular Art Shape What We Know About the Civil War* (Univ. of North Carolina Press, 2008), 8.

30. An excellent assessment of *Glory* can be found in Gallagher, *Causes Won, Lost, and Forgotten,* 95–100; the film used reenactors for the big battle scenes and trained the African American extras who portrayed the 54th MA, David Rush, "A Reenactor's 'Glory,'" *Reenactor's Journal* (February 1990), 18, 23; see the *Glory* sidebar in Mitchell, "Theater of War," 33; Bob Zeller, *Fighting the Second Civil War: The History of Battlefield Preservation and the Emergence of the Civil War Trust* (The Civil War Trust, 2017), 134–49; for a detailed discussion of the Disney controversy and the 1988 mall threat that preceded it, see chapters 10 and 11 in Joan M. Zenzen, *Battling for Manassas: The Fifty-Year Preservation Struggle at Manassas National Battlefield Park* (Pennsylvania State Univ. Press, 1998); see also Timothy B. Smith, *Altogether Fitting and Proper: Civil War Battlefield Preservation in History, Memory, and Policy, 1861–2015* (Knoxville: The Univ. of Tennessee Press, 2017) and Bradley Keefer, "Collective Memory, Civil War Reenacting, and Battlefield Preservation" in *Lesser Civil Wars: Civilians Defining War and the Memory of War,* ed. Marsha Robinson (Cambridge Scholars Publishing, 2012), 129–50, from which partial sources/notes for this section of the essay were drawn (LCW).

31. This author was a member of the 5th NY during Pohanka's stint as commander, Snell, *My Gettysburg,* 169; Anderson, *Living History Handbook,* 302; films included *Glory, Gettysburg* (1992), *Gods and Generals* (2002), and *Cold Mountain* (2003); "true believer" quote, and account of his death in Zeller, *Second Civil War,* 31, 293–94; Pohanka appears in uniform along with other reenactors as secretary of the interior, Manuel Lujuan, Jr. announces the formation of the ABPP, "Giving History a Fighting Chance," Third Battle of Manassas, The Old Museum at Manassas, http://nps-vip.net/history/museum/3rdbattle/pannel5 .htm; tributes to Pohanka in Deborah Fits, "Friends and Family Gather to Remember Brian Pohanka's Life," *Civil War News* (August 2005); 1999 quote in "Personal Struggles and Triumphs, the Zouaves and 9/11," *A Memorial Tribute to Brian C. Pohanka* (March 20, 1955–June 15, 2005), The Soul of an Idealistic, Noble Soldier, http://dragoon1st.tripod.com/cw /files/bcp_mem4.html; "Prior to his death, he had been named 2004 CWPT Preservationist of the Year," "CWPT Receives Major Bequest from Late Historian, Preservationist Brian Pohanka," *Hallowed Ground* 7, no. 2 (Summer 2006): 12 (LCW).

32. Promotional material for "Antietam: The Bloodiest Day, 135th Commemoration Reenactment, featuring The Cornfield, Bloody Lane, AP Hill's Assault," *Hallowed Ground* 10, no. 2 (Summer 1997): 12; 135th Antietam drew thirteen thousand reenactors and raised $100,00 for preservation, "Extra, Extra! Nearly 100,000 spectators witness largest 'live' Civil War educational event in history!" *Hallowed Ground* 10, no. 3 (Fall 1997): 7; "APCWS

Educational Event: Antietam 135th Anniversary Commemoration," *Hallowed Ground* 1, no. 1 (January 1998): 22–24; Thompson, *War Games*, 33; "Leading Pickett's Charge! Gettysburg Alive with Reenactors," *Civil War Courier* 18, no. 5 (June 2002): 1, 23; "1999 Reenactment of Cedar Creek a Major Success!" *Cedar Creek Courier* (Winter 2000) reported six thousand for this 135th event; Robert Lee Hodge, "Education, Preservation, and Appreciation: Spotsylvania 140th Anniversary, May 7, 8, and 9, 2004," *Camp Chase Gazette* 31, no. 5 (April 2004): 46–48 (LCW).

33. "Upcoming Campaigns," *Camp Chase Gazette* 26, no. 3 (Winter 1999):10–35; "Upcoming Campaigns," *Camp Chase Gazette* 31, no. 2 (Holiday 2003): 10–19; "12th Annual Cedar Creek Reenactment, October 20–21, 2001," *Cedar Creek Courier* (Summer 2001); both the reenactment and preservation needs are mentioned in *Cedar Creek Courier* (Winter 2001); a "Photo Essay" and report of 140th Cedar Creek in 2004 appears in *Camp Chase Gazette* 32, no. 3 (Jan–Feb 2005): 34–39; the APCWS devoted an entire issue to Perryville, *Hallowed Ground* 1, no. 2 (Spring 1998) (LCW).

34. Weeks discussed this development in a less than enthusiastic light as part of what he felt was the NPS move toward "heritage tourism," *Gettysburg Memory*, 188–94; for a concise review of battlefield usage and interpretation, see Barbara J. Platt, *This is holy ground: A history of the Gettysburg Battlefield* (Published by Barbara Platt, 2001).

35. Carol Reardon, *Pickett's Charge in History and Memory* (Chapel Hill: Univ. of North Carolina Press, 1997), 1–4; "conscious work of art" quote from Philip Van Doren Stern, "Gettysburg: The Climax—Pickett Leads His Men Across and Field of Agony," *Chronicle* "Civil War" 3; the battlefield's role in the reconciliation theme is apparent in a souvenir pamphlet, "DEDICATED TO THE CITIZENS OF THE NORTH AND TO THE CITIZENS OF THE SOUTH . . . UNITED IN ONE NATION," *Gettysburg The National Shrine: People's Pictorial Edition* (Gettysburg: N.A. Meligakis, 1948, reprinted 1952).

36. Stan Cohen, *Hands Across the Wall: The 50th and 75th Reunions of the Gettysburg Battle* (Charleston, WV: Pictorial Histories Publishing Company, 3rd printing, 1997), 32, 37, 64–65; Linenthal, *Sacred Ground*, 94–96; the introduction focuses on the 1913 handshake at the wall but does not mention the one at 1938 event, Murray, *On a Great Battlefield*, 14–16, 35–36.

37. J. Christian Spielvogel, *Interpreting Sacred Ground: The Rhetoric of National Civil War Parks and Battlefields* (Tuscaloosa: Univ. of Alabama Press, 2013), 130; edited quote (my editing) from a post by author Eric Wittenberg on a Civil War forum about the 150th anniversary, "William Faulkner on Pickett's Charge," https://civilwartalk.com/threads/william-faulkner -on-picketts-charge.86240/ (Jan. 2018).

38. As mentioned in note 19, the centennial-era events also include reenactments in 1959 and 1960, Murray, *On A Great Battlefield*, 91; for an account of the marines at Gettysburg in 1922, see Richard D. L. Fulton and James Rada, Jr., *The Last to Fall: The 1922 March, Battles, & Deaths of U.S. Marines at Gettysburg* (AIM Publishing Group, 2015).

39. Scholarly discussions of the impact of *Killer Angels* and *Gettysburg* can be found in Thomas A. Desjardin, *These Honored Dead: How the Story of Gettysburg Shaped American Memory* (De Capo Press, 2003), 145–52; Weeks, *Gettysburg Memory*, 171–214; Reardon notes the Virginia-centric nature of the film, *Pickett's Charge*, 211; and Gallagher, *Causes Won, Lost, and*

Forgotten, 56–59; Maxwell, Sheen, and Elliot quotes from "The Reenactor's Commemorative Journal of the Epic TNT Production of Gettysburg," *The Gettysburg Journal* (1993), 8, 13, 14.

40. Much of this paragraph is personal experience after a week filming Pickett's Charge and portraying Confederates for all but one day. I kept a scrapbook with photos, reviews, meal passes, and other material from the experience. Lang quote from "Reenactor's Commemorative Journal," 30, where all participants were listed individually along with cast and crew.

41. While proud of their work, many reenactors who participated in the filming and watched *Gettysburg* repeatedly make fun of the more over-the-top scenes, like Buford's admonition to "hold the high ground," Hood's plaintive wailing, Ted Turner's "come on boys" before taking his fatal wound during the charge, and Fremantle's funny hat, garish uniform, and silly prattling. Conversely, many still get goosebumps when Armistead puts his hat on his sword and shouts to his division, "With me . . . who will come with me?" before leading the final rush to The Angle and tear up when he laments upon hearing of Hancock's wounding "not all of us!"

42. Filming on the battlefield is described, along with the Pohanka quote, in "Reenactor's Commemorative Journal," 30–41 (italics added); Weeks, *Gettysburg Memory*, 190; Gallagher argues that the Virginia-centric view of the charge in the film contradicts notions of Confederate nationalism, *Causes Won, Lost, and Forgotten*, 58–59.

43. The APCWS spent a portion of that money to purchase part of the Tom's Brook battlefield in the Shenandoah Valley, while the rest, along with $5,000 collected from the reenactors themselves, went to the Malvern Hill site on the Virginia Peninsula, "Reenactor's Commemorative Journal," 3; a follow up can be found at "Revisit the 'Woodstock Races' at Tom's Brook," *Hallowed Ground* 2, no. 1 (Winter 1999): 17 (LCW); and Snell, *My Gettysburg*, 173–75.

44. Quoted in Glenn W. Lafantasie, *Gettysburg Heroes: Perfect Soldiers, Hallowed Ground* (Bloomington: Indiana Univ. Press, 2008), 35; see also Frank L. Byrne and Andrew T. Weaver, *Haskell of Gettysburg: His Life and Papers* (Kent: Kent State Univ. Press, 1970, paperback ed. 1989); Spielvogel, *Interpreting Sacred Ground*, 85–119; Murray, *On A Great Battlefield*, 138–39.

45. In addition to Reardon's book, other histories of the charge include Gary Gallagher, ed., *The Third Day of Gettysburg and Beyond: Military Campaigns of the Civil War* (Chapel Hill: Univ. of North Carolina Press, 1994); George R. Stewart, *Pickett's Charge: A Microhistory of the Final Attack* (New York: Houghton Mifflin, 1959, 1987); Jeffery Wert, *Gettysburg, Day Three* (New York: Simon and Schuster, 2001); and Phillip Thomas Tucker, *Pickett's Charge: A New Look at Gettysburg's Final Attack* (New York: Skyhorse Publishing, 2016).

46. Members of the reenactor 8th Ohio like to think they helped put the unit on the map via regular participation in NPS living histories and Remembrance Day commemorations at the regiment's monument on the Emmitsburg Road, Gallagher, *Causes Won, Lost and Forgotten*, 135–206; Spielvogel, *Interpreting Sacred Ground*, 155–56; a discussion of recent interpretive changes is in Murray, *On a Great Battlefield*, 187–93.

47. Thomas R. Pero, *Gettysburg 1863—Seething Hell: The Epic Battle of the Civil War in the Soldiers' Own Words* (Mill Creek, WA: Wild River Press, 2016).

48. Charles R. Knight, *Valley Thunder: The Battle of New Market and the Opening of the Shenandoah Valley Campaign, May 1864* (New York: Savas Beatie, 2010), xi–xii; for the larger context and another account of the battle, see Mark Grimsley, *And Keep Moving On: The Virginia Campaign, May–June 1864* (Lincoln: Univ. of Nebraska Press, 2002), 102–10.

49. Knight, *Valley Thunder*, 39–40.

50. Knight, *Valley Thunder*, 13–29; Lt. Colonel Troy Marshall, "The Battle of New Market Reenactment—the Tradition Continues," http://vmi.edu/media/content-assets/documents/museums/va-museum-of-civil-war/The-Battle-of-New-Market-The-Tradition-Continues-2017.pdf; Col. Marshall also e-mailed me a copy of this during our correspondence in the summer of 2017.

51. Quoted in Marshall, "The Battle of New Market"; another account of the campaign and battle can be accessed from the Virginia Museum of the Civil War website, Joseph W. A. Whitehorne, *The Battle of New Market—A Self-Guided Tour* (Washington, DC: Center for Military Studies, 1988), https://history.army.mil/books/Staff-Rides/NewMarket/NM-fm.htm.

52. Knight, *Valley Thunder*, 198, 238.

53. Marshall, "The Battle of New Market"; see also "The Battle," http://vmi.edu/museums-and-archives/virginia-museum-of-the-civil-war/the-battle/; items pertaining to commemorations at VMI and the Battle of New Market, including "The 125th Anniversary of the Virginia Military Institute, founded November 11, 1839" pamphlet, Lexington, VA, May 15, 1965, and origins of the roll call tradition found in Julia Martin to the Superintendent, "The New Market Day Ceremony," 1975, can be found in New Market Reenactment Folder, Virginia Military Institute Archives, Lexington, VA (New Market Folder, VMIA).

54. Video clip, http://vmi.edu/museums-and-archives/virginia-museum-of-the-civil-war/the-battle/; the author noted the photographs leading to the Hall of Honor on a visit to the museum in June 2017.

55. Clemons, "Functions of Battle Reenacting," 17; quoted in Elson and Stein, *Battlefields of Honor*, 17; quoted from Earle Lutz, "Rattle of Rifles and Crash of Heavy Guns Heard at New Market," *Richmond Times-Dispatch*, September 20, 1923, both in New Market Folder, VMIA; the file includes numerous clippings copied onto several pages from newspapers in Baltimore, MD and Lynchburg, VA, several of which repeated the *Times* report of the marine reenactment, which was the only one not held in May on the anniversary of the battle; Jonathan A. Noyalas makes a case for New Market being one of many Civil War sites in the valley that enabled reconciliation between veterans in *Civil War Legacy in the Shenandoah: Remembrance, Reunion & Reconciliation* (Charleston, SC: The History Press, 2015), 116–17.

56. Donald Gilliland, "Should Civil War Re-enactments be abandoned?" *Marching Towards Gettysburg*, July 11, 2013 (updated July 6, 2016), http://blog.pennlive.com/gettysburg-150/2013/07/should_civil_war_re-enactments.html.

57. At a recent Civil War Collector's show the author encountered the Quantrill's Raiders Chapter of the SUV, whose booth and literature personify the dubious extremes of Lost Cause "true believers." Dressed as "yahoos" (complete with cowboy boots, a six-shooter, and the plume) they impersonate reenactors and occupy an aisle alongside mainstream units like the 8th Ohio and 4th Kentucky. Their flyers have headings like "WANTED: Honest Abe Lincoln, 1st Ruler and Tyrant of the American Empire" and "the Morrill Tariff:

Northern Provocation to Southern Secession." They defend Quantrill from his historically established reputation as a "ruthless outlaw" and quote Missourian Harry Truman's claim that "Quantrill's men were no more bandits than the men on the other side," literature by Quantrill's Raiders SUV Chapter #2086, Ohio Division (May 2010), acquired by the author at the Mansfield Civil War Show, Mansfield, Ohio, May 6, 2017.

58. For a fuller analysis of the flag, see John Coski, *The Confederate Battle Flag: America's Most Embattled Emblem* (Cambridge, MA: Belknap Press, 2006) and Robert J. Bonner, *Colors of Blood: Flag Passions of the Confederate South* (Princeton: Princeton Univ. Press, 2002).

59. The home page of the NPS Appomattox site reads, "Beginning Peace and Reunion: On April 9, 1865, the surrender of the Army of Northern Virginia in the McLean House in the village of Appomattox Court House, Virginia signaled the end of the nation's largest war. Two important questions about its future were answered. Could the nation survive a civil war intact, and would that nation exist without slavery? The answer to both was yes and a new nation was born." https://www.nps.gov/apco/index.htm; Richard Kreitner, "A Victory Parade 150 Years in the Making: The African American Civil War Memorial & Museum will honor black soldiers who were not welcome at the original Grand Review celebration," *The Nation*, May 11, 2015, https://www.thenation.com/article/victory-parade-150-years-making/.

60. Despite its obvious flaws, I used Wikipedia as a way of summarizing multiple issues surrounding this event, since news coverage at the time was erratic, "Charleston Church Shooting," https://en.wikipedia.org/wiki/Charleston_church_shooting; fortunately, the list of banned or discontinued items did not initially include reenactors' flags, "Modern Display of the Confederate Flag," https://en.wikipedia.org/wiki/Modern_display_of_the_Confederate_flag.

61. Karl Plume, "Civil War buffs argue we shouldn't 'present some water-down' version of history," *Reuters*, June 29, 2015, http://www.businessinsider.com/r-civil-war-buffs-on-confederate-flag-debate-its-complicated-2015-6.

62. Photos that accompanied this story showed several versions of the Confederate battle flag amidst the white-supremacist symbols, "Virginia Governor to white nationalists: 'go home—shame on you,'" August 13, 2017, https://www.cnn.com/2017/08/12/us/charlottesville-white-nationalists-rally/index.html.

63. Wilbert Cooper quoted in Anna Mussmann, "Banning Civil War Reenactments will only Increase Ignorance and Prejudice," http://thefederalist.com/2017/08/29/banning-civil-war-re-enactments-will-increase-ignorance-prejudice/.

64. Mussmann, "Banning Reenactments"; To Our Friends in Civil War Reenacting from Brigadier General Darrell Markijohn, August 23, 2017, letter used by permission.

65. *Cedar Creek Battlefield Foundation*, https://www.ccbf.us/; *Cedar Creek and Belle Grove National Historical Park*, https://www.nps.gov/cebe/index.htm; the site of many modern reenactments, the battlefield was also central to early reconciliation efforts, Noyalas, *Legacy in the Shenandoah*, 90–95; Jayme Metzgar, "Anti-History Fury Hits Virginia Civil War Reenactment with Threats, Pipe Bombs," October 16, 2017, https://thefederalist.com/2017/10/16/anti-history-fury-hits-virginia-civil-war-re-enactment-threats-pipe-bombs/.

66. Markijohn issued two reports after the battle, both with the heading "Report of Brig. General Darrell N. Markijohn, USV, commanding, October 14–15, 2017—The Battle of

First Winchester and Cedar Creek"; the second report had the subheading "Report of the Pipe-bomb evacuation and its aftermath." Both are dated October 17, 2017 and used with permission.

67. Jim Gerhaghty, "Is Someone trying to Blow up Civil War Reenactors?" October 17, 2017, http://www.nationalreview.com/corner/452696/someone-trying-blow-civil-war -reenactors; Don Morse and Michael E. Miller, "'We wanted to send a message': Reenactors stage Civil War battle despite threat," October 15, 2017, https://www.washingtonpost.com /local/we-wanted-to-send-a-message-reenactors-stage-civil-war-battle-despite-threat/2017/10 /15/77dd0348-b1c4–11e7-a908-a3470754bbb9_story.html?utm_term=.ef108258c431.

68. Markijohn, "Cedar Creek Reports."

69. The authors include an entire chapter to "Women Reenactors" in Elson and Stein, *Battlefields of Honor*, 81–97; the presence of women as soldiers has always triggered debate but is upheld by plenty of evidence; Deanne Blanton and Lauren McCook, *They Fought Like Demons: Women Soldiers in the Civil War* (New York: Vintage Books, 2002); quoted in Metzgar, "Anti-history fury"; current scholarship that paints a darker picture of Civil War veterans includes Christopher Phillips, *The Rivers Ran Backwards: The Civil War and the Making of the American Middle Border* (Oxford Univ. Press, 2016) and Brian Matthew Jordan, *Marching Home: Union Veterans and Their Unending Civil War* (New York: Liveright Publishing Corporation, 2016).

The Ongoing Lost Cause of Southern Cultural Superiority and Its Impact on SBC Home Missions in the Mid-1900s

ED STETZER

Since 1845, Southern Baptists have sought to extend their particular understanding of Christianity through domestic missions. Not only did Baptist missionaries establish congregations outside the former Confederacy, these fellowships often benefitted from migrations by Southern Baptists in search of economic opportunities, especially from the 1930s to the 1960s. Historians have documented how Baptists, and Southern Evangelicals generally, transported their cultural beliefs, along with their material aspirations, to their new homes. Scholars have particularly focused on issues like race and missions, where Southern racial mores seem at odds with both the Bible and with social customs and expectations outside of Dixie. But the extent to which culture impacted missiology begs for further scholarly appraisal. The pattern of Southern Baptists' efforts at home missions in North America is at once a missionary endeavor and an exercise in cultural exportation.[1]

Indeed, the Southern Baptist Convention, influenced by the Lost Cause, engaged in a mission strategy that implicitly and explicitly exported this cultural philosophy outside of the American South. Embracing and shaping the concept of the Lost Cause, a concept central to the historiography of the ending of the Civil War and the emergence of a postwar Southern culture, the Lost Cause also expressed itself consistently in SBC home missions strategy and philosophy. Influenced by the notion that Southern culture was superior and worth preserving, Southern Baptists engaged in a mission strategy that, intentionally or unintentionally, exported their culture in ways that propagated the Lost Cause.

THE LOST CAUSE AND THE
SOUTHERN BAPTIST CONVENTION

A welter of scholars have traced the origin and various expressions of the Lost Cause, but few have connected its persistence to missiology. Missiology is a field that helps Christians understand and engage different cultures, and a common expression of missiology is Southern Baptist church planting. But such efforts, while central to evangelism, are not culturally neutral. Indeed, Southern Baptist captivity to the tragic elements in Southern history has been harming the work of missions. Southern Baptists have been inapproachably enamored with Southern culture for reasons that are rooted in the Lost Cause, and this attachment impacts the manner in which Southern Baptists perform evangelism and missions.[2]

In the wake of the Civil War and Reconstruction Southern Baptists began to reassert themselves as national and even international leaders in missions in the early decades of the twentieth century. This reassertion produced several fissures in their relationship to their Northern counterparts, highlighted by the conflict between I. T. Tichenor, head of the Home Mission Board, and Henry Morehouse, head of the American Baptist Home Mission Society, over the scope of both.[3] As a result, Southern Baptists began to exert greater autonomy in their missions outside the American South, as exemplified in the ministry of R. E. Milam in the American Pacific Northwest. As demonstrated in Milam's and other SBC church planters' activities, the SBC wove themes of cultural superiority and preservation into their ministry philosophy, where the exportation of culture was too connected with the advance of mission.

THE LOST CAUSE

At the outbreak of the Civil War, the South argued that the battle was over the institution of slavery. In an address to the Confederate Congress dated April 29, 1861, Confederate President Jefferson Davis claimed that Lincoln's election in 1860 set the stage for the South to be excluded from national decision making and, consequently, "rendering the property in slaves so insecure as to be comparatively worthless, and thereby annihilating in effect property worth thousands of millions of dollars."[4]

Confederate Vice President Alexander H. Stephens was even more blunt, stating that slavery was "the immediate cause of the late rupture and the present revolution."[5] Stephens saw slavery not just as an economic necessity, but as the linchpin of the Confederacy and a rule of nature. Concerning the Confederate government, he states, "Its foundations are laid, its corner-stone rests, upon the great truth that the negro is not equal to the white man; that slavery subordination to the superior race is his natural and normal condition. This, our new government, is the first, in the history of the world, based upon this great physical, philosophical, and moral truth." He ends this section of this particular speech by stating that the anti-slavery Northerners "were attempting to make things equal which the Creator had made unequal."[6] The rationale for secession is clear and well documented. However, by the time the Civil War ended and the Confederacy lost, their stated reasons for rebelling had shifted.

Instead of fighting to protect the institution of human bondage, the war was over preserving states' rights and Southern culture. The term "Lost Cause" came to encapsulate the myth that the South, though defeated on the battlefield, was victorious where it mattered most—a surviving culture[7] built on honor, chivalry, and traditions that could never be overcome by Northern invaders.[8] The South might not realize their dreams by political means through the establishment of a new country, but they would define themselves by a "separate *cultural* identity."

This concept of a separate culture helped them to justify their choice to rebel, even in defeat. With a land decimated by war, an economy wrecked with the loss of slave labor, and the South's war heroes humiliated in defeat, a new narrative needed to be written. According to Gary Gallagher:

> White Southerners emerged from the Civil War thoroughly beaten but largely unrepentant. . . . During the decades following surrender at Appomattox, they nurtured a public memory of the Confederacy that placed their wartime sacrifice and shattering defeat in the best possible light. This interpretation addressed the nature of antebellum Southern society and the institution of slavery, the constitutionality of secession, the causes of the Civil War, the characteristics of their wartime society, and the reasons for their defeat. Widely known then and now as the Lost Cause explanation of the Confederate experience.[9]

The narrative of the Lost Cause was used to provide future generations with a "proper" perspective on the events of the war.

Southerners were so committed to telling stories from their perspective and honoring Confederate soldiers, both local and national, that in the 1920s tens of thousands bought commemorative coins to finance the sculpting of Robert E. Lee, Jefferson Davis, and Stonewall Jackson onto the face of Stone Mountain east of Atlanta. The University of Alabama's victory over the University of Washington in the 1926 Rose Bowl was called "the greatest victory for the South since the first Battle of Bull Run."[10] The narrative of the Lost Cause permeated Southern society.

For Baptists (as well as other denominations) in the South who had split from their Northern brethren over the issue of slavery before the Civil War, the Lost Cause offered a way to understand their religion within a framework of their culture. They had a justification to remain separate, even after the issue of slavery was settled. The Lost Cause was "the story of the linking of two profound forces, religion and history . . . it was a Southern civil religion, which tied together Christian churches and Southern culture."[11] Southern churches helped provide the framework for a postwar South by reminding congregants of their moral superiority over the North, that southern culture was virtuous compared to the atheistic North, and that it was their duty to preserve "religious, political, societal, and economic orthodoxy."[12] According to social historian Rufus Spain, while Southern Baptists eventually welcomed a fraternal relationship with Northern Baptists at the end of the nineteenth century, "they refused to repudiate the Lost Cause and chose to retain their denominational entity along sectional lines."[13] Southern Baptists continued to identify with Southern culture as the wounds of the war began to heal.

SOUTHERN BAPTIST HOME MISSIONS AND SOUTHERN CULTURE

Baptists in the South had long struggled with the task of being in but not of the world, and that task early on involved missions. Baptists in the United States first gathered corporately for the sake of foreign missions in Philadelphia on May 18, 1814, with the creation of the General Missionary Convention of the Baptist Denomination in the United States for Foreign Missions. They agreed to convene every three years, thus taking the unofficial name of the Triennial Convention. At the subsequent meeting in 1817, they added home missions to their evangelistic repertoire. For the next

238 / Ed Stetzer

twenty-seven years, Baptists in northern and southern regions of the country worked cooperatively to spread the gospel all across the United States.

The split between the Northern and Southern Baptists in 1845 was over the issue of slavery. It should be noted that sectionalism (regional allegiance vs. national allegiance) and political concepts (in particular, the states being the ultimate political authority) certainly did play a role in the split. However, both of these issues were tied to, and had as their root, slavery. Concerning the time just before the split, William Johnson, the first president of the SBC, noted that "an evil hour has arrived . . . in the last two Triennial Conventions, slavery and anti-slavery men began to draw off on different sides."[14]

Despite the split, it is interesting to note that both sides agreed they held no animosity toward each other. Johnson himself urged that the split not be "exaggerated." He stated, "At the present time it involves only the Foreign and Domestic Missions of the denomination. Northern and Southern Baptists are still brethren. They differ in no article of faith. They are guided by the same principles of gospel order."[15]

Many in the North also expressed similar thoughts, including Francis Wayland, the president of Brown University. He sent a letter to the delegates that were meeting in Augusta, Georgia to discuss the creation of the SBC. In the letter he says, "You will separate of course. I could not ask otherwise. Your rights have been infringed. I will take the liberty of offering one or two suggestions. We have shown how Christians ought not to act. It remains for you to show us how they ought to act. Put away all violence, act with dignity and firmness and the world will approve your course."[16]

And, as a result, "The adoption of a new name and the shifting of allegiance from nationwide to Southwide agencies by no means required the construction of a new organization."[17] Baptists saw their similarities as outweighing their differences and each had their own territories to evangelize. But by 1862 the Northern Home Missions Society reassigned Northern Baptist missionaries into southern areas, claiming "its original birthright to the cultivation of this entire continent."[18] By the time Lee surrendered to Grant in 1865, the Southern economy was in shambles, thereby causing missions funding, both foreign and domestic, to wither. During Reconstruction, Northern Baptists sent a large percentage of their missionaries to the South in order to fill the missionary vacuum. One Baptist historian estimates that one third of Home Missions Society missionaries were working below the

Mason-Dixon line.[19] To many Southern Baptists, it was as if their Northern counterparts were following in the footsteps of the Union Army in the invasion of their land, not with a rifle in hand but with a Bible.

Northern Baptists saw the spiritual needs of both blacks and whites in the South and the perceived inability of Southern Baptists to meet those needs as they sent many missionaries South. Seeing Northern Baptists in the South delivered a blow to Southern pride. As Rufus Spain notes, "Southern Baptists were homogeneous members of Southern society."[20] To be Southern Baptist was to be just as Southern as one was Baptist.

No more clearly can their Southern identity be seen than in the 1861 SBC Annual, published just after the start of the Civil War, where the convention approved a motion to strike the term "United States" in its constitution and replace it with "Southern States of North America." Likewise, at the same meeting, another motion passed to change "United States to Confederate States" in all SBC documents and minutes. The motion was amended to include the justification: "growing out of the recent formation of the Southern Confederacy." These motions highlight how important identity was to Southern Baptists from the beginning.[21]

As one considers the role of religion in society, it is not unusual for culture to be shaped by religion and religion by culture. This is especially evident in displaced people, and migrating Southern Baptists illustrate this phenomenon. In his study of initial Southern Baptist settlement and mission in New Mexico, Daniel Richard Carnett argues that the persistent desire of transplanted Southerners for churches that reflected their culture proved a major initial flashpoint between Northern and Southern denominations. Even as Northern Baptists voiced their opposition to this "unwarranted invasion" of Southern Baptists, the Home Mission Board continued to offer aid to churches that wished to align with the SBC. As Carnett observes, this represented strategy on the part of the Home Mission Board that was focused on cultural replication rather than the conversionism traditionally associated with Christian mission. "During the period from 1900 to 1930, for every one member added by conversion, four were admitted to fellowship who had already been members of other Baptist churches. This means Southern Baptist presence in New Mexico is best viewed as a geographical extension of the South. . . . This continuing allowed Southern religion to be 're-created' in a new territory. Southern Baptists did not ignore the exceptional populations, they simply did not feel it necessary to adjust to them."

New Mexico proved merely the opening skirmish in missions-related conflict between Northern and Southern Baptists. For Southerners displaced from their homes, religion proved a useful tool in transplanting their culture without significant adaption. Dissatisfied with the Northern churches, the uprooted Southerners would either leave the church completely or find a church that reminded them of the South.[22]

In his analysis of the SBC and Southern culture, Baptist historian Bill Leonard notes the following: "Samuel Hill, Jr., whose numerous works on the South have made him a major analyst of that culture, insists that the 'religion of the Southern people and their culture have been linked by the tightest bonds. That culture, particularly in its moral aspects, could not have survived without a legitimating impetus provided by religion. . . . ' For the South to stand its people had to be religious and its churches the purest anywhere."[23] And one way to ensure Southern culture survived and thrived was to spread Southern religion through agencies such as the Home Mission Board. But spreading Southern religion was perhaps more about maintaining the comforts of those leaving the South than anything else. Leonard continues, "Since the 1950s, Southern Baptists have taken their faith to so-called 'pioneer' areas beyond the South. Often these efforts were begun by transplanted Southerners who wanted a little piece of Alabama or Texas to provide security in the backside of the American desert (Chicago, New York, or Boston)."[24] Many Southerners believed their culture to be superior to the rest of the country and wanted to take wherever they traveled home with them.[25]

Southern Baptists were comfortable in the culture that they helped to build. Barry Hankins argues that while Southern Baptists did not make the South distinctly Christian, they did identify with Southern culture and therefore supported its norms—so much so that religious historian Martin Marty called the SBC "the Catholic Church of the South."[26] It is important to note, however, that most people believe their culture is superior. When people participate in cultural patterns, they become indebted and connected to them. Thus, by nature of being in a culture, Southern Baptists see that culture's norms or mores as normal even better. The tension around how to understand the relationship between religion and culture took on a new dynamic in the wake of the Civil War.[27]

COMITY AGREEMENTS AND FALLOUT

In a letter dated January 14, 1864, the War Department directed Union generals to award to the Northern Baptist Home Missions Society possession of all Baptist churches in the South "in which a loyal minister of said church does not officiate." Confiscation of church buildings was justified on the basis that "to restore tranquility to the community and peace to the nation, that Christian ministers should, by example and precept, support and foster the loyal sentiment of the people."[28] Soon, the Home Missions Society "relocated missionaries in Kentucky, Louisiana, Tennessee, Virginia, Missouri, and South Carolina. Northern Baptists felt that this was consistent with the whole underlying moral theme of the Civil War, that is to free the slaves, and most of their work was done among freed slaves."[29] The missionaries of the Home Missions Society stepped into a gap that they believed Southern Baptists were neglecting as they ministered to the freed slaves.

Before the Civil War, estimates show that up to 90 percent of slaves were illiterate. After the achievement of liberty, freed people of color thirsted for education. Reconstruction era historian Eric Foner notes, "Perhaps the most striking illustration of the freedmen's quest for self-improvement was their seemingly unquenchable thirst for education."[30] Before the war, every southern state but Tennessee prohibited instruction to slaves. The Home Missions Society took note and paid special attention to ministering to former slaves through education. They set up schools both to teach them basic literacy and to train them for pastoral ministry. Through the 1880s, this proved to be a successful ministry, though debate and friction often arose as some blacks felt Northern whites would never give up control of the schools they had created, thereby keeping freed blacks in bondage.

That the Home Missions Society remained in Southern states for so many years proved troublesome for the Southern Baptist Convention Home Mission Board. Southern churches began to trust and appreciate the Home Missions Society and questioned the need for the Home Mission Board. In 1882, in large measure due to lack of interest in the current Home Mission Board, the Southern Baptist Convention voted to dismiss the secretary and board of the Home Mission Board and relocate the agency from Marion, Alabama to its present location of Atlanta, Georgia.[31] With the re-establishment of the Home Mission Board under I. T. Tichenor, Southern Baptists had a domestic missions agency they could be proud of and the first opportunity to push back against the intrusion of the Home Missions Society. Tichenor began chiding Southern churches and state conventions for partnering with the Home Missions Society, implying that such disloyalty towards the SBC was immeasurably harmful. Tensions between Northern and Southern mission agencies were somewhat resolved in 1894.[32]

Due to the war-torn and weakened state of the South, from the start of the Civil War until the 1890s, Southern Baptists were in no position to negotiate the expulsion of Northern Baptists from their region. As H. Leon McBeth quips, "For thirty years Southern Baptists could only deplore this 'invasion' of their territory and make snide remarks about the 'pretty Yankee girls' who came South to teach in the Baptist schools. But by the 1890's they could do more than deplore; they could deploy their own missionary forces to challenge Northern Baptist occupation of Dixie."[33] Thus, by 1894, Southern Baptists had enough missions collateral to leverage a negotiation with Northern Baptists.

At Fortress Monroe, Virginia, representatives from both Baptist groups met for the purpose of determining how to share the missions load together with as little overlap and frustration as possible. "The meeting featured a veritable Who's Who of white Baptist leadership including six denominational agency representatives, four college/seminary professors, two college presidents, an editor, a pastor, and a former Lt. Governor of Connecticut."[34] The conference determined that "for the promotion of fraternal feelings, and of the best interests of the Redeemer's Kingdom it is inexpedient for two different organizations of Baptists to solicit contributions, or to establish missions in the same localities."[35] The agreement laid out boundaries the SBC had been arguing for since the 1840s. "In effect, the Northern society agreed to work in the North while the SBC would work in the South."[36] Interestingly, the agreement also called both sides to recommend the application for admission of Oregon Baptists into the SBC. While there were other comity agreements that followed Fortress-Monroe, none were as groundbreaking or foundational.

As a result of the different comity agreements, by the time Tichenor resigned from the Home Mission Board in 1899, the Board supported 671 missionaries, up from forty-one after his first year in 1893.[37] Southern Baptists had expanded out of their region due to their financial strength. Around the turn of the century, the SBC had established relationships with Baptist bodies in Illinois, Arkansas, Texas, Oklahoma, and New Mexico, demonstrating a successful westward movement. Compounding this westward expansion by Southern Baptists was the migration brought on by the Great Depression, including those individuals from Arkansas and Oklahoma who were impacted by Landmarkism and did not feel comfortable in the Northern Baptist churches they found in the West. [38] Thus, these transient Southerners created their own Southern churches in their new homes.

Northern and Southern Baptists met again in 1912 at Hot Springs, Arkansas and called for "a fresh recognition of some of the simple and fundamental principles for which Baptists stand." [39] Additionally, the committee agreed that Baptists in New Mexico, formerly associated with the Northern Baptist Convention (who changed to this name in 1907), should now align with the SBC because each state should have only one Baptist convention and, more importantly, because the values and preferences of New Mexico Baptists aligned more with Southern than Northern Baptists: "The chief consideration in the minds of the committee was the fact that the tide of immigration into New Mexico from Texas and other Southern States in recent years has been so great. The result has been that the population of New Mexico has become largely Southern in tradition and sympathy and preference. This condition, taken in connection with the others which have been mentioned, seemed to the committee a sufficient ground to warrant it in adopting the plan above outlined."[40] With the Southern Baptist Convention's capture of New Mexico in 1912, specifically because of "tradition and sympathy and preference," and Oklahoma right after in 1914, state convention after state convention began to shift their allegiance from Northern to Southern Baptist over the next thirty years.

California, however, was the linchpin that opened the floodgates to Southern Baptist expansion outside of previously agreed upon areas by various comity arrangements. Since the 1850s, California had received more than its fair share of westward migration. From the gold rush of 1849 to the Dust Bowl in the 1930s, scores of people from Texas, Oklahoma, and Arkansas made their way to the Golden State. [41] In 1940, fourteen churches formed a state convention and applied to join the SBC the following year. In response, the SBC formed a Committee on the Petition from the Baptist General Convention of California to consider their admission to the convention, which requested opportunity to investigate the matter and report back in 1942.[42]

The California Committee was due to present their findings on the second day of the 1942 convention. The chairman, Arthur J. Barton, was ill and so the committee recommended postponing their report until 1943. McBeth states the committee "clearly leaned toward refusing the California messengers."[43] J. B. Rounds, a member of the committee, proposed a minority report calling for immediate acceptance of the California Convention. Louisiana pastor and committee member M. E. Dodd spoke against Rounds's motion, as did a California pastor named Louis J. Julianel. Julianel, pastor of First Baptist Church in San Francisco, opposed the motion on the grounds that membership into the SBC would be an "invasion of Southern Baptists into Northern Baptist territory."[44] Despite opposition and a long debate over the issue, Rounds's motion was approved by messengers:

> After a careful study of the situation and in consideration of the provisions of the constitution and By-Laws of this Convention, we recommend that the Southern Baptist General Convention of the state of California be admitted to membership in the Southern Baptist Convention.
>
> They have thirty-one cooperating churches with an approximate membership of 3,000, fifteen of these churches having been organized during the past twelve months. They have sent $560.23 during the past twelve months to the Southwide causes. They give 20% of all cooperative program receipts to the Southwide causes.[45]

The decision to include California Baptists within the SBC did not sit well with everyone.

Northern Baptists were immediately troubled, understandably accusing the SBC of violating the terms of the 1912 comity agreement. The SBC responded by admitting the 1942 vote was "an action unprecedented in the history of our Convention" and that it was wrong of them to admit the California Convention when they should have only admitted individual California Baptist churches. By the 1944 convention, the SBC agreed to continue with the terms of the 1912 comity agreement of Hot Springs, Arkansas.[46] Despite expansion in multiple directions, Southern Baptists still employed language that demarcated territories between the two Baptist groups.[47] The Home Mission Board was encouraged in 1944 to "strengthen their evangelistic forces in order that we may more thoroughly reach the needs of our territory, both urban and rural."[48] The Home Mission

Board and the Sunday School Board encouraged "evangelist efforts in our Southern Baptist Zion."[49]

But by 1949, the SBC put away any pretense that comity agreements based on territorial demarcations would hold them back. That year, SBC messengers meeting in Oklahoma City decided the opposite of the 1894 Convention. The Committee to Investigate the Oregon Petition recommended "that the Baptist churches in Oregon and Washington that have petitioned for affiliation with the Southern Baptist Convention be received," and the motion was adopted.[50] The solidification of the West to Southern Baptist mission work reversed the role Northern Baptists had played almost a century before when they "invaded" the South in 1862, claiming their birthright to minister to the entire nation.[51] This was only seven years after Baptists in California had been received into the fold and closed a decade when the sentiments behind the comity agreements had passed.

Southern Baptists did, however, set their own boundaries a few years later. In a letter written on November 1, 1955, R. E. Milam (the executive secretary of the Baptist General Convention of Oregon-Washington), James E. Frost (president and chairman of the Executive Committee), and other members of the Executive Committee made the following argument against comity agreements:

1. Christianity is doctrinal and spiritual, and not territorial. The Great Commission knows no national boundaries.
2. Southern Baptist mission money should be spent in the building of New Testament churches and institutions that follow our own pattern and support our own Cooperative Program and should be spent under the supervision of our own Boards and agencies.
3. Southern Baptists are not in sympathy with comity arrangements which bar the door to needy fields, either in the United States or in Canada or any other place.
4. The Southern Baptist Convention does not wish to turn a deaf ear to those who share our continent, our common ancestry, and who believe in our doctrines, practice our methods, carry out our programs and support our work.

The report went on to argue that mission work in Canada is no different than mission work in various states within America and that certain SBC entities are within their mission to assist any church that is affiliated with a Southern Baptist state convention.[52] Yet despite the plea to include Canadian Baptists within the fold of the SBC, messengers rejected their request and chose to keep in place the requirement of being geographically located in the United States.[53]

What was the reason Southern Baptists had for expanding outside of their territory? Part of it was genuine zeal for spreading the news of Jesus in unplowed fields. But that does not explain why Southern Baptist churches were planted in places where other Baptist churches already existed. Even as Southern Baptists left their residences for new territories, they didn't want to leave home; they preferred to bring it with them. In an address to Northern Baptists in 1959, Southern Baptist pastor Blake Smith offered three arguments:

> Why Southerners feel justified in establishing churches in the North: They don't feel at home in Northern churches when they move, so they set up their own style and then petition for affiliation with the Southern Convention; they fear the ecumenical connections of American Baptists; and they suspect American Baptists are doctrinally unsound. Smith warned that the first reason was valid; he chided American Baptists for not welcoming transplanted Southerners, and suggested in passing that the Northern group might well follow its people when they move to the South. The other two reasons are less valid, he said.[54]

Smith makes a de facto claim that Southerners felt out of place when they moved out from Dixie and a means of recapturing a part of their lost home was to bring their churches with them, their southern churches.[55]

The editor of the *California Southern Baptist*, the Southern Baptist state paper, took umbrage with Rev. Smith's comments. In the following week's edition, the editor dismissed comity agreements as invalid when God calls someone to plant a church, and claimed any territorial agreements between Northern and Southern Baptists were similar to the territorial agreement Abraham and Lot came to in Genesis 13, reminding the reader that Lot got the better end of the deal but "his 'ecumenical' tendencies got him into trouble and Abraham had to 'invade' his territory and go to his rescue."[56]

One commentator, writing before Baptist churches in California were admitted into the SBC, made an astute observation: "The Southern Baptist Convention may well argue that if it officially enters California it will be doing so because many of its members have insisted on bringing their church with them into their new place of residence."[57] In fact, often that is precisely what happened. Instead of Southern Baptists preaching to the lost in the West, they became enclaves of Southern transplants who wanted a piece of home in their current setting. As Southerners migrated to various parts of the country, Southern Baptist churches sprang up like weeds in a garden.

One Southern Baptist pastor in Tacoma, Washington wrote in 1952 of the prevailing method of church planting outside of the South:

> My own church is typical of the new churches that are being established every week or so. It is a middle-class-and-above suburban area with over 30,000 residents. The seven churches (three community, and one Catholic, one Lutheran, one Congregational, and one Episcopal) have less than 2,000 total membership. When a Southern Baptist church is first organized, an effort is made to enlist every transplanted Southern Baptist (and there are usually a few in any town), and then reach out in every widening circles to the native population. That we are succeeding is proven by the better than 100% gain in membership reported for the association during the past year.[58]

Southerners were recruited to be the foundation of the church, to be the means of recruiting locals. Part and parcel with these first members being exclusively Southerners was that Southern Baptist churches were mimicking the culture of their members, not the culture of their surroundings.

In analyzing the growth of evangelicals (of which Southern Baptists belong) in one particular state in the Northwest, David Jepsen recently wrote: "The current strength of evangelical churches in the region is due mostly to migration. Rather than bringing a southern brand of evangelism to the Northwest, ministers brought evangelism to southerners who had migrated there. Most southerners worshipped with other southerners, while native northwesterners worshiped as they had in the past or not at all."[59] Specifically about Southern Baptists, Jepsen noted they "struggled to convert native northwesterners. Most newcomers worked with or lived near long-time northwesterners, but when Sundays rolled around they sought the familiarity of fellow Oklahomans, Texans, or anyone 'who talked their language.'"[60] Southern Baptists worked in whatever context brought them to the Northwest but worshiped in the context that they left behind.[61]

The most helpful aspect of Jepsen's article was his personal interview with retired Southern Baptist pastor Cecil Sims. Speaking from personal experience, Sims described most Southern Baptist churches in the Northwest during the 1950s as "'Southern clubs,' and he admitted that 'nine out of ten' of his members were former southerners. 'They were people who grew up in one area and were trying to adjust in another element,' he remembered. 'I was the type of preacher they were accustomed to.' Sims said he tried not to neglect northerners, but they 'did not feel at home worshipping with Southerners. They would say to me, "I would love being a part of your church, but I don't think I could be part of an Arkansas community.""[62] Sims went on to admit that most Southern Baptist churches in the Northwest struggled to grow in the 1960s because they had already "discovered most of the pockets of Southern origin" and were unsuccessful at converting natives to their churches or their style of religion. Pastors and denominational leaders tried to "transition Southern Baptist heritage clubs into cosmopolitan New Testament churches," but rarely did they achieve their goal.[63]

Professor Cal Guy explained how people planted churches, specifically in Chicago. He noted they would wait at the one grocery store in town that sold grits, and then talk to anyone who bought them. Cal Guy called it "chasing license plates," but it was really chasing people of common culture. Guy told the story knowing it was not a good strategy, but acknowledging it was the common practice. This same strategy of chasing people of common culture was stressed in the work of the Pacific Northwest.

THE CASE STUDY OF OREGON AND R. E. MILAM

The labors of R. E. Milam, the first leader of the combined Oregon-Washington Convention, illustrate Guy's point. Milam proved tireless in his efforts to call Southern Baptists to rethink their strategy of home missions and bring their movement to the West in full force. It was not simply about adding more people to their numbers; it was also about keeping the ones who had geographically left the fold. The migration of church members was a reason for expansion of the pews. In his work so aptly named *Win American Now*, he stated, "It is conservatively estimated that there are hundreds of thousands of Southern Baptist laymen and their families who have moved into these [western and pioneer] states and that most of them will be lost to the Baptist cause unless we follow them immediately with an aggressive missionary program."[64]

Baptist churches were not new to the Pacific Northwest. In fact, the East Oregon Baptist Convention petitioned the Southern Baptist Convention for admission into its cooperative body in 1894. The Southern Baptist Convention politely declined, with an appointed committee stating, "It is inexpedient to accede to their request." [65] This request from Baptists in the Northwest led directly to the Fortress-Monroe Conference previously discussed.

By the middle of the twentieth century, things had changed. The South had come to the West, and the Southern Baptist borders of home had officially expanded. The mission field was on the horizon and they could see it, but their identity was in part defined by their place. Going to the horizon could not simply be a new adventure in a new location. When identity is defined by place, place travels with identity. For Southern Baptists, they could not simply go to a faraway land and take a timeless message to a new culture. They brought their Southern culture along with them.

W. M. Vines, a Southern Baptist pastor in the early twentieth century, wrote about this spread of culture along with the Gospel in a very direct way. Writing in a publication for the Home Mission Board, he states, "[As we] contemplate the opportunity of our Home Mission Board we cannot but feel that it is a task at once magnificent and appalling, for it means nothing less than to preserve and perpetuate the Christian spirit of the South until it permeates and prevails through and over all the spheres of life in this great and growing nation and the destiny of the world."[66]

Vines is an example of those who saw the South as the religious exemplar of the nation. Many Southern Baptists of that day saw the South as not only as a stronghold of biblical truth, what Vines called "the citadel of our Baptist position,"[67] but also the one hope (at least humanly speaking) for the nation and the world.

As people would move from the South for the military or for career opportunities, they took their culture with them. They were going to new places but they had no desire to leave behind the South, so the South came with them. They planted churches not so much to reach people but to find home. And believing that their home was superior, they were more than hospitable to share it with their neighbors. But they needed help from back home to expand fully and transform the culture around them. They used conquest language to call workers to the harvest.

In late 1954, A. C. Turner wrote in an editorial entitled "Preachers Going West." It was released in Baptist Press and distributed throughout Baptist state papers:

If large churches in the South would underwrite good strong preachers who feel called to this field, this great West would become a Baptist empire in the years to come. But don't send us your misfits. We need your best men—"Give me men to match my mountains" (inscription on the California state capitol building). Whoever builds Sunday schools in the West and preaches a positive New Testament gospel can win the West and we know of no people on earth better qualified for these very things than Southern Baptists. Thus far the burden of our mission work has rested upon the shoulders of God-fearing preachers and their families. It is time that mission minded churches come to their help. Without any question, the future of our country is vitally related to the development of the West in which she is already pouring millions of her most energetic citizens. The same can be said for the future of Southern Baptists. We were ten million people late in getting started out here but we are now on the ground floor, getting ready for the twenty million yet to come.[68]

In 1956, C. E. Boyle wrote an editorial about the contributions of Oregon-Washington Baptists to the SBC:

We have been able to preserve for Southern Baptists a good part of their constituency that has moved into the Northwest. Beginning with the great movement of population northward during the World War II from the southern states, great numbers of Southern Baptists have come from every state in the Southern Baptist Convention. Many of them found their places in churches of other affiliations and faiths. Others felt very content in forgetting about church all together. Still others found themselves dissatisfied with other churches and found no church attendance at all to be intolerable. These are the people who have made up the nucleus of many of our churches, especially in our early beginnings. These people represent the measure in which Oregon-Washington Baptists have been able to preserve for Southern Baptists a constituency that would otherwise have been a total loss to the cause.

These people made up the major part of our membership at the time that the Baptist General Convention of Oregon was recognized by the Southern Baptist Convention in 1949 at Oklahoma City. In reality, that recognition was primarily toward a people who had been Southern Baptists for many years.[69]

In other words, when these churches in the West would come together and form a critical mass to constitute their own state conventions, they wanted to partner with the national entity. Their argument was that these state conventions, while geographically located outside the South, were just as Southern Baptist as the states in Dixie. They should be part of the Southern

Baptist Convention because the Southern Baptist Convention was already a part of them. And as more people came, the more they grew. They were happy to add to their numbers and to spread their unique message among their new neighbors. But their first step in planting churches was to look for each other.

Glen Braswell, the pastor of the first Southern Baptist church in Montana, explained, "Montana is still in a pioneer stage in every way and I believe will grow rapidly in the next years. More Southern Baptists are moving to the section—and in addition, we are reaching those who have never been Southern Baptists. . . . There are some missions in addition to these churches. We have no way of knowing how many Southern Baptists there are living with these states. However, it is a growing number as more people move this way."[70] In a sense, Southern Baptists' first priority wasn't to tell the story to those who had never heard; it was to find the people who already knew their stories. They were outsiders in their neighborhoods looking to build churches where they could be the insiders.

R. E. Milam was instrumental in organizing the Oregon-Washington Baptist Convention. He also was a catalyst for expanding the Southern Baptist Mission into Canada. Milam was tireless in his efforts to call churches to send people from the South to support the mission. He didn't just see the cultural exportation of the Southern Baptist experience as a comfort to those who had relocated; he saw those very relocations as leverage for a greater conquest. Southern Baptists could win the entire nation for God. They were certainly preserving a way of life, but as natural migration spread across the nation it became about more than preserving. It was now about transforming the surrounding culture into a better one.

Publishing books with titles such as *Blueprint for Victory* and *Win America Now*, Milam outlined the need for a comprehensive strategy:

1. Never Were the Opportunities so Great
2. From all over North America hands are outstretched to the Home Mission Board.
   a. There are the pleading hands of our own laymen who have moved all over the continent and are begging for help that they may found New Testament churches.
   b. There are the hands of the lost millions on this vast continent which is now the hope of the whole world.

    c. There are the hands of thousands of our ministers who have "heard the wind moving in the mulberry trees" and feel strangely led to help win America.

    d. There are the hands of the people in 25,000 communities where there is need of a Baptist church.

3. The shackles of a century have been broken.

    a. The shackle of sectionalism which narrowed the "Bible belt" to the South is no more.

    b. The shackle of universal poverty has been lifted from a people who are learning stewardship. The automobile and the factory have moved Southern Baptists everywhere and with them will go the genius for building their New Testament church centered program, with all that that means[71]

In Milam's recounting of the origins of the Southern Baptist Convention, he explained away its proslavery beginnings in an almost dismissive tone, admitting that it was not preferable and it was a rather uncomfortable truth, but he stopped short of anything resembling a forthright acknowledgement of oppression and bondage. The hubris that the Southern Baptist Convention was somehow chosen by God made it difficult to express deep regret over the issue of slavery. If Southern Baptists were God's hope for America, then it was inconvenient to admit that they began in sin. This same difficulty to view and repudiate sin comes up as well when discussing other areas of United States history, including its founding.

For Southern Baptists trying to make sense of these events, the working of God in the Old Testament gave an analogy to lean on: "The Southern Baptist Convention was born in an hour of confusion," asserted Milam. "When Southern Baptist ministers sought to uphold slavery from the Scriptures! Here is something as strange as the brothers of Joseph selling him into slavery. Yes, as strange as God's liberator for Israel, Moses, beginning his career by murdering the Egyptian. Yet God turned these things for good. May it not be true that God will yet use the suffering of the Civil War to bless America?"[72] Milam wrapped Southern culture in the mission of God, downplaying the failures of Southern Baptists with the argument that God could turn them for good to bless America.

THE SOUTHERN BAPTIST DILEMMA
OF CULTURE AND MISSIONS

Reviewing other Southern Baptist leaders during this time reveals that Milam was only one amid many who mixed Southern culture and missions. For example, leaders of the Home Mission Board prioritized cultural preservation as well. J. B. Lawrence stated in his *History of the Home Mission Board*, "The importance of having a distinctive Southern Baptist type of church-centered evangelism was emphasized by the board."[73] In the Home Mission Board's pamphlet titled "Alaska: A Baptist Opportunity," Courts Redford explained: "There are many Baptists from the Southern Baptist Convention living in the larger cities and their numbers are greatly augmented by the military forces stationed in these centers. During World War II these Southern Baptists felt a definite need for Sunday schools and churches of their own, and, as a result, missions sprang up and some have become strong enough to be constituted into churches. The work thus was started by people in the territory who felt the need. Support from the outside came only after local forces had taken the initiative in establishing such mission centers."[74] Of course, the desire to engage in missionary work was hardly pretextual. But that focus came after Southern Baptists moved to new areas and desired "Sunday schools and churches of their own." The missionary impulse started with a longing for home.

Yet another executive secretary-treasurer of the Home Mission Board, Arthur Rutledge, explained westward migration as key in *Mission to America*:

> One may well ask, what caused a previously regional Baptist convention to become nation-wide? The answer must include the factors of national population growth and shift; the relatively smaller number of Baptists and Baptist churches in the western and northern states in proportion to population; the need for additional churches to minister to the growing cities; the denominational loyalty of many Southern Baptists causing them to desire a Southern Baptist church wherever they live; theological and ecclesiological differences in some cases; a strong emphasis on evangelism; and sufficient strength of numbers and finances to undertake such a task. The Southern Baptist Convention had never officially set geographical limits upon its field, though during the first forty years of its existence the Home Mission Board had to struggle for the right to serve even the southern states. The Board's service in California before the Civil War, with the encouragement and approval of the Southern Baptist Convention, illustrated this sense of geographical freedom.[75]

Despite the sense of geographical freedom, the Southern Baptist presence as a mission effort was not always received well. In some cases, the people in these locations knew the cultural differences and had concerns. Foy Valentine, executive director of the Christian Life Commission, discovered an editorial from the *Hawaii Herald* in 1947 responding to the arrival of summer missionaries from the Home Mission Board:

> We find it very interesting that the young missionaries who arrived in Hawaii with so much fanfare to bring the light of truth to the benighted come as representatives of a division of their sect which bears the word "Southern" as part of its title. This sect split about the time of the Civil War, with the southern branch breaking off because of the unwillingness of its members to face the evils of the caste system.
>
> We do not allege that these young visitors intend to introduce, or to try to introduce, into Hawaii the undemocratic prejudices which are unquestioned in their homeland. Nor do we charge that their sect takes a stand in favor of racial prejudice. But we do reserve the right to question the appropriateness of missionaries coming from a bi-racial, segregation-hamstrung, caste culture to bring the light of truth to us.
>
> If religion is, as we believe it to be, the organization of basic values around which man builds his life and toward which he orients his endeavors, we can't get very much excited about a religion which remains silent about, and thereby condones, injustice and the cruelties and undemocratic indignities of the caste system.
>
> Somehow, we could really see more point in sending missionaries from Hawaii to Arkansas and Texas, and Tennessee and Mississippi.[76]

Valentine underscored an important point in noting the link between missionary endeavors and white Southern cultural predilections. One indicator is in how they looked back on the history of their efforts. J. B. Lawrence was leading the Home Mission Board when he described the mission effort to African Americans, sharing his understanding of the relationship going back to antebellum days in the SBC:

> While all the home missionaries were instructed to devote a portion of their time and services to the spiritual welfare of the Negro people within their fields of labor, two were appointed to give their full time to this work. Efforts were made to get the churches to make provision in their houses of worship to seat the slaves so that they could hear the sermons. This was done in many churches, with the result that the slaves had the advantage of the ministry

> of the churches as they attended services with their masters. Reports to the
> Convention in 1850 and 1851 indicate the success of the work.
>
> Many pastors were accustomed to preaching special sermons to the Negroes
> regularly and to providing for their spiritual needs. These efforts were crowned
> with such rich blessings that when the slaves were set free, not less than 150,000
> belonged to the Baptist churches of the South.
>
> The estrangement of reconstruction days hindered for a while the flow of
> sympathies between the two races and retarded somewhat the organized mis-
> sion work for Negroes. But Southern Baptists have never ceased to have a pro-
> found interest in the spiritual welfare of the Negroes.[77]

While evangelistic zeal was obvious in his understanding of mission, the
cultural distinction was also obvious in his understanding of home. And as
the mission of Southern Baptists advanced, so did this sense of home, with
all of its baggage in hand.

MISSIOLOGICAL CONCLUSIONS

While missiologists have long recognized the ways culture shapes and influences missions, the Southern Baptist Home Mission Board strategy for
domestic missions proved far more aggressive and intentional in their cultural replication.[78] For much of the twentieth century, Southern Baptists
intertwined Southern culture with their theology, effectively exporting
Southern culture to other parts of North America. Initially focused upon
"expatriated Southerners," this cultural diaspora formed an ideal core by
which Southern Baptists could protect and disseminate their culture in foreign contexts.

In many cases, the methodology and practices of these church plants outside of the South maintained the Southern culture to not only continue to
appeal to displaced Southerners in the area, but also because of the believed
superiority of the Southern way of "doing church." David Jepsen observes
that "evangelical ministers, especially Southern Baptists, struggled to convert
native north-westerners, but when Sundays rolled around they sought the
familiarity of fellow Oklahomans, Texans, or anyone 'who talked their language.' Living under a sea of change in a postwar economy in a new region,
both the ministers and their fellow southerners were drawn to each other."[79]

Southern Baptist missions was never articulated as a return to the
Confederacy or a spread of the Confederacy. It played out in much more

subtle ways, and while it certainly involved proclamation of the Christian faith in the Southern Baptist understanding, it also included the perception that the methodology, the practices, and the ways of interacting in the South were better and worth exporting to the North and to the West. The manifest destiny of Southern Baptists brought with it a gospel that should always transcend culture, but that unfortunately is sometimes packaged in a culture.

Throughout the records of the Southern Baptist Convention and in the minutes of the Home Mission Board there is probably no record of a church being planted specifically to carry on the struggle of "the War of Northern Aggression." Even as Southern pastors extolled the virtue of Southern culture both in and out of the South, it is unlikely that historians will uncover instances of these pastors using their pulpits to implore the South back to arms. Rather, every indication suggests that Southern Baptist leaders and pastors were committed to the conversion of the individual to faith in the gospel of Jesus.

Yet even as the prospect of the South as a nation died, the idea of the South as a distinct people and way of life continued to linger. It permeated every aspect of Southern culture and, over time, found purchase in Southern Baptist theology and mission. Even as historians and pastors reflect on the success of Southern Baptists in evangelizing and institution building throughout the twentieth century, we must wrestle with how this growth in many ways served to reinforce the Lost Cause within the broader American cultural and religious consciousness.

NOTES

1. See generally, Darren Dochuk, *From Bible Belt To Sunbelt: Plain-Folk Religion, Grassroots Politics, and the Rise of Evangelical Conservativism* (New York: W. W. Norton, 2010) and Alan Scot Willis, *All According to God's Plan: Southern Baptist Missions and Race, 1945–1970* (Lexington: Univ. Press of Kentucky, 2005). Dochuck's volume especially demonstrates how cultural and racial ideas forged in white Southern history remade political culture in California. I consider myself a participant observer in this scholarly endeavor, as I was introduced to the Southern Baptist faith in a church in New York and have been vocal in speaking and writing about the negative impacts of white Southern culture on missiology at home and abroad.

2. I would like to thank Andrew MacDonald, Amy Whitefield, and Jason Sampler for their research on this project as well as their notes on early drafts. Their help proved invaluable and made this chapter far stronger than it would have been otherwise. In

addition, several researchers assisted with or consulted on this writing, including Greg Moore, Justin Clark, Mark Clifton, and Keith Harper.

3. H. Leon McBeth, *The Baptist Heritage: Four Centuries of Baptist Witness* (Nashville: B&H Academic, 1987), 429.

4. Jefferson Davis, *Constitutionalist: His Letters, Papers, and Speeches* 5, ed. Dunbar Rowland (Jackson: Mississippi Department of Archives and History, 1923), 72.

5. Alexander H. Stephens, Augusta *Daily Constitutionalist*, March 30, 1861.

6. Stephens, *Daily Constitutionalist*, March 30, 1861.

7. Charles Reagan Wilson, *Baptized in Blood: The Religion of the Lost Cause, 1865–1920* (Athens: Univ. of Georgia Press, 1980), 1.

8. By myth, I do not mean an untruth, but a metanarrative, a worldview around which a society understands its story and place in history.

9. Gary W. Gallagher and Alan T. Nolan, eds., *The Myth of the Lost Cause and Civil War History* (Bloomington: Indiana Univ. Press, 2000), 1.

10. Andrew Doyle, "College Football and Southern Progressivism," in *The Sporting World of the Modern South*, ed. Patrick Miller (Urbana: Univ. of Illinois Press, 2002), 110.

11. Wilson, *Baptized in Blood*, 1. Christopher Moore has demonstrated how Southern Baptists such as J. William Jones led the way in this regard, adapting Confederate heroes to fit the ideals of Southern piety. In doing so, Jones interwove cultural and religious themes in order to spur revivals that solidified the prominence of Southern culture within a broad Southern Baptist identity. Christopher Moore Christopher Moore, "Apostle of the Confederacy: J. William Jones and the Question of Ecumenism and Denominational Identity in the Development of Lost Cause Mythology," (PhD diss., Baylor Univ., 2016).

12. Wilson, *Baptized in Blood*, 7–8.

13. Rufus Spain, *At Ease in Zion: Social History of Southern Baptists 1865–1900*, 2nd ed. (Tuscaloosa: Univ. of Alabama Press, 2016), 32.

14. William Johnson, "Address Explaining Why the Southern Baptist Convention was Organized," in *Readings in Baptist History: Four Generations of Selected Documents*, ed. Joseph Early (Nashville: B&H Publishing Group, 2008), 113.

15. Johnson, "Address," 112.

16. Robert A. Baker, *Southern Baptist Convention and Its People*, (Nashville: Broadman, 1974), 170.

17. Spain, *At Ease in Zion*, 7.

18. *Home Missions Monthly*, New York, VI, 225f. Cited in Robert A. Baker, *Relations Between Northern and Southern Baptists* (n.p., 1948), 99.

19. Robert G. Torbet, *A History of the Baptists*, 3rd ed. (Valley Forge, PA: Judson Press, 1963), 362.

20. Spain, *At Ease in Zion*, 10.

21. SBC Annual, 1861, 57.

22. Daniel Richard Carnett, "A History of Southern Baptists in New Mexico, 1938–1995" (PhD diss., Univ. of New Mexico, 2000), 57–58, 70–71.

23. Bill J. Leonard, "Southern Baptists and Southern Culture," *American Baptist Quarterly* 4, no. 2 (June 1, 1985): 203.

24. Leonard, "Southern Baptists and Southern Culture," 209.

25. Sociologist T. Edwin Bowling frames the issue differently, arguing that southerners who moved to the North were "socially marginal and alienated from the more established religious orders of their new communities. Therefore, they would likely seek a religious group that would serve as a cushion against 'culture shock' by providing a meaningful tie with their rural past." "Southern Baptists in the North," *The Review of Religious Research* 8, no. 2 (Winter 1967): 96.

26. Hankins, Barry. *Uneasy in Babylon: Southern Baptist Conservatives and American Culture* (Tuscaloosa: Univ. of Alabama Press, 2002), 1.

27. In a dissertation on the evolution and cohesion of Southern Baptists in the generations following the Civil War, Wayne Bodiford counters that scholars have been overzealous in depicting the prominence of the Lost Cause in Southern Baptist consciousness. Bodiford argues, "To portray the denomination as an attempt to sanctify the 'lost cause,' however, provides at best an incomplete understanding of Southern Baptists." The Lost Cause only provides a "veneer of unity for Southern Baptists," belying their significant cultural and theological diversity. However, even Bodiford acknowledges that it was the rise of the Home Mission Board under the direction of Tichenor that became the centralizing identity within the SBC at the turn of the century. Bodiford notes that the combination of western expansion, funding for Southern revival campaigns and church buildings, and the noticeable decline of Northern Baptist mission societies empowered the Home Mission Board to set the theological and cultural pace within the SBC. Carl Wayne Bodiford, "The Process of Denominational Cohesion within the Southern Baptist Convention, 1845–1927" (PhD diss., Texas Christian Univ., 1998).

28. Robert A. Baker, *A Baptist Sourcebook, with Particular Reference to Southern Baptists* (Nashville: Broadman Press, 1966), 126, citing "Minutes of the American Baptist Home Mission Society" (1864), 15.

29. Jesse C. Fletcher, *The Southern Baptist Convention: A Sesquicentennial History* (Nashville: Broadman and Holman Publishers, 1994), 71.

30. Eric Foner, *A Short History of Reconstruction, 1863–1877* (New York: Harper and Row Publishers, 1988), 43.

31. SBC Annual, 1882, 29.

32. Tichenor is a complex figure in Southern Baptist history, almost single-handedly responsible for the revival of the Home Mission Board at the end of the nineteenth century. In his study of Tichenor, Michael Williams paints him as a prophet of the "New South" with all of its tensions and apparent contradictions. Unlike previous generations, Tichenor embraced urbanization and industrialization, depicting them as necessary to fuel the revival and expansion of the Home Mission Board. At the same time, this expansion was accomplished under the broader mission of claiming and subsequently defending missionary territory as distinctly Southern Baptist. As Williams notes, Tichenor consciously sought to "link his New South vision for Southern Baptists with old South culture." In this sense, Tichenor proved a pivotal figure in the transition of the Southern Baptists from the mythology of the Lost Cause during Reconstruction to its twentieth century manifestation, untethered to the specifics of the Civil War and instead emphasizing the cultural and spiritual distinctiveness (if not superiority) of the American South. Michael Edward Williams

Sr., "Isaac Taylor Tichenor: The contributions of a nineteenth-century denominationalist to the preservation and extension of the Southern Baptist Convention" (PhD diss., Southwestern Baptist Theological Seminary, 1993).

33. McBeth, "Expansion of the Southern Baptist Convention to 1951," 33.

34. Keith Harper, "The Fortress Monroe Conference and the Shaping of Baptist Life in America at the End of the Nineteenth Century," 21. Paper delivered at the International Conference on Baptist Studies, 2012, Southeastern Baptist Theological Seminary, Wake Forest, NC.

35. "Fortress Monroe resolutions, 1894," 2. *American Baptist Historical Society Digital Collections*, accessed April 13, 2018, http://abhsarchives.org/digital/items/show/20.

36. H. Leon McBeth, *The Baptist Heritage* (Nashville: Broadman Press, 1987), 431.

37. Cf. Fletcher, *The Southern Baptist Convention*, 101; Torbet, *A History of the Baptists*, 373.

38. For a brief overview of Landmarkism, see McBeth, *The Baptist Heritage*, 447–61; for an in-depth understanding, see James E. Tull, *A History of Southern Baptist Landmarkism in the Light of Historical Baptist Ecclesiology* (New York: Arno Press, 1980).

39. SBC Annual, 1912, 49.

40. SBC Annual, 1912, 54. Emphasis mine.

41. McBeth, *The Baptist Heritage*, 627.

42. SBC Annual, 1941, 68.

43. McBeth, *The Baptist Heritage*, 627. This information is not in the SBC annual for that year, though he may have procured the information from different sources.

44. "California, Southern Baptist General Convention Of," in *Encyclopedia of Southern Baptists*, vol. 1 Ab–Ken (Nashville: Broadman Press, 1958), 219–20.

45. SBC Annual, 1942, 50.

46. SBC Annual, 1944, 50–53.

47. For the sake of space, this essay has not investigated the issues surrounding SBC encroachment in Illinois, which caused feelings of resentment among Northern Baptists as they had similarly felt when California churches migrated to the Southern Convention. For a brief overview of Illinois Baptists, see McBeth, "Expansion of the Southern Baptist Convention to 1951," 35–36.

48. SBC Annual, 1944, 79. Emphasis mine.

49. SBC Annual.

50. SBC Annual, 1949, 49.

51. SBC Annual.

52. "A Petition to the Home Mission Board and Other Supporting Agencies of the Southern Baptist Convention by the Executive Committee of the Baptist General Convention of Oregon-Washington," Box 10, Folder 11, Home Mission Board Executive Office Files, Southern Baptist Historical Library and Archives, Nashville, Tennessee. In a motion made to the SBC Convention in 1953, Milam argues that through the Home Mission Board, Southern Baptists support work in Cuba and Panama and there is no reason to reject the needs of Canadian Baptists, especially where there is no language barrier (SBC Annual, 1954, 53).

53. The motion was made during the 1958 Convention (SBC Annual, 1958, 50) and pulled before it could be voted (down) during the 1959 Convention (SBC Annual, 1959,

59). Again in 1984, the question was posed to include Canada within the SBC structure, but it was rejected once more (SBC Annual, 1984, 54).

54. "'Southern Invasion' American Baptist Topic," *California Southern Baptist* 18, no. 23 (June 18, 1959): 4.

55. As an ironic aside, the first Baptist church in the South came out of a Baptist congregation from Kittery, Maine that was transplanted to Charleston, South Carolina.

56. "Competition, Invasion or Pioneering, Which?" *California Southern Baptist* 18, no. 24 (June 25, 1959): 2.

57. W. Edgar Gregory, "Southern Baptist Invasion?: Choice of San Francisco as Convention Site for 1951 Indicates Trend," *Christian Century* 67, no. 3 (January 18, 1950): 92.

58. Austin Lovin, "Correspondence: Great Need and Opportunity in Northwest," *Biblical Recorder* (October 18, 1952), 18.

59. David J. Jepsen, "'Old Fashion Revival': Religion, Migration, and a New Identity," *Oregon Historical Quarterly* 107, no. 3 (Fall 2006): 356.

60. Jepsen, "'Old Fashion Revival': Religion, Migration, and a New Identity," 372.

61. For more on the distinctions and similarities between Evangelicals and Southern Baptists, a crucial text in the historiography is James Leo Garrett, E. Glenn Hinson, and James E. Tull, *Are Southern Baptists "Evangelicals"?* (Macon: Mercer Univ. Press, 1983). For a more recent treatment of this question, see David S. Dockery, Ray Van Neste, Jerry N. Tidwell, and R. Albert Mohler, *Southern Baptists, Evangelicals, and the Future of Denominationalism* (Nashville: B & H Academic, 2011). In particular, see Nathan Finn's chapter, "Southern Baptists and Evangelicals: Passing on the Faith to the Next Generation," 231–59. For a contrarian position, see Barry Hankins, "Southern Baptists and Northern Evangelicals: Cultural Factors and the Nature of Religious Alliances," *Religion and American Culture: A Journal of Interpretation* 7, no. 2 (1997): 271–98 and the more recent Barry Hankins, *Uneasy in Babylon*, 14–40. Hankins argues that while sharing a similar theological identity to evangelicals, Southern Baptists were largely distinct until broader shifts in American culture made them necessary allies and blurred historical-cultural differences.

62. Jepsen, "'Old Fashioned Revival': Religion, Migration, and a New Identity," 372.

63. Jepsen, 373.

64. R. E. Milam, *Win America Now: God's Call to Southern Baptists* (Shawnee, OK: The Bison Press, 1954), 36.

65. SBC Annual, 1894, 27.

66. *The Home Mission Task*, 134.

67. *The Home Mission Task*, 136.

68. *Baptist Press*, October 25, 1954.

69. C.E. Boyle, "Contribution of Oregon-Washington Baptists to Southern Baptists," *Pacific Coast Baptist* (May 1956), 2.

70. Glen Braswell, "Future Bright for Northwest Baptists," *Pacific Coast Baptist* (August 1956), 2.

71. R. E. Milam, *Blueprint for Victory* (Shawnee, OK: The Bison Press, 1956), 88.

72. Milam, *Win America Now*, 17.

73. J. B. Lawrence, *History of the Home Mission Board* (Nashville: Broadman Press, 1958), 142–43.

74. Courts Redford, "Alaska: a Baptist Opportunity" (Atlanta: Home Mission Board, n.d.), 6.

75. Arthur Rutledge, *Mission to America* (Nashville: Broadman Press: 1969), 123–24.

76. Foy Valentine, *A Historical Study of Southern Baptists and Race Relations 1917–1947* (New York: Arno Press, 1980), 3–4.

77. Lawrence, *History of the Home Mission Board*, 40–41.

78. The late missiologist David Hesselgrave advanced this thesis that culture is a central, if often obscured, horizon in missions. See David Hesselgrave, "The Three Horizons: Culture, Integration, and Communication," *JETS* 28, no. 4 (December 1985): 443–54.

79. Jepsen, "'Old Fashioned Revival': Religion, Migration, and a New Identity," 372.

Redeemer Nation and Lost Cause Religion: Making America Great Again (For the First Time)

BILL J. LEONARD

"An intelligent foreigner, making his observations at Washington at this time, would be puzzled to determine whether the Americans had a Government, or not. There are the names: The Executive, the Congress, the Judiciary; but what is the executive question, what the congressional question, what the judicial question, it appears impossible to decide. It is a remarkable fact that at Washington today, there is not a single well-de-fined department of political power!"[1]

Southerner Edward Pollard wrote those words in 1867 in a volume in which he coined the term Lost Cause, initiating a re-mythologizing of the post-Appomattox Confederacy. Efforts to "make America great again" are not unique to the era of Donald Trump, who centered his presidential campaign in that slogan. In almost every era of the country's history, some-one has lamented the departure of American "greatness" and fretted that national oblivion, if not divine retribution, was at hand. Still others, dissenters mostly, have warned that claims of greatness themselves betray a certain national hubris, even blindness, to promises made but not yet kept. Their alternative demand might well be, "Making America great again for the first time."

AMERICAN NATIONAL IDENTITY: THEN AND NOW

The rhetoric of American exceptionalism was there from the start, even linked to a covenant with the Divine, a specific concern of various Prot-estant immigrants. Arriving in 1630, a group of non-separating English Puritans disembarked from the *Arabella* in Boston Harbor having affirmed John Winthrop's shipboard composition, "A Modell of Christian Charity." Among other things it declared, "Wee shall finde that the God of Israel is among us, when tenn of us shall be a led to resist a thousand of our enemies, when hee shall make us a prayse and glory, that men shall say of succeeding plantacions: the lord make it like that of New England: for we must Consider that wee shall be as a Citty upon a Hill, the eies of all people are upon us."[1]

Barely thirty years later, however, Boston clergyman Michael Wigglesworth issued his mournful 1662 jeremiad denouncing the colony's spiritual and political shortcomings. Written in the form of an epic poem entitled "God's Controversy with New England," it began by affirming a divine plan for the discovery and settlement of this new land:

> This region was in darkness plac't
> Far off from heavens light,
> Amidst the shadows of grim death
> And of eternal night.
> For there the Sun of righteousness
> Had never made to shine
> The light of his sweet countenance,
> And grace which is divine:
> Until the time drew nigh wherein
> The glorious Lord of Hostes
> Was pleasd to lead his armies forth
> Into those forrein coastes.

The poem's conclusion, however, reflects Reverend Wigglesworth's warning that the grand, God-ordained vision was already corrupt, if not lost altogether.

> Beware, O sinful Land, beware;
> And do not think it strange
> That sorer judgements are at hand,
> Unless thou quickly change.
> Or God, or thou, must quickly change;
> Or else thou are undon[e]:
> Wrath cannot cease, if sin remain,
> Where judgement is begun.[2]

American history is filled with exceptionalism and lost causes, sources of national or regional identity repeatedly mythologized, demythologized, and remythologized. "A myth," Mark Shorer wrote, "is a large, controlling image that gives philosophical meaning to the facts of ordinary life; that is, which has organizing value for experience."[3] Myths assist a nation, a society, an institution, or an individual in giving meaning to the facts of common existence. They are collective guides for knowing who we are and where we fit (or where we don't) in whatever context in which we live. The details of the myth do not have to be factual for the myth to be "true"—that is, a story, idea, or method for defining identity.

But such mythic identity may not hold forever; there are always prophets and other dissenting weirdos who challenge them on the spot. The same myths that write people in can also write other people out. The Redeemer Nation myth linked American exceptionalism with divine election, but deciding what groups or ideas are "elected" remains elusive and controversial. The Lost Cause myth was useful for writing white Southerners back into a collective national identity after their defeat in the Civil War, but it was secured at the expense of African Americans, who were written out through the collective racism of Jim Crow legislation, the denial of voting rights, and separate but equal facilities. Collective identity, especially in a democracy, is difficult to develop and to sustain.

Why is such communal consciousness worth exploring at this moment in American politics and religion? Perhaps because in 2017, an Associated Press—NORC Center for Public Affairs poll suggested that seven out of ten Americans—regardless of political affiliation—agreed that the land of the free and the home of the brave was losing its sense of shared identity, even the most basic consensus on who we are as a people and what holds us together. Yet respondents also disagreed as to the nature of national identity. The report noted:

> About 65 percent of Democrats said a mix of global cultures was extremely or very important to American identity, compared with 35 percent of Republicans. Twenty-nine percent of Democrats saw Christianity as that important, compared with 57 percent of Republicans.
>
> Democrats are far more likely than Republicans to say that the ability of people to come to escape violence and persecution is very important, 74 percent to 55 percent. Also, 25 percent of Democrats said the culture of the country's early European immigrants [is] very important, versus 46 percent of Republicans.[4]

This sense of lost vision and identity is also present in the church as denominations and congregations experience decline, division, debate, and disengagement across the theological spectrum. Likewise, successive surveys reflect unrelenting increase of the "nones," or "nons," individuals who self-identify as having no significant engagement with traditional religious communities. Recent studies indicate that the number of religiously unaffiliated Americans increases annually—currently the largest single religious identification at 25 percent, in contrast with white evangelicals, at some 17 percent.[5] Thus one in five Americans claims no engagement with a religious community. That number increases to one in three for millennials, ages 18 to 30. Those demographic and religion-related developments create major identity issues for American churches and denominations. Baptismal, membership, financial, and institutional declines in the Southern Baptist Convention are a dramatic case in point.[6] Likewise, the rise in religion-related hate crimes, white supremacy rhetoric, KKK diatribes, and race-related changes in voting laws suggest that some of the worst Lost Cause-related ideologies are not lost at all in twenty-first-century America.

In many ways, rethinking the myth of America was at the heart of Donald Trump's election as forty-fifth president of the United States. Indeed, his campaign slogan, "Make America Great Again," captures two great themes of national identity: a belief in American exceptionalism, the unique place of the US in history and among other nations; and Trump's own Lost Cause "deconstruction," articulating, even reinterpreting, national identity as a candidate, and, as president, seeking to actualize that identity throughout the national bureaucracy.

Exploring the religious roots and contemporary implications of American exceptionalism and the Lost Cause reveals how national and regional identity work to reinforce one another. The actual term "American exceptionalism" appeared rather late in American history, coined in the 1950s by Communist organizer Jay Lovestone to explain "why working-class Americans found communism less appealing than did their European counterparts."[7] American exceptionalism, Godfrey Hodgson writes, "is the idea that the United States has a destiny and a duty to expand its power and the influence of its institutions and its beliefs until they dominate the world."[8] Ideas of such national exceptionalism were there from the beginning, often shaped by what Stephen Walt calls the sense that "the United States has a divinely ordained mission to lead the rest of the world."[9]

As Thomas Connelly and Barbara Bellows suggest, the phrase "Lost Cause" originated "as a byword for the perpetuation of the Confederate ideal." Edward Pollard's initial use of the term set in motion additional publications, speeches, and populist mindsets for "justifying the southern experience."[10] The Lost Cause ideology is multifaceted, born initially as a way in which Southern writers, preachers, and politicians sought to explain the Civil War defeat and memorialize the honored dead. It later served as a way of explaining the nature of Southernness, particularly on matters of race and religion, sexuality, and Americanism.

The language of divine entitlement cast America as Holy Experiment, City on a Hill, God's New Israel, Righteous Empire, and Redeemer Nation.[11] In the 2016 presidential election, certain Trump supporters, many no doubt among the 81 percent of evangelical voters who cast ballots for him, understood the Trumpian phrase "make America great again" as a reaffirmation, even restoration, of the nation's faith foundation in Christian orthodoxy and morality, concerns not unrelated to Redeemer Nation identity. Indeed, Franklin Graham, a son of evangelist Billy Graham, touted Trump's election as evidence of a "Divine hand" in American political affairs. In an election day sermon entitled "When God Chooses a Leader," Robert Jeffress, pastor of First Baptist Church, Dallas, compared Trump to Nehemiah, who built a wall to protect Jerusalem.[12] The language of the American Zion continues.

REDEEMER NATION AND AMERICAN EXCEPTIONALISM

This on-going sense of American chosenness, historian Earnest Lee Tuveson wrote, had "two kinds of expectations" for early North American settlers who touted them: America as "New Rome" or as "Promised Land of a chosen people." As New Rome, America would compete with historically superior cultures in matters of literature, art, and overall cultural ascendency. As chosen people, America was called to resist, even transcend, the corrupting influences of the Old World. Very quickly concerns developed regarding foreigners who might bring such corruption inside the New Land—religious groups that included Baptists, Quakers, Catholics, Jews, Mormons, Jehovah's Witnesses, and Muslims, as well as ethnic groups from Irish and Italians, to Germans and Japanese, to Vietnamese and Arabs. Many Protestants understood a Redeemer Nation as an important "next step" for the churches of the Reformation, forging at last a true Christian civilization and nationhood.[13]

This latter understanding of American identity was centered in a covenant between God and God's righteous people. It required that they keep the biblical, moral, and national covenant or face divine retribution. John Winthrop's treatise, "A Modell of Christian Charity," summed it up in this classic assertion: "If wee shall deale falsely with our god in this worke wee have undertaken and soe cause him to withdrawe his present help from us, wee shall shame the faces of many of gods worthy servants, and cause theire prayers to be turned into Cursses upon us."[14]

This spiritual mission appears throughout American Protestantism, echoed, for example, in Jonathan Edwards's eighteenth-century optimistic assertion that colonial religious awakenings, particularly in New England, would renew the church, usher in a postmillennial golden age, and prepare for Christ's return after one thousand years of peace. Edwards concluded, "And, if these things be so, it gives us more abundant reason to hope that what is now seen in America, and especially in New England, may prove the dawn of that glorious day."[15]

Nineteenth-century preacher and educator, Lyman Beecher, the father of thirteen little Beechers, including Harriet Beecher Stowe, cited Edwards's vision in his 1835 treatise, "A Plea for the West," writing, "It was the opinion of [Jonathan] Edwards, that the millennium would commence in America. When I first encountered this opinion, I thought it chimerical, but all providential developments since, and all the existing signs of the times, lend corroboration to it." Thus Beecher declared, "There is not a place upon earth which, in fifty years, can by all possible reformation place itself in circumstances so favorable as our own for the free, unembarrassed applications of physical effort . . . and moral power to evangelize the world."[16]

By the late nineteenth and early twentieth century, Edwards's postmillennial views had been overshadowed by a premillennial idea that the state of the world could only worsen as a prelude to Christ's immediate return to establish his reign on earth for a thousand years. In his study of American Evangelicalism, Matthew Sutton cites twentieth-century Pentecostal Frederick Childe's belief that the US was the nation "with two wings of a great eagle," referenced in Revelation 12:14, and among those Protestants who "believed that the United States' support of a Jewish homeland in Palestine was evidence of Americans' prophetic role in the last days." Childe wrote, "Perhaps it is more than a coincidence that U.S.A. is in the middle of Jerusalem! (Jer-USA-lem)."[17]

During World War II, evangelical leaders often reasserted the nation's divine mission. Harold Ockenga, pastor of Park Street Church in Boston, declared in a 1943 sermon, "The United States of America has been assigned a destiny comparable to that of ancient Israel which was favored, preserved, endowed, guided and used of God." Ockenga contended that the nation had two destinies: "One is the road of the rescue of western civilization by a re-emphasis on and revival of evangelical Christianity. The other is a return to the Dark Ages of heathendom."[18]

Anyone who reads the newspaper or various forms of social media recognizes that debates over the religious nature of the American Republic know no end. Is America a Christian nation? A Judeo-Christian nation? A nation grounded in three great Abrahamic faiths? A formerly Christian nation, rapidly "going secular?" Or a materialistic Banana Republic that uses religion as expedient political sound and fury signifying nothing?

CHALLENGING THE REDEEMER NATION MYTH: AMERICAN DISSENT

Also from the beginning there were the dissenters, challenging the Redeemer Nation metaphor and presumed action. First, voices of dissent against the idea of America as an elect nation were there from the beginning, most notably in the quintessential dissenter Roger Williams. Williams was clear: there are no Christian nations, only Christian people, united to Christ not by citizenship, but by faith. Historian Edmund Morgan wrote that for Williams, "the sword of state could make a whole nation of hypocrites, but only God could make Christians, and God's grace simply did not operate on a national scale."[19] Williams himself wrote in 1652, "I ask, where was the truth the true Authority and power of Christ Jesus, Whether in the stately assembly of Kings, Nobles, and Bishops, or in the two-edged Sword of the Word and Spirit of God, in the mouth of that one single, and yet most faithful witness of Christ Jesus?"[20]

Second, Williams's own critique of national chosenness was predicated on the idea that whenever a nation claims to be elected, it excludes some citizens, either because they are not Christian or because they are the wrong kind of Christians. Even the briefest list illustrates the pluralism of American faith traditions and the tendency of Americans to grudgingly grant much-touted religious liberty to faith-based newcomers, sectarians or outsiders.

- Colonial Baptists exiled from Massachusetts; jailed as nonconformists; churches sometimes boarded up, 1640s.
- Colonial Quakers exiled to the Caribbean; Mary Dyer, Quaker preacher, executed in Boston for preaching Quaker views, 1660.
- Shaker Founder Mother Ann Lee, preaching celibacy and communal living in Massachusetts, attacked by mobs, severely weakened, died in 1784.
- Joseph Smith, Mormon founder, mayor of Nauvoo, Illinois, shot by an anti-Mormon mob while jailed in Carthage, Illinois, June 27, 1844.
- Bloody Monday, August 6, 1855, Louisville, Kentucky, Anti-Catholic mobs attack German and Italian immigrants to keep them from voting, Catholic churches ransacked; twenty-two killed.
- *Minersville School District v. Gobitis,* 1940, Supreme Court ruled that public schools could compel Jehovah's Witness-oriented students to say the pledge of allegiance to the US flag. Numerous children expelled from schools throughout the country.
- KKK bombing of the Sixteenth Street Baptist Church, Birmingham, Alabama, September 15, 1963, resulted in the deaths of four elementary school age girls in a Sunday School class.
- Sikh Temple, Oak Creek, Wisconsin, six people killed by white supremacist, August 5, 2012.
- June 17, 2015, Emanuel African Methodist Episcopal Church, Charleston, SC, nine people shot to death by a white supremacist.
- August 11–12, 2017, Charlottesville, Virginia, white nationalists and Neo-Nazi protesters march around a church chanting "Jews will not replace us." A self-professed white supremacist drives a car into a crowd of counter-protestors, killing a young woman.

Thus the racial, ethnic, and immigrant issues of a Redeemer Nation contained elements of the myth of the Lost Cause, when one region of the country sought to make its case in a literally divided nation, in part by excluding some people and inconvenient facts from consideration.

THE LOST CAUSE: A THEOLOGY FOR RACISM

In her study of Ladies' Memorial Associations in the postwar South, Carolyn Janney suggests that the Lost Cause became a way in which the defeated Southerners shaped a collective memory that cast "the war and its outcome in the best possible terms," "often factually and chronologically distorting the way in which the past would be remembered." These "alternative facts" minimized or overlooked the role of slavery in the culture and as a reason for the war, instead asserting that Northern Reconstruction efforts were signs of "'Yankee aggression,' and black 'betrayal.'"[21] In words that sound strangely parallel to issues and ideologies in twenty-first-century culture, Janney writes, "The Lost Cause provided a sense of relief to white southerners who feared being dishonored by defeat, and its rituals and rhetoric celebrated the memory of personal sacrifice in a region rapidly experiencing change and disorder."[22]

Thomas Connelly and Barbara Bellows note that the Lost Cause "embodied the mental processes of an entire generation of southerners in the late nineteenth century. Many such southerners were involved in Confederate military and political circles. So they attempted, during the years of defeat, to justify secession and military catastrophe."[23]

In an essay entitled "The Anatomy of the Myth," Alan T. Nolan insists that "the Lost Cause was expressly a rationalization, a cover-up." Nolan summarizes the elements that shaped Lost Cause ideology beyond simply memorializing the dead or responding to veterans. First, he suggests, the Lost Cause created a sense of advocacy to perpetuate the Southern cause over against and beyond defeat. It preserved the South's "defensive posture" over slavery and later Jim Crow segregationist laws.[24] Second, Nolan insists that the Lost Cause promoters minimized slavery as a cause of the war and a major source of Southern cultural ethos. Thus the primary issue of the war was not the defense of chattel slavery, but to defend the autonomy of states' rights, a "sectionalism" that included even the power of secession.

Third, Lost Cause creators declared that the South wasn't actually defeated but rather betrayed by Yankee "trickery and unfairness"—blockading harbors and overwhelming brave rebel troops with far superior arms. Thus, Nolan comments, "if the Confederacy could not have won, it somehow did not lose."[25] In the early days of Lost Cause mythologizing, groups such as the Southern Historical Society, the Lee Memorial Association, and the United Daughters of the Confederacy promoted memorials to the fallen, and to the leaders of the CSA, particularly military officers.

Fourth, religion, specifically Protestant Christianity, was a major force in shaping the theology and mythology of the Southern Lost Cause. As Connelly and Bellows write, "The rising tide of evangelical faith, witnessed

in the phenomenal growth of the Southern Baptist Church and other funda-
mentalist churches, gave solace and structure to the defeated Confederate
generation." Likewise, school textbooks were carefully monitored by
"watchdog committees of veterans' organizations" determined that the
young would be offered the "true story" of the Civil War and its origins.[26]
Well into the twentieth century, veterans' periodicals touted Southern gentility and ethical rigor as compared to "Yankee amorality, boorishness, and
even cowardice."[27]

In his assessment of the Lost Cause, historian Gaines Foster wrote that
"few southerners expressed any guilt over the owning or the mistreatment
of slaves, even though they had been raised in a society that encouraged
the public confession of sin." Not only did Southerners refuse to repent
of participation in slave culture, "many reaffirmed their belief in its justness. In an 1865 sermon, Mississippi Presbyterian minister James Lyon acknowledged that southerners might "'lament before God' their neglect
of duty toward our servants," but there was no need to "bow the head in
humiliation before men" for their use of slaves since biblical heroes the
likes of "Abraham, Isaac, and Jacob" did as well.[28] Indeed, Edward Pollard
understood the Emancipation Proclamation as an economic travesty, writing that the South was "a spectacle of ruin" with "the fruits of the toil of
generations all swept into a chaos of destruction; their slave property taken
away by a stroke of the pen; a pecuniary loss of two thousand millions of
dollars involved in one single measure of spoliation—a penalty embraced
in one edict."[29]

As the Lost Cause mythology gained momentum in the late nineteenth
and early twentieth century, Southern ministers got into the act. In his
monumental study, *Baptized in Blood, the Religion of the Lost Cause,* Charles
Reagan Wilson writes that "as guardians of the region's spiritual and moral
heritage," Southern ministers "used the Lost Cause to buttress this heritage." He contends that "Christian clergymen were the prime celebrants of
the religion of the Lost Cause." Thus Wilson concluded that these ministers
"used the Lost Cause to warn Southerners of their decline from past virtue,
to promote moral reform, to encourage conversion to Christianity, and to
educate the young in Southern traditions; [and] in the fullness of time,
they related it to American values."[30]

While Lost Cause mythologists attempted to rewrite the South back into
national identity, they also portrayed the South as the prime preserver of

the original myth of America as Redeemer Nation. For these Protestants, the Lost Cause meant that the people who lost the war retained the vision. The defeated people, even in defeat, would be more moral, more "Christian," and more "American" than their Northern counterparts had been or ever could be.[31]

The earliest Lost Cause concerns sought to help a defeated people come to terms with the reality of a defeat few thought possible. This effort was in many ways inseparable from the fact that the idea of Redeemer Nation was transferred from the nation as a whole to the South itself. By the war's end, "The Civil War became a jihad, a holy war, against the decay of northern industrialization, the mongrel races from Europe that swelled Yankee ranks, Jacobin theories of excessive democracy and racial disorder."[32]

Yet underneath the rhetoric of moralism, sectionalism, and theological orthodoxy was the abiding scourge of racism. Lost Cause myths facilitated the formation of the Ku Klux Klan, a group whose racism was romanticized in books like *The Clansman*, written in 1905 by Baptist preacher and Wake Forest University graduate Thomas Dixon. In his introduction to the novel, Dixon set forth the plight of the Reconstructionist-devastated South and the deliverance offered by the Ku Klux Klan in two idealized paragraphs:

> In the darkest hour of the life of the South, when her wounded people lay helpless amid rags and ashes under the beak and talon of the Vulture, suddenly from the mists of the mountains appeared a white cloud the size of a man's hand. It grew until its mantle of mystery enfolded the stricken earth and sky. An "Invisible Empire" had risen from the field of Death and challenged the Visible to mortal combat. How the young South, led by the reincarnated souls of the Clansmen of Old Scotland, went forth under this cover and against overwhelming odds, daring exile, imprisonment, and a felon's death, and saved the life of a people, forms one of the most dramatic chapters in the history of the Aryan race.[33]

In an earlier novel entitled *The Leopard's Spots* (1902), Dixon allowed the Reverend John Durham, his Baptist preacher character, to make the case for sectionalism as the primary explanation for Southern secession, minimizing slavery as a cause for the Civil War. Speaking to a "Deacon" from a Northern Baptist church, Reverend Durham declares:

> The South did not fight to hold slaves. Our Confederate Government at Richmond offered to guarantee to Europe the freedom of every slave for

the recognition of our independence. Slavery was bound of its own weight to fall. . . . But for the frenzy of your Abolition fanatics, who first sought to destroy the Union by Secession and then forced Secession on the South, we would have freed the slaves before this without war, from the very necessities of the progress of the material world, to say nothing of its moral progress. We fought for the rights we held under the old constitution, made by a slave-holding aristocracy. But we collided with the resistless movement of humanity from the idea of local sovereignty toward nationalism, centralization, solidarity.[34]

In many ways, Dixon's novels mark a second stage of Lost Cause mythology, glorifying the Klan as an agent of Southern deliverance and the war as a states' rights issue, not a battle over slavery.

Likewise, the Lost Cause became a vehicle for reasserting white supremacy as the divinely ordained division between the superior Aryan race and the lesser, darker races around the world and in the United States. Again, Dixon's novels link the Lost Cause irrevocably with white supremacy. In *The Leopard's Spots*, a central character, Baptist politician Charles Gaston, is crystal clear in his analysis of the South's postwar challenge: "My boy, the future American must be an Anglo-Saxon or a Mulatto. We are now deciding which it shall be. The future of the world depends on the future of this Republic. This Republic can have no future if racial lines are broken and its proud citizenship sinks to the level of a mongrel breed of Mulattoes. The South must fight this battle to a finish. Two thousand years look down upon the struggle, and two thousand years of the future bend low to catch the message of life or death."[35] Dixon as the novel's narrator extends the racial mongrelization threat with equal clarity: "With the Anglo-Saxon race guarding the door of marriage with fire and sword, the effort was being made to build a nation inside a nation of two antagonistic races. No such thing had ever been done in the history of the human race, even under the development of the monarchial and aristocratic forms of society."[36] For Reverend Dixon and other Lost Cause advocates, Reconstructionist attempts to bring the races together politically, regionally, and biologically would ultimately destroy the Republic. The result of their futile attempts was "the complete alienation of the white and black and white races as compared with the old familiar trust of [slavery-based] domestic life."[37] Dixon's novels redefine the nature of the Civil War from slavery to sectionalism as the primary cause. They glorify the work of the Ku Klux Klan as the protectors of the South in general and Southern womanhood in particular. They "stand for one thing at least, the supremacy of Anglo-Saxon civilization."[38]

Other Baptists picked up such supremacist and sectionalist elements perpetuating and in some ways institutionalizing the Lost Cause in various Southern religious institutions. Mercer University professor Robert Nash documents that ecclesiastical collusion with the case of James Franklin Love, corresponding secretary of the Foreign Mission Board of the Southern Baptist Convention from 1915 to 1928. Nash notes that Love "was profoundly influenced by the concept of Anglo-Saxon supremacy, the belief that white races possessed a superior intellect, religion, and civilization." He shows that during Love's tenure at the Baptist mission board, "the basic premises of Anglo-Saxon supremacy were adopted with considerable intentionality as mission strategy. In an effort to encourage Baptist expansion into Europe, Love argued that world evangelization, could be accomplished more quickly if the aggressive white races were evangelized first."[39] In laying out his strategy for that kind of white-dominated evangelism, he wrote, "Let us not forget that to the white man God gave the instinct and talent to disseminate His ideals among other people and that he did not, to the same degree, give this instinct and talent to the yellow, brown or black race. The white race only has the genius to introduce Christianity into all lands and among all people."[40]

Love went so far as to link white supremacy with divine chosenness, insisting that the Spirit's call to St. Paul redirected him from Asia to evangelization in Europe, noting that before that time "the Jews were the chosen race; since then the Anglo-Saxon race has been God's favored people." Love concluded, "There is not a colored race in the world which could evangelize the white race. . . . All of Africa could not evangelize one county of American white people."[41] Thus, for a time in the twentieth century, Southern Baptist mission strategy was formulated by a leader who had drunk deeply at the wells of the Lost Cause, undergirding white supremacy with a form of racial election that he believed to be the will and work of the God of Abraham, Moses, and Jesus.

The sectionalism argument endured throughout much of the twentieth century, often in the work of Southern historians. In his 1954 book, *The History of the Southern Baptist Convention, 1845–1953*, W. W. Barnes, church history professor at Southwestern Baptist Theological Seminary in Fort Worth, Texas, referenced sectionalism as a significant rationale for regional and denominational secession, North and South. Barnes went to great lengths to cite early Baptist efforts to remain united in spite of the divisions over slavery. In a footnote, Barnes himself reflects the argument made by Thomas Dixon, writing, "The probability is that these [Maryland, Virginia, Kentucky] and other states would have freed the slaves had not abolitionists fomented slave rebellions, such as Nat Turner's rebellion in Virginia, 1831."[42] Describing the situation leading to the founding of the Southern Baptist Convention (1845) and the Civil War, Barnes insisted, "The principle and practice of slavery were not divisive issues when the national government was established on the basis of the federal Constitution. There was opposition to slavery in the South and in the North. It had not become a *sectional issue*."[43]

Barnes acknowledged that amid a myriad of national struggles in nineteenth-century America, the slavery issue "cut the deepest because it was at once a political, economic, social, moral and religious issue. But not until the opposition took the form of abolitionism in the 1830's did the issue begin to portend those divisions in the religious and political spheres." As Barnes saw it, the General Convention of the Baptist Denomination in the United States (Triennial Convention) had managed to stay together amid differences over slavery until abolitionists forced the Northerners to make slavery the deciding issue. Barnes was no advocate of slavery, but he seems to have accepted the Lost Cause argument that abolitionist radicalism galvanized North and South, creating the sectionalism dichotomy that divided the denomination and the nation.

CHALLENGING THE MYTHS:
MARTIN LUTHER KING, JR.

A new kind of radicalism challenged the regional and racial status quo, as well as the tropes of national exceptionalism and the Lost Cause, in the years following World War II. The civil rights movement of the 1960s represented a momentous challenge, not only to the Jim Crow legacy of Lost Cause mythology, but also as a call to extend the promise of America to persons long left out because of race, poverty, and injustice. That challenge to the nation is clearly represented in the 1963 March on Washington. In that year, a century after passage of the Emancipation Proclamation, another Baptist preacher, Martin Luther King, Jr., standing before the Lincoln

276 / Bill J. Leonard

Memorial, assessed the inadequacies of Redeemer Nation and Lost Cause mythologies, challenging the nation to make America great again for the first time. Before Dr. King reached the soaring rhetoric of "the dream," he laid out the nation's failures—failures fostered by elements of the Lost Cause. Said King:

> Five score years ago, a great American, in whose symbolic shadow we stand to-day, signed the Emancipation Proclamation. This momentous decree came as a great beacon light of hope to millions of Negro slaves who had been seared in the flames of withering injustice. It came as a joyous daybreak to end the long night of their captivity.
>
> But one hundred years later, the Negro still is not free. One hundred years later, the life of the Negro is still sadly crippled by the manacles of segregation and the chains of discrimination. One hundred years later, the Negro lives on a lonely island of poverty in the midst of a vast ocean of material prosperity. One hundred years later, the Negro is still languished in the corners of American society and finds himself an exile in his own land. And so we've come here today to dramatize a shameful condition.
>
> In a sense we've come to our nation's capital to cash a check. When the architects of our republic wrote the magnificent words of the Constitution and the Declaration of Independence, they were signing a promissory note to which every American was to fall heir. This note was a promise that all men, yes, black men as well as white men, would be guaranteed the "unalienable Rights" of "Life, Liberty and the pursuit of Happiness." It is obvious today that America has defaulted on this promissory note, insofar as her citizens of color are concerned. Instead of honoring this sacred obligation, America has given the Negro people a bad check, a check which has come back marked "insufficient funds."[44]

Those "insufficient funds" blocked the fulfillment of the grand American myth, as King notes in his lyrical conclusions: "I have a dream that one day this nation will rise up and live out the true meaning of its creed: 'We hold these truths to be self-evident, that all men are created equal.'"[45] Thus the promised covenant was broken from the start.

Likewise, the language and action of the Lost Cause thwarts the grand dream. King calls it out when he declares, "I have a dream that one day, down in Alabama, with its vicious racists, with its governor having his lips dripping with the words of "interposition" and "nullification"—one day right there in Alabama little black boys and black girls will be able to join hands with little white boys and white girls as sisters and brothers."[46] Sectionalism and states' rights were no excuse for segregation any more than for support of chattel slavery. King's dream for America captured elements of the Redeemer Nation, calling the nation to "live out the meaning of its creed" that all are created equal, a promise unfulfilled until every American was "free at last, free at last." At the same time, he rejected Lost Cause ideology and the racist, white supremacist ideology and actions that accompanied it.

CONCLUSIONS: NOW WHAT?

Dr. King's words prompt debate and discussion, and possibly action, as an increasingly diverse US population grapples with the promise of the American dream—material and moral manifestation of national exceptionalism—and with the continued power of the Lost Cause narrative, with its persistent racial overtones. Four things seem clear.

First, such engagement requires learning to read contemporary culture in the United States with a sense of history. It necessitates locating contemporary rhetoric of American exceptionalism, claims of being a Christian nation, or racism masquerading as voter reform within the historical context that birthed them. It mandates informed analysis and comprehension of the roots of white supremacy, internet racism, and ongoing anti-Semitism, and, perhaps most importantly, distinguishing "alternative facts" from "alternative interpretations."

Second, for church members and citizens in general, learning to distinguish between Christian conviction and cultural prejudice, especially when both are articulated in biblical rhetoric, has acquired increased imperative. Many elements of Redeemer Nation and Lost Cause mythology were rooted in distorted biblical hermeneutics, interpretative methods that gave proof texts for supporting Manifest Destiny, exploitation of Indians, chattel slavery, Jim Crow segregation, and white supremacy. Such malformed biblicism was evident in 2017 when Robert Jeffress, pastor of First Baptist Church in Dallas, touted Romans 13 as divine sanction for a US President to "take out" the South Korean leader using assassination and other dark arts as necessary.[47]

Third, churches and church members must cultivate anew gospel dissent, contesting the ways in which religious communities cut deals with the larger culture. Edwin Gaustad wrote, "This reform of religion in the name of religion, this growing edge, this refusal to let well enough alone, is the role of dissent." It "may also be a manifestation of the unfettered human spirit."[48] And sometimes essential dissent becomes irrevocably prophetic. Cathleen Kaveny writes that prophets provide a "kind of *moral chemotherapy* . . . a brutal but necessary response to aggressive forms of moral malignancy."[49] In the church and in the world the religiously faithful must stand ready to dissent at a moment's notice with a prophetic voice so transformative that when the times get so out of hand, in the spirit of Luke 19:40, "the stones will cry out."

Finally, Roger Williams and Ann Hutchinson, Frederick Douglass and Harriet Tubman, Dorothy Day and Martin Luther King, Jr., and oh yes, Jesus, offer instruction in re-mythologizing America, not as Redeemer Nation, but as Beloved Community. In segregated America of 1963, Dr. King reminded the nation that the existence of slavery meant that the mythic covenant of a Redeemer Nation was broken from the start, a promissory note of "insufficient funds." But King did not lose hope: "I have a dream," he said, "that one day this nation will rise up and live out the true meaning of its creed: 'We hold these truths to be self-evident, that all . . . are created equal.'"[50] More than a half century later, that creed remains unfulfilled for so many. Fulfilling that promise requires mirroring Dr. King's courage by confronting a renewed Lost Cause ideology spewed out in Charlottesville, Virginia, in white supremacy-KKK-Nazi bigotry made tangible in torch light parades, in "blood and soil" mantras, and in the murder of a thirty-two-year-old dissenter. If the hope of a Beloved Community means anything at all, then Heather Heyer must not have died in vain.[51]

Resisting that kind of perpetual racism requires commitment as "agents of justice, reconciliation, and compassion." That's the language of a Beloved Community: language and action that can never be a Lost Cause.

NOTES

1. Edward A. Pollard, *A New Southern History of the War of the Confederates* (New York: E. B. Treat & Co., 1867), 749.

2. John Winthrop, "A Modell of Christian Charity," in *God's New Israel: Religious Interpretations of American Destiny*, ed. Conrad Cherry (Englewood Cliffs, NJ: Prentice-Hall,

Inc., 1971), 43. 3. Michael Wigglesworth, "God's Controversy with New England," in *God's New Israel: Religious Interpretations of American Destiny*, ed. Conrad Cherry (1662), 44, 54.

4. Mark Shorer, "The Necessity for Myth," in *Myth and Mythmaking*, ed. Henry A. Murray (Boston: Beacon, 1960), 355.5. "Poll: Americans fret losing identity," *Winston-Salem Journal*, March 6, 2017, A8.

6. Betsy Cooper, Daniel Cox, Rachel Lienesch, Robert P. Jones, "Exodus: Why Americans are Leaving Religion—and Why They're Unlikely to Come Back," PRRI, September 22, 2016, http://www.prri.org/research/prri-rns-poll-nones-atheist-leaving-religion/. See also Daniel Cox and Robert P. Jones, "America's Changing Religious Identity," PRRI, September 6, 2017, www.prri.org/research/american-religiouus-landscape-christian-religiously -unaffiliated, 1/26.

7. While the number of SBC-related congregations increased, reported membership declined by more than two hundred thousand, down 1.32 percent to 15.3 million members. Average weekly worship attendance declined by 1.72 percent to 5.6 million worshippers. Southern Baptists also experienced a decline in baptisms, down 3.3 percent to 295,212. The number of churches affiliated with the Southern Baptist Convention grew by 294 to 46,793, a 0.63 percent increase over 2014. This is the seventeenth year in a row the number of SBC churches has grown. https://www.getreligion.org/getreligion/2016/6/8 /news-in-those-southern-baptist-statistics-baptisms-babies-and-crucial-ethnic-churches.

8. Peter Beinart, "How Trump Wants to Make America Exceptional Again," *The Atlantic*, Feb. 2, 2017.

9. Godfrey Hodgson, *The Myth of American Exceptionalism* (New Haven: Yale Univ. Press, 2009), 10.

10. Stephen M. Walt, "The Myth of American Exceptionalism," *Foreign Policy* no. 189 (November 2011): 74.

11. Thomas L. Connelly and Barbara L. Bellows, *God and General Longstreet: The Lost Cause and the Southern Mind* (Baton Rouge: Louisiana State Univ. Press, 1982), 2–3.

12. Martin E. Marty, *Righteous Empire* (New York: The Dial Press, 1970), 5–56; Ernest Lee Tuveson, *Redeemer Nation: The Idea of America's Millennial Role* (Chicago: Univ. of Chicago Press, 1968); Conrad Cherry, *God's New Israel: Religious Interpretations of American Destiny* (Englewood Cliffs, NJ: Prentice-Hall, 1971).

13. "Rev. Jeffress: Trump Like Jeremiah who God Called to build Wall Around Jerusalem," http://insider.foxnews.com/2017/01/20/robert-jeffress-trump-nehemiah-god-called-build -wall-jerusalem.

14. Ernest Lee Tuveson, *Redeemer Nation*, 24.

15. John Winthrop, "A Modell of Christian Charity," 1630, in *God's New Israel: Religious Interpretations of American Destiny*, ed. Conrad Cherry (Englewood Cliffs, NJ: Prentice-Hall, Inc., 1971), 43.

16. Jonathan Edwards, "Some Thoughts Concerning the Present Revival of Religion in New England," cited in *God's New Israel*, ed. Conrad Cherry, 59.

17. Lyman Beecher, "A Plea for the West," in *God's New Israel*, ed. Conrad Cherry, 120.

18. Matthew Avery Sutton, *American Apocalypse: A History of Modern Evangelicalism* (Cambridge: The Belknap Press of Harvard Univ. Press, 2014), 224.

19. Harold J. Ockenga, "Christ for America," May 1943, 11, 13–14, sermon manuscript, cited in Matthew Avery Sutton, *American Apocalypse: A History of Modern Evangelicalism* (Cambridge: The Belknap Press of Harvard Univ. Press, 2014), 283.

20. Edmund S. Morgan, *Roger Williams: The Church and the State* (New York: Harcourt, Brace & World, Inc., 1967), 101.

21. Roger Williams, *Collected Works* VII, 225–26, in Edmund S. Morgan, *Roger Williams*, 22. 101 Carolyn E. Janney, *Burying the 'Dead but Not the Past': Ladies' Memorial Associations and the Lost Cause* (Chapel Hill: The Univ. of North Carolina Press, 2008), 3.

23. Janney, *Burying the 'Dead but Not the Past,'* 3.

24. Thomas L. Connelly and Barbara L. Bellows, *God and General Longstreet: The Lost Cause and the Southern Mind* (Baton Rouge: Louisiana State Univ. Press, 1982), 3.

25. Alan T. Nolan, "The Anatomy of the Myth," in *The Myth of the Lost Cause and Civil War History*, ed. Gary W. Gallagher and Alan T. Nolan (Bloomington: Indiana Univ. Press, 2000), 14.

26. Nolan, "The Anatomy of the Myth," 17.

27. Connelly and Bellows, *God and General Longstreet*, 6.

28. Gaines M. Foster, *Ghosts of the Confederacy: Defeat, the Lost Cause, and the Emergence of the New South 1865 to 1913* (New York: Oxford Univ. Press, 1987), 23–24.

29. Pollard, *The Lost Cause*, 743.

30. Charles Reagan Wilson, *Baptized in Blood: The Religion of the Lost Cause* (Athens: Univ. of Georgia Press, 1980), 11.

31. Bill J. Leonard, *God's Last and Only Hope: The Fragmentation of the Southern Baptist Convention* (Grand Rapids: William Eerdmans Publishing, 1990).

32. Connelly and Bellows, *God and General Longstreet*, 11.

33. Thomas Dixon, *The Clansman: An Historical Romance of the Ku Klux Klan* (Lexington: The Univ. Press of Kentucky, 1970, 1905), 2. *The Clansman* was a source for the silent film *Birth of a Nation*, a cinematic attempt to romanticize the South and the Klan.

34. Thomas Dixon, Jr., *The Leopard's Spots* (New York: Doubleday, Page & Company, 1902), 335.

35. Dixon, *The Leopard's Spots*, 200. Italics are Dixon's.

36. Dixon, 203.

37. Dixon, 202.

38. Dixon, 312.

39. Robert N. Nash, Jr., "Peculiarly Chosen: Anglo-Saxon Supremacy and Baptist Missions in the South," in *Perspectives in Religious Studies* 38, no. 2 (Summer 2011): 164–65.

40. Nash, "Peculiarly Chosen," 165, citing James Franklin Love, *The Appeal of the Baptist Program for Europe* (Richmond, VA: Foreign Mission Board of the Southern Baptist Convention, 1920), 14–15.

41. Nash, "Peculiarly Chosen," citing Love, *The Mission of our Nation* (New York: Fleming H. Revell, Co., 1912), 18, 21, 64–65.

42. W.W. Barnes, *The Southern Baptist Convention, 1845–1953* (Nashville: Broadman Press, 1954), 20n.

43. Barnes, *The Southern Baptist Convention*, 18. Italics added. Barnes's work was the first full history of the Southern Baptist Convention.

44. Martin Luther King, Jr., "I Have a Dream," http://www.americanrhetoric.com/speeches/mlkihaveadream.htm.

45. King, "I Have a Dream."

46. King, "I Have a Dream."

47. "Pastor Robert Jeffress, 'God has Given Trump Authority to Take out Kim Jong-Un,'" August 8, 2017, www.firstdallas.org.

48. "Pastor Robert Jeffress," 4–5.

49. Cathleen Kaveny, *Prophecy Without Contempt: Religious Discourse in the Public Square* (Cambridge: Harvard Univ. Press, 2016), 312.

50. Kaveny, *Prophecy Without Contempt*, 312.

51. Heather Hyer was slain in Charlottesville when a self-described white supremacist drove his automobile into a crowd of counter-protesters, killing Hyer and injuring numerous others.

"Skewed Too Far": Social Studies Standards and the Lost Cause in Texas

EDWARD R. CROWTHER

State-level academic content standards rarely make national news, but in 2010 the work of the Texas Board of Education to craft new social studies standards garnered attention from *The New York Times* and *The Washington Post*. Perhaps more remarkably, the issue even reached *The Colbert Report*, with Dr. Don McLeroy, who chaired the Texas Board of Education, appearing more than once as a guest. The debate over the social studies curricular standards, which shape everything from teachers' lesson plans to content reflected in commercially produced textbooks, was part of a larger expression of the culture wars, largely pitting evangelical conservatives against teachers and academics, and followed earlier efforts in Texas to ensure that creation science appeared alongside evolution in the science curriculum. In the social studies arena, conservative culture warriors wanted to enshrine their cherished values and beliefs, including the religious nature of the US Revolution, and see that the "unintended consequences" of governmental programs, such as the New Deal, received prominent places in the curricular standards. While not central to these efforts, Lost Cause themes made their way into the standards.[1]

"We are adding balance" to the standards, said McLeroy. "History has already been skewed. Academia is skewed too far to the left." Despite objections, the State Board of Education approved the standards on a party-line vote, and four years later it approved some eighty-nine textbooks, supplements, and software packages for Texas schools written to the standards. A year later, a text in world geography written to these standards added fuel to the fracas. One caption referred to enslaved Africans as immigrant "workers," adding tinder to the fiery dispute over the standards and their implications. Academics joined in the debate over the standards as a framework and the curricular materials that were sure to ensue. Pulitzer Prize winning historian Eric Foner believed the Texas Social Studies Standards were flawed:

> The Texas Board of Education seeks to inculcate children with a history that celebrates the achievements of our past while ignoring its shortcomings and that largely ignores those who have struggled to make this a fairer, more equal society. I have lectured on a number of occasions to Texas precollege teachers and have found them as competent, dedicated and open-minded as the best teachers anywhere. But if they are required to adhere to the revised curriculum, the students of our second most populous state will emerge ill prepared for life in Texas, America and the world in the twenty-first century.[2]

He and other scholars noted many shortcomings with the standards including a focus on coverage models and memorization. Even at its best, the democratic process producing standards deteriorated into an effort to "accommodate everyone's wishes." And as Edward H. Sebesta noted, where slavery and the Civil War featured in the standards, a strong bias for "Lost Cause Ideology and Neo-Confederate History" revealed itself. While such perspectives were already present in the curricular standards adopted in 1998, changes in the 2010 standards made this viewpoint much more prominent. This Neo-Confederate viewpoint now appeared "mainstream" in the new social studies curriculum.[3]

While members of heritage groups such as the League of the South or the Sons of Confederate Veterans may have celebrated this result, they do not appear to have impacted the decisions by the Texas State Board of Education. The views of a majority of the Texas board came from the larger conservative political culture in Texas, and in Sebesta's determination, the Christian textbook industry for Christian academies and homeschooled students shaped these beliefs more than literature from Confederate heritage groups. Lost Cause ideology has grafted itself onto the larger conservative cultural movement, where its presence is simply accepted and forms just one element of those concerned citizens about United States identity. Those directly engaging the social studies curriculum in Texas seemed much more concerned with whether the United States was a Christian nation, whether it was white or multi-cultural, whether the curriculum focused on the ongoing struggles between American capitalism and the multitude of threatening isms within, and whether it truly demonstrated the exceptional status of the United States. The persistence of the Lost Cause in the standards debate reflects its peculiar place in the Lone Star State since the Civil War, but that ironic place perpetuates a fantasy rather than the rich and contingent history of Texas.[4]

As Laura Lyons McLemore has recently argued, there is a Lost Cause tradition in Texas, but it was and is much less central to white Texan identity than to whites in most of the other former states of the Confederacy. A republic before it was a state and one that warred for its sovereignty from Mexico just twenty-five years before it seceded from the United States, Texas's Southernness is less central to its identity than its Westernness and its value of rugged individualism. The Lost Cause in Texas matters both as commemoration of the Confederate experience but also, and more centrally, in its utility in supporting forward-looking Texas values. The core Lost Cause apologists—E. A. Pollard, Jubal A. Early, and J. William Jones—and the crusader for the Lost Cause in the public school curriculum, Mildred Lewis Rutherford, shape the apparition in the Texas social studies curriculum much less than Texas boosterism that uses the Lost Cause to "honor our past and draw from it the courage, strength, and wisdom to go forward into the future together as Texans and Americans," as resolved by the Texas Senate in 1999 when it set aside April as Confederate History and Heritage Month.[5]

And yet this very boosterism perpetuates much of the essence of the Lost Cause and, as the Senate Resolution makes very clear, "It is important for all Texans to reflect upon our state's past and to respect the devotion of her Confederate leaders, soldiers, and citizens to the cause of Southern liberty," who did not fight to perpetuate slavery, a view foisted upon Texans by "politically correct revisionists."[6] A Republican Party resolution in a Republican state, this version of the Texas Lost Cause forms a part of a larger political culture that drove a majority on the Texas Board of Education to revise its curricular standards.

Consider the case of Bill Ames, a conservative Republican from Dallas who served on one of the social studies review teams. He began his efforts to align Texas's social studies curriculum "with the majority of Texas parents, citizens, and taxpayers." He worked with Don McLeroy and the conservative group, the Texas Public Policy Foundation, to adjust curricular standards in the social studies around particular issues, including rehabilitating the image of Senator Joseph McCarthy. An aeronautical engineer by training, Ames worked tirelessly to ensure that the Texas standards were free of bias from revisionist historians. He supported efforts (discussed more thoroughly below) to keep Jefferson Davis's inaugural address paired with Abraham Lincoln's inaugural address in the standards. Ames delights in the language of Lincoln, who stated, "I have no purpose, directly or indirectly, to intervene with the institution of slavery in the States where it exists"—a statement Ames believes proves that secession and the Civil War did not result from a debate over slavery. He suggests that "the left" would have deleted the entire exercise had they known what Lincoln said in his inaugural. Curiously, Ames does not appear to know what many antebellum white Texans and many other Southern slaveholders understood Lincoln to have meant in this often quoted passage as the flip side of the Republican Party's cordon strategy for ending slavery. But for Ames, the Civil War curriculum was less important than correcting the pro-government bias in the history curriculum in the twentieth century. He considered the standards, once adopted, as a "victory for conservatism," noting cautiously that "the education culture war rages on." A native of Minnesota transplanted to Texas, Ames's Lost Cause beliefs seem part of a larger patriotic, libertarian nationalism, one that equates Texas's secession in 1861 with his version of United States patriotism in the twenty-first century.[7]

TEXTBOOK WARS

But his devoted activism in the service of ensuring that school children learn correct points of view has long antecedents in Texas and elsewhere in the former Confederacy. In the wake of the 1960s, perceived anti-family and anti-Christian bias in school textbooks propelled Texans Mel and Norma Gabler to create Education Research Analysts, a textbook watchdog group, to pressure school boards into adopting appropriate texts for school children. They were not the first textbook warriors, however. Immediately after the Civil War, Confederate Vice President Alexander Hamilton Stephens wrote *A Compendium of the History of the United States from the Earliest Settlements to 1872* to counter the anti-Southern, anti-Confederate bias he found in Thomas Wentworth Higginson's *Young Folks History of the United States*. His was among the first efforts to ensure that Lost Cause themes informed public school curricula. For Stephens, the Civil War resulted when Abraham Lincoln ignored the true nature of the Federal Compact of 1787, compelling South Carolina to claim its property (Fort Sumter) by force. Stephens focused on Lincoln's suspension of the writ of habeas corpus and his calling for troops. Slavery appeared not to figure into Stephens's postbellum account of the war, a marked contrast to his "Cornerstone Speech," delivered in March 1861. There he celebrated the secession of seven Confederate States that had created a government based upon the "truth" of African American inferiority and slavery "as his natural and normal condition." Lest there be any doubt, intoned Stephens, "African slavery as it exists amongst us . . . was the immediate cause of the late rupture and present revolution." Stephens's politically correct postbellum revision minimized slavery as a cause of the war, his own antebellum words notwithstanding, and made peace with the political outcome of the Civil War, but he warned that Congressional Reconstruction, as enforced by President Ulysses Grant, continued to threaten popular liberty and the newly restored constitutional republic.[8]

Public schools in Texas were no stranger to these early textbook wars. In 1902, the schools in Bonham, Texas ceased to use David Henry Montgomery, *The Beginner's History of the United States*, due to his "false" portrayal of Southern and Confederate history. The Confederate veterans organization in Fannin County hoped to make the ban on the popular, Northern-authored text general throughout Texas.[9]

Sporadic efforts to portray the Lost Cause took more programmatic form, and in the process, codified the major themes that school boards were to demand in their history textbooks. Mildred Lewis Rutherford, "historian general" of the United Daughters of the Confederacy, articulated eleven core themes in her twenty-three page pamphlet, *A Measuring Rod to Test Text Books, and Reference Books in Schools, Colleges and Libraries*. The federal union was a compact among states; secession was a right, not a rebellion; the North caused the war; the war was not fought over slavery; slaves were not "ill-treated" in the slaveholding states; restoring the Union by force violated the Constitution; the Lincoln government caused the "horrors" at Andersonville; the party of Lincoln "was not friendly to the South"; the South sought peace, not war; the North waged a destructive war on property; and the current writing about the war excluded the truth of the Southern viewpoint.[10]

Thirty years later, John S. Tilley, an Alabama Lawyer and Lost Causer, published *Facts the Historians Leave Out: A Confederate Youth's Primer*. After asserting the disproportionate role Southerners had played in creating an independent United States, it asked and answered four questions. To answer the first, "Was the War of the Sixties Fought over slavery," Tilley used Lincoln's words about non-interference with slavery to demonstrate that slavery did not cause the Civil War. The second question, "Did the Southern Armies Fight to Preserve Slavery?" resurrects both Generals Lee and Jackson as noble men who wanted slavery to end under the "mild and melting influence of Christianity." Anti-slavery-general-led armies were comprised of non-slaveholders, who could not therefore have fought to preserve slavery. And "Who imported the Slaves brought from Africa?" Although many slaves came on Dutch and British ships, others came on American ships, the vast majority "owned and operated by Northerners." The fourth question, "Were Southern Masters Brutal to Their Slaves," invited a litany of responses. Sometime parents spank children who need it and sometimes a few parents are brutal, but those cases do not indict all parents. Moreover, many Northerners who traveled south noted the benevolence of slaveholders. Besides, irrespective of the cruelties in slavery, it resulted in the Christianization of African slaves.[11]

Most of these features of the Lost Cause find reflection in the beliefs about slavery and the Civil War held by many members of the Texas State Board of Education. In debating the fifth grade standard detailing the causes of the Civil War, board member Patricia Hardy, a career social studies educator, wished to delete slavery, leaving only sectionalism and states' rights as the sources of conflict. She allegedly said that "slavery was a side issue" in the conflict between slaveholding and non-slaveholding states, a point of view subsequently endorsed by textbook activist Bill Ames. Education Research Analysts, the textbook watchdog group founded by Mel and Norma Gabler, urged the board of education to note the parallels between British violation of North American colonists' rights as Englishmen and the repeated violation of Southern whites' constitutional rights during Reconstruction. Determination to defend their constitutional rights, not racism, explained Southern white opposition to Congressional Reconstruction. David Bradley, another board member, worked to ensure that the standards required instruction about Confederate heroes and Civil War battles.[12]

THE LOST CAUSE AND THE CULTURE WAR

And yet this significant foray into enshrining the Lost Cause was not an end in itself, but simply a tactical thrust in the larger culture war. Sanitizing the Civil War and Texas's role in it was less about redeeming the Confederate cause than it was about promoting US exceptionalism, or "true American History," according to Don McLeroy. The central theme of US history under providential direction—according to both McLeroy and Ames—is freedom, and that history faces an assault by the twin agendas of "the Left" to "paint United States history in as negative light as possible" and to introduce "as much multicultural content as possible." Education reform in Texas required a return to the basics of teaching English grammar, dethroning Darwinism in science, and restoring a triumphalist narrative of United States history—including the engrafting of the Lost Cause into a Reconcilationist narrative of the forward march of United States history. With no ironic intent, McLeroy described his own hopes with the words of Lincoln: "This nation, under God, shall have a new birth of freedom—and that government of the people, by the people, for the people, shall not perish from the earth," once the critical naysayers on the ideological left had been routed. And, no doubt, McLeroy's religious beliefs provided his central motivation. As he told one journalist, "We wanted to remove the liberal bias from the standards and restore the biblical foundations of our country. . . . I think we did that."[13]

Once approved by the Texas State Board of Education, the standards became codified as Chapter 113 of the *Texas Essential Knowledge and Skills for Social Studies* (abbreviated as *TEKS* and pronounced "teaks" in the parlance of practitioners). In essence, the standards become targets to which textbook language and classroom curricular activities must demonstrate alignment. Middle school standards include two courses that embrace the origins and course of the Civil War, among other topics. Texas's seventh-graders take a course in the history of Texas from "early times to the present," and eighth grade students "study the history of the United States from the early colonial period through Reconstruction." When the *TEKS* was adopted, critics feared that the standards would infuse a Lost Cause narrative into Texas's social studies curriculum, and as new textbooks were written and adopted by the Texas State Board of Education, that appears to have happened, although in sometimes subtle ways.[14]

CURRICULAR MATERIALS

Although the term Lost Cause occurs nowhere in the standards, its influences shape key components of the standards framing the curriculum in United States history. Consider the United States Revolution. The governing standard requires the student to "analyze causes of the American Revolution, including the Proclamation of 1763, the Intolerable Acts, the Stamp Act, mercantilism, lack of representation in Parliament, and British economic policies following the French and Indian War," the standard litany of grievances in the traditional Whiggish narrative of the Revolution. And the board-approved volume by McGraw-Hill, *United States History to 1877*, discharges that duty quite well, noting how the implementation of the New Imperial Policy violated white colonials' rights as Englishmen and how a sense of grievance led to boycotts and collective action. But because of the tenor of the standard, fifteen pages pass before students encounter division among white colonials in the colonies, "loyalists" versus "patriots," although to the immense credit of the text, it also describes the "patriots" as "rebels" and refers to their conflict as a "civil war." The narrative is crisp and the teacher's edition is splendidly aligned to curricular themes and skills that spiral though the social studies curriculum, including a comparison of arguments for and against independence. And yet the thrust remains on imperial violation of colonial rights, as dictated by the standard. And in Texas, the ideological legitimacy of the American Revolution matters most of all because it serves the twin purposes of establishing United States exceptionalism and providing historic precedent of the right of the Confederate States to secede from the governing compact of 1787. The contingencies on the battlefield, in diplomacy, and in English politics that resulted in the actual independence of the United States are less important. The basic content of these textbooks comes from highly reputable historians whose work is consistently reliable; publishing companies make slight alterations, sometimes inserting standards-driven language to make a book adoptable by a board of education. In the case of Texas, these subtle edits create interpretations and conclusions historians never intended.[15]

Consider the discussion of the protective tariff. The McGraw-Hill text makes it solely a discussion over the cost of goods imported from Europe versus goods produced from US manufacturers. The guiding question asks students to consider how a debate of high versus low tariffs became a debate about "states' rights versus federal rights." The students are prompted to speculate how factory workers in protected industries might "react to the lowering of the tariff." The section, driven by the standard to analyze "the impact of tariff policies on the sections of the United States before the Civil War," reduces the tariff to a question of rates rather than a proxy for a set of antebellum concerns that historians have been discussing for fifty years. Planters constructed the tariff question as a proxy for the power of the national government to regulate slavery itself, not simply as an issue that affected the cost of consumer goods. Perhaps introducing the complex historiography over the nullification crisis, in addition to the daunting content required to understand it, demands too much of most eighth-graders. But ignoring the connection of the protective tariff to planters' concerns about the future of slavery misrepresents history—at least antebellum history practiced by terminally qualified historians.[16]

The Texas standards require students to understand how "political, social, and economic factors" impacted "slaves and free blacks." Hence, McGraw-Hill education follows a long-established pattern of comparing the economic systems of the antebellum "North and South." No narrative or images depicting happy slaves chopping cotton appears anywhere in the text; indeed, the text characterizes the life of "enslaved African-Americans as one of hardship and misery." Chief among these wretched conditions include separation of loved ones by sale, working for free, and little likelihood of obtaining freedom. The text notes how the enslaved set up "a network of relatives and friends" to deal with the abuses in slavery, especially forced separation. The text carries the famous image of the whip-scarred back of Gordon (a.k.a. Peter), who escaped his vicious owner before enlisting in the United States Colored Troops. The caption for the picture refers to whippings as possible punishments, which they were, but the caption seems to downplay the meaning of whipping: it was torture, it humiliated, it extorted extra labor, and it enforced the power relationships. The reference to punishment seems to imply that an enslaved person might actually deserve chastisement. The text nowhere depicts the rape or deliberate mutilation of the enslaved. Furthermore, because the standard does not require it, students may only infer that slavery was the unfortunate result of the need of an agrarian south for labor. The text represents slavery as cruel, far from the benign institution imagined by its antebellum and postbellum apologists, but its utterly abhorrent nature—and the gymnastics its practitioners performed to justify it—remains underdeveloped. In the same manner, the relation between slavery and non-slaveholding whites receives no mention, because the standards do not require it.[17]

Texas standards require students to "identify the provisions and compare the effects of congressional conflicts and compromises prior to the Civil War, including the roles of John Quincy Adams, John C. Calhoun, Henry Clay, and Daniel Webster." The McGraw-Hill text discharges this responsibility in two chapters, one on Manifest Destiny, and the other over the question of slavery in lands acquired by the United States in its war with Mexico. The Manifest Destiny chapter understandably centers on Texas, but it includes the admission of Florida as a slave state, opposite the free state of Iowa. Calhoun emerges as the champion of congressional non-interference with slavery in the lands acquired from Mexico and as an opponent of Henry Clay's Omnibus Proposal in the spring of 1850. Clay and Webster receive brief mention in the run-up to the Compromise of 1850. Key to all of these sections is the directive to focus on the theme of compromise. Slavery fueled debate, one reads, but "each time this debate flared, the nation's leaders struck some form of compromise." And it was the failure of "Northern juries" to convict "people accused of breaking" the Fugitive Slave Act of 1850 that reflected one sectional departure from this spirit of compromise. Other than inference, a reader struggles with why the Fugitive Slave Act proved injurious to a national culture of trade-offs.[18]

The tortured link between slavery in the territories and secession continues in the text. The Kansas-Nebraska Act begat violence in Kansas and birthed the Republican Party. The Dred Scott case pleased "many white Southerners" and angered "Republicans and anti-slavery groups." Contrary to the sentiments of some in the Neo-Confederate movement, the text accurately indicates the centrality of slavery in the Lincoln-Douglas debates and how his performance in those debates made Lincoln a national figure. The section on why John Brown's raid mattered is simply splendid. Perhaps these sections read well because the Texas standards are silent about this content. The Thomas B. Fordham foundation report skewering the 2010 standards especially chided the Texas Board of Education for this oversight: "The issue of slavery in the territories—the actual trigger for the sectional crisis—is never mentioned at all." On further review it seems that the otherwise quality book that McGraw-Hill modified to meet state standards shines brightest when not darkened by Texas's "politicized distortion of history."[19]

The perversion driven by Texas standards re-emerges when the standards compel contortion. The Civil War resulted from "sectionalism, states' rights and slavery." So the McGraw-Hill text inserts this line: "Southerners used states' right to justify secession," a line that virtually every Lost Cause apology for secession repeats. When applied to Texas, there is but one problem, one magnified by the standards that require the use of "a variety of rich primary . . . source material." Even the most sympathetic reading of "A Declaration of the Causes which impel the State of Texas to Secede from the Federal Union" does not provide documentary support the justification of states' rights. The oft-quoted document begins with the unique history of Texas's annexation by the United States, noting especially that "she was received as a commonwealth holding, maintaining and protecting the institution known as negro slavery—the servitude of the African to the white race within her limits—a relation that had existed from the first settlement of her wilderness by the white race, and which her people intended should exist in all future time." Since that time, "the non-slaveholding states" have worked to exclude slavery from the federal territories and violently violated the rights of slaveholders in the Territory of Kansas (which had just been admitted to the Union as a free state). The free-state dominated national government had consistently failed to protect Texans from "Indian savages" and "murderous forays of banditti from the neighboring territory of Mexico," which white Texans have been forced to repel without repayment from the federal government. But perhaps there are more complaints related to states' rights.[20]

There are, and they are legion. States' rights, at the core of the concept, involve the right of a state in the Union to determine if the national government is acting within the scope of its authority under the Constitution. According to Thomas Jefferson: "That the several states who formed that instrument, being sovereign and independent, have the unquestionable right to judge of its infraction; and that a nullification, by those sovereignties, of all unauthorized acts done under colour of that instrument, is the rightful remedy." In its "Declaration of the Causes," secessionist Texas complained that twelve non-slaveholding states had violated the rendition clause of the Constitution and the Fugitive Slave Act of 1850 passed by Congress under that constitutional authorization. Texans justified secession because non-slaveholding states exercised their right to block enforcement of a federal law. The citizens of the non-slaveholding states had created a Republican party, one sectional in nature, demanding an abolition of slavery everywhere. Citizens of these states acting collectively have jeopardized slavery through the underground railroad and John Brown's raid. They have mailed abolition pamphlets "to stir up servile insurrection and bring blood and carnage to our firesides." In a reference to the fire and slave insurrection scare in summer 1860, the "Declaration of the Causes" blamed abolitionists for procuring "emissaries among us to burn our towns and distribute arms and poison to our slaves for the same purpose." In short, when secessionist Texans justified secession, they blamed abolitionists and their machinations to end slavery. When states' rights were an issue, it was the deployment of states' rights by states invoking the right of interposition to block the interests of slaveholders that irked Texans. It was not, as the McGraw-Hill text claims, that "the national government had broken the compact by refusing to enforce the fugitive slave act." It was the "controlling majority of the Federal Government," the "non-slaveholding states," that denied "Southern states equal rights to the territories." A fairer reading of the "Declaration of the Causes" compels a tortured reading of the McGraw-Hill text. Texas seceded because non-slaveholding states resorted to states' rights as an anti-slavery tactic in the national debate over the future of slavery. Texas did not secede because the national government ignored the rights of the state of Texas.[21]

The Thomas B. Ford Foundation criticized the Texas standards for "avoiding clear historical explanation while offering misrepresentations at every turn." Not only are states' rights presented as an explanation for secession; they compound this exercise by subjecting eighth-graders to a comparison between Lincoln's and Jefferson Davis's ideas about "liberty, equality, union, and government." Since the standards permit relying only on Davis's first inaugural address as a source of his ideas, McGraw-Hill simply compared the two inaugural addresses. Davis's address, delivered two full weeks before Lincoln's inauguration, simply asserted the "right of the people to alter or abolish a government whenever it becomes destructive of the ends for which it was established." Reciting the Preamble to the United States Constitution, Davis avers that the United States government had violated the terms of the Constitution to which seven Southern states had agreed. Nowhere in the text does Davis assert what precisely these violations were. A student lacking context may simply conclude that the discontent of seven lower-South slave states had something to do with violated states' rights.[22]

Given the standards-driven comparison, McGraw-Hill understandably chose to focus only on the small portion of Davis's first inaugural address that parallels that of President Lincoln. Since Davis did not mention slavery, Lincoln's evocation of the potential harm to slavery caused by his election as the source of lower South "apprehension" does not appear in the exercise for the sake of curricular balance. Since Davis only in the most oblique way addresses states' rights, Lincoln's recitation of the "rights of states" to control their own domestic institution receives no mention. Since Davis seemed to assert that Southern states could secede, that is the union could be dissolved, Lincoln is left with claiming that the Union was "perpetual," but even this discourse does not appear in the text. The text contains only a brief passage that suggests that Lincoln cannot, as president, accede to secession because the "people" have not amended the Constitution to allow the president such a power. Because the standards do not require it, the obvious irony of the comparison as presented remains latent. Lincoln's belief that the Union was perpetual rested precisely on his reading of the Declaration of Independence. He believed the people of the United States abolished their allegiance to Great Britain. The people indivisible, the nation, preceded and was superior to the Constitution. But the apparent goal of the standards was to reduce the crisis of secession to the merits of the various arguments about the rights of secession rather than to explore the actual reasons for the secession of the lower South or the even more complex but explicable reasons why Lincoln, and scores of his supporters, might not only believe the Union was perpetual, but that the Union embodied "a Nation worth fighting for."[23]

As Edward Sebesta has noted, the linking of Lincoln and Davis, in essence two equal presidents, echoes a Lost Cause idea, dating at least to Mildred Rutherford. She thought Lincoln a coarse ruffian compared to the cultured, West Point-educated Davis. She believed that biased school curricula unfairly focused on Lincoln and ignored Davis. She advocated for the inclusion of Davis in history courses, a cause taken up by United Daughters of the Confederacy chapters since the 1920s.[24]

The standards-driven hodgepodge continues with the prescriptions it applies to understanding the course of the Civil War itself. The standards specifically mention battles—Antietam, Gettysburg, and Vicksburg; significant individuals—Jefferson Davis, Ulysses S. Grant, Robert E. Lee, and Abraham Lincoln; and heroes like "congressional Medal of Honor recipients William

Carney and Philip Bazaar." The narrative menagerie must also include "the announcement of the Emancipation Proclamation; Lee's surrender at Appomattox Court House; and the assassination of Abraham Lincoln." Given the importance of the actual outcome of the war on the future of the United States and the role of evolving US military strategy on emancipation and the Thirteenth Amendment, about which the standards are completely silent, it seems strange that the standards do not require students to understand the complexities leading to the US victory in the military phase of the war, nor to one of the most useful concepts in combatting Appomattox Syndrome, the tendency to see the ultimate outcome of the war as inevitable by deploying the interpretive idea that James M. McPherson termed "contingency."[25]

And yet, the chapter on the Civil War itself seems impervious to the strictures of the standards. The McGraw-Hill text slogs through the massive scope and complexities of the Civil War in a worthy fashion. It reminds students that the term "casualties" means "people killed, wounded, captured, or missing," an important and often misapplied concept. It admirably and succinctly describes the uncertain path toward the Emancipation Proclamation, though not precisely connecting the timing of Lincoln's announcement with the Battle of Antietam. It provides a cogent narrative and articulates sound conclusions about the outcomes of the fight at Gettysburg and the fall of Vicksburg. It links the outcome of the presidential election of 1864 with the effort to approve the Thirteenth Amendment. The text concludes wisely that the war ended with a military victory that "saved the Union" but that left undecided two vexing questions: determining how the rebelling states would be restored and deciding the status of "newly freed African Americans." The standard Lost Cause fare of "the South" fighting "against overwhelming numbers and resources . . . until exhausted" appears nowhere in the text. In fact, the narrative of the military and material assets and liabilities of the North and South notes that "how each side used its strengths and weaknesses would determine the war's outcome." The reflection of the standards in the McGraw-Hill text indicates a much greater concern for de-emphasizing slavery as a cause for secession and Civil War and postulating that the struggle was simply about states' rights rather than infusing other Lost Cause tropes into the narrative about the war itself.[26]

Similarly the standards for Reconstruction simply require students to understand and evaluate the welter of Reconstruction policies typically described as wartime, presidential, and congressional (or radical) Reconstruction and how these agendas operated. Important, transformative pieces of legislation, the Morrill Land Grant Act and the Homestead Act, what Leonard Curry called the "blueprint for modern America," find specific mention in the standard. The inclusion of the Dawes Severalty Act in a Reconstruction standard makes sense from a Texas perspective. But the standards contain one peculiar specificity: "Evaluate the impact of the election of Hiram Rhodes Revels." Other prescriptions include modifications like the phrase "such as," or list individuals to be included in the curriculum. This standard does not read: "Evaluate the impact of the election of African Americans to local, state, and national offices." It specifically focuses on Revels, and the McGraw-Hill text makes a plausible case for specifying him. He was the first African American elected to the United States Senate, and his election can be seen as marking "the way for other African Americans to follow." The McGraw-Hill text places Revels quite appropriately in a section headed "African Americans in Government." Given the Texas-centered focus of other standards, there seems to be more to this prescription. African Americans who won state-level offices in Texas, such as G. T. Ruby and Matthew Gaines, are not mentioned. Revels is required. Perhaps it was the result of his criticism of congressional Reconstruction and specifically those he called "unprincipled adventurers" (the context makes it clear he meant carpetbaggers), who, in his view, used Reconstruction for personal gain. Nothing in the McGraw-Hill text makes this Dunningite-like connection, but the inclusion of Revels—and the exclusion of other African American officeholders such as John Roy Lynch—appears to subtly preserve some Lost Cause elements in the Reconstruction standards in Texas.[27]

TEXAS HISTORY AND THE LOST CAUSE

The standards likewise infuse Lost Cause ideas and shape curricular materials for the Texas history course required of seventh-graders. The standards delineate the "Civil War and Reconstruction" as one of twelve epochs in Texas history. They specify the holy trinity of Civil War causation—"states' rights, sectionalism, and slavery"—call for students to understand the "political, economic, and social effects" of this era in Texas, and articulate a litany of people and events to include "John Bell Hood, John Reagan, Francis Lubbock, Thomas Green, John Magruder," and the battles of Galveston,

Sabine Pass, and Palmito Ranch. Nothing requires Texas seventh-graders to understand how the Civil War resulted in a military victory by the United States. Furthermore, and more glaring perhaps, are sins of omission. Sam Houston, who appears twice, previously in the standards, is conspicuously absent in the chapter on disunion, perhaps because he opposed the efforts of secessionists in Texas in early 1861.[28]

How the veneer of certain key Lost Cause ideas covers an otherwise reasonable curriculum in Texas history becomes apparent by examining textbooks written to the Texas history standards. Chapter 13 in the McGraw-Hill Texas history volume deals with social and economic conditions in Texas after its independence from Mexico. It stresses the growth of Texas's population due to immigration, and the skills organizer does ask students to think about "daily life" for enslaved people in Texas. But the chapter also addresses how "slavery and states' rights" began to divide the United States.[29]

In important ways, this chapter succeeds in capturing diversity and complexity, including change over time among the status of people, including free blacks:

> Even though most white people in Texas did not own slaves, they generally supported the institution of slavery. They claimed that slavery was needed to support the economy of the South. In the North, by contrast, the economy was based on industry and manufacturing and had never become dependent on slavery. In fact, the economy of the Southern states did depend on the work of slaves to help produce cash crops. However, many groups in Texas, including German immigrants and Tejanos, opposed slavery. They argued that it was morally wrong for one person to own another person.[30]

But the overarching tenor of economic need and states' rights overshadows the brief mention of moral opposition to slavery, and the text does not ask students to analyze the racial arguments employed by African American slavery's many defenders. Most whites simply believed African Americans (and Mexicans and Native Americans) were biologically inferior. The chapter notes that Texans were angry at Sam Houston for his refusal to endorse the Kansas-Nebraska Act, noting that it would have opened up the possibility of Kansas becoming slave territory, but the chapter concludes strongly: "Most Texans still preferred secession to losing states' rights." The text does not ignore slavery as an issue, but rather links it to the right of Texans to

determine the future of slavery in Texas, which of course is not what seced-
ing Texans claimed motivated them in 1861. Given the staccato repetition
of this phrase, one might readily forgive a student who would say that they
learned the real cause of secession and the Civil War was states' rights.[31]

The Lost Cause casts a dark shadow over chapter 14, which deals with
secession and civil war. Here, a collage of facts and how they are arranged
obscure the pivotal moment when white Texans debated secession. Age-
appropriate pedagogy adds to the textual gloss. Quite understandably the
text directs students to develop an empathy with those people confronting the "momentous issue of civil war," and the prompt asks students to
think about how they felt when someone challenged a deeply held belief.
"Were you hurt, angry, or confused? Did you try to understand the other
person's point of view, or did you jump to defend your beliefs?" The section
concludes with asking students to think of contemporary issues over which
people disagree and "effective" and "ineffective" ways to handle dispute.
Texas's seventh-graders are clearly positioned to understand that the Civil
War resulted from differing beliefs of many white people in Texas with others over two important issues: states' rights and slavery.[32]

The section continues: "Southern states, including Texas, depended on
slave labor to maintain their agricultural economy. Northern states were
more industrialized and opposed to slave labor. Many Texans, like other
Southerners, strongly believed that their first loyalty belonged to their state.
In fact, many Texans were willing to go to war in the defense of these beliefs." The passage minimizes the devotion of white Texans to slavery and
maximizes Texans' patriotism to Texas. Slavery was necessary, but Texans
fought to defend their deeply held loyalty to their state.[33] Obscured by the
textual fog is precisely why Texans seceded. Despite the instructions in the
standards to use primary sources, the text does not direct students to read
what Texans actually said motivated them to secede and to fight.

As dictated by the standards, the chapter emphasizes the "main idea:
Political and social issues divided the country in the early 1860s. Many
Southern states, including Texas, decided to separate themselves from
the United States." The chapter sets out to define these ideas, beginning
with the "tariff." Not only does the section not distinguish between a reve-
nue tariff and a protective tariff, but it makes no effort to link the abstract
debate over the constitutionality of a protective tariff with the power of
the national government to regulate slavery. Instead, it simply reduces

the sectional struggle to a debate between the economic self-interests of the North and the South over industry versus agriculture. And then it links this economic sectionalism expressed in the debate over the tariff with the emergence of the Republican Party, which "would destroy the Southern economy, which depended on foreign trade and slave labor." The implication is clear: the tariff favored by Republicans hurt Texas. This inference is plausible, but ignores what the Republican Party actually planned to do to threaten slavery, a threat well-acknowledged in Texas's own ordinance of secession but not acknowledged as a cause of secession in this passage.[34]

This tariff-centered partisan debate furthered "other arguments over states' rights." The text offers two examples: federal regulation of slavery in the states and the right of states to secede. Lost in this discussion is the evidence, such as Lincoln's own letter to his former congressional colleague and Confederate Vice President, Alexander Stephens: "One section of our country believes slavery is right and ought to be extended, while the other believes it is wrong and ought not to be extended. This is the only substantial dispute." Texas partisans may dismiss Lincoln as a self-interested and untrustworthy figure, but the Texas ordinance of secession made clear what Texas's concerns about slavery were, while the seventh-grade text ignores the effort by Southern Democrats to create a federal slave code for the federal territories, preferring to treat the schism between Northern and Southern Democrats as a debate over whether they "should officially endorse slavery."[35]

The narrative then covers the 1860 presidential election and the movement for secession in Texas, including a brief mention of Governor Sam Houston's opposition to secession. It then invites students to learn the word "ordinance" and notes the overwhelming passage of the Texas Ordinance of Secession in late January 1861. But nothing in the actual ordinance of secession appears in the text and the sidebar, accurately noting that not all white Texans supported secession, invites students to wonder "why might Texans from the upper South and Europe oppose secession?" The prompt directs students to think about economic interests, ignoring the moral opposition of German immigrants to slavery briefly mentioned in the previous section. Nowhere are students asked to read and reflect on what those many white Texans who supported secession thought they were doing and why they were doing it. The text does mention the revised Texas State

Constitution, noting that it "defended states' rights and slavery. It stated that the freeing of slaves was illegal." The text does not ask students to reflect on why the State of Texas might instruct property owners on what they may not do with their property.[36]

In dealing with the Civil War years, the text does note dissent in Texas and makes specific reference to the hangings of Unionists at Gainesville and to the Battle of the Nueces between Germans loyal to the United States and Texans loyal to the Confederacy. It identifies Texas as a locus of slaveholders from other states refugeeing with their slaves, directly citing Kate Stone, one of the best known of these refugees. As the standards directed, the text specifically refers to Tom Green, John Magruder, and the Battle of Palmito Ranch. [37]

Chapter 15 deals with Reconstruction and avoids the Dunningite myth of a heroic, vanquished people subjected to "Negro Rule" by vengeful radical Republicans. It mentions Juneteenth and notes that many white Confederates did not support Reconstruction because they remained loyal to the cause for which they fought and were not of a mind to seek reconciliation with their former foes. It describes opposition to African American rights and violent efforts by the Ku Klux Klan to repress those rights. It characterizes in positive terms the Constitution of 1869, which "declared the Constitution of the United States the law . . . guaranteed the right of all men to vote, regardless of 'race, color, or former condition' . . . established the foundation for a public school system for all children, a centralized system of law enforcement, and the number and length of terms for state government offices." But it concludes that this constitution was too detailed and too costly to maintain. There is no mention of redemption and no discussion of race or racism at all in this chapter; instead, the text uses Texas resistance to alien military rule—not resistance to black political equality—as a grounds for its opposition to Reconstruction. The promise of civil equality for black men is obscured by linking that equality with an African American quest for "more rights," which of course is true only if one knows that under slavery black men had no rights.[38]

Textbook companies addressed *TEKS* standards, many of which reflect the quality work of expert panels, but others embodied the idiosyncratic viewpoints of an apparently partisan state board of education. The McGraw-Hill texts dampen but do not extinguish some of the concerns raised by Edward Sebesta about the Neo-Confederate biases in *TEKS*, especially the selection of Confederates like John Magruder, who went on to fight in the service of Emperor Maximilian rather than surrender to the United States, and the catalog of Civil War battles that treat Texas as a victim of Yankee aggression. The texts do not make these connections and, given the coverage model teachers follow, they are not likely to urge students to make such links. But some Neo-Confederate and Lost Cause ideas persist in more prominent ways. *TEKS* ignores slavery's racial dimensions and its routinized violent operation, reducing it to an economic system about which white Northerners and Southerners disagreed. While slavery is not the benign institution depicted by Lost Cause apologists, the standards make it less brutal than it really was. States' rights persist as the umbrella cause for the Civil War because the ordering in the standards almost guarantees that outcome. General Thomas J. Jackson lurks in the standards as "Stonewall" Jackson, a sobriquet he earned while fighting against the United States military, as an example of a United States military leader.[39]

CONCLUSION

Those responsible for amending the proposed standards to include Lost Cause references were not diehard Confederate sympathizers, but rather culture warriors who had absorbed a potpourri of ideas that they associated with traditional United States history, a mixture that included core Lost Cause nostrums. They believed their fragrant metanarrative to be under assault from "the Left," which they had a duty to counter with the truth. These ideas were part of a larger cultural narrative of a lily-white US exceptionalism they sought to enshrine throughout Texas's social studies curriculum. Led by a "seemingly unassuming dentist in control of the Texas State Board of Education, these ideologues" sought to refashion a history for Texas school children, believing that "all history that challenges their interpretations should simply be erased, forever ignored as politically inconvenient." To a great degree, they enacted their belief into Texas curricular standards, which like the Texas Confederate Monument erected a century earlier on the grounds of the state capitol stands as a sentinel to an enduring Lost Cause.[40]

NOTES

1. *The New York Times*, March 12, 2010, http://www.nytimes.com/2010/03/13 /education/13texas.html; *The Washington Post*, May 22, 2010, http://www.washingtonpost .com/wp-dyn/content/article/2010/05/21/AR2010052104365.html; *The Colbert Report*, http://www.cc.com/video-clips/14wyxm/the-colbert-report-don-mcleroy.

2. McLeroy in *The New York Times*, March 12, 2010. *The New York Times*, November 22, 2014, A22; Eric Foner, "The Nation: Twisting Texas History," NPR, March 19, 2010, https://www.npr.org/templates/story/story.php?storyId=124861233.

3. Edward H. Sebesta, "Neo-Confederate Ideology in the Texas History Standards," in *Politics and the History Curriculum: The Struggle over Standards in Texas and the Nation*, ed. Keith A. Erekson (New York: Palgrave McMillan 2012), 149.

4. Sebesta, "Neo-Confederate Ideology," 163; Gene B. Preuss, "'As Texas Goes, So Goes the Nation': Conservatism and Culture Wars in the Lone Star State," in *Politics and the History Curriculum*, ed. Erekson, (New York: Palgrave McMillan 2012), 21.

5. Laura Lyons McLemore, "Gray Ghost: Creating a Collective Memory of a Confederate Texas," in *Lone Star Unionism, Dissent, and Resistance: Other Sides of Civil War Texas*, ed. Jesú F. de la Teja (Norman: Univ. of Oklahoma Press, 2016), 15–36.

6. Senate Resolution No. 526, http://www.legis.state.tx.us/tlodocs/76R/billtext/html /SR00526F.htm.

7. Bill Ames, *Texas Trounces the Left's War on History* (Dallas: Taylor Publishing for Bill Ames, 2012), 19, 36, 106, 229, 231, 237, 281.

8. Joseph Moreau, *Schoolbook Nation: Conflicts Over American History Textbooks From the Civil War to the Present* (Ann Arbor: Univ. of Michigan Press, 2003), 52–54.

9. "False Histories Ousted in Texas," *Confederate Veteran* 10 (September 1902): 1.

10. Mildred Lewis Rutherford, *A Measuring Rod to Test Text Books, and Reference Books in Schools, Colleges and Libraries* (n.p., 1919); See James M. McPherson, "Long-Legged Yankee Lies: The Southern Textbook Crusade," in *The Memory of the Civil War in American Culture*, ed. Alice Fahs & Joan Waugh (Chapel Hill: Univ. of North Carolina Press, 2004), 72.

11. John S. Tilley, *Facts the Historians Leave Out: A Confederate Youth's Primer* (Montgomery: Paragon Press, 1951).

12. Dan Quinn, "Coming Soon to Texas Classrooms?" Texas Freedom Network, July, 1, 2010, http://tfn.org/coming-soon-to-texas-classrooms; Dan Quin, "Far-right Org Wants Textbooks to Portray Southern Whites as Victims after the U.S. Civil War," Texas Freedom Network, April 24, 2014, http://tfn.org/far-right-org-wants-textbooks -to-portray-southern-whites-as-victims-after-the-u-s-civil-war/; Steven Schafersman ,"State Board of Education Begins Meeting to Revise and Adopt Social Studies Standards," *Texas Observer*, May 20, 2010, https://www.texasobserver.org/state-board-of-education -begins-meeting-to-revise-and-adopt-social-studies-standards/.

13. Bill Ames, "Insertion of Liberal's Texas History Warrants SBOE Action," *Texas Insider*, September 9, 2009, http://www.texasinsider.org/insertion-of-liberal%e2%80%99s-texas -history-warrants-sboe-action; Don McLeroy, "Teaching Our Children What it Means to Be American in 2011," Constitutional Coalition, St. Louis, January 28, 2011, http://www

.donmcleroy.com/; John Savage, "Where the Confederacy is Rising Again," *Politico Magazine*, August 10, 2016, https://www.politico.com/magazine/story/2016/08 /texas-confederacy-rising-again-214159.

14. *Texas Essential Knowledge and Skills for Social Studies Subchapter B. Middle School* (hereafter *TEKS*), chapter 113, §113.19 and §113.20; Savage, "Where the Confederacy is Rising Again," *Politico Magazine*.

15. *TEKS*, 16; *United States History to 1877, Teacher Edition* (Bothwell, WA and other cities: McGraw Hill Education, 2016), 159–90.

16. *TEKS*, 17; *United States History to 1877*, 379. See generally William W. Freehling, *Prelude to Civil War: The Nullification Controversy in South Carolina, 1816–1836* (New York: Harper & Row, 1966); Freehling, *The Road to Disunion: Secessionists at Bay, 1776–1854* (New York: Oxford Univ. Press, 1990), 259; Lacy K. Ford, *Origins of Southern Radicalism: The South Carolina Upcountry, 1800–1860* (New York: Oxford Univ. Press, 1988), 125–41.

17. *TEKS*, 17; *United States History to 1877*, 442–44.

18. *TEKS*, 17; *United States History to 1877*, 402–4, 279–81.

19. *United States History to 1877*, 481–88; Thomas B. Ford Foundation, "The State of Texas U.S. History Standards, 2011," 141–42.

20. *TEKS*, 14; "A Declaration of the Causes which impel the State of Texas to Secede from the Federal Union," https://www.tsl.texas.gov/ref/abouttx/secession/2feb1861.html.

21. *TEKS*, 14; "A Declaration of the Causes which impel the State of Texas to Secede from the Federal Union," https://www.tsl.texas.gov/ref/abouttx/secession/2feb1861.html. *United States History to 1877*, 490.

22. *United States History to 1877*, 494.

23. *United States History to 1877*, 494–95. David Herbert Donald, *Lincoln* (New York: Simon and Schuster, 1995), 269.

24. Sebesta, "Neo-Confederate Ideology," 156.

25. *TEKS*, 17; James M. McPherson, *Battle Cry of Freedom: The Civil War Era* (New York: Oxford Univ. Press, 1988), 858.

26. *United States History to 1877*, 502, 510, 513–14, 528–30, 534, 537. Lost Cause fare taken from the inscription on the Texas Confederate Monument on the Texas State Capitol grounds.

27. *TEKS*, 17; Sebesta, "Neo Confederate Ideology," 162. See Revels's letter to Grant in James Wilford Garner, *Reconstruction in Mississippi* (New York: McMillan, 1902), 399–400.

28. *TEKS*, 7, 9–10.

29. *Texas History* (Columbus, OH: McGraw-Hill Education, 2016), 285, 295.

30. *Texas History*, 296.

31. *Texas History*, 298.

32. *Texas History*, 303.

33. *Texas History*.

34. *Texas History*, 304.

35. *Texas History*, 304; Lincoln to Stephens, December 22, 1860, in *The Collected Works of Abraham Lincoln* IV, ed. Roy P. Basler (New Brunswick: Rutgers Univ. Press, 1953), 160.

36. *Texas History*, 305–7.

37. *Texas History*, 312–18.

38. *Texas History*, 328–31.

39. Sebesta, "Neo-Confederate Ideology," 156–57.

40. Fritz Fischer, *The Memory Hole: The U. S. History Curriculum Under Siege* (Charlotte, NC: Information Age Publishing, 2014), x. In November 2018, the Texas State Board of Education voted to streamline the Social Studies Standards, but the Lost Cause emphasis on states' rights and sectionalism remained as central causes of the Civil War. Kritika Agarwal, "Texas Revises History Education, Again," *Perspectives on History,* January 11, 2019, https:// www.historians.org/publications-and-directories/perspectives-on-history/january-2019 /texas-revises-history-education-again-how-a-good-faith-process-became-political.

Contributors

COLIN CHAPELL is graduate coordinator for University College at the University of Memphis.

EDWARD R. CROWTHER is emeritus professor of history at Adams State University.

CAROLYN DuPONT is associate professor of history at Eastern Kentucky University.

KEITH HARPER is senior professor of Baptist studies at Southeastern Baptist Theological Seminary, Wake Forest, North Carolina.

BRADLEY KEEFER is associate professor of history at the Kent State University Ashtabula Campus.

BILL J. LEONARD is Dunn Professor of Baptist Studies and professor of church history emeritus at Wake Forest University.

SANDY DEWAYNE MARTIN is professor and head of the Department of Religion at the University of Georgia.

LEIGH McWHITE is political papers archivist and associate professor in the Archives and Special Collections at the University of Mississippi.

CHRISTOPHER C. MOORE is instructor of history and religion at Catawba Valley Community College, Hickory, North Carolina.

ED STETZER holds the Billy Graham Distinguished Chair at Wheaton College Graduate School.

ALAN SCOT WILLIS is professor of history at Northern Michigan University.

CHARLES REAGAN WILSON is professor emeritus of history and Southern studies at the Center for the Study of Southern Culture at the University of Mississippi.

Index